NEW YORK FASHION

THE EVOLUTION OF AMERICAN STYLE

NEW YORK FASHION

THE EVOLUTION OF AMERICAN STYLE

BY CAROLINE RENNOLDS MILBANK

HARRY N. ABRAMS, INC., PUBLISHERS, NEW YORK

PROJECT MANAGER: *Leta Bostelman*
EDITOR: *Lory Frankel*
DESIGNER: *Raymond P. Hooper*
ADJUNCT PHOTO RESEARCH: *J. Susan Sherman*

Library of Congress Cataloging-in-Publication Data
Milbank, Caroline Rennolds.
New York fashion: the evolution of American style/by Caroline
Rennolds Milbank.
p.   cm.
Bibliography: p. 298
Includes index.
ISBN 0–8109–1388–7
1. Costume—New York (N.Y.)—History.   2. Costume designers—New
York (N.Y.)—History.   3. Clothing trade—New York (N.Y.)—History.
4. Costume—United States—History.   I. Title.
GT617.N4M55   1989
391′.009747′1—dc19   89–60

A Times Mirror Company
Printed and bound in Japan

FOR MY PARENTS

Seymour Rives Laughon and

John Kerr Branch Rennolds

C O N T E N T S

hether or not there is such a thing as American fashion is still being debated, and misconceptions about what is designed in this country abound. It is not true that America invented ready-to-wear, or sportswear, or even the concept of department stores. It is not true that Americans merely copied the French, or that American clothes were less well made than those from Europe. It is especially untrue that American fashion would never have come into its own if Paris hadn't been occupied by the Germans during World War II.

What is true is that American fashion existed long before the 1940s and was centered in New York by the middle of the nineteenth century. The first American fashion was made to order, and when ready-to-wear came into being, it supplemented rather than replaced custom-made clothes. Fashion in this country was a blend of hand and machine work, with the distinction between retailers, manufacturers, and designers blurred. Out of this group, designers rose to prominence during World War II.

Before there was an American fashion, there was an American style. It had its genesis in the patriotic determination, after the Revolutionary War, to wear homegrown, homespun, and homesewn clothes, following the example of George and Martha Washington as well as such religious groups that had sought freedom in this country as the Amish and the Quakers. Relying on imported goods reflected poorly on America's independence, and ostentation in dress was viewed as epitomizing the rigidly delineated way of life under a monarchy. Simplicity in dress celebrated both self-sufficiency and the freedoms inherent in a democracy.

However, as the country prospered, a taste for opulence grew, and beginning around the middle of the nineteenth century ostentation served as an outward and visible sign of an inward and invisible ability to get ahead. Those amassing vast fortunes built European-style houses, collected French, Italian, and English art and furniture, and dressed in Paris clothes. In doing so, they displayed a pervasive native inferiority complex about America's capacity to produce its own art and, along with art, luxury goods. It is

interesting to note that when Americans were criticized for lacking taste, it was almost always when they were aping Europeans.

The nineteenth-century preoccupation with French fashion had grown out of a desire to avoid importing goods from England, so recently America's nemesis. France had long enjoyed a reputation for marvelous fabrics and trimmings, as well as for the wonderful clothes made out of them and worn by French beauties, particularly at court. However, it was not until Charles Frederick Worth in the 1860s established himself as an artist of fashion that the couture became a unified entity in which a dress, as created by an artist, was greater than the sum of its parts. Worth acted as the catalyst to transform French fashion (composed of products from around the country) into Paris fashion. New York was already the center of American fashion.

New York supplanted previously fashionable centers like Boston and Philadelphia when, with the invention of the steam-powered ship in the 1820s, the Hudson River became easily navigable, making New York's port doubly convenient. Within two decades, the number of merchants purveying all kinds of fashion-related wares greatly increased, although their primary trade was in imported materials and trimmings rather than actual clothing. Along with these dry-goods stores, which would develop into mammoth bazaars selling everything from $2,500 shawls to fabrics available for a penny a yard, catering to every level of society, there were by the 1850s grand dressmaking-import houses that made luxurious clothes to order.

While Paris dresses were displayed prominently in the windows of emporiums like A. T. Stewart, Lord & Taylor, or Mme Demorest—just as magazines and newspapers published fashion plates showing couturier clothes—what was actually available to buy was a store-made version of the dress in the window or plate. Paris dresses were rarely copied faithfully; instead, they served as departure points to American seamstresses, custom dressmakers, and the first ready-to-wear manufacturers. New York stores, which sold on both a retail basis to their own clients and wholesale to merchants around the country, served, along with the fashion magazines that were based in New York, to inform the rest of America about what was in fashion.

New York didn't copy Paris, it used it. The very words *French*

Gingham, a term that originally applied to a plain weave of fabric but has now come to mean the plaid formed when two equal-size stripes are woven together, is not indigenous to America. However, it has long been popular here, both in imported and homespun versions, and American designers of the twentieth century have often been inspired by it to make clothes that combine innocence, or a kind of naive charm, and sophistication. This formal visiting or street ensemble was made around 1870.

This gingham checked coat was made in the triangular transitional silhouette of World War I by Max Meyer, one of New York's earliest and best ready-to-wear companies. The Library, Fashion Institute of Technology, New York

This mid-1920s day dress in black and white, highlighted by red accessories, was made in the typical period silhouette—almost entirely straight and barely covering the knees. The Irene Lewisohn Library, the Costume Institute, The Metropolitan Museum of Art, New York

and *imported* meant money in the till, and it is the rare nineteenth-century label that does not read Mme————, Importer, or———— & Co., New York and Paris. As the Paris couturiers became known by name, New York designers/custom dressmakers effaced themselves all the more. They downplayed their own participation in their designs, content to imply that Paris had been responsible. By the twentieth century false Paris labels were being sewn into New York couture designs. Ready-to-wear clothes, clearly not comparable to the products of the Paris couture, bore on their labels only the names of the stores in which they were sold, not those of manufacturers or designers.

Part of why Paris cachet was so important was that the fashions themselves were not always pertinent to American women, who, by the Civil War, had begun to be interested in getting an education, in trying their hands at jobs previously held almost exclusively by men, and in engaging in athletic endeavors. Their growing independence was hampered not only by the more ornate and restrictive nineteenth-century fashions themselves but also by the convention of following fashion, easily a full-time occupation. As American

Compatible with the 1930s taste for a lean, long, and fluid silhouette, pants or pajamas became a favorite sartorial item for the beach or at-home wear. This New York socialite was photographed in her gingham checked silk coat and hip-wrapped handkerchief at Newport in the early 1930s.

This black and white checked silk crepe shirtwaist dress of 1942 with a black patent leather belt was one of Norman Norell's first big successes after he began designing under the label Traina-Norell in 1941.

Adrian, the Hollywood costumer turned ready-to-wear and custom designer, was fond of American fabrics and references. Here he combined two shades of gingham in a 1944 bustle-backed evening dress. Photograph: John Rawlings. Courtesy the Edward C. Blum Design Laboratory, Fashion Institute of Technology, New York, and Vogue

women began to establish a preference for simpler clothes, like shorter skirts for walking and jackets and/or shirtwaists and skirts for all-day wear, the ready-to-wear industry was finding that just such simple clothes best suited the limitations of its rudimentary machinery. Simplicity is an element of American fashion, in terms of both manufacture and style, that cannot be overemphasized. By the end of the nineteenth century, supply and demand had resulted in a style that would be epitomized by the Gibson girl's shirtwaist and skirt, a fashion that was easily manufactured and appropriate to all classes.

Even as American style and fashion were rising to the fore, many Americans had found Paris a difficult habit to break. Before World War I there were rumblings about whether American designers should be given more credit. More than a decade later Lois Long, the fashion writer for the just-established magazine the *New Yorker*,

Betsy Pickering modeled this gingham sundress with overall-strap bodice in Miami Beach in 1954.

For this 1962 suit, modeled by Peggy Moffitt, Rudi Gernreich paired a table-cloth check with gingham. The cardigan jacket is lined in gingham. Photograph: William Claxton

broke precedent by covering those designers previously known by name only within the industry. And it was a bold move when Dorothy Shaver at Lord & Taylor in 1932 began promoting American designers in various ways, including having such couturieres as Elizabeth Hawes and Muriel King branch out into ready-to-wear. Throughout the 1930s awareness of American fashion grew, and in 1938 *Vogue* initiated its annual Americana issue.

This slow but sure progress toward recognition of American fashion accelerated during World War II. Since Paris was actually occupied, its couture was much more curtailed than it had been during World War I. New York fashion magazines promoted local talent, not simply because it was patriotic and the fashions themselves good, but because they had no choice. And so at last designers who had long been known within the industry, like Claire McCardell, became familiar to American women. Although the couture regained its position after the war, especially once Christian Dior opened his own house and showed his successful New Look, New York's reputation, so firmly established, remained secure.

New York was not just a center of high fashion, although it had numerous couturiers, including Mainbocher, Charles James, and Valentina, along with deluxe ready-to-wear designers like Norell, but of quality fashion at every level. Just as there were several different types of American women, so there was great variety in what was being designed. The most important category of fashion, and the one unique to America, was that of sportswear. Claire McCardell, Tina Leser, Clare Potter, and Tom Brigance brought a tremendous inventiveness to their clothes, which sold for a twentieth, thirtieth, and even fortieth of couture prices.

Fashions were produced elsewhere in America, in Chicago and particularly in California, where an industry had grown up around the active sports scene and the Hollywood movies, but New York was where Americans wanted to shop. It was where the American fashion magazines were published and where the vast majority of clothes were produced. It was a magnet that drew art students from around the country to study, many to discover that their creativity would be best put to use designing clothes. New York was the place to be. New York was where style and fashion were most closely synchronized. New York dressed America.

Bill Blass used taffeta woven in a pale pink gingham check and tucked it at the bodice for a striped effect in this 1988 short evening dress and bolero trimmed with black lace.

During the nineteenth century, when New York City occupied the bottom tip of Manhattan Island, the widest, most elegant thoroughfare was Broadway. It had grand houses as well as the best shops, and New York residents and visitors taking their constitutionals there could not only see and be seen but also amuse themselves window-shopping. As the city progressed northward, houses were built farther and farther away from the bustle of commerce, only to be followed anew by merchants, again drawing crowds in their wake. This view of New York's answer to Paris's rue de la Paix and London's Bond Street was drawn by W. S. L. Jewett for Harper's Weekly in 1868.

Nineteenth-century America was the scene of rampant growth and opportunity. Nowhere was this truer than in New York City, which rapidly surpassed other cities as a center of trade, culture, and fashion. Here could be found theaters, restaurants, grand hotels, museums, as well as such spectacles as the 1853 exposition in the Crystal Palace. New York residents, along with masses of tourists, could be seen riding in their carriages or taking their constitutionals along the avenues. By the mid-nineteenth century, New York's shops and early department stores were so splendid and varied that the city was said to equal any European center as a purveyor of style and luxury.

Fashion was the most immediate and obvious sign of success. As the middle classes grew wealthier, their clothes reflected their changing social status as much as the great houses they built in New York along Broadway, around such open spaces as Union and Washington squares, and, eventually, on Fifth Avenue. Upwardly mobile women dressed according to their station, and there was also another aspect of mobility to their lives. American women spent more time outside their homes, particularly in cities, where they could engage in shopping, going out to lunch, attending lectures, and visiting museums and galleries. They traveled more, within America and to Europe. They continued to hold their own in recitals of poetry, reading, and discussions of politics with their husbands and fathers, while women's finishing and boarding schools, seminaries, and even colleges were founded, opening up more opportunities for education.

By the mid-nineteenth century, women were becoming more physically active, not only riding but also taking up brisk walking, swimming, calisthenics, and croquet. They also worked outside the home, in factories and, up the social scale, in offices, schools, in their own businesses, and even, occasionally, as doctors, lawyers, and ministers. For every type of activity, whether serious or leisure, specific clothes were decreed.

At the same time that women's lives became more complicated with all these new activities, they also became easier, with more and more newly invented machines lifting the burden of housework from them. Ironically, the sewing machine and related inventions had the direct result of rendering fashion more complicated, as designs incorporated new methods and techniques in order to sate the desire for a labor-intensive look so gratifying to the status seeker. The newly wealthy welcomed complicated activities as well as the clothes that went with them. They paid attention to new fashion, and fashion accordingly upped its tempo, aided by the plethora of technological inventions, the rise in quality and variety of retail establishments, the development of the ready-to-wear industry, and the increasingly rapid communication of new styles.

From being isolated, something that existed in a private relationship between seamstress or tailor and customer, especially for those who lived in rural areas, fashion became the province of city shops, burgeoning depart-

BROADWAY, FEBRUARY, 1868.—[Drawn by W. S. L. JEWETT.]

ment stores, small or grand dressmaking houses, and even manufacturers. Fashion ideas were disseminated throughout America from Europe in a variety of ways: fashion plates, detailed descriptions in magazines and daily newspapers, and word of mouth. Actual ready-made garments imported from Europe could be seen here and purchased, and women could also learn about the new styles, and even order them, through corresponding with friends and family abroad.

In the late 1850s the sized paper dress pattern was invented; this, coupled with the increasing use of the recently introduced and constantly-being-improved sewing machine, meant that a dress worn in a big city, either here or across the ocean, could be copied in any hamlet. The pattern's inventor, Ellen Curtis Demorest, professionally known as Mme Demorest, was as important to American nineteenth-century fashion as Charles Frederick Worth would be to the development of the Paris couture. More than anyone else, she foresaw the structure of American fashion as the combination of invention, production, education, marketing, distribution, and an allegiance to quality.

Besides the sewing machine and the pattern, nineteenth-century inventions included machines that made lace, covered buttons, wove special fabrics on power-driven looms, printed on fabrics in many layers of color, specialized in tucking or embroidery, and cut through several layers of fabric at once. Aniline dyes came into being, which made previously expensive bright, rich colors more accessible. Countless fashion ideas held patents. Although fully mechanized production was used first for men's clothing and then boys' clothing, any of these inventions, when applied to women's clothing, lowered its cost.

Nineteenth-century women's clothes were for the most part too ornate to lend themselves easily to mass production. The dress dominated fashion, and although the silhouette remained fairly constant, its changing ornamentation was complex, and therefore better suited to the handwork skills of dressmakers and home sewers. Although ready-to-wear, or dresses made for a nonspecific customer to be altered to the final buyer's figure, was available throughout the nineteenth century, as it had been since America was settled, the women's ready-to-wear industry, or clothes made in large numbers, did not start up until the 1850s, when loosely fitted wraps and outerwear began to be manufactured, by hand and machine, in quantity. Gradually, those articles that most resembled menswear in style and the technique required, such as shirtwaists, tailored skirts, and jackets, began to be manufactured in increasing numbers as demand for such styles among the upper classes grew.

From the 1860s to the 1890s, except in the 1870s, the tailored costume or suit became an alternative to the various types of dresses as an appropriate daytime costume. Like ready-to-wear itself, the tailor-made was not an American invention. However, it was in America, specifically in New York, that mass manufacture was perfected, and ready-to-wear clothes became not only acceptable but desirable. By the beginning of the twentieth century, the quality of American ready-to-wear was internationally recognized.

In America, fashion-related invention tended to concentrate on facilitating the production of clothing, whether for the manufacturing industry or for the home sewer. Fashion innovation itself, as in specific new styles, originated in European centers, whose manufacturers of materials, laces, accessories, and garments relied heavily on the American appetite for imported goods. America was capable of producing its own silk (beginning in the late eighteenth century), as well as linen and wool, its own leather goods and furs (both raw materials were plentiful here), and such accessories as straw bonnets and beaded pocketbooks. The most important native raw product was cotton, whose production increased a purported thousandfold in the three decades after the invention of the cotton gin in 1793. The fact that labor was more expensive in this country made the development of technology imperative and meant that European imports were priced competitively with comparable American goods. European materials and clothing were generally superior in quality to our early efforts, but it was novelty that would tip the scale. Improvements in ocean travel, like the steamship, saw to it that the latest bonnets, gloves, parasols, shawls, collars, cloaks, dresses, silk flowers, and fans arrived on these shores quickly enough to fuel fads.

There is no doubt that American women followed European fashions throughout the nineteenth century, but the extent to which they relied on European styles, especially in the first half of the century, will never be fully known. One indication that women here adapted rather than copied outright the clothes illustrated in fashion plates is that the plates rarely give any information about the materials or techniques used in the design depicted. Terms for clothing changed constantly, and the lengthy, complex descriptions of clothes offered in magazines and newspapers did not include specifics about construction. Someone wanting to make an exact version of a dress from a fashion plate would have had a difficult time of it.

Another factor indicating that American women adapted rather than copied French, German, or British fashions is the fairly simple nature of American life, even in the sophisticated cities of New Orleans, Charleston, Richmond, Washington, Baltimore, Philadelphia, New York, and Boston. The White House, no matter who was in residence, bore little resemblance to one of the European royal courts. When seen in one of these elegant American centers, the newest fashions usually appeared somewhat outlandish. Most social gatherings featured women in a variety of dresses, from those in the latest style to those that had been remade many times.

By the middle of the nineteenth century it became very clear that the American version of European fashions suited American temperaments and habits far more than the originals. Magazines published in this country (*Godey's Lady's Book* was the first, beginning in 1837) were not only quick to describe the latest styles but also especially quick to offer modifications or, for those who slavishly followed any trend, admonitions. In 1846, *Godey's* published fashion plates with the caption "Godey's Paris Fashions Americanized." In her magazine, Mme Demorest actively promoted American fashions. That there remains today a lingering tradition of Bostonians or Virginians storing their new clothes in order to let them age a bit before wearing them supports the notion that American style has at its backbone a taste for a sort of dateless classicism.

The appetite for European imports and an emerging American taste for simplicity were not mutually exclusive, since European merchandise had quality going for it as well as novelty, and during a time in which every woman knew at least the basics of sewing and embroidery, workmanship was very important. Naturally, it was the most extreme fashions that were described in the press (as is true today), and prior to the widespread use of photography, it

Although the country's appetite for imported goods was great, America could and did manufacture textiles, as well as such accessories as leghorn bonnets, furs, leather shoes, and beaded bags. The pocketbook shown here was made in the mid-nineteenth century by American Indians using native techniques in a pattern designed to appeal to fans of European styles. Museum of the City of New York. Gift of Mrs. Richard Devens

Demorest's Monthly Magazine *was published by Mme Demorest, inventor of the paper dress pattern, and her husband and partner. These 1876 afternoon or visiting costumes, designed especially for their magazine and available in patterns for women to make at home, featured the then-current silhouette of narrow, curved front and elaborate back with both train and bustle. The Irene Lewisohn Library, the Costume Institute, The Metropolitan Museum of Art, New York*

OPPOSITE

As stores grew they typically took over adjoining buildings, as was the case in 1878 of R. H. Macy & Co., which was conveniently located near the elevated railway at Sixth Avenue and Fourteenth Street to take advantage of customers using public transportation as well as the carriage trade.

A. T. Stewart was New York's most ambitious merchant, and those rivals who could emulated his grand architectural statements. This was his last great emporium, built in 1862 at a cost of nearly three million dollars, and it occupied an entire block between Broadway and Fourth Avenue and Ninth and Tenth streets. Besides its five arch-windowed stories, each measuring two and a half acres in area of floor space, it also boasted two full basements. Museum of the City of New York

Although small in size, the Demorest emporium was tremendously important. It reached customers all over the world with its patterns, which were illustrated in its magazine and also available at countless outlets in the United States and abroad. From their store, the Demorests also sold custom-made clothes, including the trousseau made for the highly publicized marriage of Tom Thumb, such inventions as Mme Demorest's for a skirt elevator, useful for crossing a muddy street, and a range of perfumes and cosmetics. The New-York Historical Society, New York

DESIGNED AND ENGRAVED EXPRESSLY FOR
DEMOREST'S MONTHLY MAGAZINE.

21

is impossible to determine the difference between the most press-worthy innovations and their interpretation by individual women.

While the American preference for French over other European clothes was settling into a firm habit, New York was establishing its precedence over other American cities in commerce, business, and fashion. For every American who dressed in Paris, there were hundreds, if not thousands, for whom New York represented the last word (also still true today). Americans who didn't travel to New York patronized shopkeepers who did; early New York merchants sold goods wholesale to out-of-town store owners as well as on a retail basis. By the 1850s, New York's hundreds of stores contained the most interesting wares in the country, and its avenues contained the most fashionably dressed citizens. Its retail leadership was cemented by the practice of twice-a-year Opening Days, when all the merchants, seamstresses, milliners, and importers showed off their wares for the coming season.

Poised at the bottom of Manhattan Island between two waterways, one of which by 1825 would provide access as far inland as the Great Lakes via the Erie Canal, New York City was geographically well positioned to become a retailing hub, and it was also, since the 1820s census, the nation's largest city. Ships arriving constantly not only supplied goods continuously for the proliferating shops, they also created a market of sailors who needed clothes and other necessities between voyages. The clothing produced for them was the first American ready-to-wear (other than uniforms).

One of the stores that sold men's clothing, both made-to-order and ready-to-wear, was Brooks Brothers, founded by Henry Sands Brooks at Catherine and Cherry streets. Also located in the still-partially residential area were jewelers, booksellers, hatters and milliners, furriers, which were concentrated on Water Street, and leather-goods merchants on Ferry Street. Dry-goods stores, which sold household and clothing-related items, including imported fabrics, depended on the dockside auctions for their stocks of merchandise. Such stores, whose success hinged on selling the greatest possible variety, would develop into department stores with a largely female clientele; early ones were located on Maiden Lane, William Street, and Chatham Street.

Gunther, for furs, was established in 1820 on Chatham Street. Aaron Arnold's 1827 store, located on Pine Street, would eventually merge with that of Constable on Canal, forming Arnold & Constable. Lord & Taylor was founded in 1826 on Catherine Street and the Bowery by English immigrants Samuel Lord and George Washington Taylor, his cousin by marriage.

In eighteenth-century maps of lower Manhattan, Broadway stands out as the most prominent boulevard, running north to just west of the center of the island. Various businesses began to migrate to Broadway as early as 1805, with commercial concerns sprinkled among some of the grandest residences in the city. Any store located on Broadway enjoyed the advantages of a great stream of traffic—commercial vehicles, private carriages, and people promenading on foot. The first important merchant to establish himself on Broadway was Alexander T. Stewart, an Irishman who moved to New York as an adult and who started his business in 1823 at number 283 with three-thousand-dollars' worth of Irish linens and laces. As he grew more and more successful, other merchants wanted their stores to be clustered near his.

By 1830 A. T. Stewart had moved into larger quarters slightly south of the first Broadway location, and in 1837 James McCreery opened at 82 Canal

By the mid-nineteenth century New York stores were offering both custom-made clothes and such easily fitted ready-to-wear items as mantles and cloaks, all of which were usually made on the premises. Workrooms, such as these of A. T. Stewart in 1875, shown in Frank Leslie's Illustrated Newspaper, *necessarily occupied a large part of the space in any given retail operation.*

This 1880s interior view of the Hill Brothers Millinery Goods main salesroom shows customers choosing from a vast array of partially blocked hat forms and trimmings in order to have their headgear made to their own specifications. The New-York Historical Society, New York

Street, a northern boundary of the retail trade that gave way to new ones as New York residents, inspired by dense population and the fire of 1835, moved their homes farther and farther north.

In the 1840s Gunther & Sons was in Maiden Lane, and in 1842 George A. Hearne, a dry-goods store, was established by the former partner of Aaron Arnold at 425 Broadway. In 1846 A. T. Stewart opened his Italianate marble palazzo at the northeast corner of Broadway and City Hall Park. This building, which still stands, was the largest structure ever built solely for retail. Other merchants were constantly moving from one rented location to another, working out of buildings that had originally been constructed as dwellings.

According to Charles Lockwood, author of *Manhattan Moves Uptown*, Stewart's building introduced the Italianate architectural style to New York, where it would dominate residential and commercial architecture well into the 1870s. The store also changed the perception that the west side of Broadway, which caught the afternoon sun and was therefore the preferred place for ladies to walk, was the glamorous, or dollar side, the east side being the shabbier, or shilling side, with less attractive stores. At Stewart's marble palace, the sales help was primarily handsome men, and novelties included floor-length mirrors for the Ladies Parlor and the fashion shows.

In the 1850s the commercial area shifted northward and westward to encompass Greenwich Village, now a part of New York City, and a pattern was firmly established. Well-to-do New Yorkers anxious to get away from the noise, dirt, and bustle when their residential streets gave way to trade would move uptown to less populated areas, only to be followed again by businesses anxious to be conveniently located near their customers. This is what had happened to Broadway.

An important new residential area in the 1850s was the newly developed Union Square. Canal Street, instead of the northern border it had once been, became the southern boundary for shopping. Stores were located on Bleecker Street and Waverly Place, not far from Washington Square, as well as on Charles Street in the center of Greenwich Village. By the end of the decade R. H. Macy would open on Sixth Avenue south of Fourteenth Street; the next retail progressions would follow Sixth Avenue up into the Teens and, on the other side of Fifth, University Place and Broadway, just below Union Square. Fifth Avenue was for the moment reserved for the most elegant residences, although some people predicted that it would become commercial as well.

In 1852 Lord & Taylor followed A. T. Stewart's lead and erected a luxurious new emporium at the corner of Grand and Chrystie streets. By 1859 the business had grown so much as to require an even more luxurious and spacious building. The new five-story, white marble–faced building with its rows of arched windows was located at Broadway and Grand streets. Lord & Taylor and A. T. Stewart, along with other former dry-goods places, were by the 1850s manufacturing some of their own women's clothing as well as selling imported dresses, accessories, children's clothing, and vast quantities of dress materials and trimmings. On Canal Street could be found Arnold & Constable, Aitken, Genin, described as an immense bazaar of imported goods and mourning clothes, and Brodie, whose wraps and other articles of clothing were regularly depicted in *Godey's Lady's Book*. On Broadway, besides A. T. Stewart, were Brooks Brothers, which moved to number 464 in 1857, Hearne, at 775 in 1856, Mrs. Erickson, a dressmaker, and Bowen

McNamee, who sold dry goods at Broadway and Pearl Street. Other 1850s stores included Gray Beekman & Co., Lichtenstein, Lambert, LeBoutillier Brothers, Elliott, Miller & Grant, Tucker, and Jackson and McCutcheon, for linens.

Mrs. Davidson and Mme Pinorse were among the smaller dressmaking and millinery establishments in Bleecker Street. Most of the dressmakers who used the title Mme or Mlle were seeking to imbue their establishments and themselves with some French cachet. Although New York had some actual Parisian dressmakers who had emigrated from Paris, the majority were trading on the American blind spot that deemed native fashions inferior to those from Europe.

The major innovation in fashion retailing in the mid-nineteenth century was the instigation of Opening Days, which occurred each spring and fall. Although some stores and dressmaking establishments tried to promote themselves as being elite by refusing to participate, most of the stores banded together in preparing Opening Day displays, and New York residents and visitors dressed to the nines to promenade up and down Broadway and along the side streets, examining each other's costumes as well as what was arranged in all the windows. A contemporary observer commented, "On that day hundreds, thousands of charming, domestic ladies, devoted housekeepers, watchful mothers, tender wives, leave husband and child and household cares behind them and rush in all directions through the streets of New York. . . ." (*New York Times*, March 25, 1859).

In 1862 A. T. Stewart spent almost three million dollars on his newest and final store, which occupied the entire block between Broadway and Fourth Avenue and Ninth and Tenth streets. Standing five stories tall with two basements, each floor occupying two and a half acres, and boasting a cast-iron facade and a glass-domed rotunda, it was by far the largest and grandest of New York stores. It had the added attraction of continuous organ music. Among Stewart's most renowned customers was Mary Todd Lincoln, the nation's First Lady, who was capable of running up huge accounts; she reportedly worried that if her husband were not reelected, A. T. Stewart would call in its invoice. The store was joined on this new reach of upper Broadway by Arnold & Constable at Nineteenth Street in 1868 and Lord & Taylor at Twentieth in 1869. Also taking advantage of this new stretch of retail territory was Mme Demorest, who kept her store at number 473 Broadway as well as opening a new one at Eleventh Street in 1867.

Although the Demorests—Ellen Curtis and William Jennings, who were married and parents as well as working partners—never built any marble palaces, their influence was widespread. Shortly after their marriage in 1858 they lived in Philadelphia, where, from the front room of their house, they sold Mme Demorest's paper patterns for women's and children's clothing. It was an idea whose time had come, since it complemented the increasing home use of the sewing machine. Machines that could stitch seams had been invented over a period of decades in England, France, and America, but it was here that Elias Howe first put them into mass production in the 1840s; by 1860 there were more than one hundred thousand sewing machines in American homes.

The Demorests' success with their patterns led them to New York, where they opened a shop at 375 Broadway. They moved in 1860 to 473, where they

Department stores were major attractions in the nineteenth century, offering such diverse entertainments as continual organ music, fashion shows, lectures, and the thrill of riding up and down in an elevator. The opening of a new one, especially such a grand store as Siegel-Cooper in 1896, could—as this one did—draw crowds of more than one hundred thousand people. Museum of the City of New York

The shirtwaist and skirt was suitable for a wide range of activities, including performing calisthenics, as proved by this group of Siegel-Cooper employees enjoying the fresh air on the roof of the store. Simple as the costume was, it offered many opportunities for individualization. The Byron Collection, Museum of the City of New York

The first fashions of the nineteenth century were carried over from the end of the eighteenth century and featured Empire waistlines, a narrow silhouette, and lightweight fabrics such as muslin and calico, even in winter. This typical Empire dress, United States, circa 1805–10, is shown with the favored accessories of the period: self-embroidered muslin shawl and beaded pocketbook. Cincinnati Art Museum. Gift of Alice B. Pollack, by exchange

displayed dresses made from their patterns, in addition to designing and selling made-to-order clothes, corsets, and bathing and other athletic costumes, and offered materials and such sundries as Mme Demorest's invention of a skirt elevator, with which the crinoline skirt could be raised to cross a muddy street. In 1860 they began publishing a quarterly fashion magazine that featured plates of their dress patterns. The patterns could then be ordered by mail at a cost of twelve cents for a child's dress to five dollars for a complete lady's wardrobe. Eventually the magazine became a monthly, and the patterns were available at more than one thousand authorized outlets here and abroad. Their major rival was the firm founded by Ebenezer Butterick, which had begun a booming business selling patterns in 1863 and is usually credited with their invention.

Both the Demorests dabbled in inventions; Mr. Demorest's achievements include a version of the sewing machine that sewed backward as well as forward and a variation on the bicycle. Mme Demorest realized, decades before any French couturier, that a fashion name could be applied to beauty preparations; in the 1860s she offered for sale Mme Demorest's Roseate Bloom, a rouge, along with other skin products and a whole line of floral perfumes. The Demorests also participated in the feminist cause of giving female employees responsible positions, good wages, and pleasant surroundings. Especially unusual was their policy that black and white workers work and socialize together at company functions.

In a sense, the Demorests were nineteenth-century versions of today's couture-calibre designers whose top-of-the-line work is aimed at a chosen few but whose licensed products are mass distributed. While they didn't operate a custom salon in order to sell great quantities of inexpensive patterns or skin creams, the Demorests perceived the importance of a reputation for quality as it pertained to mass marketing, and they were as interested in dressing their wealthy patrons as they were in helping the rest of America dress itself. Since American fashion did not just progress from made-to-order clothes to ready-to-wear, as both existed in tandem almost to the present, the Demorest contribution was important.

By the 1870s, thinking similar to theirs had produced another way in which to dress the country: that of offering ready-to-wear and made-to-individual-measure clothing through catalogues, which were distributed by New York's luxury stores. Clients sent in their measurements, according to the directions given, and could order anything from walking suits to dinner and bridal dresses, mourning clothes, underwear, hats, shoes, shawls, and wraps, as well as dress materials, laces, and trimmings. Ready-made clothes, which could be ordered simply by bust size and skirt length, as opposed to the dozen or so measurements required for made-to-order, cost about the same as the cheapest custom clothes.

In the meantime, New York retail establishments, all falling into certain categories, continued to spring up. Some, like A. T. Stewart and Lord & Taylor, offered more and more kinds of merchandise as they grew in size; others specialized in millinery or dressmaking. Sometimes the smallest stores were the most exclusive. Almost every type of store sold items that could be bought ready-made (that did not need to be individually fit), the first such items being mantillas, shawls, capes, cloaks, and collars. By 1868 ready-made suits, with skirts and loose-fitting sacque jackets, were available. The prices ranged from twenty-five to two hundred and fifty dollars, including the cost of material for the waist. Waists were not offered ready-made because they required the most careful and individual fit. The *New York Times* of September 19, 1867, predicted that ready-made dresses and costumes would soon be offered, stating, "There is no reason why ladies should not be able to choose from as large a stock of ready-made clothing as men" (page 8).

Every category of store was represented on Broadway. Mme Diede, a dressmaker, could be found at number 15; at 407, S. T. Taylor sold patterns; at 425 was Hearne for Paris wraps; and W. Lockwood at 551B sold widow's weeds and second mourning. Number 461 housed Lord & Taylor before it moved to Broadway and Twentieth. Bereman & Co. sold embroideries, breakfast sets, and mantles, or wraps, at 478, Mrs. Kahn millinery at 499, and Genin luxurious imported goods at 513. Gunther's furs were available at number 502 in 1866. L. Binn, which specialized in millinery, moved from 555 to 579 in 1868. At Broadway and Waverly Place were Mme Harris & Sons, possibly the most exclusive millinery house in the city, with hats ranging in price from twenty-five to one hundred dollars, and also James Gray & Co. Mrs. Cripp, a dressmaker, was at 571, Mrs. Simmons at 637, Wilkes & Moynan at 691, and Mme Havais at 729. Also located on Broadway were Mrs. Lovett, Mathilde, Lambert, Clark & McLoghan, R. Thompson & Co., and F. Mather.

On Sixth Avenue, which was considered a little less chic than Broadway, were Macy, growing rapidly and beginning to take over other buildings fronting Fourteenth and Thirteenth streets, Stern, which sold a variety of goods at number 367, B. Altman, which had been founded in 1864 on Third Avenue but moved to 645 Sixth in 1868, and dressmakers Mrs. Ringold, Mrs. Higgins, Mrs. Ryer, Miss Shugg, and Mrs. Lovett, who moved from Broadway.

Shops were also clustered on side streets to take advantage of major avenue traffic. Mrs. Davidson, known for the simplicity of her clothes, operated at 125 Bleecker Street and later moved to University Place. Mme Burlmeyer took over the popular business of dressmaker Mme Ferrero on Great Jones Street, and Mme Ferrero later returned with her own shop. Mme Regnier was at 9 Fifth Avenue, and 148 East Ninth Street was the address of Natalie Tilman, who, as she expanded her imported millinery business, added departments for made-to-order cloaks, dresses, and costumes, as well as lingerie and laces and such jewelry as dog collars of jet, amber, crystal, and even pearls. Mme Rallings, one of the retail world's arbiters of taste, continued to operate out of 318 Canal, where Brodie was also located. Brooks Brothers, which had moved to Fourteenth Street in 1867, moved in 1869 to Union Square.

By the 1870s what is now remembered as Ladies Mile was firmly in place. This was not just a single mile-long stretch of great luxury stores but encompassed an area through which Broadway ran as a diagonal line, forming the eastern boundary, and bordered at the south by Fourteenth Street, on the north by Twenty-third, and on the west by Sixth Avenue. According to the *New York Times* in 1878, Fifth Avenue was comparable to Paris's rue de la Paix or London's Regent Street, so fashionable were the establishments there. Perhaps most important on Fifth was Mrs. C. Donovan, one of the city's top dressmakers.

On Broadway below Fourteenth Street there was A. T. Stewart, which,

The Empire silhouette deliberately recalled classical Greek costume. This New York belle of around 1820 is wearing a high-waisted dress based on a toga.

At the beginning of the 1830s, when this fashion plate was published, Boston and, to a lesser extent, Philadelphia were fashion centers along with New York. These dresses show the natural waist, top-heavy sleeves, wide shoulder line, and bell-shaped skirt that followed the Empire silhouette, keeping the ground-clearing hemline.

FASHIONS FOR SEPTEMBER.
Pub by Kane & Co 127 Washington Street Boston.

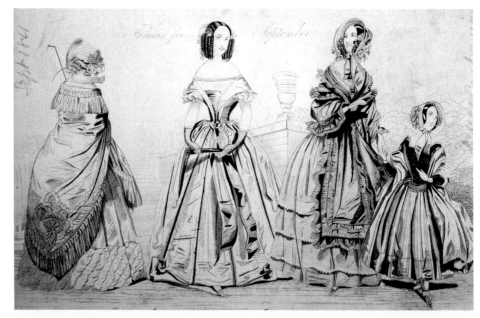

ABOVE, LEFT AND RIGHT

By the 1840s dresses were still made in the bell-skirted silhouette, but hems were longer and sleeves smaller than in the previous decade. The shoulder line continued to be wide, with dropped sleeves and off-the-shoulder necklines prevailing. The Irene Lewisohn Library, the Costume Institute, The Metropolitan Museum of Art, New York

The clothes depicted in European fashion plates differ greatly from dresses known to have been made in America and now in museum collections. While the silhouettes were usually up to date and the fabrics as fine as the owner could afford, the dresses themselves are usually much simpler. This printed wool afternoon dress and capelet, circa 1838–43, created interest by using the stripe in different ways rather than by adding on ribbons, ruffles, or flowers. Cincinnati Art Museum. Purchase by exchange

This two-piece evening dress, made in New York circa 1856–58, was composed of fairly narrow bands of striped silk, probably originally intended to be sewn together in two widths for shawls, and trimmed effectively with self fringe. The dropped shoulder line, a holdover from the 1830s and 1840s, is still in evidence, but the circumference of the skirt, especially at the hem, has grown. Cincinnati Art Museum. Gift of Mrs. Jesse Whitley

These mantillas, or cape wraps, triangular in shape in order to accommodate the widening skirt, were illustrated in 1854 in Frank Leslie's Ladies' Gazette. *Available at a New York store called Bulpin, they were probably produced to be sold ready-to-wear. The Irene Lewisohn Library, the Costume Institute, The Metropolitan Museum of Art, New York*

This 1860s summer day or afternoon crinoline dress of white organdy ornamented with green-leaved scarlet rosebuds, from A. T. Stewart, was a forerunner of the classic American shirtwaist dress.

after Stewart's death in 1876, was taken over by his manager, becoming F. J. Denning & Co. Also on Broadway were Best & Co., Thurn, dressmakers and importers, Rogers Peet, Lord & Taylor, and Arnold, Constable & Co. On Fourteenth Street were Hearne and Demorest, which took over an old mansion at number 17. Sixth Avenue became the site of massive buildings, many of which still stand, that housed, among others, B. Altman, Stern, Simpson-Crawford-Simpson, Ehrich Brothers, and Adams. Dressmakers and importers of Ladies Mile included M. A. Connelly, Albert Guerin, and Marian Dick.

Once it was established, the Ladies Mile district remained fairly stable, with less new building and moving around of stores. New names in the department store category included Bonwit Teller and Hilton Hughes, which took over F. J. Denning & Co. in 1892 and then was taken over by Wanamaker in 1896 for a New York branch of that renowned Philadelphia store. Redfern, a British couture house known for its superb tailoring, opened a New York branch near the fashionable restaurant Delmonico's. The important category of dressmaker-import houses in the 1880s and 1890s included L. P. Hollander, Mrs. C. Donovan, White-Howard & Company, Macheret, who provided the trousseau for Consuelo Vanderbilt's marriage in 1896, and T. M. and J. M. Fox, which was founded in 1885 by the four Fox sisters on Thirty-fourth Street and which was so exclusive that it shunned all publicity.

Some dressmaking establishments invaded the East Fifties and Sixties; the elegant Mme A. E. Sauer was located as far north as East Sixty-fourth Street. In 1896 the Siegel-Cooper department store, between Eighteenth and Nineteenth streets off Sixth Avenue, contributed the grandest opening of the end of the century. More than a hundred thousand people thronged the streets clamoring to see its interiors, which boasted a copy of the Daniel Chester French sculpture *The Republic*, an important sight at the World's Columbian Exposition in Chicago in 1893.

A statue celebrating the Republic was a curiously suitable device for a new department store at the end of the nineteenth century. The great emporiums were monuments to free enterprise, both in that they reflected the visionary business thinking of their founders and in the way they catered to all of society, including an elite but not excluding others.

Progress was reflected in nineteenth-century American fashion in two ways. There was the on-again, off-again simplification of women's clothing, which mirrored their uneven course toward eventual emancipation. It finally led to the shirtwaist and skirt becoming an all-day uniform for all classes, widely available in ready-to-wear, by the 1890s, which was suitable for both working at a job and participating in a sport. The simplified look gained the approval of women who were discovering the joys of independence and want-

FROM MADAME RALLINGS'S ESTABLISHMENT, 779 BROADWAY.   PAGE 225.

In 1868 the crinoline became smaller and triangular rather than belled. These two dresses with wraps from Mme Rallings in New York, shown in Frank Leslie's Magazine, *belong to this transitional period: poised on the brink of the coming bustle. The Irene Lewisohn Library, the Costume Institute, The Metropolitan Museum of Art, New York*

ed to present themselves as capable individuals.

The second strain was the idea of ostentation in dress, which reflected the growth of the middle classes and the success of a new country. As America's biggest and fastest-growing center, New York was emblematic of the land of opportunity. The parade of fashionably dressed folk promenading up and down Broadway signified a general condition of prosperity and demonstrated that America was no longer a wild, uncivilized place. The women who dressed to the hilt in order to prove their positions in society, usually the wives of successful businessmen, earned ample criticism for all the showy display. Slaves to fashion were perceived of as vain and silly, especially during the periods of the nineteenth century when clothes were excessively constricting and ornamental.

In a way, the nineteenth-century woman was torn between two worlds, the past and the future. Etiquette upheld the ways of the past, and the marvels of technology pointed the way to the future. Already transportation had become much less difficult; steamships, trains, and trolleys enabled people to move about more easily between and within cities. Indoor plumbing, gas light and heat, inventions like that of the washing machine all facilitated the job of managing a house. The effect of progress was to open up women's lives. While this was reflected in their style of dress, it was even more important in their role as the major consumers of the household. And what they consumed most was fashion.

Tall buildings, elevators, electric light, steam engines for ships and trains, sewing machines, and many other nineteenth-century innovations affected how fashion was produced and distributed in this country. Curiously, the prevailing spirit of expansion and invention had little effect on how fashion actually looked. The opening decades featured styles that had their genesis in the political ideals of the French Revolution, but ensuing looks reflected little of what was new in the world. Instead, as machines made the production of clothing easier, more of everything went into its making: more fabric, more detail, more intricacy of silhouette. The greatest influence on fashion was the desire of the large new middle classes to get away from the overcrowded cities. They valued fresh air and took their leisure activities seriously. In the end, these activities—swimming, riding, tennis, walking, croquet, golf, boating, and bicycling—did more to change the look of fashion than did technology.

The nineteenth century began with the Empire dress, with its very high waistline, located just under the breasts. Dresses were one piece and fitted by means of drawstrings, with the gathering centered at the back. Around 1810 a closer fit in the bodice began to be achieved by means of gores, or panels of fabric, sewn together. Dresses were narrow, although they were worn fuller here and in England than in France, and they came to just above the ground for daytime, breaking on the ground, with a train, for grand occasions. The evening décolletage was low and extended straight across the breasts, forming a square neckline with the short sleeves. The high daytime neckline sometimes had a ruff collar, and day clothes were often worn with the very short-waisted, long-sleeved jacket called a spencer. Other wraps included the narrow, long pelisse coat, made in much the same shape as a dress, the short cape mantelet, and the cape-collared redingote. Most of these wraps were given deep or dark solid colors; otherwise, fashionable tones were very pale, with white predominating. Small-scale patterns, sometimes ending in border designs, replaced the large and fairly bold floral fabrics of the eighteenth century. An interesting note about the Empire style is that it looked just as charming interpreted in materials like printed calico, plain gauze, or a fairly heavy white cotton as it did in silks embroidered in gold or silver with the small shaped sequins called spangles.

Accessories included flat slippers, small fabric purses called reticules, and, above all, shawls, which could be rectangular as well as any other shape and made of any material, although the most desirable were in Indian hand-woven paisley or Scottish or French imitation paisley. For at least fifty years shawls remained the most important element of a woman's wardrobe—and the most expensive. Accounts of shawls that sold for one thousand dollars, especially in the mid-nineteenth century, are not uncommon; one was described as costing about the same amount as a small farm. Perhaps to offset the relative simplicity of early-nineteenth-century clothes, accessories like muffs and hats were large; poke bonnets had brims that protruded from the forehead in the shape of a hood. Turbans were also popular; Dolley Madison was known for hers. Into the 1820s favored decorations on dresses consisted of unusual sewing techniques like puffs and other three-dimensional appliqués, ruching, scallops, shirring, and trapunto used in tiers at the bodice and hem.

Around 1818 the waistline began to drop, reaching the natural waistline by the end of the 1820s. Skirts were bell-shaped and became more gathered as

The period of Reconstruction after the Civil War brought with it a taste for lavish ornament, in furniture and the decorative arts as well as in dress. This two-piece visiting costume was decorated primarily with shirred bands and panels, an especially popular device by the time sewing machines had come into general use as the edges of the panels could easily be machine-stitched and then gathered. The Valentine Museum, Richmond, Virginia

they increased in width. For both day and evening, hemlines were short; the feet, in flat slippers, could be glimpsed under the skirt. There was an increasing element of width to the bodice of dresses, with bateau necklines, opened surplice treatments, and cape collars creating a visual contrast with the small waist. The shoulder line was dropped into puffed sleeves for evening or puffed sleeves over long sleeves for day. Decorations took the form of wide bands at the skirt and yokes of clustered lappets, scallops, flounces, or embroideries. To accommodate the larger skirts, wraps were made in the form of cloaks or capes that almost reached to the hem. Hats were wide-brimmed or toque-shaped, trimmed with ribbons and ostrich plumes.

Dresses of the 1830s were decidedly top-heavy. Leg-of-mutton sleeves grew to enormous size by 1835 before they began to dwindle. The sleeve continued to jut out of a lowered shoulder line. Full skirts, longer than they had been for some time, set off tiny, corseted waists. Hats, made in the shape of bonnets, trimmed with lace and flowers, tied under the chin with wide silk ribbons. Coats followed the shape of dresses, with fitted bodices, big sleeves, and full skirts. While flat shoes were still the norm, slippers with heels began to appear.

The major novelty of fashion in the 1840s was the elongated, pointed bodice. The fairly plain bodices sometimes buttoned down the front or opened with lapels or revers over a white shirt front. Skirts were wide and gathered to either side of the pointed bodice, as well as in back. The dropped shoulder line continued, sometimes ending in caps over long, close sleeves. Bertha collars, especially in lace, were prevalent, along with tiered skirts. Widening skirts were held out over petticoats stiffened at the hem, called crinolines. Bonnets were smaller and sometimes worn with lace lappets on either side of the face. By this time somewhat weighty fabrics, such as brocades and velvets, came into favor, and patterned materials were woven or printed with designs on a larger scale than those preferred in the early part of the century.

Bell-shaped skirts, closely gathered into small waistlines, expanded throughout the 1850s. At first they were supported by layers of petticoats with caning or wicker hoops sewn into them and then, later in the decade, by cages, also called crinolines or skeleton skirts, which were made of steel, whalebone, or wicker hoops connected by cloth tapes. Women loved the lightweight frames, as they alleviated the need for so many bulky underskirts. Dresses had fitted bodices and bigger sleeves, although not at the shoulder line; instead, the pagoda sleeve, which widened toward the wrist, was popular, usually with separate undersleeves of white batiste or cotton trimmed with lace or embroidery, which might match a separate collar. Over the huge, skirted dresses women donned tent wraps, usually about hip-length, made as jackets or capes. During this time ladies' cloaks and other outerwear began to be manufactured in this country.

Trends in the 1850s included using pale or white tulle or a transparent muslin fabric called tarlatan, ornamented with silk flowers, for ball gowns; this evening look would stay in fashion for some time before becoming the exclusive province of young ladies. Although Queen Victoria did not exert the kind of sartorial influence that the French empress Eugénie did (Eugénie's every clothing novelty was endlessly discussed in the press), the queen undoubtedly contributed to the enthusiasm for tartans, which were brought out every fall. The development of aniline dyes, man-made from a coal base, led

MARCH, 1870.

FRANK LESLIE'S LADY'S MAGAZINE

to brighter colors; patterned fabrics of all kinds were more complex and deep in color, and many patterns were combined with plaid backgrounds. Greek motifs, especially in braid sewn around the hems of skirts or sleeves, were much in evidence; women who read *Godey's Lady's Book* or any of the other fashion magazines could choose designs for passementerie and work them out themselves. In the late 1850s the various conflicts in Europe occasioned several war-related fashions: Zouave jackets were among the many military-inspired styles trimmed with braid and buttons; the colors solferino (a shade of rose) and magenta were named in honor of battles. An 1859 predilection for color combinations of red, white, and green expressed appreciation of the Italians' effort to unify their country.

The rage for military fashions, Greek key patterns in decoration, tartans or plaids, and the pale, soft ball gowns continued into the 1860s. Far from affecting New York shoppers' spending habits, the Civil War may have created as much wealth as it destroyed. A. T. Stewart was one of the near-obligatory stops for visitors to New York, and as they took in the many floors of merchandise, the giant skylight, and the country's first fashion shows, they almost inevitably ended up making a purchase.

During the Civil War women in both the North and South necessarily shouldered many of the responsibilities left behind by soldiers. They managed farms, plantations, even businesses, and filled the thousands of vacancies in factories and plants. Since so many men were either killed or permanently disabled, women continued after the war to hold jobs in order to support their families. Women who did not work for pay outside the home were, in the absence of slaves or servants, performing more of the physical tasks involved in keeping their families fed and clothed, their houses clean, and crops and livestock in order.

The 1880s bustle-backed dress was the most restrictive of all nineteenth-century styles. The bodice was closely fitted to well below the waist, calling for a boned lining or a corset, and the skirt was elaborately draped. The Irene Lewisohn Library, the Costume Institute, The Metropolitan Museum of Art, New York

THE YOUNG LADIES JOURNAL MONTHLY DOUBLE PANORAMA OF FASHION OCTOBER 1883

New fashions accommodated the needs of these women, who were of all ages and classes. The first change was in the size and shape of the skirt, which became narrower and was cut in gores, so that copious amounts of material were no longer gathered into a tiny waistband. By 1867 the *New York Times* reported that if crinolines were worn at all, they had to be imperceptible. The most practical change was the introduction of the street suit—a matching skirt and jacket—which could be worn indoors or out, nine months out of the year, requiring an overcoat only when it was very cold or wet. Even more of an improvement was the street skirt in the new (as of 1867) short length, which cleared the ground. Short skirts could be worn for all but the most formal occasions, when a train was customary.

Women demonstrated that they were physically stronger than had previously been supposed, first at work and, increasingly, at play. The tremendous growth in the size and density of American cities spawned a movement to seek fresh air and open spaces to maintain good health, and women began to walk for exercise, as well as to engage in calisthenics and skating. At watering places or in the country, they played croquet and bathed in the sea. For calisthenics and swimming they wore versions of the tunic and pantaloon costume first created by Amelia Bloomer around 1850. This style, introduced with the intention that it replace the huge skirt and bulky underskirts, was ridiculed as a masculine-looking atrocity. The gored, short skirt was viewed as much more feminine and practical. As a basis for an athletic costume, however, the bloomer lasted until the first decade of the twentieth century, and gym tunics with bloomers underneath continue to be worn today in a few private schools.

The simple and practical styles of the 1860s gave way to antebellum tastes for elaborately constructed clothing, equally elaborate crimped and curled hairstyles on which were perched teensy hats, high-heeled boots, and much ostentation in jewelry and accessories. On March 29, 1868, the *New York Times* noted that "the man milliner Worth" of Paris had come out with a new invention described as a pannier or bustle. The bustle silhouette, known at the time as the Grecian bend, gathered the material of a dress into the back, creating an elaborate arrangement of drapery. A. T. Stewart was quick to import the pannier gown; a gray poplin walking version with a drawstring overskirt that could be pulled up to form the pannier sold for $250, although it was suggested that black silk copies could be made for $125.

As a fashion phenomenon, the ornate bustle silhouette can be compared to the New Look of 1947. Both the Civil War and World War II implemented fashion changes that reflected the new responsibilities and freedoms of women, and both were followed by periods of extreme femininity and ornamentation. While women had long worn hats, shawls, and gloves and carried fans, pocketbooks, sunshades, and muffs, what was objectionable about the post–Civil War taste for ornament was that it was so purposely showy. A certain degree of ostentation had always been permissible in private and at night—in carriages, at receptions, or in opera boxes—but in the late 1860s, women decked themselves out in glitter for the streets. Daytime jewelry included chains of tortoise or jet; beads made of coral, amber, and garnet; suites of necklaces, brooches, bracelets, and dangling earrings set with cameos or made in dull gold chased with Etruscan or Greek Revival motifs. Lockets were popular, as were all the sentimental pieces of jewelry made from or set

This formal reception dress of yellow silk faille, brown velvet, and beaded net was made in 1885 by New York dressmaker M. C. Blanck. Chicago Historical Society. Gift of Mrs. Charles F. Barchelder

Introduced first in the 1860s and very popular with American women by the end of the century, tailor-made suits fulfilled a variety of sartorial needs. These 1897 versions by the JNO J. Mitchell Company were made with modified leg-of-mutton sleeves and flared skirts gathered to the center of the back. The Irene Lewisohn Library, the Costume Institute, The Metropolitan Museum of Art, New York

with plaques containing braided strands of loved ones' hair. As the wearing of jewelry proliferated, women who could not afford costly brooches or bracelets bought and wore pinchbeck and paste. Critics mourned the loss of women who had striven to appear demure and well-groomed and had also seemed above following fads.

The bustle silhouette featured an unbroken line in front, very fitted, and in back the dress of the 1870s jutted out over a support of a half-cage crinoline. Plain fabrics were often combined with patterned ones. Daytime dresses were

40

street-length, and evening dresses had trains that continued from the bustle. Wraps, cut to fit around the bustle, were hip-length. Relief from the extremely constricting narrow silhouette came in the form of *déshabillés*, which were novelties in 1878; these precursors of the tea gown were comfortable dresses for at-home wear that did not require a corset yet were elegant enough for receiving visitors. The practice of putting belladonna in the eyes to brighten them had begun, and fashion was decried for having excused "false trinkets, false hair, false light in the eyes, false tints upon the flesh" (*New York Times*, March 28, 1875).

As the 1880s began the dress lost its actual bustle and substituted a concentration of fullness at the back of the skirt midpoint between the waist and the floor. Around 1884 the full bustle returned to favor, and for the rest of the decade the new bustle silhouette was interpreted in a fairly rigid way. An observer of the time noted a similarity between fashions in dress and interior decoration. He remarked on the use of cut velvets, damasks, and brocade for screens, cushions, and dresses and compared the taste for assemblages of antiques, travel souvenirs, and other objets d'art with that for antique lace (the less white and new-looking the better), buttons, and buckles. Tailored clothes, particularly suits, were very popular and purposely made to resemble men's clothing, with man-tailored jackets opening onto vests and simple blouses. Dress bodices were made to look like open jackets showing vests, with revers framing a center placket of a contrasting material. On morning, or indoor, dresses that were cut princess style, the placket continued all the way down the front. In a single formal ensemble up to four different fabrics were combined, which could be trimmed further with piping; petaled or crenellated bands; bands of beading, embroidery, or passementerie; lace, pleated ruffles, bows, and fancy buttons.

The *New York Times* gave a typical period description of an evening dress on October 17, 1880 (page 5):

This 1895 evening dress bodice of orchid ribbed silk and white chiffon trimmed with festoons of glass pearls and beads was made by Mme O'Donovan, one of New York's finest custom dressmakers, and featured the gigot, or leg-of-mutton, sleeve, by then beginning to wane. Museum of the City of New York. Gift of Francis Delancey Cunningham

> Another evening dress is of pink surah. The apron consists of three deep flounces bordered with white lace. They are fastened down in the middle to form on the top a deep puffing. Showing under the lace is a ruby colored plaiting. Above the third flounce, from the lower part of the hip to the waist, are very close shirrs. The waist is of ruby colored faconné. The long basque is cut open in front, to show the shirring. The waist is open at the neck; down the front is a pink surah plaited piece. Around the neck is a band of ruby colored velvet. The faconné waist laces down the front over the plaiting. On the sides of the skirt is a faconné quille, bordered with a large surah and velvet shell-shaped plaiting. The velvet forms the lining. The train is covered with narrow ruby and pink flounces, alternating. On the side of the skirt is a large ruby colored bow, with ends trimmed with fringe. The sleeves terminate at the elbow, and have inserted puffings on the outside of the arm. On one side of the square opening of the neck is a spray of flowers.

Evening clothes, while quite elaborate, were often made in softer materials, rendering the bustle silhouette less harsh and rigid. Wraps, often trimmed with ruffled lace or chenille fringes, were cut in points to accommodate the bustle or made like long, fitted coats. It is interesting to note that the

As they had in the 1860s for croquet, women in the 1890s wore shortened versions of their regular street clothes for cycling, the new rage. The New-York Historical Society, New York

Lingerie dresses, so named because they were made of various plain or patterned cottons and linens and ornamented with such underwear trimmings as ruffles, ribbon beading, bows, embroideries, and lace, were worn for most daytime occasions in the summer, particularly in resorts like White Sulphur Springs, where this group photograph was taken in the early 1890s. The Valentine Museum, Richmond, Virginia

Compared with the idealized version of a skating costume shown in a contemporary plate published by the Ladies Tailor (opposite), these women, photographed playing ice hockey in the 1890s, are wearing much looser jackets and skirts that clear the ice by several inches (The Valentine Museum, Richmond, Virginia).

bustle was not worn by many sports enthusiasts; they adopted what were known as tennis skirts for most sports. These were plain, white, floor-length or somewhat shorter skirts gathered into waistbands and worn without corsets. Tops included shirtwaist blouses and shirts copied from sailors' jerseys. Swimming costumes consisted of tunics worn above fairly straight pants cropped below the knee, accompanied by stockings, rubber-soled bathing shoes, and mobcaps.

The prevailing 1890s silhouette was the hourglass, based on a narrow waist, a flared, gored skirt, and a blouse with sleeves puffed high at the shoulder. These last increased in size, becoming immense leg-of-mutton sleeves by 1895. Larger-sleeved bodices were more ornamental in every way. Bands of ribbon tied in bows, ruffles of lace, and other three-dimensional decorative effects followed the line of the sleeves across the bodice. Tailored suits continued to be popular, but blouses began to be worn more and more on their own. The outfit of a plain dark skirt (light in summer), a belt, and a crisp white blouse was suitable for working women and college students, for street wear and lunching in a restaurant, and also for golf, tennis, boating, and other summer sports.

For some summer sports, but more specifically for leisure activities such as picnics, women wore the costume of a white skirt and white blouse. Made of lawn, batiste, or heavy linen inset and decorated with bands of lace and white-on-white embroidery, these two-piece lingerie dresses were immensely popular and available in ready-to-wear and custom-made versions. They were both ornamental and practical, since various blouses could be combined with different skirts and, especially important for summer, they could be washed and ironed quickly and easily.

Winter sports seemed to have more definite costumes; these were based on tailored suits but were quite short, below the knee in length, and worn over pants that had been bloused into high boots. The most popular wraps were capes, which were hip- or waist-length and had cape or ruff collars. By the end of the decade blouses and bodices were beginning to be bloused into the waistband of the skirt, a look that would form the S curve at the beginning of the new century.

The course of fashion in the nineteenth century, as in the twentieth, took the form of a series of fashion progressions followed by regressions. Comfort, practicality, and an easy elegance would take women two steps forward, and then newly restrictive, highly ornamental clothing would come in again and force them at least one step backward.

The nineteenth century began with the rather pure Empire dress, which made the wearing of a corset optional. In its most fashionable form, made out of very sheer fabrics and cut very close to the body, it was not easy to wear, as it was very revealing, but as it was adapted, it was a fairly natural-looking style, and it was worn with flat shoes. As the century wore on, elaborate decoration became more and more the norm, as did a waistline placed closer to the natural one, necessitating a corset. By the 1830s women typically wore fitted bodices, full skirts, and gigantic sleeves. The 1840s style, while still small-waisted, was fairly sober, but by the middle of the 1850s skirts had ballooned. The wire-cage crinoline was viewed as an actual boon to women, as it replaced weighty, bulky petticoats, but it could cause embarrassment or even danger if it got caught on a carriage wheel or fireplace fender.

The period of the Civil War ushered in three important innovations in women's clothing: the less wide skirt, the short skirt, and the tailored suit for women. And then in 1868 the bustle came into fashion. Besides making the business of sitting down and standing up awkward, the bustle look encased women in tightly swathed materials, as the front was extremely fitted. Although skirts were still full and worn with a small waistband in the 1890s, the suit and the look of a skirt and blouse emerged as the first practical women's uniforms. Dress reformers, who often supported classical flowing gowns instead of up-to-date styles, had in their thinking missed a point. Since women were becoming as active as men, they needed to have a small amount of clothes work for a variety of occasions. The tailored suit and the skirt and blouse provided a woman with appropriate dress for any kind of daytime occasion, no matter what the weather. And, since tailored jackets, skirts, and shirtwaist blouses formed the basis of the first women's ready-to-wear industries, this look could be bought and worn by almost everyone.

World War I was the first instance in which women played such active roles as to require their own uniforms; this illustration by Paul Stahr, which appeared on the cover of Life *magazine in 1919, shows different uniforms that might have been worn by nurses, ambulance drivers, and Red Cross and other volunteers. Collection of Society of Illustrators Museum of American Illustration. Gift of Lowell M. Schulman*

The new century would see radical transformations in women's lives. While World War I effected sweeping changes, with women shouldering traditionally male jobs and employers becoming accustomed to female competence and ability, the war actually served to intensify conditions that were already in place. According to the November 1911 issue of a magazine called the *American Businesswoman*, there were five million self-supporting women in the United States employed in 295 occupations. The job titles included "agriculturists, dairy women, florists, women engaged in domestic and personal service, restaurant keepers, bankers, brokers, bookbinders, dressmakers, merchants, milliners, glovemakers, stenographers and typewriters [as typists used to be called]. There are professional women, actresses, artists, clergymen, dentists, journalists, lawyers, writers, physicians, surgeons, teachers and civil engineers." Although women were regularly paid a fraction of what men earned for the same job, and many jobs were hardly stimulating, particularly those manning machinery, the emergence of more cerebral opportunities made the idea of working more appealing to women. As the prejudice against women attending college decreased, more and more women sought an education, and the graduates went looking for an occupation.

Many gravitated to the New York fashion world, which offered a great variety of pink-collar jobs. Magazines like *Vogue, Harper's Bazaar,* and *Ladies' Home Journal* employed female editors, and women writers were responsible for most of the fashion copy in newspapers. Women worked as sketch artists, designers, mannequins, and buyers, traveling to Europe to choose and purchase Paris clothes. They also continued to be entrepreneurs, running their own import, custom millinery, and custom dressmaking houses.

The stigma attached to nineteenth-century women who overcame obstacles to enter male-dominated professions had gradually fallen away. Their examples served to inspire more and more women to search for avocations in which their skills and talents could be put to meaningful use. Gradually, in the twentieth century, society would come to look down upon women who seemed to lead unproductive lives. American women had long had a reputation for being independent, expressed both mentally and physically in their curiosity and athleticism, and it became the hallmark of their fashion style as well.

The women who didn't have to work contributed the most to the growing expectation that women put their minds and talents to use. In America more than any other country, society ladies who had honed their organizational skills promoting temperance and running garden and women's clubs, literary and arts societies turned increasingly to philanthropy. They founded free hospitals, schools, and asylums, where they contributed enormously as volunteers and also as fund-raisers, through organizations like the Junior League. They also participated in suffragette marches, lending their impressive names to advance the cause of the vote for women, and, to a limited extent, supported workers' strikes for better wages, hours, and workplaces. Deplorable working conditions became an even more important concern after the

tragedy of the Triangle Shirtwaist fire, in which many seamstresses died because there were inadequate fire safety devices. When war broke out in Europe, American women stepped up their volunteer work and even went abroad to start hospitals and ambulance services.

Fashion reflected this new professionalism of women's lives by replacing the concept of *novel* with that of *modern*. Automobiles and airplanes were among the phenomena that ushered in new styles (driving was the latest sport). However, the main influence on fashion was the working woman's need for simple, unrestrictive clothing that could be worn all day. The late-nineteenth-century innovations of the shirtwaist, worn with a skirt (and, for factory workers, an apron), and the suit, which was still known as a tailor-made, would be even more pertinent in the twentieth century. Mass manufacture made shirtwaists available for as little as $1.50 and suits for $10.00 to $20.00, and, although prices were equally low for some custom-made versions, they could climb into the hundreds. The importance of these two costumes cannot be underestimated. That they were available to all classes established America's reputation for a well-dressed "average woman." That they were good-looking as well as well made despite being mass-produced established America's superiority in the field of ready-to-wear. And that they continued to be popular, despite the efforts of couturiers to supplant them with more ornate styles, established American women as having a mind, and a style, of their own.

Because tailor-mades featured skirts that cleared the ground, as well as fairly narrow lines that didn't call for unnecessary and unwieldy yardage, they made it easy for women to get around, whether in motorcars or by subway or streetcar. They changed the attitude of women toward their wardrobes, as a woman could dress in a tailor-made in the morning and not have to think about her clothes again until evening. This concept, important today, was even more crucial at the turn of the century; clothing then was still divided into rigid categories governed by intricate etiquette.

For morning, a lady of leisure could wear a tailored suit if she expected to go out, or, if staying home, a morning dress, which was relatively simple. Since she was not involved in housework, she might wear, in her room or to breakfast, various kinds of the ever more elaborate peignoirs, combing jackets, or other kinds of wrapper. For afternoon, if paying a call or attending a reception, she was required to wear a formal afternoon costume called a reception gown, which was as ornate as an evening dress, possibly featuring a sweeping skirt and a train, though not décolleté. For receiving visitors at home during the afternoon a tea gown, if respectably made, was an alternative to the reception dress. Dinners at home required dinner clothes, slightly more formal or décolleté than afternoon ones, and going to the opera, a ball, or a private dinner party called for the most formal of clothes, as well as the most fashionable. These delineations were further qualified by whether one was yet to be married, newly married, long married, or never married; the weather; the season; one's location—in town, in the country, or at a resort; and, of course, whether one was in mourning or half-mourning.

An all-day costume was somewhat radical in that it ignored these customary divisions of social life and even those between classes. A society woman who wore a tailor-made for most of her activities was viewed at first as flouting convention. In 1910 the new newspaper *Women's Wear* lampooned the idea of

Although lingerie dresses continued to be popular, women also wore summer versions, usually made in linen, of their favorite tailor-mades. This woman, a member of the Social Register, was photographed at a lawn fete held behind the Lenox Library in New York City in 1909.

The sparse attendance at this 1910 State Fair Votes for Women booth indicates the long road still ahead for suffragettes and other supporters of women's rights to participate in their country's elections. The Valentine Museum, Richmond, Virginia

a costume that could be worn all day and even into the evening by adjusting certain accessories. The cartoon, titled "The Transformable Quadruple Gown," showed four drawings of a woman. In the first three, she is dressed in a suit with increasingly elaborate jabots at her neck and wears a hat. The last drawing, for evening, carries the punchline: that she has been wearing a satin evening gown underneath her suit all day, with its train looped through the waistband on the inside.

World War I blurred the distinctions between categories of dress. Full evening rig began to be considered pretentious. As there continued to be numerous evening events, notably benefits for the war effort, women began to wear afternoon dresses at night. These were silk dresses, with sleeves and not-too-revealing necklines, embroidered subtly with beads or silk to match the dress. Wool, needed for uniforms, became scarce during the war, and the American government restricted its use for women's clothes. This led to a new category, the all-day dress, to supplement the tailored suit. An American designer, E. M. A. Steinmetz (always known as Miss E. M. A. Steinmetz), who worked as a fashion artist and designer for the New York store Stein & Blaine beginning around 1917, showed in an early collection a group of silk dresses, made in dotted or foulard silks with white organdy collars, that could be worn for practically any occasion. In keeping with the prevailing silhouette, these dresses were one piece, loosely fitted with gently gathered skirts, and fairly short, skimming the top of the boot. As wool came slowly back into use in the 1920s, women were left with two uniforms that reflected their more independent lives. The suit and the little silk (and, later, rayon) dress, both appropriate to mass manufacture, became major staples of American fashion.

In a sense these were clothes that didn't require too much designing. Therefore, it was natural for couturiers to try and promote more ornate styles. Between 1900 and 1920 a discernible pattern emerged in the way fashions were introduced, adopted by a very few, ignored by most, and then gradually absorbed into a new look or silhouette.

In 1900 the S-curve silhouette was in full swing. Dressed in a shirtwaist and skirt or in two-piece dresses, the corseted female figure, with her bodice bloused over her waistline and her skirt gathered in back over a slightly protruding rear end, resembled in profile the letter S. The silhouette was exaggerated in photographs because the shape of the corset induced a somewhat swaybacked posture. Other than being gathered in the center back, skirts were gored so that they fit closely around the hips, flaring toward the hem, which was above the ground for street clothes and grazed the ground, with a train, in reception and evening gowns. Evening dresses were made with low necklines and scanty sleeves, but for daytime collars were high and supported with interlinings, wire, or celluloid bones.

For summer, lingerie frocks continued to be extremely popular, as they had been in the nineteenth century, especially at resorts, where white was the premier color. Made of cotton or linen, these got their name from their decorations of inset Valenciennes lace, tucks, white-on-white embroidery, and ruffles. Lingerie dresses owed much of their appeal to being easy to care for; they were washable and thus could stand up to fairly rigorous athletic activities. In town they were worn when the season resumed in September. Along with the lingerie dress, lingerie became more decorative, ornate, and varied.

In 1902 and 1903 rumors abounded that the shirtwaist was about to go out

American women loved the practicality of shirtwaists, which were easy to launder, and skirts, and they resisted attempts by couturiers to introduce blouses, of silk or other materials. These shirtwaists, from a 1902 American Waist Album, feature the then-prevalent high collars and pouter-pigeon blousing at the waistline. The skirts, from the American Skirt Album of 1903, show the great variety available within the same flared silhouette with a slight train. The Library, Fashion Institute of Technology, New York

of style. The tailor-made was similarly threatened with extinction, yet women refused to give up either one. By 1904 a more feminine, decorative mode was being pushed, but it was viewed by Americans as less elegant than the simple tailored look. Another important look came from the sport of automobiling; the loose fit of automobile coats, called dusters, influenced all other forms of wraps. Naturally, those who didn't have cars wanted to look as if they did, so unfitted, long coats in linen or pongee in summer and wool or tweed, fur-lined wool, and all-fur coats for winter were the rage. With the coats went motoring veils, worn over the hat and around the face beekeeper style to protect the face while driving in open cars on dusty roads. As hats were fairly large, the veils, of sheer silk inset with a lace panel for the face or mesh worked with chenille dots or embroidered patterns, followed suit. The most desirable ornaments for hats were entire preserved birds, their wings sweeping the air. Bird of paradise, with its cinnamon, emerald, yellow, and cream plumage, was the favorite; a hat with one of these could cost more than one hundred dollars. However, the hatmakers (among others) became so predatory that by 1910 laws were passed that prohibited them from using certain species of birds for millinery in order to keep them from dying out.

In 1905 the S curve remained the reigning shape. As it was considered chic not to wear color in the street, navy serge, brown tweeds, or black wool were popular for tailor-mades. The jackets, which might be double-breasted, were short, ending just past the waist. Some suits, influenced by the style of the lingerie frock, were made in pale wools decorated with heavy laces like Irish crochet, guipure, Renaissance, and Battenberg. These laces, used in combinations with shirred, ruffled panels and piping, found their way into afternoon and evening dresses in subtle colors: dove gray, robin's-egg blue, pale rose, ice green.

Paris caused a stir by introducing a form of the Empire dress in 1906; this was not worn exactly as shown by designers except by some very fashionable women, who wore the most extreme versions of Empire evening dresses or tea gowns. Within two years, the Empire dress and its corresponding look, the princess dress (a one-piece paneled or gored fitted dress with a flared skirt), changed the silhouette by doing away with the monobosom, which was low and bloused at the waist, the minute waistline, and the two-piece dress. Although still curvy, the Empire silhouette was narrower than the S curve, and its waistline was slightly raised. Suit jackets lengthened, and dresses with jackets began to appear, particularly in linen, lawn, or Irish crochet in summer.

In 1907 the great news was the new short skirt, especially for tailor-mades; it grazed the top of the boot. Boots, which laced or buttoned up to above the ankle or had gaiters, had Cuban heels, about an inch and a half high and curved, also used for other shoes. In jewelry, bar brooches fell from favor, replaced by oblong or round pins. A prevailing style in necklaces was pendants suspended in festoons from a chain, the center pendant the longest, set with semiprecious stones like amethyst or topaz.

In 1908 the *New York Times* lampooned such fashions as the one-piece dress featuring rows of hundreds of buttons, hats shaped like upside-down buckets, and earrings as large as parrots swinging on their bars or vases filled with flowers. In 1909, Parisians became infatuated with all things Russian or Near Eastern. Evening dresses of coarse metallic net were embroidered in large paillettes and beads, with tunic effects and breastplates over the long,

For her 1902 role in the play A Country Mouse, *Ethel Barrymore wore a lingerie dress for a croquet scene and an evening dress made with the same taste for pale tones, fluid lines, and self embroidery. As was typical at the time, the older women are wearing much more luxuriously embroidered and decorated dresses; it would have been unseemly for a young woman, especially one who wasn't married, to appear to be trying to lure men by her rich dress.*

one-piece Empire dress. In contrast, Americans were inspired by the North Pole expedition to wear bright blue wool Hudson Fulton capes, Cook bonnets, Eskimo hats, and Peary coats. The *New York Times* of October 24, 1909, noted that "it's all very well to say the one-piece dress is universal, but just as many coat-suits have been ordered this fall as ever." Nonetheless, the one-piece dress had ushered in newly narrow underwear, and the combination, made with attached cache-corset (also known as corset cover) or camisole and petticoat skirt or knickers, while not new, became more important to wear under fitted clothes.

The Parisian trend for elaborately beaded evening and reception clothes in the Roman, Egyptian, Byzantine, Moorish, or Turkish taste accelerated, and couturiers like the Callot Soeurs and Mme Paquin caught up with Paul Poiret, who started it all. Upholstery materials like glittering brocades and large-scale patterned damasks became the base for narrow dresses adorned with swathes of beading and worn with cocoon-shaped wraps. The hobble skirt was introduced during the spring, and the general consensus in America was that those who wore it were merely copying the mannequins hired by the couturiers to wear their latest creations at fashionable French spots, like the races. In October the hobble skirt gave way to a more practical narrow skirt that often featured buttons at the hem, which could be unbuttoned for walking.

In October the American Ladies' Tailors' Association exhibition in New York highlighted the "suffragette suit," designed in protest of the hobble skirt. It featured a jacket with plenty of pockets and a separated or divided skirt with creases and cuffs, just like male trousers. It did not catch on, but by October 31 two sightings of "near trousers" were reported, one at the Plaza at teatime and another on a Miss Mary Garden. Surprisingly, her costume had been made for her by Doucet of Paris, who told her it was the first costume of its sort to leave the Place Vendôme and dared her to wear it. At about the same time, Poiret brought out his version, which he called the pantaloon skirt. In New York, a dress reformer lectured wearing a long dress open up the sides over pants tucked into high boots. She announced her plan to have the costume made for evening in black velvet as well as white satin, with the pants embroidered in gold, and matching boots, so that she would never again have to worry about what to wear. As with most dress reform items, this ensemble was too radical to enter directly into fashion. Within twenty years, however, pants, especially in pajama versions, were popular for beachwear or in at-home outfits. The divided skirt continued to exist as a novelty; women wore pants tucked into boots for shooting or other winter sports, and American women stuck with the narrow skirt, which they preferred to voluminous ones.

All through 1910, as England mourned King Edward VII—and Mme Paquin in Paris mourned her husband—black and white dominated as the color scheme. Not always combined, both colors also stood on their own, all-white evening dresses being as popular as all-black ones. Other popular colors included strong but not quite vivid tones appropriated from Near Eastern sources: cerise, coral pink, violet, sapphire. The ethnic look also brought in a new version of the shirtwaist; based on a peasant blouse, it was made in soft materials like gauze, crepe de chine, or silk chiffon, and was sometimes embroidered at the front and down the sleeves. By this time the high collar had disappeared, to be replaced by daytime necklines that were round, boat-shaped, or cut like a sailor collar with an inserted panel. Americans were

This evening dress ending in dhoti, or harem, slits for the feet was an example of the many experiments with trouser-legged fashions around 1910.

Going to the races, in this case Belmont Park, meant much simpler and more tailored clothes than would have been worn to the races in France. These two tailormades show a decidedly more relaxed fit than had previously been in fashion; although long and belted at the natural waist, these suits look ahead to the chemise silhouette of the 1920s.

OPPOSITE
This New York beauty wears a dress, circa 1905, that was the apogee of Edwardian taste—made with sinuous lines, in delicate tones, with embroidered decoration that was both subtle and lavish.

By 1909, the Empire line had been incorporated into the S-curve silhouette. Dresses were one piece, with slightly raised waistlines, but the exaggerated posture and the sweep of the train retained the previous curve. Enthusiasm for the gigantic brimmed hat trimmed with ostrich, egret, or bird of paradise—and requiring the longest hatpins in history—peaked in 1909 and 1910.

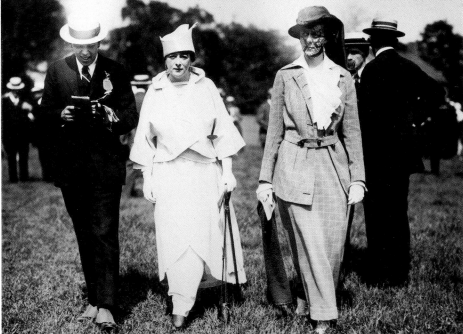

Irene and Vernon Castle were the nation's most famous ballroom dancers. Irene Castle, who often dressed at Lucile's New York branch, had great influence on women all over the country, who copied her short hairstyle and her favorite dress silhouette, which, with its not-too-closely-fitted bodice and a fairly short, bell-shaped skirt, was easy to dance in.

These two New York evening dresses, circa 1911–12, show the prevalence of black and white, either together or alone, and are made in the slightly high-waisted, one-piece, narrow silhouette that was the legacy of the short-lived Empire revival. The ivory silk dress, trimmed with black net, velvet, and jet, was made by Mme Helene, a New York dressmaker; the cream silk satin dress embroidered in white and silver was by Bonwit Teller & Co. The Bruce Museum, Greenwich, Connecticut

confused by these blouses, and fashion writers decreed that white shirtwaists could still be worn with tweed coat-suits, but that suits in colors demanded matching blouses of silk.

In 1911 the black-and-white look continued to dominate fashion. Skirts were narrow, worn quite short for daytime, and bodices of evening dresses were draped like fichus. Couturiers experimented with vaguely Victorian- or Colonial-inspired wider skirts, and Poiret showed his lampshade dress, with its wire hoop–edged tunic. While both the bell-shaped or crinoline skirts and the lampshade tunic were considered freakish, they eventually influenced accepted silhouettes. The lampshade induced a taste for tunic effects, which were often formed by the fabric of the skirt being draped into folds at the hip, and dresses with fuller, fluttering skirts of chiffon or tulle became fashionable along with Irene Castle, who, as half of the husband-and-wife team that popularized ballroom dancing, favored them over the restrictive narrow skirt for gliding across the floor. Irene Castle, who was extremely photogenic, had a slim, girlish figure, and, along with actresses appearing in the new medium of film like Mary Pickford and the Gish sisters, she exuded a youthful charm that resulted in a new standard of beauty. Inspired to cut her hair by the prospect of a hospital stay for an appendectomy in 1914, Irene Castle next appeared in public wearing a seed-pearl necklace around her forehead to keep her coiffure in place, spawning a new hairstyle. In her autobiography she reported that two hundred and fifty women cut their hair the next week, and twenty-five hundred the week after.

The freedom of short hair and short skirts was joined in 1913 by an unconfining silhouette described at the time as triangular or pear-shaped. Sports clothes and day clothes consisted of flared skirts worn with hip-length jackets or cardigan sweaters with wide, unfitted belts. Less-defined waistlines alleviated the need for a tightly laced corset, and the straight, less-fitted corset ushered in the need for a brassiere, both of which were depicted in magazines as being worn over chemises or camisoles. By 1914 the shirtwaist had become a tunic worn outside the skirt, and it was not until the 1930s that shirts would again be tucked into the waistband. For the duration of the war, the prevailing looks were a loosely fitted blouse or jacket worn with a skirt, a one-piece dress for day or afternoon with a gently defined waistline, and an evening dress with a wide bandeau bodice over a slightly full skirt. These styles evolved naturally into the low-waisted chemise dress and suit of the 1920s.

Ever since the turn of the century, when couturiers kept trying to replace the simple American shirtwaist and walking skirt with more ornate garments, the idea that there was a native American fashion suitable for independent American women had been brewing. American-made clothes rose in favor, helped by the rise in the taxes imposed on foreign imports. (By 1907 customs officials routinely captured smugglers of Parisian finery; a stout woman was apprehended who, by the time the yards and yards of lace were unwrapped from around her waist, was found to be quite slender.) Also in 1907 the *New York Times* reported that American tailor-mades were being copied abroad; at the same time, fashionable women who could afford custom clothes were buying ready-to-wear. Supposedly, women who used to take the ready-to-wear labels out of their clothes so that no one would know that they had been reduced to buying cheaper clothing continued to remove them for a new reason: they didn't want anyone else running to the store to buy the same outfit.

According to the fashion press, in 1909 American custom-dressed women continued to rely on ready-to-wear suits for day clothes, and manufacturers claimed that their tailored ready-to-wear was selling well abroad. In 1910 the American Ladies' Tailors' Association exhibition on the Astor Hotel roof featured the press-worthy suffragette suit, as well as "aeroplane suits," which mannequins modeled sitting in an airplane. American manufacturers and retailers wisely realized that they would get more attention offering very modern items than trying to compete with the exotic luxuriousness of Paris.

Saks & Company (which would become Saks Fifth Avenue) advertised in 1911 that its clothes were the products of two continents. "No mere generalization can cover the supreme artistry of American workmanship. And those who tailor our women's apparel are as expert not only in following original ideas from abroad, but also in carrying out our own individual ideas." From here on it became increasingly common for stores to tout their own creations—but they almost always added that they also carried the best imports. In 1912 the actress Geraldine Farrar, asked at an interview that appeared in the *New York Times* of December 29 if American fashion was any good, replied, "I understand that there are houses right here in New York where beautiful clothes are created, but I don't know anything about them. And why? That is just the point." At the same time that the achievements of American or New York designers were creeping into editorial copy, attributions to French designers were soaring. Previously, most dresses depicted in newspapers or magazines had been anonymous.

In December 1912 the *New York Times* sparked off a pleasant controversy by announcing an American fashion design contest, with cash prizes for the top three styles in the categories of evening dress, afternoon dress, and hat. While many people countered that American fashion did not exist, various experts rushed to give their endorsements. Louis M. Fisher of the American Fabric Company wrote in the issue of December 15 that American fashion was not new, but that it had never gotten much attention because it was designed with the average rather than the society woman in mind. Alexandre M. Grean, temporary chairman of the hastily formed Society of American Fashions, opined in the paper of December 17, "We have the art, we have the created product right here in New York. What we want is recognition of it. We want New York dressmakers to stop using false labels . . . and also American manufacturers of silk not to send their fabrics to Europe to be bought and then returned here." Sewing Paris labels into New York–made dresses was a new practice engaged in not by ready-to-wear manufacturers but by the small, exclusive import-custom houses. The head of one of these, Thurn, admitted to the newspaper of December 22 that he had been forced to sew New York–made copies of Paris labels into his designs because "American women have been brainwashed into thinking French clothes are superior." This practice apparently had nothing to do with the copying of French clothes, which was fairly rampant, and which ready-to-wear manufacturers indulged in as well. When Poiret visited New York around 1916, the numerous clothing items with Poiret labels that bore no resemblance to any of his designs prompted him to try and establish regulations concerning copying and false labels.

Finally, in the Sunday, February 23, 1913, issue of the *New York Times*, the winners were announced. The first prize for an evening dress went to Ethel Traphagen, who had studied art at the National Academy of Design,

L. P. Hollander, a store that was a cross between a specialty shop and a custom dressmaking house, created this 1912 evening dress of canary yellow and white chiffon trimmed with silver braid and beads. Chicago Historical Society. Gift of Mrs. John O. Vieta

By World War I, when this military-inspired khaki suit was produced by the New York ready-to-wear manufacturer Max Meyer, the softer, more easily fitted silhouette had become somewhat pear-shaped or triangular. The Library, Fashion Institute of Technology, New York

In this 1919 photograph the author Anita Loos, appearing with John Emerson, is dressed for a ball in Irene Castle–style headband and in an evening dress that was slightly longer, more décolleté, and more ornate, with its embroidered apron effect, than the typical day dress. Her Louis-heeled pumps were fairly new to fashion and would remain in style for more than a decade.

New York, had worked as an illustrator for the publishing house Doubleday, Page & Co., and had been a designer for such custom houses as Joseph, Thurn, Mrs. Osborn, and Maison Jacqueline. (She went on to found the fashion school that still bears her name.) Her design, based on one of James McNeill Whistler's Nocturne paintings, featured blue chiffon layered over putty silk to emulate the painter's nighttime palette and was softly draped and embroidered with garlands of blue and yellow wooden beads.

The first prize for an afternoon dress was awarded to Ruth Turner Wilcox, who later established herself as a writer and illustrator of books on the history of costume. Her dress was of pale blush champagne silk satin, overlaid with an open-front tunic of dull blue chiffon embroidered with pinkish roses, its loosely tied girdle, or cloth belt, finished with tassels. The second prize for an

Not only were these Lower East Side clothing stores of about 1910 (right) crowded together, but the mannequins in the windows, dressed in ready-to-wear suits, are densely packed, in high contrast to the displays in the uptown store J. M. Gidding & Co. (left: Museum of the City of New York).

afternoon gown, won by one of Lord & Taylor's in-house designers, Irma Campbell, was patterned after a Quaker dress and made out of gray silk chiffon with a white lace-edged collar.

The first-prize hat, perhaps most American of all, was made out of white tulle and brown velvet to resemble a cotton boll. Gimbel Bros., which advertised in the same edition of the paper that it would be selling the following day one of the prize-winning hats, wisely opted to offer the second-prize winner, which was inspired by the American Beauty rose.

Bonwit Teller took advantage of the contest by advertising "an American-made Bonwit Teller creation," announcing that there were further domestic as well as foreign models to be seen at the store. Bloomingdale's and Arnold, Constable & Co. also placed ads celebrating American designers (albeit leaving them anonymous). *Ladies' Home Journal* took out an ad proclaiming that it had been the first magazine, four years previously, to advocate and publish American design and that its upcoming issue featured Mrs. Woodrow Wilson (the First Lady) and her daughters dressed in American designs.

The *New York Times* contest considerably increased awareness of New York shops, manufacturers, specialty shops, and designers. Although French clothes continued to be emphasized, American designs were also pushed. Poiret startled his confreres by announcing that he was having his

Henri Bendel, at 520 Fifth Avenue between Forty-third and Forty-fourth streets here, was one of many New York merchants who offered exact copies of Paris dresses as well as in-house designs and costumes for the theater. Everything he sold had the reputation of being of the very finest quality. The New-York Historical Society, New York

By the turn of the century, Fifth Avenue had replaced Broadway as New York's premier shopping street. Custom dressmakers were the first to locate themselves adjacent to the elegant houses being built there, and they were soon followed by department stores, mostly clustered in the Teens not far from Union Square. Lord & Taylor built a branch at Fifth Avenue and Nineteenth Street, which it had already outgrown when this photograph was taken, and in 1914 it moved to Fifth at Thirty-eighth Street (its current site). The fact that Fifth Avenue fronts Central Park above Fifty-ninth Street, where it is not zoned for commercial activity, has kept the retail section fairly stable ever since. Museum of the City of New York

Martine School prints made up into fabrics by a New York silk manufacturer. Dresses made from these prints were sold at Wanamaker, in the grand, expanded former A. T. Stewart store on Broadway.

In 1914, when war erupted in Europe, the couture houses were shaken. Male designers were called to the front, and as the war raged, mills were destroyed, supplies cut off, and shipping and transport presented formidable obstacles. Nonetheless, many of the couture houses managed to remain open, showing limited collections. John Wanamaker ran a two-page ad in *Harper's Bazaar* describing the difficulty with which he managed to get almost two hundred French models out of France despite the couture's state of havoc. Expecting to hear no more from Paris, Edna Woolman Chase, a well-known *Vogue* editor, planned a Fashion Fête showing New York designs as a charity benefit. Henri Bendel, Herman Patrick Tappé, Kurzman, Bergdorf & Goodman, and the Maison Jacqueline all participated. However, as soon as it became clear that the French were still operating their couture houses, *Vogue* again turned its attention to supporting their efforts. New York buyers continued to go to Paris, but Charles Kurzman reported in 1915 that only about fifty New York store representatives, as opposed to the usual two hundred, made the trip to examine the French collections.

Although the Paris houses remained in operation, New York store buyers made fewer purchases there, relying more on New York originals. Designer-importers Tappé, Bendel, and Hickson wrote articles for *Harper's Bazaar* describing not only French fashions but also their own designs, which were copyrighted. Hickson made a splash in 1917 with his bustle-back frocks; Bendel continued to exert a tremendous influence through his costuming for the theater; and Tappé accompanied his somewhat outlandish designs for hats with poems and prose in his decorative script. Several branches of European couture houses located in New York, including Lucile, the Boué Soeurs, Redfern, and Revillon, contributed to the field of original custom work being done here. By the time the war was over, several of the French couturiers found it impossible to recover their prewar cachet. Poiret, Paquin, and the Callot Soeurs, responsible for the most extreme of the so-called freakish fashions, dwindled in popularity and were replaced by a group, among them Gabrielle Chanel, Jean Patou, Edouard Molyneux, and Madeleine Vionnet, who sensed better how to dress the modern woman.

New York fashion continued to be divided into several categories. There were ready-to-wear manufacturers, mostly in the area of the shirtwaist and the coat-and-suit; department stores that ranged from very thrifty to very luxurious; ladies' tailors, who made custom suits; dressmakers, who produced custom reception and evening dresses; and specialty shops, or custom-import houses, that sold imported models, adaptations of imports made according to customers' directions, and original designs. These last stores were the most exclusive, luxurious, and creative. Some of them, like Henri Bendel and Bergdorf & Goodman, eventually became top-of-the-line department stores.

For the most part, manufacturers were anonymous, but some had their tailor-mades acknowledged in *Women's Wear*. In the 1910s, Max Grab Co. made typical suits of wool or velvet, decorated simply. In 1916 this company advertised authorized Poiret copies, which bore a special label and which may or may not have been actually authorized. Wm. H. Davidow & Sons, a firm of coat-and-suit specialists founded in 1880, would remain in business

Particularly American is the tendency, apparent in this mid-1910s ready-to-wear skating costume by Max Meyer, to design clothes for fairly vigorous activities in an intentionally feminine idiom. European sports clothes for ladies were usually translated literally from those worn by men. The Library, Fashion Institute of Technology, New York

for many decades. Max M. Schwarcz was another wholesale manufacturer of tailored costumes. Max Schwarcz was a man of rarefied tastes, an art collector and opera aficionado, whose company produced all the copies of Paris models for the import-custom house J. Lichtenstein. A. Beller & Co., which had been founded in 1890, copied tailored clothes from Berlin and Vienna for New York retail stores. Max Meyer, a partner in the firm, told M. D. C. Crawford in the latter's book *The Ways of Fashion* that the tailor-made manufacturers were much more dependent on Berlin and Vienna for inspiration than on Paris, but that they began to be more independent by 1905. Wilkins & Adler manufactured Golfex suits for sports that were sold around the country. Perhaps the most highly regarded ready-to-wear manufacturer was Edward L. Mayer, a native Chicagoan who started his business in New York. Mayer was known for his allegiance to creative design, workmanship, and, above all, expert fit. In 1915 Main Rousseau Bocher, who eventually became the couturier Mainbocher, was a student in New York supporting himself by selling sketches of his own designs to the Mayer company.

The National Cloak & Suit Company on West Twenty-fourth Street, despite its utilitarian-sounding name, offered no ready-to-wear. Founded in 1888, it operated out of its own eleven-story fireproof building, built in 1907, where 1,500 employees produced suits, two-piece dresses, shirtwaists and skirts, cloaks, and underwear, all of which could be ordered made to individual measure through its catalogues. Other custom tailors included Nardi, on West Forty-seventh Street, which specialized in riding habits, Berkowitz, whose custom-made habits were fitted as the customer sat astride a wooden horse, Joseph Fiore on Forty-sixth Street, H. Blumberg on West Thirty-sixth, Wm. Naddelman on West Forty-eighth, and J. Winter on East Thirty-eighth.

During the first two decades of the century, the best establishments for shopping relocated to be near Fifth Avenue in the Thirties, Forties, and Fifties. Some department stores, which at the time sold everything from Paris originals to store-made copies and adaptations to ready-made clothing that had been manufactured by outside contractors, still occupied the downtown areas of Sixth Avenue in the high Teens and low Twenties or Fourteenth Street, and a new shopping area, Herald Square, at Thirty-fourth Street and Broadway, centered around Macy, Saks & Company, and Gimbel Bros. Downtown, on Broadway between Eighth and Tenth streets, was Wanamaker, which had taken over the A. T. Stewart emporium in 1896, greatly enlarged it by building another structure next to it, and added shopping bridges above the street connecting the two. A brilliant retailer, John Wanamaker drew customers downtown by offering the finest imports and exclusive designs by couturiers like Poiret, and he also launched his own designer, called Diana, who specialized in the then-untried area of young ladies' clothes.

Other department stores included Oppenheim & Collins at Broadway and Twenty-first Street, which moved to Thirty-fourth Street in 1916, Simpson-Crawford-Simpson at Sixth Avenue between Nineteenth and Twentieth streets, O'Neill Adams Co. at Sixth between Twentieth and Twenty-second streets, and Stern, which moved from the Twenties up to between Forty-second and Forty-third streets. On Fifth Avenue were B. Altman at Thirty-fourth Street, Bonwit Teller, which moved to Thirty-eighth in 1911, Lord & Taylor, which moved to Fifth at Thirty-eighth in 1914 and offered French models ranging in price from $235 to $650, Franklin Simon, between Thirty-seventh

This turn-of-the-century opera wrap of velvet and lace embroidered with chenille was made by T. M. and J. M. Fox, a custom dressmaking establishment so exclusive that there was no shingle above the door and such socially questionable women as actresses were discouraged from coming there to have their clothes made. Museum of the City of New York. Gift of Mrs. Paul Moore

This 1914 evening dress of salmon velvet trimmed with silver lace and pink tulle was custom-made by Hope & Co., New York. Chicago Historical Society. Gift of Mrs. James M. Hopkins

and Thirty-eighth, McCreery at Thirty-fourth, Stewart & Co. at Thirty-seventh, and Best & Co. at Thirty-fifth.

The specialty shops were numerous, and most were headed by savvy designer-importers who boasted a real knack for choosing Parisian imports and whose own staffs were capable of top workmanship and quality. Besides Bendel, Bergdorf & Goodman, Tappé, Hickson, Joseph, and Kurzman, there were houses whose names were lesser known by choice. Among these, perhaps the best was T. M. and J. M. Fox, which was owned by Mrs. Edward Douglas (the mother of Carmel Snow, famous editor of *Harper's Bazaar*), who had bought the firm from the Fox sisters. In 1911 Mrs. Douglas moved the company to 10 West Fifty-seventh Street into the Havemeyer house, for which she paid $220,000. She kept the staff at 225 and prided herself on employing only American designers, although the house was known to go to Paris for inspiration. Jake Lichtenstein, whose business had begun in the mid-nineteenth century on Canal Street, was one of the best importers, and he distinguished himself by discovering Jean Patou, buying from him when the designer was using the name Parry.

Although Fifty-seventh Street was becoming important, with residents T. M. and J. M. Fox as well as Lucile, most of the specialty shops were located on or just off Fifth Avenue. These included Frances Clyne at Fiftieth Street, Estelle Mershon, J. M. Gidding, and Maison Bernard between Thirty-second and Thirty-third, Maison Maurice at Forty-third, Russeks at number 326, and L. P. Hollander at 552. Frances, an importer-designer who had her own building at Fifth and Fifty-third, would later be described by Anita Loos as dressing gold diggers. Four other establishments operated out of her building: Mary Anderson Warner, Hope & Co., Balcom, and Faibisy, who advertised that one of his clients was Irene Castle.

It is hard to know where to draw the line between dressmaker and importer-custom house, since dressmakers could import clothes either by buying them in Paris or through import agencies, but the best dressmaker in New York was considered to be Mrs. Dunstan. Another top-notch house was run by Mrs. Osborn. It was patronized by the interior decorator Elsie de Wolfe, who had been a minor stage actress in the 1890s, known for her perfect taste in Paris dresses and her grace when wearing them. That she ordered clothes from Mrs. Osborn indicates that the quality there equaled that of her favorite French couturiers. In 1912 Elsie de Wolfe ordered a suit hemmed to six inches above the floor. She wore it in Paris, and later she liked to tell the tale that it started a fad for "le walking suit." Other dressmaker-importers included Mollie O'Hara, Jo Ford, Jeanne Dimelow, formerly with Mrs. Osborn, Simcox, Mrs. Clarke, an early pioneer on Madison Avenue at number 182, Julia Boyd Bacon, and Ruszit, directed by Margaret Smith, formerly of Aitken.

Style watchers reported on what was available at New York stores as well as what was worn to weddings, in restaurants, onstage, at dances or teas, and American women waited to see which Parisian novelties would be adopted or rejected by Manhattan. Every kind of clothing, from the most regal to the most plebeian, was available here, and in great variety. It was seeing New York society women buying ready-made suits that did away with the stigma attached to buying off the peg. Whether or not New York compared to Paris was an issue that could not be resolved, at least for several decades. That New York was the capital of the American fashion world was indisputable.

The biggest change in fashion during World War I was the emergence of the dress as a casual, all-day item that was as comfortable and practical as a shirtwaist and skirt or a tailor-made. Wartime wool shortages had seen to it that silks and other fabrics came to the fore, and the tailored, rather than formal, silk dress, such as the one shown here of around 1920, became a fashion staple that lasted well into the 1920s and beyond.

THE 1920s

The 1920s brought a mood of frenetic change and dissatisfaction with the ways of the past. Suddenly, man had become airborne; communication moved rapidly via telephone, radio, and movies; and automobile travel had opened up new vistas to be explored. Three specific occurrences in the first year of the decade added greatly to its flavor: on January 16, Prohibition went into effect; on August 20, the first licensed radio broadcasting began; and on August 26, women officially won the right to vote.

Prohibition altered much more than national drinking habits. At all levels of society, but most strikingly in the always emulatable upper classes and the newly influential café society, breaking this particular law was so common as

to be fashionable—and ignoring the Volstead Act fostered the flouting of other conventions. In addition, alcohol was no longer solely a male vice. Having already proven that they could perform well in the workplace and that they deserved the right to vote, women set about establishing another relationship as equals to men: that of pals, or partners in crime. Women boasted about holding their liquor and enjoyed complaining of hangovers; they competed vigorously with men in sports and in performing acts of bravado; they took up swearing and smoking. If it didn't sully men's reputations to engage in petting parties, then women wouldn't let it bother them either.

The automobile and advances in housekeeping technology had liberated women from the home, and they spent their newfound time acting not like the equals of mature men but like adolescent boys. Not every woman in America ran in a fast crowd, but those who did not could shock their elders merely by bobbing their hair (it would be years before emotional reactions to shorn hair abated), using slang, raising their hemlines, or putting on lipstick in public. Visually, women transformed themselves into only slightly feminized versions of their male cohorts, and the gamine was born. Also known as a flapper

The widespread use of the automobile was one of many reasons why 1920s women spent so little time tending the hearth. As they raced around town, and for sports and evening as well, they wore streamlined clothes—almost brimless cloche hats, short, narrow skirts, and flat shoes—and bobbed hairstyles, appropriate for the speedy modern pace of the time.

Dancing was so popular during the 1920s that tea, or afternoon, dances came into vogue. These suited the casual air of the times, since men were appropriately dressed in blazers and flannels or suits, and women could waltz or fox-trot in afternoon frocks.

The University of Kansas coeds shown here modeling the correct costumes for such activities as golf, riding, traveling, and attending classes demonstrate how uniform 1920s fashions were. The one- or two-piece chemise dress or the cardigan suit, depending on how dressy or sporty it was, could be worn anywhere.

These maillot-clad bathing beauties demonstrate that 1928 was a leap year. By this time, women were wearing the exact same bathing costume as men, who did not abandon the tank tops of their swimsuits until the 1930s. For women, second-skin maillots signaled a radical change from the knee-length dresses with bloomers worn with mobcaps, dark stockings, and rubber-soled shoes seen in the water as recently as World War I.

and a Bright Young Thing, the twenties type was characterized by a boyish figure, leggy and straight of torso; by her shining cap of hair; and by such youthful features as wide-open eyes, tiny lips, and rosy cheeks.

The rise of radio brought music into most households, and popular music, particularly the more risqué forms of blues and jazz, took hold of the 1920s, in much the same way that rock and roll, and then rock, colored the 1950s and 1960s. The fascination with dancing, already intense, accelerated, and to add to the hours in a day in which it could be practiced, tea dancing became all the rage. Popular flappers could go from dancing all afternoon to dinner to dancing all night. In some parts of the country, dance marathons enjoyed a vogue that would diminish only in the 1930s; in stuffy places, new dances were banned as soon as they were introduced. Those who could not afford to patronize a hotel dance room rolled up the rug at home, accompanied by whatever band was being broadcast live over the airwaves. The dances that became crazes were exhibitionist and athletic in nature, and the energetic American girl who could work all day and play all night set the tone for the ideal woman of the period.

The changes in women's lives during and after World War I were paralleled by fashion changes that made for clothes that were much freer-fitting and much less formal than ever before. World War I also altered the role of the Paris couture. Previously, styles had been slow to change, with silhouettes evolving over decades. New each season, arriving by steamer from France, or each month, described in cables printed in American newspapers and magazines, was the odd detail of fashion rather than any entire look. Manufacturers and custom-design houses as well as women who made their own clothes or had them made by a dressmaker followed the news of the components of fashion, ready to incorporate into a dress that already existed or was being made up the latest in colors, materials, collar or sleeve shape, length in train. These ideas came anonymously from France, usually in reports of what was seen on fashionable women, along with the materials with which to execute them: silk brocades, embroideries, laces, ribbons, trimmings, beads, feathers, and silk flowers. Although beautiful laces could be imported from Belgium, England, or Ireland, shawls from Scotland or Kashmir, and beads and crystals from Austria, France was the only country to develop so completely all the different areas of fashion into a self-sufficient whole, and it did so with the highest level of artistry and cachet. France was also the only country to promote new modes successfully in order to sell the components that went into them.

Fashions in accessories typically changed frequently, because, to offset the slower pace of silhouette change, women wanted novelty, and also because such smalls as capelets, kid gloves, paste jewels, and, especially, hats could be transported, displayed, tried on, and incorporated into American clothes-wearing habits far more easily than the couture's whole costumes, which had to be made individually and to order. In addition, the limited clientele of the couturiers included only those Americans who could travel to Paris for their clothes or who, having already established a relationship and a file of measurements with a couture house, could order through the mails. The couturiers, therefore, were unimportant to the average American woman, who cared only that her new fichu or silk bouquet or embroidered stockings be Parisian. Being French guaranteed an article's quality as well as its de-

pendability as a status symbol. Parisian flavor aside, the French article was likely far finer than any American counterpart; manufacturers here could not produce the gossamer silks for flower petals, the fine laces, the hand-done trimmings, ribbons, and so on, as these small, artisan-dependent industries had never been established here. In order to attract customers, New York stores had only to advertise that a Paris shipment had cleared customs; there the next morning would be waiting scores of women who didn't care who Worth was but could appreciate the finer points of point lace.

The radically simpler clothes that sprang up during and after World War I "re-shuffled the great couturiers" (*Fortune*, 1932), and a new group of French designers emerged whose clothes were less complicated, less "French," and therefore much more appealing and meaningful to Americans. Fashion magazines that had previously mentioned sparingly such names as Paquin, Worth, or Doucet now touted Chanel jersey suits, Patou golf ensembles, Molyneux chemise frocks, Vionnet crepe de chine afternoon dresses, Jane Regny bathing suits, and even Schiaparelli's first clever homemade sweaters. Because they were designing simpler clothes that reflected a more democratic general attitude, and because these simpler clothes were by their very nature much more copiable, French designers became, for the first time, household names in this country. Women for whom a Poiret lampshade tunic or a Callot Soeurs evening dress in the Chinese taste had just been something to admire (or scoff at) from a distance went from coveting the latest French silk ribbon as a sash for their American-made lingerie dress to planning their wardrobes around Chanel's beige tricot dress no. 811 or its American adaptation.

American clients had never been unimportant to couturiers (Worth had described them as having the desirable attributes of "faith, figures and francs"), and in the 1920s they assumed a new role—that of dictating fashions rather than being dictated to. The boom years here had started with the war, and Americans spent money in the 1920s at a dizzying rate. With the decline in value of the French franc, Paris clothes and accessories became more accessible and affordable than ever before. The couturiers realized that they had to keep their American clientele satisfied. Although they tried repeatedly to lengthen skirts in the 1920s, preferring to make their clothes less sporty and more elegant, American women adored the freedom of the short skirt and rejected all Parisian attempts to persuade them to give it up.

At a time when American fashion should have been rising to the fore, since it had always been based on now-popular notions of comfort and ease, the French, inspired by a difficult fiscal situation, managed to make their position in fashion invincible—and they achieved this not by developing the artistry of the couture but by "designing American." Jean Patou pulled off one of the greatest fashion publicity coups ever when he imported six American models to Paris to work as fitting models (American women were built differently from Frenchwomen—they were taller and less curvaceous) and also to wear his jaunty, American-inspired designs in his shows. American designers and manufacturers here had yet to learn the art of self-promotion, and since they were doing so well copying, or claiming to copy (they had found that they could sell a $19.95 suit for $24.95 by appending the description "after a Chanel *tailleur*"), they stuck for the moment with the "bird in the hand."

Twenties fashion can be summed up in a single garment: the short, straight, figure-skimming, low-waisted chemise frock. First known as the tu-

This two-piece golf chemise of tan and brown wool flannel was made with an asymmetric neckline embroidered with a flower.

Mme Eta, a New York wholesale, or ready-to-wear, designer, created these six variations on the chemise theme in 1923. She softened the straight silhouette by using lace, circular skirts, and floating scarves. The Brooklyn Museum Library Collection, New York

bular dress, it did not burst immediately onto the scene, however, nor was it worn for the entire decade. It evolved fairly slowly and peaked during 1925 and 1926. Despite the best efforts of couturiers, hemlines rose steadily. The most notable aspect of the decade was the softness and relative lack of construction in all the clothes. Two factors contributed to this relaxation of the silhouette. The new allegiance to freedom of movement opposed rigid construction and corsetry; at the same time, there was a dearth of heavier, stiffer materials like wool and cotton because so many French mills had been damaged in the war. By the end of the 1920s both wool, particularly the non-French-produced Scottish tweeds, and cotton would be so popular as to constitute fads, but until then silk was the predominant material. It led to a fashion characterized by easy fit, blouson waistlines, flowing scarves and other panels, circular skirts, and shirring in lieu of more rigid tailoring. Even coats and the blazers of suits were soft and unconstructed.

Day dresses and suits were made of silk jersey, foulard, limp faille, and georgette; afternoon dresses of crepe de chine or chiffon; evening dresses of silk brocades, lamés, satins, and velvets. The importance of silk to twenties fashion was demonstrated by its extensive use for underwear (pale peach, dark peach, and bright peach were the colors of choice for bandeaux, camisoles, chemises, teddies, peignoirs, even boudoir pillows, chaise throws, and counterpanes) and for active sportswear. Even women who were playing to win adopted silk tennis dresses, bathing suits, and golf frocks.

Rayon, officially baptized in 1924 but extant before then, was first experimented with as a replacement for silk in printed dress materials and in underwear, and it also was an integral element of the new shiny, thin velvet hybrid known as transparent velvet. This material, which was used for afternoon and evening dresses, capes with shirred, fold-over collars, and evening coats with ermine or rabbit trim, became so ubiquitous that the *New Yorker*'s fashion writer Lois Long was driven in September 1928 to describe it as "that slinking, drooping, glistening velvet, the sight of which is torture now."

At the beginning of the 1920s, women were still wearing dresses with waistlines slightly lowered but not yet at the hip, barrel-shaped skirts, and hemlines that hovered between knee and ankle, favoring the ankle. These dresses featured some trailing, trainlike draperies and pannier side or apron-front panels. Suits had long, blazerlike jackets, harbingers of the very low waistline. Coats with wrap (surplice) fronts were common and would remain so for the remainder of the decade. Women accessorized their clothes with deep-crowned hats, some with wide brims and some made as crushed turban-toques, trimmed with long swatches of egret, bird of paradise, or ostrich, and with Louis-heeled pumps, often with rectangular buckles set with marcasite or paste. At night, continuing in the Irene Castle tradition, glittering bandeaux were worn around the head across the forehead, and hair, whether long or, more frequently, short, was dressed low about the brow, usually combed sideways across the forehead in loose waves. In fashion magazines women were depicted with smudgily outlined eyes, and the emphasis for all the features was on roundness: spherical eyes, circles of color in the middle of cheeks, and bright red lips painted to look as if they were pursed for a kiss. Although King Tut's tomb would not be excavated for several years, Egyptomania was already the rage in 1920, led on in New York by Charles Kurzman, at whose store one could find Egyptian jewelry, embroideries, and scarab orna-

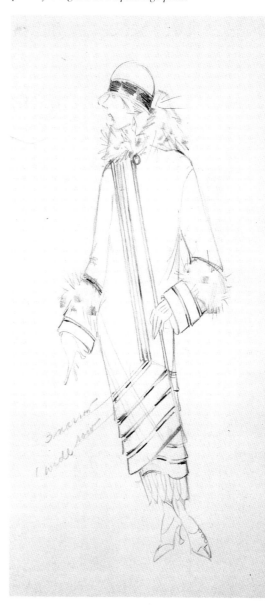

Shortly after the little silk dress came into being, the little printed silk dress, considered very practical, followed. This 1928 example with its tire-tread pattern was especially designed as a Speed Age print.

Just as the chemise dress dominated fashion, so did the fur-trimmed, wrap-front coat, and it was available in such sporty fabrics as leather or jersey or tweed on up to luxurious chiffon velvet, lamé brocade, and beaded or embroidered silk. This 1920 coat was from Bonwit Teller. The Irene Lewisohn Library, the Costume Institute, The Metropolitan Museum of Art, New York

ments, as well as fabrics woven to capture the nacreous quality of faience.

In 1921 waistlines stabilized at the hip and skirts were fairly narrow, although not yet short. The straightish line struck a medieval note, and designers studied the Middle Ages for details like long, trailing sleeves, bateau necklines, low, girdling belt effects, deep tones, and slightly crude pre-eighteenth-century-style embroideries. The medieval look was popular throughout the decade for brides' and bridesmaids' dresses, as it was in architecture and interior decoration. Barer bodices for evening started to appear, including one-shouldered and camisole necklines. In shoes, pumps started to be replaced by the more ornate T-strap and the demisandal, both of which were considered to lend more support when dancing vigorously. Although plain shoes would be described throughout the decade as the most "smart" (an important style word in the 1920s), with short skirts highlighting the foot, increasingly elaborate combinations of colors, textures, and rhinestones or other ornaments were to be found. As evening dresses became simpler in style (but not necessarily in surface decoration), wraps and cloaks became more sumptuous.

Attempts in 1922 to lower hemlines failed miserably. To provide more interest in the short skirts women wanted, designers introduced godets and other inset panel treatments that would allow skirts to fall gracefully in folds from the low waistline. Beige and tan were fast becoming the chic colors, next to black, for daytime wear. The flapper's coiffure was beginning to look less unruly, worn close to the head in a shingle and ashine (like a man's) with pomade or brilliantine.

In August 1922 the couturier Paul Poiret visited America and set off a spark of controversy about American taste and style. Congress was contemplating raising the import tax on clothes from 60 to 90 percent, and Poiret told the *New York Times* (August 30, page 10) that the high tariffs would prohibit French designers from selling their clothes to Americans and that this country would suffer, because American designers did not "have the spark of genius that is necessary," and, furthermore, American women were always three years behind the times. New York couturier and importer Nathaniel Giddings countered in the next day's paper that "the American designers have made wonderful progress, and, outside of six or eight of the famous ones in Paris, we have just as good designers here" and added that "our Fifth Avenue shops are superior to the shops on the Rue de la Paix ten to one." Most of the ensuing letters defended American women for not being slaves to fashion; for having eschewed unwieldy long skirts; for being well dressed at all price levels, not just at the top; for looking well in business; and even for being ahead of fashion—having worn the beaded evening dress two seasons before it was shown in Paris. Poiret, ever mindful that publicity serves to sell clothes, finally conceded that American women had indeed improved since his 1913 visit.

By 1923 fashion seemed to be splitting off into two directions. One, led by such couturiers as Chanel, advocated the straight-hanging frock for day and evening, eight inches from the floor for the conservative, ten inches for the daring. In January 1923 Baron de Meyer, bon vivant and fashion photographer and observer, used the phrase "extravagant poverty" to describe the ever more streamlined and sleek silhouette whose spareness was balanced by the most opulent of materials: brocades, embroideries, and, especially, all-

DAVY GEORGETTE and TAFFETTA   NO.11617   TAN NET and LACE FLAME RIBBON GIRDLE NO.41628

As the 1920s progressed, the waistline dropped and dresses became straighter in cut. These afternoon dresses, one of which was made along middy blouse lines, were worn to watch the tennis matches at the Newport Casino.

This sales album page from the top-quality wholesale firm Edward L. Mayer shows the back and front views of two 1921 afternoon dresses. The waistline has not yet hit the hips, but otherwise the 1920s silhouette is in place. The Brooklyn Museum Library Collection, New York

over beading. Day and evening clothes differed only in the degree of bareness (although bare arms were creeping into daytime dress via the sports dress) and in the materials used.

The second direction was a more nostalgic and feminine look, exemplified by the designs of Poiret, Lanvin, Madeleine et Madeleine, and the Callot Soeurs, as well as by New York–based designers Herman Patrick Tappé, Lucile, and the Boué Soeurs. These romantic and occasionally exotic fashions, often based on details from paintings or from the history of costume, included the full-skirted *robe de style*, made in paper taffetas or silk organdies and embellished with feminine ribbons, flowers, ruchings, and lace.

Harper's Bazaar wrote in October 1923 that "the cloche (like the chemise dress) is so youthful that women simply will not relinquish it," and the prediction proved true. Either entirely brimless or with a small visorlike attachment, the cloche was worn very low on the brow, over hair even flatter than before, with spit curls peeping out on one or both sides. Suspended from mostly hidden earlobes were longer and longer dangling earrings. Accessories of all kinds in this period were highly designed, even when worn by the most severely smart women. Smoking had ushered in the use of cigarette cases, lighters, and holders, and the open wearing of makeup called for compacts, lipstick cases, or vanities (precursors of minaudières) that had compartments for rouge, lipstick, and comb as well as dimes and quarters. They were made in precious, semiprecious, or base metal, especially in combinations of various colors of gold or silver and copper and brass. As in the decorative arts, lacquered finishes were popular, in shades of coral, black, eggshell, and shagreen. Some featured chinoiserie motifs, others were whimsical, inscribed with cartoon characters or private jokes. The bracelet watch, typically twenties in that it combined sportiness with feminine decorations, set with sparkling stones, was much seen, and designers resuscitated the fan as a chic accessory, making it in unusual asymmetric shapes or materials. Spanish shawls were frequently worn as evening wraps.

Although in 1924 the Paris Exposition des Arts Décoratifs, which gave its name to the style Art Deco, was still a year off, geometric patterns were everywhere in fashion. Beaded dresses were decorated with triangles, overlapping circles, ziggurats, lots of fringes, and dark-light contrasts. Spectator and active sports clothes featured striped and checked materials, appliquéd geometrics, squared-off monograms, and bright colors used in striking combinations. In New York, a designer named Berthe Holley, who had trained in Paris and worked as a designer here for twelve years, presented a collection at the Plaza Hotel that featured the new idea of having clothes designed in sets. The dresses, composed of tunics and slips, were planned so that a group of pieces could be interchangeable, making a few dresses seem like many. This early example of the separates concept was peculiarly American: women here had continued the shirtwaist tradition into the twentieth century by buying and wearing sweaters and blouses with skirts to make up ensembles. Since twenties evening, day, and sports clothes all looked so similar, a skirt and top in a matching or contrasting color was easy to coordinate. It resembled a dress and was tidy and comfortable. Unlike in Paris, entire New York manufacturing houses were devoted to separates, like blouses or skirts.

Underneath their clothes, twenties women wore camisoles or chemises and step-ins, or teddies, and a brief, straight girdle to hold up their stockings. A

Along with the sporty flapper style existed a more romantic look, usually but not always worn by debutantes and other young women. This velvet dress features a somewhat gathered skirt and a bertha collar made of pieced gros point and other laces.

lighter version of this last item was made to wear for dancing, but racier flappers stashed their girdles in the cloakrooms so as not to disappoint their dancing partners, who had come to expect women not to feel rigidly encased in corsets. Without anything to hold them up, stockings had to be rolled at the knee. This was an *outré* look often depicted in the drawings of popular cartoonist John Held, Jr. Other lingerie followed the lines of clothing. Nightgowns were cut in straight lines like dresses and came with little self belts to be worn low on the hip. Peignoirs, which appeared in silk, lace, or transparent cut velvet, were shaped like evening coats, usually wrapping and sometimes slightly cocoon in shape. Pajama costumes were worn by the mid-1920s in place of tea gowns for at home, or dishabille.

In 1925 the quantity of stockings produced in this country, at 12,300,000 dozen pairs, had increased by almost 100 percent since 1919. Not only were the numbers greater but also the proportion of seamless to seamed stockings was reversed. Made of cotton and knitted in the shape of a straight cylinder, seamless stockings bagged at the ankles and stretched out at the knees. Seamed stockings were made in two shaped pieces sewn together, a much more expensive process; prior to 1920, it accounted for only 20 percent of stocking production in this country. According to *Fortune* magazine's January 1932 issue (page 49), "silk stockings made short skirts wearable," which is true, since women never would have raised their hemlines just to show opaque, drooping leg coverings. The most desirable stockings in this country were beige or flesh-colored, plain, and, most important, sheer; French stockings, made with clocks (patterns along the wide of the leg) or allover designs, were not as popular here.

Other fashion-related businesses grew rapidly in the 1920s. Short hairstyles, although they gave the illusion of being carefree, actually required more upkeep than long hair, despite the fact that women typically had assistance piling their tresses on top of their heads. The bob and the shingle had to be trimmed regularly and treated with permanent and/or finger waves. Beauty shops mushroomed, providing all sorts of hair-related services (including dyeing, which was still a furtive affair) and also facial treatments, massage, and applications of the newest form of makeup: nail lacquer. The first nail polishes, which came in shades of red as well as blue, green, and purple, had no staying power—the tints ran when women washed their hands. Young companies like Revlon, Elizabeth Arden, and Helena Rubinstein competed with each other in the search for long-lasting enamels.

The mid-1920s also saw the hat industry move toward mass production. Machines were devised that could construct, block, and even trim hats, and as a result prices went down and availability grew. Women no longer had to save their good custom-made hats for years, retrimming them for novelty, as they could buy a new one instead. By the 1930s, mass production allowed hat styles to change rapidly.

The Art Deco phenomenon, already in the air in terms of fashion by the time of the great 1925 exposition, exerted a definite influence on the architecture, interior decoration, and display design of department and specialty stores. Hattie Carnegie announced in 1925 that her new five-story building would be designed by the same mastermind who had decorated the atelier of Lucien Lelong, and Lord & Taylor in 1926 planned entire windows around a group of screens by the artist Drian, painted with his signature *élégantes*

As the predominant dress silhouette of the 1920s grew simpler and straighter, its forms of decoration grew more ornate. Beaded dresses became immensely popular; they were available in gauze with restrained ornamentation for afternoon or in silks, chiffons, and velvets entirely pavé with rhinestones and bugle beads for black tie. Just as pleats were used to add movement to daytime styles, fringes were worn at night for dancing. This beaded, fringed evening dress was modeled by a Hollywood starlet and is thus more fitted than the usual chemise frock; film actresses were loath to hide their figures, no matter what the going style, whereas on Broadway, a chic and up-to-the-moment look was more important.

posed in chic locales against backgrounds of silver and gold. Milgrim moved in 1928 to 6 East Fifty-seventh Street and furnished its interiors with high-gloss woods combined with matte-finish silver metal, and B. Altman conducted an exhibition of twentieth-century taste that included furniture, objets d'art, and fashion. In window display the modern style banished old-fashioned lifelike mannequins and postures, substituting the new wax dummies with ultrastylized faces set into avant-garde environments. By the 1930s, artistic windows would be a matter of course.

The peak period for the short, tubular chemise frock lasted into 1926, although *Women's World*, "the Magazine for the Middle West," was just beginning to show the below-the-knee-length skirt, indicating that New York (and, of course, Paris) was rather ahead of the rest of the country. Almost every skirt of daytime costumes shown anywhere was pleated, whether all around or in clustered box pleats. Evening and afternoon clothes featured trailing draperies that tempered the harsh lines and bands of fox or ostrich on hems and sleeves. The most prevalent neckline for tuniclike blouses and the bodices of dresses was a scarf band tied in a bow or a knot at the end of a V. Rectangular, square, or triangular scarves were as important to the flapper as paisley shawls and lace fichus were to the Victorian lady. Hats were worn slightly less close to the head, with crushed folds or other shapes of sculptural interest and ornaments of Bakelite set in metal with brilliants.

What was then known as couturier jewelry was the rage of 1926. There are several reasons for its widespread acceptance. First, there was the booming predilection for pearls, set in motion by the invention in Japan of the cultured-pearl process. Natural pearls, rare and more costly by far than any other precious stone, had previously been worn only by royalty and the very wealthiest of women. Cultured pearls were available to a whole new segment of society and therefore became a fashion in and of themselves, making imitation pearls also desirable as a look. Hardly any woman photographed in the 1920s is without her slightly-longer-than-a-choker strand of graduated pearl beads. Among the first pieces of costume jewelry designed by Chanel, generally acknowledged as the originator of couturier jewels, was a 1924 pair of Zuleika Dobson (one black and one white) pearl earrings.

Costume jewelry was also important in light of the prevailing simplicity of clothes. In Paris, the accessories houses, like Alexandrine for gloves, Hellstern & Sons for shoes, and Caroline Reboux for hats, had always been independent entities, with the majority of the couture houses concentrating solely on clothes. As the appeal of clothing came to be based more on style and less on artistry, couturiers were more or less forced into showing their clothes fully accessorized in order to make any impact, and what they designed to show on their little nothing dresses became a big lure for New York department stores, who all set up couturier jewelry departments. The latest in pearls were triple strands in tints of gold, silver, or *café crème;* crystal was popular for long, dangling earrings and in chains; and, as couturiers became more inventive, they experimented with various combinations of wood, cork beads, "exotic seeds," and dull gold rondels and made necklaces with chiffon or tulle and paste-set spheres. Costume jewelry parures (matching sets) might include jeweled shoulder straps and belt buckles to be sewn onto dresses. New York dress manufacturers began to make use of Art Deco rhinestone-set clips and buckles to enliven otherwise simple designs.

Although this tweed suit is accessorized with a shotgun, it would more likely have been worn for spectator sport. As wools again started to become plentiful, tweeds became all the rage.

Lois Long wrote in the *New Yorker* in 1927, "As regards the new jewelry, I have opinions that are both violent and definite, and I might as well express them now as later. I accepted the artificial pearls after a year's struggle, but the new Chanel 'diamond' necklaces are too, too much for me. To my mind, these are glassy and flashy, though the Parisienne who loves glitter, will doubtless adore them." Between fake and precious jewelry was a range of semiprecious styles made of silver or silver gilt set with carnelian, black or green onyx, coral, or cabochon glass, and this was considered more tasteful than pieces in strass, or paste. Part of the appeal of couturier jewelry lay in its ability to shock the older generation, which had been brought up to consider imitation jewels cheap. Carmel Snow, famed editor of *Harper's Bazaar*, recalled in her autobiography how shocked her mother was to see her in the latest Paris mode of extremely plain Chanel jersey adorned with masses of baubles.

Asymmetry gradually became the keynote of 1927. Surplice necklines draped to one side of the hip; bias-cut, almost flat ruffles zigzagged across skirts. Allover beaded patterns began to be supplanted by motifs sprinkled down one side of a dress. Triangular scarves called Deauville handkerchiefs, worn with the points hanging down over one shoulder and tied in a knot over the other, were seen in fashion illustrations as well as on women on city and resort boulevards. Some women wore these at the shoulder—or at the hip— over tailored one- or two-piece dresses. Evening clothes began to show signs of the coming transformation of silhouette: when viewed from the front, some designs looked short and straight; from the back, with their trailing draperies below bustle bows, they appeared long.

Paris introduced gray as the new important color for spring—to replace beige—and was ignored by American women, who thought the shade too drab. By 1927 suntans were so common that colors that set them off, like marigold, tangerine, shades of green, and white, became popular. At night, lamés and lamé brocades were considered flattering to sun-kissed complexions, and these were woven in combinations of black or white with silver or gold in either large-scale geometric or stylized floral patterns. Lamé brocade was used for evening clothes as well as for cloaks and coats and, in 1928, would be reported as an element of day clothes. The latest coiffure, like the half-short, half-long dress, seemed to waver between the new femininity and the old modernity: carefully arranged curls were juxtaposed with smooth expanses. Hats were tilted over one eye, and women continued to wear silk flowers at their shoulders or hips.

By 1928 fashion editors were advising women to wear the skirts of their formal clothes somewhat longer, and in New York, at stylish roof gardens atop tall hotel buildings, the most elegantly attired women were wearing dresses with irregular hems that floated and whirled as they danced. Suggestions for wedding parties included long, romantic *robes de style* for the bridesmaids and short, straight dresses for the brides, with train or veil behind them to the ground. The French midseason collections, held in late spring, sponsored slightly raised waistlines along with the longer skirts. Other signs of femininity were plucked eyebrows in the shape of arcs over eyes made up to look elongated rather than round. Pocketbooks, even those with a handle, were carried in the hand or the crook of the elbow. They tended to be rectangular and were made with Art Deco appliqués of alligator, lizard, or calf. Pocketbook frames, like costume jewelry, were set with stones, in geometric designs. Cartier's Indian-inspired cabochon ruby, sapphire, or emerald beads made a splash on the Continent, and other jewelry trends included combining lots of mismatched bracelets and rings with single, large stones. Heels of shoes, particularly pumps, were still curved, but they were much higher. Tangee introduced a new lipstick that changed from orange to rose on application.

The Paris spring, midseason, and fall-winter collections for 1929 all included longer hemlines, higher waistlines, fitted torsos, and wider hat brims—and all met with strong resistance. (New York custom houses and stores advertised the same range of straightish day clothes, fluttery afternoon frocks, and partially or fully floor-length evening dresses.) In April, *Harper's Bazaar*'s Marjorie Howard noted that the longer skirts and tighter bodices were being shown more by male designers than female, and she reasoned, "I suppose they cannot bear it any longer that our clothes should be so much more comfortable and easy to get into than their own." In the July issue of *Harper's Bazaar*, John R. Tunis defended the short skirt as the "greatest of all blessings to the modern woman in sport or in business," incidentally crediting its acceptance to the tennis champion Helen Wills, who, as she grew up, "refused to lengthen her skirts upon the court and handicap herself in her matches." In its September 28 issue, *Vogue* magazine hesitated to take a stand, writing, "These are troubled times in Paris. There is a general upheaval. No one is having an easy time, neither creator or client. Everyone knows that fashion has changed. Yet very few are sure what it's all about. There is a general feeling in the air that simplicity isn't the thing anymore; that clothes are more complex, and of course that waists are high and that skirts are long."

The *New Yorker*'s Lois Long was more pragmatic when she wrote on October 29 (coincidentally the day of the New York stock market crash), "Since even the raging Vox Populi and Mrs. C.M.G.'s (Bronxville, N.Y.) have had their say in print pro and con, about long skirts, it seems only fitting that I should pipe up and have done with it. For daytime, skirts that zigzag up and down and trail on the pavements and get droopy are in just as bad taste as skirts above the kneecap formerly were. 'They' are wearing them, on the street at least, in a modest inconspicuous length, four inches below the knee if you are tallish. After all, your height has something to do with what is the most becoming length of skirt, let the saleslady say what she may; and the utilitarian aspect of our daily life demands that smart day clothes look trig [right]. For evening, you can go as far as you like—four inches below the knee or trailing on the floor, whatever you happen to fancy."

Although long skirts had clearly come on the scene prior to the crash, observers were uncertain as to what they signified about the modern woman or whether they would prove adaptable to modern life. *Vogue* finally made up its mind about the new silhouette in a November 9 piece called "The Revival of the Lady," writing that "she had almost expired, that fragile, dainty, much adored person, the lady. The bustling life of the day, so hard on elegant fragility, had much to do with it. But even more responsible was the new found freedom of the Modern Woman, which had gone to the head of that energetic person and made her push to the wall anyone less aggressive." The Modern Woman wasn't so much supplanted by the Lady as she was tamed by the financial crisis. Aggressive, reckless behavior, like that which had caused stock market speculation to go awry, waned, and women stopped protesting the more modest, or conservative, silhouette and began looking more de-

Lace was popular in the late 1920s, especially when it was used in a modern, or unfussy, way, as in this spare afternoon or evening dress. The oversize silk flower sewn to the left hip was a ubiquitous ornament. The Irene Lewisohn Library, the Costume Institute, The Metropolitan Museum of Art, New York

Surplice, or wrap, fronts were used on dresses as well as coats. This dress features a surplice, scarflike collar. The Irene Lewisohn Library, the Costume Institute, The Metropolitan Museum of Art, New York

Handkerchiefs or scarves relieved the severe lines of the chemise and were sometimes incorporated into the dress design itself, as in this pink afternoon frock, possibly by Frances Clyne. The Irene Lewisohn Library, the Costume Institute. The Metropolitan Museum of Art, New York

mure, not necessarily because of Paris but because the new silhouette canni-ly suited more subdued behavior.

The Paris couture had, by the end of the 1920s, fully developed its reputa-tion as the center of high style, but in actuality many French ideas were con-sidered too extreme, or inappropriate, or simply unappealing for Americans, and these did not catch on here. Nevertheless, American fashion, concentrat-ed in New York, concerned itself during the decade with profiting from French cachet even as it was (sometimes) ignoring French dictation. With few exceptions, most New York stores, specialty shops, and even wholesale houses advertised their New York–made versions of French designs.

Stein & Blaine's in-house designer, known to all as Miss E. M. A. Stein-metz, was both a talented fashion illustrator and a designer whose day and evening dresses, coats, furs, and children's clothing were recognized early on as being independent of the French couture and sometimes of even better quality. All of the clothes at Stein & Blaine, which was located at 13–15 West Fifty-seventh Street, were custom-made, and fashion shows were held there twice daily. In a March 1921 interview for *Harper's Bazaar*, Miss Stein-metz mentioned individuality as her most important concern (one problem with French clothes was that everyone tended to import the same "Fords," that is, the most popular garments of a given season, and American women, unlike the French, had a real horror of running into their mirror image at a party or other event), and said that she went often to the Brooklyn Museum's costume collection in search of inspiration. Museum costume departments would be very important in helping American designers build a foundation of creative, native work.

Milgrim, which moved in 1928 from Broadway and Seventy-fourth Street to Fifty-seventh Street, also had an in-house designer who was known by name: Sally Milgrim. Her designs were sold not only at the Milgrim locations in New York and Chicago but were also available at a store in each major American city, an early example of a store designer working in the wholesale area. Mil-grim's advertisements regularly featured photographs of stage and film stars like Mae Murray, Leonora Hughes, and Marilyn Miller, posing in ensembles that had been named after them.

Herman Patrick Tappé, the Poiret of New York, was both an innovative designer and an importer, whose shop on Fifty-seventh Street was decorated, unusually for the period, in Victoriana. He wrote articles for *Harper's Bazaar*, and these were printed in his cursive script and included poems about current styles as well as sketches of his hats and other designs. Most of his clothes were imaginative and dramatic, and he gradually became known primarily as a designer of wedding, bridesmaid, and coming-out dresses. In 1922 he made the costumes for D. W. Griffith's film *Orphans of the Storm*.

Jessie Franklin Turner, a somewhat reclusive custom designer who created all of her own fabrics and never met a single one of her customers, moved in 1923 to 410 Park Avenue from Greenwich Village. She worked by draping material directly on a model and therefore was best known for sinuous, long tea gowns, which were unlike most twenties fashions. Her fabrics were culled from around the world, and she combined them in interesting ways. Prior to striking out on her own she had worked for Bonwit Teller.

Valentina, who used only her first name, opened a small couture house in New York in 1925. Two years later her backer left, and in 1928 Valentina

Geometric patterns showed up in every-thing from beaded evening dresses, theater coats, and pocketbooks to knitted pullovers and other sports clothes. This coat and two-piece dress ensemble of about 1927 of flannel and silk from the New York store Thurn features a diamond motif repeated down the front of the dress and on the sleeve of the coat.

and her husband George Schlee incorporated as Valentina Gowns at 145 West Thirtieth Street. The new custom salon was an immediate success, with $1,400 worth of business the first hour; Valentina was forced to sell dresses from her own wardrobe in order to keep up with the demand. She designed very much to suit her own personal style, making clothes with natural waistlines, flowing lines, and covered-up bodices.

Valentina was born Valentina Sanina in 1904 in Russia, where she studied drama. In Sevastopol she met her future husband, who was involved with a free university and newspaper that he had founded. In 1920 the Schlees sought refuge from Russia in Greece. They then moved to Italy and on to Paris, where Valentina's beauty and the clothes she made to highlight it were noticed by theater designer Léon Bakst, who encouraged her in her designing. The Schlees formed a theatrical company, which lasted eight months, and then moved to New York in 1923.

Another small couture house that opened in the 1920s was that of Charles James, who had been born in England, educated at Harrow, and, after moving to his mother's hometown of Chicago, opened a millinery establishment using the name Charles Boucheron. He started a dress and hat business in New York in 1928 in a carriage house. In 1929 *Harper's Bazaar* featured one of his hats, a wide-brimmed straw trimmed with a tulle cockade.

In 1928 Elizabeth Hawes and a partner, Rosemary Harden, founded Hawes-Harden as a custom dressmaking house on Fifty-sixth Street. Clever and Vassar-educated, Hawes had trained herself for her future profession by working in New York briefly at Bergdorf Goodman and then in Paris at the couture house of Nicole Groult (Poiret's sister); for Macy as a stylist in Paris (which then meant someone who was on the lookout for novelties that the store could copy or import); as the Paris correspondent for the *New Yorker*, signing her pithy cablegrams PARISITE; and for a Paris copy house. When she returned to New York, Hawes claimed that there was only one authentic couturier working in America—Jessie Franklin Turner—and set out to remedy the situation by going into business as an American designer designing for American women.

Hawes-Harden became an immediate success. One of the designers' gimmicks was to make a chiffon dress directly on the client, sending her out in it just basted together or, if she came in for the fitting early enough, having it finished by dinnertime. Rosemary Harden left the business in 1930.

The house of Kurzman moved in 1926 from Fifth Avenue and Thirty-sixth Street to Fifth between Fifty-second and Fifty-third. The new building was outfitted with staircases, walls, and paneling from various European castles, and there could be found Kurzman's own designs, Paris imports, and Kurzman Paris replicas, which sold for $95 to $425. Marion Davies was an early client. By 1928 Kurzman was concentrating more on in-house design than on reproductions, and Kurzman originals included luxurious sports clothes like crepe de chine dresses with angora cardigans and cashmere jersey ensembles as well as clothes made from fabrics inspired by Navaho textiles. In 1929 Kurzman hired a designer who had previously worked for Chanel.

Like Sally Milgrim, Peggy Hoyt was another importer-designer whose clothes were fashionable with actresses. She claimed in an ad that "the American woman is the greatest inspiration any creator of clothes could possibly wish for!" Hoyt was born in Michigan and, as a child, moved with her

Clare Boothe Luce, perfectly turned out in a photograph taken on Park Avenue in 1924, epitomized the 1920s image of smart elegance.

widowed mother to New York. She apprenticed herself to a milliner at age seventeen and then, with three hundred dollars, opened her own millinery establishment on upper Fifth Avenue, moving three years later to 16 East Fifty-fifth Street. At her height she had hundreds of employees, with one floor devoted to clothes and another to hats. In 1924 she introduced a line of perfumes called Camellia, Mimosa, and Yellow Orchid, which were followed in 1925 by Flowers and Christmas.

Bruck-Weiss, at 6–8 West Fifty-seventh Street in 1920 and 20–22 West Fifty-seventh Street by 1928, was the source for clothes that were considered somewhat theatrical. This establishment specialized in what it termed "the Mode Individual," which meant that it could dress clients more or less head-to-toe, fully accessorized, except for shoes. Hickson, at Fifth Avenue and Fifty-second Street, was known for custom-made original and imported tailored clothes with complicated detailing. In its new building, opened in 1927 and decorated formally in gold and white, the store conducted elaborate fashion shows. J. M. Gidding, who moved in 1922 from Fifth Avenue at Forty-sixth Street to Fifth between Fifty-sixth and Fifty-seventh, had an in-house designer named Evelyn McHorter, whose clothes were worn by Irene Castle. Gidding's clothes, which also included imports, tended to be fairly conservative; for the whole of the 1920s, the store's advertisements never featured really short skirts. Lucile (Lady Duff Gordon), whose reputation had been entwined with that of Irene Castle, was still operating a New York house in the 1920s, but it was beginning to wind down. She continued to write articles for *Harper's Bazaar,* showing those of her designs that were most appropriate for New York City life.

In 1926 Lilly Daché, who had been running a millinery shop on Broadway at Seventy-seventh Street for about two years, bought out her partner. Lilly Daché had been born in the Bordeaux area of France in 1907 and worked for the Paris milliner Caroline Reboux before coming to New York and taking a job selling hats at Macy in 1924. She soon opened a branch on West Eighty-second Street and a second branch on West Fifty-seventh. In 1928 she consolidated her three shops into one at 485 Madison Avenue. While she made cloches in the typical style of the 1920s, it was characteristic that the very first hat she made on her own was different from the going mode: a turban (a style for which she would be famous in the future) made of several shades of velvet twisted together.

Hats, like other accessories, were available at almost every store, but New York also had specialized shops, like Lilly Daché, where hats, pocketbooks, shoes, and so on were available on a custom-made as well as take-away basis. Joseph and Tappé were both famous for their hats, but Nathan Gibson Clark sold nothing but hats, at around seventy-five dollars each, and he amused his clients with his rude comments and wisecracks. During the 1920s, the Echo scarf company was founded, and its products were sold around the country. Koret, a company that specialized in beautifully made pocketbooks, also started up during the 1920s. Also very popular at the time were the mesh pocketbooks, sometimes enameled in patterns, by the firm of Whiting & Davis. The top store in New York for pocketbooks was Nat Lewis, where all of the wares were originals or designed in-house, and the best shoes were to be found at Delman, J. J. Slater, I. Miller, and Cammeyer.

There were also a number of New York houses that specialized in Paris

Although signs of dropping hemlines had been in the air for several seasons, 1929 gave women a reason to dress in a more sober and covered-up manner. Many of the first longer-hemmed styles were fussy, and most hems were uneven, as if to show that women and designers couldn't make up their minds. This dress of patterned lamé was made of material manufactured by the American company Cheney Brothers.

imports, putting great effort into making meticulous copies. Known for its exquisite workmanship was the Tailored Woman, which imported both models and fabrics from Paris and custom made the models in New York. Thurn, at 15 East Fifty-second Street, was a small import house, as was Joseph, at 2 West Fifty-seventh Street, which in 1921 presented Poiret's entire collection. L. P. Hollander, which in 1923 had been in business for seventy-five years, duplicated Paris originals for both custom orders and ready-to-wear. Kargère was a shop at Fifth Avenue and Fifty-first Street that maintained stores in Paris and Cannes and sold primarily lingerie and boudoir accessories as well as some sports clothes.

Gervais was a very chic small shop with predominantly custom-made versions of clothes by Chanel, Paquin, Patou, Vionnet, and Marcel Rochas, with new stock arriving weekly. In 1928 Gervais moved from 408 Madison Avenue to 16 East Forty-eighth Street, and it was about this shop that Lois Long wrote, in the *New Yorker*'s October 29, 1929, issue, "If a fairy godmother started hovering around my home, they would certainly be prominent in the amazing wardrobe I would order." Frances, at 10 West Fifty-sixth Street, was a small custom house that specialized in romantic portrait dresses with lampshade crinolines or sable-trimmed panniers. This shop was especially popular for bridesmaids' dresses trimmed with cascades of tulle and flowers and lace. Chez Ninon, at 500 Madison Avenue, had a constantly renewed stock of Paris clothes, which were copied exactly in imported fabrics and sold for under two hundred dollars. The shop's more avant-garde offerings included Schiaparelli's sweaters and the important 1927 Yvonne Davidson lamé smoking, or evening jacket. Frances Clyne was also known for extremely smart Paris imports.

Hattie Carnegie, from 1925 located in her own building at 42 East Forty-ninth Street, sold French clothes, which she bought during her seven annual trips to Paris, her own in-house designs, and, beginning in 1929, ready-to-wear from a special department. Born Hattie Kanengeiser in Vienna in 1889, she moved to America with her family as a child. She left school at the age of eleven, and worked at Macy and for a wholesale house before she and a partner, Rae Roth, in 1909 opened a shop on East Tenth Street known as Carnegie—Ladies Hatter. In 1913 the two partners relocated to Eighty-sixth Street and Broadway, where they sold dresses as well as hats to their stylish Upper West Side neighbors. Beginning in 1919 they also imported French models. After buying out her partner, Hattie Carnegie continued her Eighty-sixth Street shop, adding another address in 1923, 6 West Forty-eighth Street, from which she sold models on a wholesale basis. In 1925 she consolidated her business under one roof at 42 East Forty-ninth Street.

Although the New York–based magazines occasionally gave credit to local couturiers, they never mentioned any ready-to-wear designers. Of all the fashion press, only Lois Long writing for the *New Yorker* visited the wholesale firms and reported on their doings, although she was limited in that she could only hint at what type of stores would be carrying the clothes.

According to Lois Long, one of the most copied of the ready-to-wear designers was Jo Copeland, who had started out designing part-time for a company called Pattullo Modes in the 1920s. Born in New York, she became acquainted with fashion through her father, who was in the clothing business, and through the regular visits of a seamstress to her parents' house. She stud-

Stein & Blaine

The longer hemlines were slow to appear in sports clothes, as demonstrated by this 1929 print dress with a scarf neckline by the ready-to-wear firm Davidow. The Library, Fashion Institute of Technology, New York

Prior to 1929, the last longer hemlines had been seen in 1923, which is when this passementerie-trimmed dress and jacket ensemble was offered by Stein & Blaine, one of the first New York stores in the 1910s to showcase its own in-house designer, Miss E. M. A. Steinmetz. The Library, Fashion Institute of Technology, New York

ied at the Art Students League and at the New York School of Fine and Applied Art before working both as a fashion illustrator and as a designer. Gradually she began drawing her own ideas as well as those of others and selling them to Pattullo.

Anthony Blotta had opened his wholesale fashion house in New York in 1919, where he was, unusually, designer as well as cutter and fitter. Born in Italy, he had studied at the Academy of Fine Arts in Rome before coming to America with his family when he was a teenager. He apprenticed himself to a coat manufacturer before starting out on his own, and his specialty was tailored suits, coats, and dresses.

Philip Mangone, a seventh-generation tailor, set up his wholesale business in New York in 1916. He had started sewing at an early age when helping his father finish garments that he had brought home. As a teenager, he went to work with his father at B. Altman, and he followed him to such wholesale houses as Julius Stein, Harry Rothenberg and Levy, and Charles M. Cohen. Mangone Models were sold during the 1920s in two hundred stores around the country; unusually for the time, each one featured the Mangone label rather than the store's label. The company's 1920s styles were tailored, whether for dressy occasions, as in fur-trimmed, embroidered theater coats; for daytime, as in low-waisted jackets and skirt ensembles; or for spectator sports, as in coats and jackets made out of doeskin.

It is telling of New York's importance as a fashion mecca that one city supported not only so many luxury establishments but, additionally, so many department stores. Each of them had individual images even as they all were divided into more or less the same types of departments: imports, custom-made clothing, ready-to-wear, millinery, sports clothes, wedding clothes and trousseaux, furs, coats, lingerie, children's clothes, and men's clothes.

The merchandise at B. Altman ranged from saddle oxfords, portable bathhouses for changing on the beach, and junior-miss party frocks at twenty-five dollars to the exclusively reproduced line of seven Callot Soeurs dresses originally designed for Cecile Sorel in 1926 preparatory to her acting in a play on Broadway. B. Altman also sold Cheney silk fabrics (an American textile company) based on floral paintings by Kees van Donghen then being displayed at the Anderson Galleries and sweaters knitted with silhouettes drawn by John Held, Jr.

Henri Bendel, whose store had moved to Fifty-seventh Street, was a brilliant buyer and designer who also wrote articles on Paris fashion. He delighted in discovering new talent, and his Paris finds tended to be excitingly off-the-beaten-track. Bergdorf Goodman moved in 1928 from 616 Fifth Avenue to its present building at Fifth Avenue and Fifty-eighth Street, which was decorated at first in the Louis XV, Louis XVI, and Empire styles. Its ready-to-wear department was especially fine, with off-the-rack designs created from unusual imported fabrics. Bergdorf Goodman was one of the first stores in New York to feature the longer skirt in 1928.

Best & Co., at Fifth Avenue and Thirty-eighth Street, had its own line of hats, known as Fortmason, and wearable sports clothes called Nada. Several of the store's offerings were based not on what Parisian couturiers were doing but on what actual women had been seen wearing: for instance, a Lady Diana Manners hayseed straw hat, a daringly décolleté bathing suit copied from one worn by Lady Abdy on the Lido, and a suede jacket for passenger flights

By the late 1920s, the carriage trade traveled by motor, or even by double-decker bus, as seen in this view of Bergdorf Goodman, a luxurious department store that had begun as a custom-tailoring establishment. The New-York Historical Society, New York

By the 1920s, Fifty-seventh Street was the most luxurious and exclusive street after Fifth Avenue, and Jay-Thorpe was one of its best stores, offering custom-made clothes from French and in-house designers. Museum of the City of New York

introduced in 1928 when Amelia Earhart completed her trip across the Atlantic by plane. In 1926 Best promoted its Shirtmaker frocks, made of cotton and ready to be monogrammed; these were forerunners of the classic shirtwaist dress of the mid-twentieth century.

Bonwit Teller, at Fifth Avenue and Thirty-eighth Street, sold a wide variety of French models, but it also occasionally pushed such American-made designs as clothes from the wholesale house A. Beller & Co. (Most department stores did not give credit to wholesale houses; instead, they put their own labels in the clothes.) In 1925 and 1926, the store ran a series of advertisements depicting Bonwit-clad ladies engaged in such New York activities as tea dancing at Sherry's, attending the Westminster Kennel Club Show, and leaving for Palm Beach on the Orange Blossom Special, and these were drawn by Muriel King, who would become a fashion designer in the 1930s. In 1926 Bonwit had on display Paris hats and dresses by Redfern designed for Queen Marie of Romania and Princess Ileana. The following year New York Junior League volunteers took over the store for one day, working as salesclerks and other staff, in order to raise money for charity.

Arnold Constable, which celebrated its hundredth birthday in 1927, stood out among American stores by avoiding futuristic designs. This store also managed the amazing achievement of selling handmade, imported dresses for twenty-seven dollars. Franklin Simon sold some Paris clothes, but advertisements tended to emphasize its own, copyrighted, ready-to-wear line called Bramley. In 1927 the store sold coats made out of Fortuny cotton, and in 1928 the men's department was decorated with a mounted nine-foot sailfish caught by Mr. Simon himself.

Jay-Thorpe moved in 1920 to 24–26 West Fifty-seventh Street. There one could find imported hats from all the top Paris houses as well as hats to be custom made on the individual head and evening hats, which were considered exotic novelties. The lingerie was famous; a Jay-Thorpe negligee was once spotted at the Hotel Ritz at dinnertime. In 1929 the store hired Harry Lichtenstein to start his own custom-order department. There was also a beauty salon on the premises. Lord & Taylor, on Fifth Avenue at Thirty-eighth Street, copied rather than adapted most of its French models; it also advertised evening clothes by an anonymous "famous New York designer." In 1926 it carried the Americana collection of Stehli silks, a company that had commissioned fabric designs from John Held, Jr., Katherine Sturgis Knight, and Neysa McMein, all popular American illustrators. Lord & Taylor also came up with the interesting idea of selling sports ensembles as separates, to be put together by the customer, who could start by selecting a skirt, take it with her to the sweater counter, and then on to the jacket section.

Saks Fifth Avenue, brainchild of Adam Gimbel, opened its doors on September 15, 1924, at its present location at Fifth between Forty-ninth and Fiftieth streets. From its first day, this store emphasized modern luxury, in its interior architecture, advertising presentation, and the kinds of merchandise it offered. In 1927 Saks imported Monsieur Antoine, creator of the shingle haircut, and placed him in his own salon, where haircuts started at ten dollars and went to twenty if performed by Antoine himself. Also in 1927 the store inaugurated its Salon Moderne department, a custom department that relied on Paris but added a bit of a twist: each dress would be discarded after ten copies had been made—a level of exclusivity not available even in Paris.

French creations were also sold at Wanamaker, on Broadway and Ninth Street, in the Coin de Paris department. Wanamaker came up with an innovative arrangement with Vionnet in 1927, ordering a light wool crepe sports dress to be made in her workrooms in Paris in various colors and in regulation American sizes. It is surprising that this wasn't done more often.

Part of the reason that there were such great numbers of shops and department stores—and there were hundreds of others that, because they never advertised or were never written about, have been forgotten completely—was that American women valued variety, perhaps above even quality. Their clothing needs were based on whether or not they lived in a city or in the country, in a warm or cold climate, whether they worked or ran households, whether they were social or private. Some women's lives encompassed all of these aspects. Although Paris fashion became very important in the 1920s, it succeeded because of the couture's awareness of and adaptation to American manners and mores. The fact that women here accepted only those styles that suited them allowed American fashion to begin finally to realize its role. In the 1930s, it would shed its anonymity to become an entity in its own right.

In the 1920s Macy was beginning to enjoy a better reputation. Although it was still a bargain center, as these summer crowds attending sales show, it was also acquiring a reputation for better-quality merchandise, including imports from Paris.

THE 1930s

The 1930s was the only decade in which a new look was immediately perceptible. In contrast to the frenetic 1920s gamine, the archetypal beauty was languid and serene, with intentionally feminine make-up and hair. Hollywood, hitting its stride, provided America and the world with an ideal of feminine pulchritude. This M-G-M actress was arrayed in the kind of clothes most photogenic in black and white: monochromatic, here all in white, with the textures of her ermine coat, silk satin dress, moiré pumps, and diamond "service stripe" bracelets playing against each other.

The 1930s began with a world-wide depression that would color nearly every aspect of the decade's fashion, from the alarmingly literal drop of hemlines that mirrored the fall in the Dow-Jones average to the transformation of American fashion into a real force. The widening chasm between the haves and the have-nots, as well as the increasing numbers of the latter, brought a subdued sobriety to fashion and, at the same time, justified flashes of diverting extravagance, exemplified by Hollywood fashion, and of silliness, demonstrated by fads. The influence of the Depression on spending habits lasted throughout the decade—so much so that in 1939 President Roosevelt approved moving Thanksgiving to the fourth rather than the last Thursday in November in order to create more days of Christmas shopping.

One of the causes of the stock market crash had been speculation on margin accounts, and this, coupled with rampant joblessness, meant that people not only had less money to spend, they were no longer optimistically spending money they hoped to have. Just as the elaborately beaded chemise dresses and Cubist-patterned sportswear reflected the Jazz Age, the 1930s produced clothes that even at their most elegant reflected leaner times: for the first part of the 1930s figures were almost emaciated; clothes were narrow, long, and spare. In comparison with the flapper, the ideal woman of the 1930s was older, more sophisticated, and much less carefree.

Paris, fashion center of the world, found itself in serious trouble. Monsieur Gerber, president of the Chambre Syndicale de la Couture Parisienne, reported to the *New York Times* of March 3, 1931, that "French dress imports in 1926 were valued at $80,000,000. but they fell to $57,400,000. in 1929 and to $55,640,000. in 1930. . . . [a drop] of more than 40 per cent in four years." These figures reflect more than individual women's couture purchases, since patrons of the couture would eventually resume spending pre-Depression sums on their wardrobes. What caused a major change in the way American women were clothed is that manufacturers and retailers came to rely less on buying Paris originals that were expensive to import and to have copied by seamstresses earning American wages and more on what they could produce at home, independent of any French influence. The French announced at various points that they were lowering their prices, but otherwise their attitude remained somewhat elitist. Gerber indicated that the couture, geared as it was to the highest standards of artistry and quality, would not be able to adopt methods of mass production and that it would concentrate instead on trying to maintain a demand for the best possible clothing. Unfortunately for Paris, the American fashion industry was well versed in the intricacies of mass production, which would bloom in a climate where clients at every price level had become conscious of value.

In 1930 in New York City, there were literally thousands of dress, suit, coat, accessories, lingerie, and fur houses listed in *Fairchild's Women's Wear Directory*. From these, as well as from the city's custom design houses, specialty shops, and department stores, would emerge talented native designers,

not just at the top, as in the French couture, but at every price level. By the end of the decade American fashion names to be reckoned with included not only Elizabeth Hawes, Charles James, Valentina, Jo Copeland, and Jessie Franklin Turner but also Nettie Rosenstein, Germaine Monteil, Louise Barnes Gallagher, Muriel King, Claire McCardell, Clare Potter, Helen Cookman, Tom Brigance, Hattie Carnegie, and Lilly Daché. The fact that America's first real crop of designers was predominately female is important. Typically, when designing professionally, women have designed for themselves, understanding firsthand how clothes move and work and thinking most often of comfort and suitability. Practicality has always been an American trait, and an American dress can be considered less a work of art than a solution to a design problem. When solved well, elegance is the natural result.

One of the givens of clothing production is that the cost of manufacturing a dress affects its appearance, and the three elements of dress design that most influence its cost are: the material, the cut (in terms of making the original pattern and in terms of finishing each garment), and the decoration. Because the effects of the Depression were so far-reaching, cost became a consideration in dress design at all levels, from the couture and custom houses on down to the wholesalers. What makes thirties design so appealing in retrospect is that designers and couturiers made such creative use of materials that had previously been overlooked.

Fabrics that had been popular in the 1920s, when the cut of a chemise dress was incredibly easy to execute, included: ornately beaded and embroidered stuffs; woven lamé brocades; and fragile silk jerseys, chiffons, and velvets that are notoriously difficult to work with by machine. The Depression triggered many vogues for simple, ordinary fabrics that had previously been considered inappropriate for high fashion. Some of these new uses of existing materials originated in Paris; in 1930 Jean Patou and Gabrielle Chanel showed summery evening clothes fashioned out of such varieties of cotton as organdy, eyelet, piqué, and lace, and these were very influential in America, where there are many regions with a long warm season. Daytime materials that seemed new when used for more formal clothes also included corduroy, bouclé knit, which could have a handmade look when machine-knitted, and wool, for such evening clothes as dinner dresses and theater suits. Some designers experimented with interior fabrics like chintz and toile.

In Paris the main artificial materials to find favor were outlandish novelties like spun glass, but in America the little printed rayon or other synthetic silk dress became ubiquitous. American textile manufacturers were involved with researching, inventing, and promoting all kinds of man-made materials as well as varieties of the new wood fiber–based rayon. DuPont advertised in 1938 that it had devised "whole new schools of fabrics," and the Celanese Corporation was among the first institutions to promote American-born designs using American-born fabrics. Artificial silk had its first really widespread use in lingerie and nightgowns; slips and other underwear were more often made of peach synthetic silk than the cotton and real silk previously used. As camouflage, artificial silks were often printed or given unusual textures, particularly, in the 1930s, crepe finishes.

The early-thirties silhouette was simple to the extreme, and the most common styles were: for day, a modified shirtwaist dress with fairly straight skirt or a slim suit with below-the-waist-length fitted jacket, and for evening, a

For daytime, the newly lean silhouette entailed longer hemlines and longer, slightly more fitted jackets. Colors tended to be sober, as, for example, forest green, brick red, burgundy, brown, and eggplant, and such textured fabrics as nubby tweeds, bouclé knits, wool shantungs, and raw silks were prevalent. This 1935 suit, made with the coordinating but non-matching pieces so important in the Depression era since they could be worn with other clothes as well, was designed by Leslie Morris, in-house custom designer of Bergdorf Goodman. The Irene Lewisohn Library, the Costume Institute, The Metropolitan Museum of Art, New York

The craze for sunbathing ushered in evening styles with almost nonexistent backs so as to display as much sun-kissed skin as possible. This 1935 evening dress by Bergdorf Goodman emphasized the long line with a slight train. The Irene Lewisohn Library, the Costume Institute, The Metropolitan Museum of Art, New York

Attempts to experiment with the abbreviated silhouette of the 1920s had often failed, and designers found that the new longer, leaner looks of the 1930s were more conducive to experimentation. Many of the more elaborate alternative silhouettes harked back to the end of the nineteenth century, such as bustles, trains, and gigot sleeves, as on the bolero jacket of this evening ensemble made by Bergdorf Goodman in 1932. The Irene Lewisohn Library, the Costume Institute, The Metropolitan Museum of Art, New York

101

In the 1930s, the little print dress was
made in the new synthetic silk as well as
in real silk. Its waistline was placed at the
natural waist and given little emphasis,
and the prints were smaller and more
delicate than the patterns of the previous
decade.

dress cut like a slip, on the bias. In Paris, the top couturiers worked within these silhouettes, sometimes varying them with gigot sleeves, bustle backs, or peplum overskirts, creating designs whose ornamentation was often the cut itself—as in a Vionnet dress pieced together from brilliantly conceived widening strips of material, a complicated structure that achieved a simple effect. American manufacturers tended to work with the simple silhouette and varied the ornament for novelty. Popular details in the 1930s included silk flowers sewn to the neckline or waistline of a dress; rhinestone-set clips or brooches; and (often removable) collars and cuffs.

By the end of the decade, the American preference for a variety of silhouettes and looks over a single uniform one, particularly strong in the 1920s, was firmly in place. The narrow line continued to hold sway, but, increasingly, this silhouette was reserved for covered-up day and evening dresses in supple fabrics, many of them printed, made with various shirrings and draperies. The barer, and thus more formal evening style of the late 1930s often featured a strapless or camisole bodice, tiny waist, and long, full skirt. This style would survive the war years and emerge even more strongly as the New Look. In 1938 *Vogue* illustrated anonymous versions of the "monastic dress" Claire McCardell had devised; it was full, cut to flow from the shoulders, and could be worn belted however the wearer wished.

Day suits, along with those for evening (the theater suit was a novel 1930s concept), had cropped bolero jackets or long, sometimes flared, tunic-style ones. Sports clothes ran the gamut from tweedy man-tailored styles, shown by designers like Vera Maxwell and B. H. Wragge, to bright, feminine, and innovative separates like pants, shorts, skirts, bra or other bare-midriff tops, and backless dresses with various jackets and cover-ups, as designed by Tom Brigance and Clare Potter. The increasing ease of plane travel opened up new worlds to explore, and designers and consumers returning from places like Mexico, Bali, or India put in their design vocabulary or their closets such elements gleaned from their foreign excursions as peasant blouses, dirndl skirts, serape shawls, harem pants, sarong-shaped dresses and bathing suits, kimono-wrapped coats, and obi sashes, in fabrics hand-loomed in mountain villages or printed with native patterns.

Fit is an important consideration in mass production since the clothes have to flatter a variety of figures, and the form-fitting quality of the thirties silhouette inspired several innovations. First was the zipper, which was cheaper to install in a dress than hand-sewn hooks and eyes or snaps down one side and across the front or back. Couturiers like Schiaparelli and the American-born Charles James used zippers as a design element. A newly invented elastic substance, Lastex, began to be woven into wool and other knits, at first for such active sports clothes as bathing suits or ski pants and later as part of expanding necklines or midriffs of dresses. Belts also became an important thirties element. When she made her first foray into mass production, Elizabeth Hawes, an important American dress designer of the 1930s, complained that the manufacturers always put a belt on a dress whether it was part of the design or not. A belt gave the woman who bought the dress a little more leeway in adjusting it to her own figure. Although they could be bought as separate accessories, they most often came with the clothes, usually made in the matching fabric. Buckles became more elaborate, often mirroring tastes in costume or precious jewelry: they were set with marcasite or paste in Art

Deco patterns; enameled on metal in geometric designs; carved from plastic imitating ivory or amber; or made of Bakelite, set with crystals.

Whatever the budget of the thirties woman, her dress had to go a long way. It had to wear well, and its design had to stand up to being worn well; it couldn't look dated after several seasons. This explains the simplicity of the clothes, a mood that lasted up until the end of the decade, when fashions became more elaborate, and it also explains the rise in importance of accessories. Previously a hat, a pocketbook, a pair of shoes, gloves, and stockings complemented an ensemble and, usually, each other by matching. Thirties accessories became more dashing to perform a very important function: changing the look of a relatively simple suit or dress from one wearing to the next.

Unlike the 1920s, when all cloches looked alike, in the 1930s hats ran the gamut from cartwheel picture hats to the Eugénie, worn back on the head nineteenth-century style, to slouchy fedoras and turbans. Flat envelope pocketbooks grew also, becoming more sculptural in shape and gradually sporting shoulder straps. There was more variety in shoe styles, which incorporated exotic platform soles and complicated sandal straps. Longer gloves became popular, as did all kinds of gauntlet shapes, colors, and textures. Whereas earlier accessories were expected to be in the best of taste, in the 1930s they began to be witty and daring. Schiaparelli exerted tremendous influence with her Surrealist-inspired buttons and theme accessories.

Costume jewelry, which had become fashionable in the late 1920s under the aegis of Chanel, practically became *de rigueur* in the 1930s. It was still made in imitation of real jewelry, which was making greater use of semiprecious stones like coral, black and green onyx, and aquamarines, but might also incorporate such "found objects" as dice or strawberry-shaped pincushions. Marcasite, regarded not as sham but as real, since it was a faceted mineral, was prevalent. The American costume jewelry industry was centered in Rhode Island, and by 1930 the best-known name in American costume jewelry design, Miriam Haskell, was gaining recognition for her unusual gilt filigree pieces set with her signature baroque pearl beads.

Despite all this native activity, it still took time for stores, wholesalers, and the fashion press to shake off their allegiance to France. The entire American fashion industry remained dependent on French designs. Small wholesale houses on up to the grand department stores sent buyers to the French collections, which must have been similar in mood to major auctions. Everyone watched each other for signs of which dresses would become the next season's "Fords," or best-sellers. The French did everything they could to thwart copying; for example, anyone attending the shows was required to make at least one purchase. Since actual Paris originals could only be sold at a loss in New York, most buyers tried to soak up as many free ideas as possible. It was the job of assistant buyers, at a secret signal, to memorize every detail of a given dress and draw a picture of it later.

Women could buy in New York, sometimes only ten days after the models had arrived, the actual originals, the store-made exact copies (using the same fabrics and notions and often sold as originals), the blatant copies that did not begin to duplicate the original quality, and adaptations. Adaptations could actually be considered original American designs, since they were made with a French idea changed to suit American workmanship and tastes. As the 1930s progressed, unless a store had bought a dress specifically for a special

Although the narrow silhouette lasted well into the 1940s, by the end of the 1930s another look appeared that would become a classic, rarely going out of style. Made with a strapless bodice (a 1930s innovation), small waist, and full skirt, it would eventually be integrated into the New Look of the late 1940s and 1950s. This 1938 evening dress by Henri Bendel, made of black velvet and madonna blue silk faille, the skirt stiffened with horsehair, represented a real change from the fluid bias cut. Photograph: John Rawlings. Courtesy the Edward C. Blum Design Laboratory, Fashion Institute of Technology, New York, and Vogue

In 1932 Dorothy Shaver of Lord & Taylor made the daring move of actively promoting American fashion design. Although native designers had sporadically received credit for their talents and achievements before, Shaver launched a movement that, by World War II, had lifted American designers from anonymity. This 1936 window and interior display featured day dresses and separates by Clare Potter, a ready-to-wear designer. Museum of the City of New York

John-Frederics, a top New York millinery team that later split off into Mr. John and John-Frederics, created this sporty ensemble in 1939 featuring a plaid cotton blouse and pocketbook and a wide-brimmed straw panama with veil edged with the same plaid. Photograph: Horst. Courtesy Vogue

The 1930s saw the rise in importance of West Coast fashion, which emanated from two sources: Hollywood and such sportswear manufacturers as Jantzen—whose maillot with insignia is shown here—who sated the need for active outdoors clothes.

client and had it made to her measurements, French imports were harder and harder to sell, because fashions in the post-chemise days required much more careful fitting. Thus, store-made copies, custom-fitted, became more important, along with clothes designed by Americans for Americans to fill the gaps between the Paris major and midseason collections.

Although they had been mentioned by name in magazines and in store and textile advertisements practically from the beginning, American designers did not become well known overnight. However, a single action on the part of Dorothy Shaver proved to be instrumental in bringing designers recognition. In the spring of 1932, Shaver, then vice-president of Lord & Taylor, began to name American designers in the store's ads as part of her promotion of young talent. Photographs of the chosen designers were displayed along with each one's latest designs in the Fifth Avenue windows and in special areas set aside inside the store. As more and more editorial and advertising copy followed Shaver's lead, the public began to be more aware of who was designing its clothes. But this didn't make American clothes easier to find. In 1937 *Life* magazine profiled Nettie Rosenstein, one of the most revered American designers, finishing the article with a photograph of one of her evening dresses along with the information that it bore not Rosenstein's label but Bergdorf Goodman's.

The Lord & Taylor promotion was so successful that certain manufacturers were unable to fill orders for copies of the clothes featured. However, it reflected Dorothy Shaver's genius that she did not eschew Paris completely. She wrote in 1933 that she wanted to make it clear that Lord & Taylor's sponsorship of American fashions "does not preclude an appreciation of what Paris is and has always been." But she asserted that "American designers are best equipped by tradition, background and feeling to understand the needs and demands for American women in sports clothes" (reprinted in a brochure published by the National Retail Drygoods Association, 1935). American women had always been more athletic than their European counterparts and, as the twentieth century progressed, wore what can be called "sports clothes" increasingly frequently for a variety of occasions. Sports clothes were especially adaptable to mass production because they consisted primarily of separate items to be worn in different combinations and tended to be made in fabrics easy to work with on machines. As American style developed, it continued to comprise elements like "ease" and "comfort" and "individuality."

Besides that of Lord & Taylor, the 1930s saw many other promotions of American fashion design. In 1930, associations sponsoring fashion shows in New York included the Custom Tailors' Club, the Garment Retailers of America, the New York Modern Designers' Club, the Retail Millinery Association, the Fashion Group, and the Fashion Guild. Both the Chicago World's Fair in 1933 and the New York World's Fair in 1939 highlighted American design. The best-dressed list, which had been begun by a group of Paris couturiers, was taken over and expanded in the 1930s by fashion publicist Eleanor Lambert, and it frequently featured American women. American women on the list for 1934 included Mrs. Harrison Williams, Tallulah Bankhead, Ina Claire, Mrs. Eleanor Patterson of Washington, D.C., Mrs. William G. McAdoo, Mrs. William Vanderbilt, Mrs. Carroll Carstairs, Mrs. Frank Jay Gould, Princess Faucigny-Lucinge (formerly Caroline Foster), and Baroness Eugénie de Rothschild (formerly Kitty Spotswood). In 1937 Wallis Simpson became

the most famous American-born fashion plate in the world, wearing a dress by American-in-Paris Mainbocher at her wedding to the Duke of Windsor.

Although specific Paris-born styles would take hold in the 1930s and become internationally favored, there were other sources of fashion inspiration. America not only had its own fashion industry, it also boasted Hollywood, whose golden age can be dated as beginning with the stock market crash. Many, many more thousands of women went to the movies than studied high-fashion magazines, and one of the biggest attractions of films was seeing what the beauties of the moment were wearing. Film designers had learned, when the hemline crashed and they were left with recently canned movies featuring short-skirted actresses, that intense fashion slavery was ill-advised. They stopped trying to keep abreast of the latest modes and concentrated instead on their own version of classicism, although they kept starlets busy offscreen posing in trendy fashions for photographs that news agencies distributed around the country.

What was successful on film, in terms of clothing, was what was most flattering to the actress, what would remain timeless, and what was most photogenic in black and white or in the early temperamental color photography. Hollywood clothes, while lavish with the textures of furs and thousands of hand-sewn sequins and bugle beads so loved by the camera, were curiously very simple. Printed fabrics were rare, and dresses and ensembles were most often severely cut, with the emphasis placed on a few memorable details: a low back décolleté seen when the actress turned away from the camera, face-framing touches of white or glittery jewels, and one or two striking accessories. Manufacturers and stores soon learned to look to Hollywood for specific items to copy, and discussions of whether Hollywood was a more important style center than New York began to occur along with those comparing New York to Paris.

New York's great advantage over Hollywood was Fifth Avenue. On and off the avenue the world's greatest clothes could not only be seen, as in the movies, but also purchased. The Chrysler Building opened its Art Deco doors in 1930, followed by the Empire State Building in 1931 and the ground-breaking for Rockefeller Center in 1932. Traffic lights, as well as more and more skyscrapers, were still arriving, but the fashion landscape of New York had stabilized. Most manufacturers had their headquarters between Eighth and Madison avenues in the Twenties and Thirties. All of the department stores that still exist, with the exception of Bonwit Teller, were ensconced in their present buildings. The most exclusive shops and custom houses were clustered on and off Fifth and Madison avenues in the Fifties and Sixties, and Fifty-seventh Street, home to the most top stores per block, had been described as if Fifth Avenue had turned at a right angle. The Upper West Side was no longer a fashionable shopping district, as it had been briefly, and downtown was left with only Wanamaker, occupying the entire area bound by Broadway and Fourth Avenue and Eighth and Tenth streets. Despite its innovative retailing past and its Coin de Paris shops, which sold models by Louiseboulanger, Patou, Lanvin, and Alix, Wanamaker suffered from its distant locale. Although the store remained there until 1950, it would never again equal its Philadelphia flagship.

Next farthest south, and benefiting from their proximity to each other, were Macy's, B. Altman, Saks Thirty-fourth (which had been started by a branch of

Whereas in the 1920s casual clothes, while made in different materials, had been shaped the same as formal styles, the 1930s saw the development of fashions for sport and leisure that formed a separate entity. These included lounging pajamas—a major late-1920s and early-1930s fad—worn primarily at the seaside, and all manner of pants, shorts, playsuits, and culottes. This sporty costume, a cross between a long skirt and pants, worn with a camp-type shirt, won a prize in a California fashion show.

New York ready-to-wear designer Tom Brigance specialized in innovative and whimsical play and active sports clothes. He based these two styles from his 1938 Palm Beach, or resort, collection on overalls, made in bright shades of linen. The Irene Lewisohn Library, the Costume Institute, The Metropolitan Museum of Art, New York

the same Gimbel family that founded Saks Fifth Avenue), Franklin Simon, and Lord & Taylor. Thirty-fourth Street itself, excepting the department stores, had a "cheap" reputation: ladies did not want to look as if their clothes had been purchased there. Lois Long, fashion writer for the *New Yorker,* often mentioned Macy's, "The World's Largest Store," questioning why her readers were so surprised at the high-quality goods that could be found there. Its top department was the Little Shop, located on the third floor (where the Little Shops are still found today). There one could find French models by Lucien Lelong, Marcel Rochas, Molyneux, Schiaparelli, Paquin, Maggy Rouff, Lucille Paray, and Martial et Armand. The Little Shop for Accessories, on the first-floor balcony, was a source for pocketbooks by Vionnet or Patou as well as copies and originals of couturier jewelry. Resort clothes were sold in what was an important 1930s concept: the Little Shop for Southern Wear (Palm Beach and Miami were 1930s boomtowns, and great strides in transportation had made them popular winter spots). By 1938, however, Macy's major advertising slogan was "It's Smart to Be Thrifty," and the store would have more and more of a bargain store image throughout the next few decades.

Between Macy and B. Altman was Saks Thirty-fourth, where the newsmaking event of the early 1930s was the installation of in-house milliner Robert, who designed hats directly on the head. The store backed him so completely that there were very few French hats for sale there. Saks Thirty-fourth was quick to copy everything it found interesting, from little Princess Elizabeth's coat seen in the newspaper rotogravures to the entire Schiaparelli midseason collection that it purchased in 1931.

B. Altman, at Fifth Avenue diagonally across from the Empire State Building, continued to feature fabrics and sewing patterns on its first floor. On the third floor it sold imported couturier clothes from France and England, some custom, some ready-to-wear. Its bridal shop was famous for rare antique laces, with veils ranging in price from $95 to $15,000 (in 1931). The French hat salon carried imports by Agnès, Patou, Suzanne Talbot, and Maria Guy. Although the store featured Schiaparelli's daring newspaper-print hat and crumpled glass fan in 1935, it tended to sponsor such lesser-known or waning couture houses as Callot Soeurs, Ardanse, Chantal, Cheruit, DuTukine, Yvonne Carette, and Lucille Paray. By 1931 Altman had branches in Westchester and East Orange, New Jersey.

Advertisements and editorial copy of the period indicate that despite its forward-thinking sponsorship of American design, Lord & Taylor relied heavily on European design. In the Little Salon on the third floor, which offered special orders, were dresses and suits by Paquin, Schiaparelli, Drecoll-Beer, Chanel, Norman Hartnell, Lelong, Vionnet, Suzanne Talbot, and Patou. The Misses Department sold outright copies. In 1931 the store advertised "Contemporary prints designed by world famous artists, selected by style authorities, produced by American manufacturers, sold in the sports shop (fifth floor)." There was also a summer sports shop and a Young New Yorker's Shop. In 1936 an interior display generated much excitement: its twenty decorator windows included two inspired by couturiers—Lelong's, swathed in brown ciré satin, and Mme Grès's, draped in white silk jersey. Tom Brigance, the store's in-house designer beginning in 1938, was one of the few of his ilk to later make a name for himself on his own.

Close by Lord & Taylor, between Thirty-seventh and Thirty-eighth streets

Shoppers and passersby in front of Saks Fifth Avenue.

on Fifth Avenue, was Franklin Simon. In April 1931 *Harper's Bazaar* queried, "Did you know that Franklin Simon & Company have eighty-seven individual shops catering to the needs of smart young people and smart older ones too?" The shops included the sports department, where Lois Long found "charming costumes for the likes of you and me, who pretend we don't want to bother with fittings, but, in reality, prefer spending $35 on a little costume to $250" (October 11, 1930), as well as the Paris trousseau shop, for wedding dresses made to order, and the Women's Gown Shop on the fourth floor for reproductions of French models. As of 1930, Franklin Simon & Company proudly advertised that it had added another clothing line, called Wendell, to Bramley, both "originated and patented" by the store. More haute offerings included imported models by Vionnet, Patou, Lanvin, Molyneux, and Chanel, "to be copied immediately," accessories by Patou and Lelong, shoes by Hellstern, and the first exclusive offering of two new Worth perfumes: Je Reviens and the short-lived Honeysuckle. In 1930 Franklin Simon had a Palm Beach branch at the intersection of Worth and Hibiscus avenues and, in 1937, a store in Greenwich, Connecticut.

Off Fifth Avenue, at 42–44 East Forty-ninth Street, sat Hattie Carnegie, a specialty shop the size of a small department store, with, by 1934, branches in stores across the country. It set a high standard of quality in its clothes, whether French (custom-made models were imported from Alix, Schiaparelli, Worth, Chanel, Patou, Mainbocher, and Vionnet) or Carnegie's own (by such in-house designers as Claire McCardell, who worked there in the late 1930s before and after joining Townley, or Norman Norell, who was there at the end of the decade). Special departments included the modernistic Our Little Salon, the lower-priced Spectator Sports Shop, the hatmaking facility of a Mrs. Potts, and a custom-made pocketbook department where handbags could be ordered to match specific dresses or ensembles. Also available were perfumes, furs, and even chocolates.

Saks Fifth Avenue, a block away, boasted, by 1931, an in-house designer even more in-house than most: Sophie Gimbel, who was married to the store's owner Adam Gimbel. Designing under the fashionably elided name sophiegimbel, she was in charge of perhaps the country's single smartest store department, the Salon Moderne. Within three years, according to *Fortune* magazine, she had tripled the sales of her department, where her French purchases from such couture houses as Louiseboulanger, Chanel, Vionnet, Bruyère, Patou, and Schiaparelli were available on a made-to-order basis, along with her own three-times-a-year collections. The price range for sophiegimbel custom-made dresses by 1938 was $145 to $1,500. She also designed, along with Emmet Joyce, who had formerly worked for Hattie Carnegie and had his own business, the Saks Originals ready-to-wear collections. Her special signature in the 1930s was a subdued but striking palette; Lois Long described her colors as capable of making one swoon.

Although Saks Fifth Avenue strove for a reputation of great exclusivity, it responded to the Depression by advertising in 1930 that the Salon Moderne had lowered its prices: street dresses would start at $135 and Palm Beach dresses at $110. These "low" prices were as high as the most expensive prices ever mentioned in the advertisements of the era. Saks also sold accessories by such French designers as Agnès, Chanel, Caroline Reboux, and Callot Soeurs and shoes by the American designer LaValle. During the 1930s the store established both a shop for petites and the New Debutante's Shop.

Men's clothes were at their most elegant during the 1930s. Much of the way men dress today is based, nostalgically, on the style set during this decade. The major influence on women's clothes was Paris, but most styles for men emanated from England, specifically from the Prince of Wales, who was both particular and innovative about his attire. His appearance in anything new could set off an international fad. Among the novelties introduced by the man who would become the Duke of Windsor were double-breasted dinner jackets, midnight blue for evening, the larger Windsor knot in a necktie and the wider-set flat collar to accommodate it, the use of plaids rather than tweeds, as in the Prince of Wales glen check, argyle socks, plus fours, and vests with dinner suits. At 650 Fifth Avenue, at Fiftieth Street, could be found De-Pinna, "complete outfitters to the gentlemen of New York," which also sold tailored sports and town clothes for women, closely copied from men's clothes, designed by DePinna and produced in England.

This early 1930s window display at Franklin Simon used a clock and miniature mannequins as a device to show clothes for different times of day. The New-York Historical Society, New York

Women who wanted to look romantically exotic patronized several haunts in the low Fifties near Fifth and Madison. At 6 East Fifty-second Street was Natacha Rambova, the shop run by the ex-wife of Rudolph Valentino. Her theatrical-looking designs included tea gowns, theater wraps made from antique Persian brocades, and dresses in vaguely Oriental styles. Mariano Fortuny of Venice was represented in New York at 509 Madison Avenue, and there one could find, as the *New Yorker* described in its December 13, 1930, issue, "shimmering pleated teagowns in fine satin, rolled up and delivered in a box for violets. Also . . . evening or tea-coats of velvet stamped in silver and gold in a manner that suggests antique embroidery." A Paris follower of Fortuny, Babani, sold her own ethnic-inspired raiment exclusively through Chez Ninon, which was located in the beginning of the decade at 551 Madison Avenue, decorated in the modern style with brilliant blue glass. (Babani's perfumes were sold through Elizabeth Arden.) Chez Ninon was primarily known as a shop for off-the-beaten-track Paris originals, and among the social ladies whom the store advertised as its "chatelaines" was Mrs. Carroll Carstairs, who made the best-dressed list in 1934. Close by Fortuny, at 501 Madison Avenue, on an upper floor, was the first store run by Martha, who would later make a name for herself on Park Avenue.

Other shops sprinkled throughout the Fifties included that of Arthur Falkenstein in the Hotel Meurice, at 145 West Fifty-eighth Street, where prices for models purchased in Paris started at seventy-five dollars. At 16 East Fifty-third Street was Mrs. Franklin, who designed primarily knitted clothes and was immensely popular as long as the craze for knitted sportswear and dresses lasted. She imported some clothes from such lesser-known Paris couture houses as Goupy, had a custom millinery department, and sold styles ranging from beach pajamas to evening gowns. Dickert's, at 11 East Fifty-fifth Street, was known for French models that had been creatively transformed and adapted. At 49 West Fifty-sixth Street, briefly, was Norman Edwards, whose clothes were originals, and whom in the *New Yorker* of January 9, 1932, Lois Long called "one of our most promising blades or I quit tomorrow."

Perhaps the most elegant small store in Manhattan was that of Frances Clyne, at 6 East Fifty-sixth Street. Her clientele included members of the best-dressed list, such as Mrs. Harrison Williams, and actresses who wore her clothes on and off the stage, such as Katharine Cornell, Ina Claire, and

Better stores such as Bergdorf Goodman, where this photograph was taken in the early 1930s, held private fashion shows daily. This model is wearing a look as ubiquitous in the 1930s as the beaded dress was in the 1920s: a long, sliplike dress of lace with matching fox fur–trimmed jacket and triple strand of graduated pearls.

Ethel Barrymore. Clyne's own designs were sold along with imported dresses and accessories by Chanel, Lanvin, Molyneux, and Schiaparelli. The shop closed just prior to Clyne's death in 1944. Hermès was one of the few Paris stores that had a branch in New York, at 1 East Fifty-third Street, where the stock included leather goods, pocketbooks set with watches, sports clothes like beach ensembles of matching sunshade, hat, jacket, and handbag, and the new (in 1932) perfume Hermès No. 1, an old-fashioned scent packaged in glass surrounded by a silver stirrup.

The uptown department stores were Bloomingdale's, considered very isolated over on Lexington Avenue, Bonwit Teller, and Bergdorf Goodman, the latter two on Fifth Avenue. Bloomingdale's had not yet completed its evolution from dry-goods emporium to grand department store, but it was beginning to elevate its image when it established, in 1931, the Green Room on the third floor, where French models from Molyneux, Patou, Lyolène, and Chanel were copied exactly in imported fabrics. An interesting department was the Black and White Shop, primarily for mourning clothes but designed to appeal to any woman who liked those noncolors.

In September 1930, Bonwit Teller of New York, Paris, Philadelphia, and London advertised that it had opened its new building·at Fifth Avenue and Fifty-sixth Street. Its top department, for custom-made clothing, was run by Mme Harwick, and it also had the usual shops for Palm Beach clothes, sports clothes, and debutantes. It offered exact copies of the clothes of French couturiers Lanvin, Patou, Lelong, Vionnet, Maggy Rouff, Schiaparelli, and Marcel Rochas, among others. By 1938 Bonwit Teller had distinguished itself by giving Hortense Oldlum the job of president, making her the first woman to be in charge of a major department store.

Bergdorf Goodman was unusual in that it boasted not one but several in-house designers. Valentine Tukine was a little-known Parisian couturiere who joined Bergdorf's design staff in 1931. That same year, the Grand Duchess Marie returned to Bergdorf's from her lecture tour to resume designing for her regular clients. And, lastly, in 1931 Leslie Morris was named as the store's designer who went to the Paris collections. Morris, a talented designer, would be associated with the store for several decades. By the end of the 1930s, the names being touted by the store in an advertisement included the Countess de Robilant, who was in charge of Gabriella sports clothes, knitted to measure in Milan and delivered within a fortnight to New York; the English beauty Peggy Morris, whose forte was three-piece sports outfits and "dressing the Sargent type for evening"; Mark Mooring, "up from a Texas ranch via Paris and the New York theatre, whose specialty is getting the most drama out of yardage"; and Mrs. Gleason, "who's been with Bergdorf Goodman for twenty years, designing the loveliest clothes worn by many of America's loveliest ladies. She gets an extra special star for her tea gowns." There were also such French wares as hats by Patou and Agnès, jewelry by Vionnet, Louise-boulanger, and Lelong; dresses, coats, and suits by Vionnet, Lanvin, Schiaparelli, Paquin, Mainbocher, Maggy Rouff, and Chanel.

In just one block, between Fifth and Sixth avenues on Fifty-seventh Street, was situated a galaxy of deluxe specialty shops, starting with Dobbs at the corner of Fifth, followed by Milgrim at number 6, Henri Bendel at 10, Stein & Blaine at 13–15, Bruck-Weiss at 20, and Jay-Thorpe at 24–26. Sportswomen patronized Dobbs for riding habits made under the direction of dicta-

Surrealism replaced Art Deco as a major fashion influence in the 1930s. In 1937 Bonwit Teller carried off a real coup when Salvador Dali agreed to design a group of windows. This one features his smoking jacket covered with shot glasses. Museum of the City of New York

torial Ernest K. Fownes (he deplored the way some women insisted on wearing their riding caps back too far on their heads), as well as lounging pajamas, smart suits, and, of course, Dobbs hats.

At Milgrim, Sally Milgrim presided over her own studio, designing for private clients (she made the inaugural gowns for Mrs. Warren Harding, Mrs. Calvin Coolidge, and Eleanor Roosevelt) and for a wholesale line known as salymil, which occupied an entire floor in the store and was also sold in various other stores across the country. Next door, Henri Bendel, universally acknowledged as a genius of taste and style, advertised in 1932 that it was "impossible to truly copy a French model unless one copies its spirit, too. So truly Parisian in spirit is the House of Bendel that it is only natural that women who understand the art of reproducing French fashions should prefer them as Bendel's recreates them." Along with dresses designed or styled by Bendel himself and ready-to-wear offered in a department installed in 1931, the store carried high fashion by Chanel, Schiaparelli, Yvonne Carette, Worth, Lucille Paray, and Molyneux.

Stein & Blaine was courageous enough to rely mostly on its own talented designer, Miss E. M. A. Steinmetz, advertising her original creations more often than those of the relatively few French couturiers whose clothes it imported. Jay-Thorpe, in 1929, ensconced Harry Lichtenstein, a New York tailor, along with his entire staff, in a new custom-order department. As was usual, Lichtenstein traveled to Paris to attend the collections, and his department offered adaptations as well as exact versions of what he had chosen. The trousseau department was in the hands of Mrs. Hendrik Suydam, and Jay-Thorpe also had Renee Montaigue on staff as an in-house designer. This store

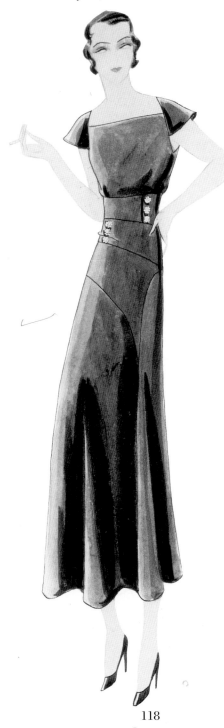

The 1930s was the first era in which different lengths were worn at different times of the day. Evening events called for long dresses, perhaps with a train for white-tie occasions, floor-length for black tie and informal dinners, while mid-calf lengths prevailed during the day. This dressy day-length frock designed by Leslie Morris of Bergdorf Goodman in 1932 is a forerunner of the cocktail or short evening dress. The Irene Lewisohn Library, the Costume Institute, The Metropolitan Museum of Art, New York

ranked with Bendel and Hattie Carnegie in terms of quality but had a more avant-garde image, not only because the Paris designers it favored were daring choices (Mirande, Augustabernard, Premet) but also because of its Art Deco interior filled with Lalique glass panels and fixtures and its Bistro on the fourth floor, where customers sat at a cocktail-type bar to watch the latest models parade back and forth. A 1933 advertisement placed by Jay-Thorpe featured a photograph by Lee Miller, photographer and model.

In 1938 Lilly Daché opened the doors to the entire building she had built at 18 East Fifty-sixth Street. At the top was her penthouse apartment, but the seven floors below were dedicated entirely to accommodating her staff of more than one hundred and fifty, her round salon upholstered in leopard, her gold fitting room for brunettes, and her silver one for blondes. Her hats were sold not only in her own building, for a top price of $165 in the 1930s, but in stores around the country, and they were "as sure to have smartness as a Steinway piano is to have tone," according to *Fortune* magazine in January 1935. Daché achieved such smartness through not only her creativity but also her sense of just how far to take it. She made a variety of hats, including profiles, which framed the face from one side, stand-up berets, peaked caps, turbans, sometimes forming snoods, and evening caps trimmed with swaths of veiling, sometimes to just one side, as well as silk flowers. She was known for unusual flowers, going beyond roses and violets to incorporate orchids, freesias, and gladioli, usually highlighted by the addition of little bugs, and for basing designs on antique or ethnic themes, as in a group of 1830s-style hats, a collection inspired by Peru, and another based on a cache of African headgear she found in a French gallery.

As is true today, a concentration of high-quality stores in an area brings in a high volume of custom, since women who like to shop like to make an outing of it. More and more, Madison Avenue was becoming a real shopping street, with small, personal stores giving it the character it still has in the 1980s.

Like Fifty-seventh Street, Sixty-seventh was the home of several special establishments, primarily located in town houses between Fifth and Park. At number 32, there was Marcel Rochas, the only French couturier in the 1930s to capitalize on the American market by installing a branch in New York for the sale of his custom-made clothes. There was also Eldridge & Garson, at 22, Elizabeth Hawes, at 21, and Valentina, at 27. By the end of the decade Valentina had moved into the recently vacated Hawes building.

Eldridge & Garson was a joint but separate venture in the same elegant premises. Mabel Eldridge was a designer as well as importer whose taste was romantic and feminine. She was known for the extremely fine quality of handwork in her clothes and for hand embroidery that equaled that of France. During a period of spare and narrow clothes, she specialized in *robes de style*, dresses with fairly fitted bodices and full, picturesque skirts. She imported from Molyneux, Patou, Vionnet, Schiaparelli, Martial et Armand, Ardanse, and Paquin. Her fellow tenant, Daisy Garson, designed, imported, and sold handmade lingerie that was either simple and tailored or lavish with beading, embroidery, and appliqué.

Valentina never stopped designing for herself, and what suited her—severe, monochromatic, beautifully cut clothes made in the finest fabrics—also suited her very elite clientele. Many of her 1930s designs featured Oriental details. As early as 1935 she was accessorizing mandarin jacket suits and

Sally Milgrim of Milgrim on Fifty-seventh Street was both a custom designer and a ready-to-wear designer, with a line named salymil that was sold around the country. She made many clothes for Eleanor Roosevelt, including her inaugural gowns, and also designed this dress for her daughter, Anna, then Mrs. Curtis B. Dall, to wear to the 1933 inauguration. Made from Chinese brocade that had been in the family for half a century, the dress featured a raised waistline, a sash-train of two shades of red silk chiffon, and embroidery at the neck and armholes of red and white crystal beads.

At Jay-Thorpe private fashion showings were informal, taking place in the in-house bar, where customers could relax with coffee or other refreshments and also sample perfumes.

The first floor of Jay-Thorpe had the most lavish Art Deco interior of any New York store. It featured chandeliers and other fittings by the crystal manufacturer Lalique. Museum of the City of New York

obi-sashed surplice dresses with pointed coolie hats. She was fond of aprons as a decorative device to change the look of a dress. One such example was a boldly printed abstract black and white silk dress with a red ciré apron. In 1937 she showed a divided, or culotte, dress, inspired by New York's windy streets. When her clothes appeared in 1930s fashion magazines, they were usually worn by performing artists like Lynn Fontanne, Gladys Swarthout, or Tamara Toumanova, and Valentina also designed frequently for the theater. Among her most notable costumes were those for Katharine Hepburn in the 1939 stage production of Philip Barry's *The Philadelphia Story*. For years Valentina received orders for Tracy Lord's white, Grecian-pleated evening dress, blue-and-white checked luncheon dress with frilled collar, and "second wedding dress" of softly draped pink and mauve mousseline de soie. Other Valentina clients were Gloria Swanson, Dorothy Parker, and Greta Garbo.

One of the major differences between French couturiers and American designers is that the French developed much more quickly into stars. Worth led the way by conducting himself like an artist, not a tradesman, and by making sure that his establishment was exclusive. By the turn of the century, couturiers like Doucet were accepted as gentlemen in society, and before World War I, Poiret held exotic parties to which everyone wanted to be invited. In America, though, even the fashion names that were known early on, like Herman Patrick Tappé, Henri Bendel, and E. M. A. Steinmetz, remained fairly anonymous. Their work may have been recognizable, but their faces, and private lives, remained enigmatic. Elizabeth Hawes was the first visible and vociferous native designer. Throughout the 1930s her actions proved newsworthy. By 1933 Elizabeth Hawes's clothing designs—simple, restrained, often colorful, and intended for intelligent women like herself— were eclipsed by the many antics that demonstrated Hawes's astute grasp of the power of publicity.

In 1932 she took a collection of twenty-five of her dresses and held a fashion show in Paris on the fourth of July. She wasn't expecting to sell them; she wanted to prove that good clothes could be designed by non-Parisians, something the American-born Mainbocher was certainly already doing, as was the British Norman Hartnell, who presented his collections in Paris as well as London. When she returned from a Paris probably more than a little irked by the drastic drop in American patronage of the couture, she received coverage in the *New York Times* by complaining that she had not been "courteously received." That same year, she was represented in the first Lord & Taylor advertisement of American fashion by a checked dress and dark coat ensemble called City Child, ready-made and priced at $10.75 (as little as one-tenth her custom prices). In 1935 she was invited by Soviet officials to give a fashion show in the Soviet Union, and, upon her return, she reported to the *New York Times* that her reception this time had been cordial, that Russian women were indeed interested in fashion, and that they wore permanent waves, painted fingernails, and (80 percent of them) berets. Her deliberately controversial book *Fashion Is Spinach*, published in 1938, was based on the premise that fashion is deplorable but that style is laudable. She went on to write several other books, including *Men Can Take It* and *It's Still Spinach*, and she eventually became less of a fashion designer and more of a fashion sage and critic.

When Muriel King was chosen as one of the first three designers for Lord & Taylor's 1932 promotion of American fashion, she had just gone into business

8 Diamond Horseshoe
ianchini silk
345.

KATHERINA
POWDER BLUE
WEDDING FEAST

model without
sleeves

36

for herself running a couture salon at 32 East Sixty-first Street. While Lord & Taylor sold her ready-to-wear designs, priced between twenty and fifty dollars, her private clientele could order dresses that were then retired from circulation so that no one else would own them.

Muriel King had been born in 1901 in Bayview, Washington, and studied art at the University of Washington, designing theater costumes on the side, before moving to New York. Her first jobs were in fashion illustration for publications like *Vogue* and *Harper's Bazaar.* In 1927 King spent the first of three annual eight-month stays in Europe, where she free-lanced as a fashion artist for *Modes and Manners, Femina,* and French *Vogue.*

Urged on by friends, whom she had long been helping with their wardrobes, she decided to begin designing clothes professionally. She worked by making her beautifully rendered drawings first, and then had the clothes made up by her sewing staff. Customers ordered from the sketches rather than from actual models. She often worked with American fabrics and even designed an entire collection of them in 1933 for B. Altman. She designed everything from bathing suits and skating clothes to evening gowns and was especially interested in interchangeable wardrobes of separates and day-into-evening clothes. Beginning in 1935, when she designed the clothes for Katharine Hepburn to wear in the movie *Sylvia Scarlett,* she worked occasionally for the movies. Her designs were worn by Hepburn off camera as well, and she designed Hepburn's as well as Ginger Rogers's clothes for the movie *Stage Door* in 1937. She moved her salon to 49 East Fifty-first Street in 1937.

Muriel King's clothes were breathtakingly elegant, with none of the intellectual gimmickry that marred other American efforts at native designs. They also reflected her painter's sense of color, and she relied more on playing transparency against opacity or in contrasting textures than she did on ornamentation.

During the 1930s fashion caught up with Jessie Franklin Turner, and there was more of a demand than ever for her flowing tea gowns and evening dresses. Typical were long, narrow dresses ending in trains and made with long angel sleeves in layered shades of chiffon. She made daytime clothes, too, usually with vaguely ethnic details with blouson waists and puffed sleeves. One suit of rough wool featured Chinese gilt filigree ball buttons. By the end of the 1930s she had redecorated her salon at 410 Park Avenue in shades of red, chartreuse, and black, and she began to pattern her evening clothes after those worn in portraits by Francisco de Goya and Sir Henry Raeburn.

A designer operating out of his or her own store had a much better chance of achieving recognition for his or her work because the clientele obviously was aware of the name behind the designs. American designers who worked in wholesale establishments were less fortunate. The businesses themselves did not necessarily reveal their designer's name; Norman Norell's deal with Traina, Inc., to be paid less in order to get his name on the label would be widely known. The wholesalers held shows of collections at least twice a year, but, unlike in Paris, these were seen only by buyers, not by the press or private clients. The press concentrated on what was being shown in the stores, and by then, any sign of the design's creator had been removed. Although several wholesale designers were well known for innovation and quality, such information tended to remain inside knowledge. This slowly began to change, as thirties designers began to get credit for their work.

This 1936 white crepe evening dress and house sketch (opposite), both in the collection of the Brooklyn Museum, New York, provide a rare opportunity to see a fashion drawing come to life. The dress (gift of the Estate of Elinor Gimbel) was by Elizabeth Hawes, one of the first American designers to become well known. Mainly a couturier, she also branched out into ready-to-wear, notably when she was included in the first group of designers to be promoted by Lord & Taylor.

OVERLEAF
Muriel King, one of New York's most talented custom designers, had started out as a fashion illustrator, and she designed in the unusual manner of making complete drawings, from which her clientele could order and which her sewing staff used as a guide. She was also one of the few New York designers who costumed Hollywood films. Katharine Hepburn often wore her clothes, on screen and off; this pair of lounging pajamas with monogrammed pocket was made for Hepburn for the 1937 film Stage Door. Her evening dress with off-the-shoulder neckline and insect-wing transparent overskirt was designed in 1938. This day dress from 1939, with its panel of hand-woven-looking fabric and coolie hat, shows the predilection for ethnic-inspired materials and styles that was just becoming important in American fashion. Muriel King used printed velvet for a dress with a surplice cape collar that was suitable for day or afternoon. The Irene Lewisohn Library, the Costume Institute, The Metropolitan Museum of Art, New York

Clare Potter was well known almost from the moment (in 1930) that she began as designer for Charles W. Nudelman, Inc., at 550 Seventh Avenue. One of the American designers featured in the Lord & Taylor promotions, she also won the store's 1937 women's sportswear award. Neiman-Marcus honored her with a fashion award in 1939. She used the elided lower-case version of her name, clarepotter, throughout the 1930s and into the 1940s. Very much an American designer, she purposely avoided Paris and instead found inspiration from vacation trips to Mexico or Bermuda and from her own suburban way of life on a New York State farm, where she and her engineer husband raised Dalmatians and vegetables.

She was born Clare Meyer in Jersey City, New Jersey, and with the intention of becoming an artist, she studied in New York at the Art Students League and at Pratt Institute, where she switched over to costume design. She left before graduating to work for Edward L. Mayer, Inc. This was in the 1920s, during the height of the vogue for elaborately beaded dresses, and her assignment was to research embroidery designs in museums. Gradually she began to suggest other design elements as well and became a designer, a post she held for three years. She then took a sabbatical to Mexico, worked briefly at another Seventh Avenue house, and moved finally to Nudelman.

Her major talent was as a colorist, and her clothes tended to concentrate on line and color combinations rather than added decoration for effect. She didn't like to make a design on paper and then have it made into a toile, or muslin pattern. Working directly with the fabric gave her a much better sense of the fall of the material and how the colors worked with each other. Although she used some printed fabrics—she even created a Dalmatian print based on her pets—she worked mostly in solid materials dyed to her specifications. Her clothes reflected the active American image and included beautifully cut pants and shorts, pajamas, and other articles of sportswear.

American designers Jo Copeland at Pattullo and Nettie Rosenstein were considered so talented that they were copied as much as the French. After becoming a full-time designer for Pattullo, which had a reputation as one of the most innovative wholesale houses, Copeland left in 1930 to found a wholesale firm of her own with Ann Sadowsky. The new firm lasted only four years, and she returned to Pattullo where, after four more years, she became a partner. Like other American designers, she found it frustrating to work with toiles; instead, she designed directly on the figure, frequently using her own. Her exceptionally well-made clothes, usually quite expensive, tended to the elegant rather than the sporty and lay outside the mainstream. Her fabric choices were luxurious and interesting, as in a thin wool woven with gold sequins, and one of her signatures was the use of "moving fabric"—flying panels and asymmetric draperies.

Nettie Rosenstein, born Nettie Rosencrans in Austria, moved with her family to New York in the 1890s. They settled in Harlem, where they ran a dry-goods store. Nettie began making her own clothes when she was eleven. In 1916 she married Saul Rosenstein, and three years later, after making clothes informally for her friends, began a dressmaking business in her house. In 1921 she moved to East Fifty-sixth Street, where she had fifty employees. She switched to wholesaling when I. Magnin approached her about selling her clothes on the West Coast. In 1929 she retired from the business but returned to design for the company Corbeau et Cie. In 1931, in partnership with her sister-in-law Eva Rosencrans and Charles Gumprecht, she began a wholesale business using her own name on West Forty-seventh Street. In 1942 she moved to 550 Seventh Avenue.

Lord & Taylor issued Rosenstein an award in 1938. At her peak she designed five hundred models a year, preferring to work by draping material directly on the figure. Unusually for ready-to-wear, each of her dresses was made by a single sewer from start to finish, except when special embroiderers were needed. Her clothes were sold around the country, but only one store in each city was allowed to use her label; the store that featured her clothes by name in New York was Bonwit Teller. Her prices ranged from $89.50 to $795.00, and her specialty was grand as well as more casual evening clothes.

Although American style was primarily considered sporty and relaxed, there was great variety among the early designers, as befitted a group that was designing for a wide range of tastes, pocketbooks, climates, and types, as well as for city and country living. There were very sophisticated designers who specialized in dressier clothes, like Germaine Monteil and Mollie Parnis; wholesale houses known for classical sportswear, like William Bloom and Helen Cookman; and designers like Tina Leser and Claire McCardell, who could run the gamut of sportswear and evening clothes without relying on the model set by men's sports clothing.

William Bloom ran a sportswear house whose clothes were sold at various department stores, including Bonwit Teller and Saks. Among his designing staff was the then-well-known Virginian Eve Bennett. William Bloom sports clothes were frequently made of cunningly knitted fabrics and used zippers innovatively as early as 1930. Most of the clothes were versions of what came to be called separates, with suits, vest-blouses, blouses, and jumpers working as components on their own or together.

Another of Lord & Taylor's advertising campaign protégées was Helen Cookman. Although she had been in the coat-and-suit business since 1924 and became director of her own company in 1928, it was not until 1930 that, out of necessity, she began designing. She was a wife, mother, designer, and businesswoman, described as small, blonde, pretty, and well groomed. Originally from Philadelphia, she attended Agnes Irwin School before moving to New York to work. She was best known for her tweeds, which she had woven specially in Scotland, and the "keynotes of her costume structure" were "fine materials, well-bred linens and classic tailoring" (from a brochure published by the National Retail Drygoods Association, 1935).

Germaine Monteil had her own wholesale house by 1930, after having designed for Harry Collins, who operated a store in New York, and for the manufacturer A. Traina. Despite the fact that she was called "the American Vionnet," she is today remembered for having founded a cosmetics empire, which began with her introduction of a lipstick as early as 1935. She was born in Paris, immigrated to America when quite young, was married to a Mr. Njorkman, and had an elegant appearance. She worked by making drawings, was very careful about cut, and concentrated primarily on evening clothes, with results that were innovative and alluring. In 1931 her clothes could be found without attribution at Henri Bendel, Bergdorf Goodman, Jay-Thorpe, Saks, Vera Sanville, Stein & Blaine, and Madame et la Jeune Fille.

More of an editor than a designer, but one astute enough to remain in business well into the 1980s, Mollie Parnis started a wholesale company in 1933 with her husband, calling it Parnis-Livingston. She experimented with high waistlines, although not every dress she made was Empire. In effect, she gave her dresses two waistlines, at the top and the bottom of the midriff, and as the decade wore on she continued using the highlighted midriff for what became her specialties: evening or dinner suits, which had long, circular-cut skirts, cropped jackets with sleeves puffed high at the shoulder, and decorative ruffled or beaded blouses. Her price range in the 1930s was $79.50 to $195.00, and her clothes were sold (without the labels) at such stores as Henri Bendel, Bergdorf Goodman, Jay-Thorpe, Saks Fifth Avenue, Vera Sanville, Stein & Blaine, and Madame et la Jeune Fille.

A wholesale designer of day-into-evening clothes, Omar Kiam was named Alexander when he was born in Mexico to Alsatian parents but nicknamed Omar when attending school in the United States. He worked during the 1930s first as a designer for his own company, at the same time designing costumes occasionally for the theater, including the play *Dinner at Eight*, and then, beginning in 1933, in Hollywood for Samuel Goldwyn and United Artists, where his credits included *A Star Is Born* and *Stella Dallas*, both of 1937. As a wholesale designer his clothes were highly regarded, especially his suits, day-in, day-out wool or crepe dresses, and coats. In the March 26, 1932, issue of the *New Yorker*, Lois Long singled out his black satin, just-above-the-ankle-length dress with cap sleeves and a matching jacket, calling it "the best cocktail-dinner-theatre-anything dress I have seen in moons."

A. Beller was considered one of the very best of the coat-and-suit manufacturers. Lois Long wrote of the company in the July 26, 1930, *New Yorker*, "When you stroll into your favorite shop, in search of a magnificent tweed coat or suit to start the autumn in style, the model which you wistfully consider mortgaging the home for is quite likely to have been designed by A. Beller." Using imported tweeds and the best furs, A. Beller made ensembles composed of a heavy tweed coat and a lighter, matching tweed dress; feminine suits with fitted waistlines; evening coats and jackets of black velvet trimmed with ermine or made of metallic brocade; and, in 1931, an early version of the culotte suit, called, unfortunately, a "pantie suit," consisting of a skirt-pants combination with front and back panels covering the pants.

Emmet Joyce had established his wholesale company in 1928 (Claire McCardell was an early employee, working as a salesperson and sketch artist), and it was so successful that he netted a million dollars the first year. He had been born in Chicago and had studied at the Art Institute there before moving to New York, where he worked for Hattie Carnegie. By 1935 he was no longer associated with his own business; instead, he designed for the establishment of Mme Frances and, eventually, for Saks Fifth Avenue. His ready-to-wear clothes tended to be very colorful, with lots of swagger and detail, and were sold at stores like Bergdorf Goodman and Jay-Thorpe or, unusually, directly from his showroom. He worked with fluid materials for his day, afternoon, and evening clothes and liked to combine several versions of a color in a single garment, such as grape, mauve, pink purple, and fuchsia.

Louise Barnes Gallagher was a ready-to-wear designer of suits, coats, and dresses, primarily for day and afternoon, who was known for one particular fabric: Gallagher mesh, a sheer wool with the feel and look of a fine hand knit. Gallagher typically used it for many-buttoned dresses with many-buttoned coats. From 1930 her business was located at 37 West Forty-seventh Street.

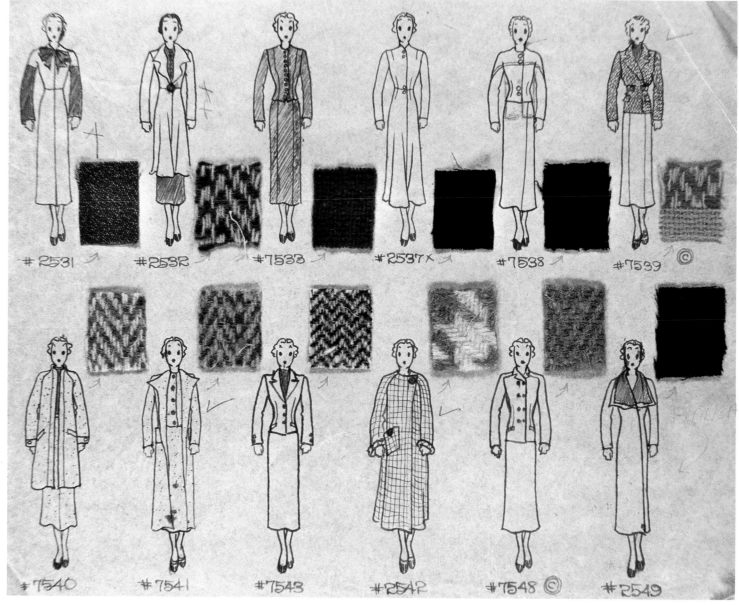

Philip Mangone continued to design his wholesale suits and coats, almost exclusively from woolens, throughout the 1930s, as he had since beginning his firm in 1916. He traveled to Europe as often as four times a year, looking for inspiration as well as the most interesting fabrics. Returning to the United States in 1937, he voyaged in the dirigible *Graf Zeppelin* and was severely burned when it exploded upon landing, although he was able to continue working.

Other ready-to-wear companies that specialized in coats and suits included Harry Frechtel; Davidow, originally founded in 1880 by William Davidow and eventually run by his sons; David Crystal, whose 1931 advertisement ran, "It's deplorable if you're not adorable in sportswear"; Anthony Blotta; Ben Zuckerman of Zuckerman & Kraus; Ben Reig, founded in 1929; and Maurice Rentner, specializing in dresses and suits. Although these houses were known within the industry for high-quality sportswear, they would not begin to be known by name until the 1940s.

Charles Armour & Bro. was a manufacturer of ready-to-wear day and evening clothes. Armour's wearable, sporty designs often made use of whimsical

details, such as red wool revers on a 1931 black silk suit or belts designed to place the visual interest in the back rather than the front. In its December 1933 issue, *Fortune* magazine described Armour as being as "temperamental as a declining opera star" and as having "a great following in the half-world between the footlights and the Social Register."

Sydney Wragge bought a company that manufactured men's shirts in 1931 and founded B. H. Wragge. He began making women's shirts as well, and by the late 1930s he had expanded into producing carefully coordinated collections of shirts, jackets, skirts, coats, dresses, and pants made in tweeds, rayon prints, solid color silks, cottons, and wools, all designed to be interchangeable.

That it has become a cliché makes it no less true that Claire McCardell's clothes are dazzlingly timeless. Like Chanel, she had a genius for making clothes that not only suited women of her own time but that continued to hold great appeal decades after her death. Originally from Maryland, McCardell studied fashion design at Parson's School of Design, spending a year at the Paris campus. After working at several insignificant jobs, she became an assistant to Robert Turk, following him when he went to design for the wholesale company Townley. Turk died in a freak sailing accident just as the first collection was getting under way, and McCardell stepped in as head designer. When Townley closed in 1938, she went to work for Hattie Carnegie, where her designs were considered too understated.

Because thirties designers were so often anonymous it is difficult to trace McCardell's early work. Her first major commercial success was the "monastic dress" of 1938, so called because it was cut like a tent (or a monk's robe) and could be worn full, swinging from the shoulders, or belted. McCardell's inspiration for the dress was an Algerian costume she had made for herself to wear to the New York Beaux Arts Ball in 1937. It was a relaxed, adaptable style that contrasted with the late-thirties look of structured clothes with fitted bodices and a feminine style that predated the postwar New Look. That it was so successful (it continued to sell for years) proved that Americans were finally ready to wear totally original designs created by Americans specifically with Americans in mind. In 1939 *Harper's Bazaar* showed a dress from Hattie Carnegie, since attributed to McCardell: it featured a rather atypical sweetheart neckline and peplum overskirt but already showed such McCardellisms as a surplice front and the use of a sporty striped material in an evening dress. During the 1940s, her innovations became widely known, beginning spectacularly with her 1940 abandonment of the exaggerated shoulder pad. No one would prove more influential than McCardell in demonstrating that ingenuity could surmount the difficulties of wartime rationing and regulations.

The years between the stock market crash of 1929 and the outbreak of World War II were the most formative for American fashion. Never again would the immense amount of native designing talent be ignored, nor would designers continue to remain anonymous. Without the foundation laid in the 1930s, New York's wartime reputation as fashion capital of the world would have dissolved as the Paris couture again became available and intriguing to fashion writers, editors, and buyers. Although New York had been compared to Paris for decades, it was not important whether American fashion equaled, or even threatened to surpass, that of France but, rather, that it existed at all. And, in the 1930s, it began, definitely, to exist.

A favorite element of American style that emerged during the 1930s was the use of traditional day fabrics, such as wool or, in this case, gingham, for evening clothes. Charles Armour, a ready-to-wear designer, made this 1939 slip dress, which is paired with a jacket of organdy. Photograph: Munkacsi. International Center of Photography, New York, Permanent Collection. Gift of Joan Munkacsi. Courtesy Harper's Bazaar

As war threatened in Europe and it began to be clear that America would be cut off from European, especially Parisian, design sources, American fashion magazines, stores, and designers realized that they would have to function independently of the couture. Fortunately, native talent abounded, and although many designers were still anonymous to the public, the 1930s had set the stage for the acceptance of American names and styles. No longer would outfits such as this 1939 two-piece dress of light and dark blue striped rayon be commonly shown without designer credit. Photograph: Munkacsi. International Center of Photography, New York, Permanent Collection. Gift of Joan Munkacsi. Courtesy Harper's Bazaar

THE 1940s

American patriotism before and during World War II extended to the fashion industry. Not only were local talents and products encouraged and, finally, fully appreciated, but fashion also played an integral part in maintaining morale. The fashion industry participated in the war effort by heeding rules about saving fabric, leather, and metal and by turning out attractive dresses to brighten the eyes of soldiers on leave. Fashion magazines did their bit for the war effort by promoting fabric-saving styles, running articles on women's war-related contributions and achievements, and showing such styles as this 1943 white linen blazer suit in such patriotic settings as this flag-making factory. Photograph: Horst. Courtesy Vogue

Since World War II was not fought in the United States, most Americans at home never experienced the horror of having their cities and towns, even the air above them, become battlefields. They endured hardships, mostly having to do with shortages of food, heating oil, gasoline, rubber for tires, metal, fabrics, and leather, but compared to the citizens of other countries, Americans had it fairly easy. Many civilians remember the war years as rather fun, and certainly full of camaraderie: everyone banded together to participate in scrap-metal or rubber drives; to assemble Bundles for Britain; to plant and tend Victory Gardens; and to entertain the military.

Women were not only active volunteers in such efforts, they also filled administrative positions in organizations like the Red Cross, served in the WAVES and WACS, and worked in defense plants. As in all wars, housewives found their jobs more involved; tending the home fires called for diligence, creativity, and cheerfulness in the face of obstacles. In fashion, as in everything else, Americans were patriotic. American women proudly wore the uniforms or coveralls that signified that they were pitching in, and they were enthusiastic about all of the excellent American designs that so ably incorporated government regulations.

From the moment Paris was occupied, there was a flurry of speculation as to whether American fashion could function cut off from the inspirations of the couture. New York was mentioned most often as the city most capable of becoming the style center of the world, and its mayor, Fiorello La Guardia, established committees to study and evaluate how best to make the city a lure for buyers and editors. According to most of the experts busily voicing their opinions, only a relatively small amount of American production consisted of out-and-out copies—a reasonable assumption, given that the couture turned out relatively few models compared to the 125,000 garments designed in New York annually, as of 1940, to be made up in the millions. As it happened, the French couture didn't shut down completely, but it might as well have, since fashion editors and buyers were unable to see most of its offerings. And so they shifted their attention to design that originated here.

The major American fashion magazines, *Vogue* and *Harper's Bazaar*, along with all the periodicals or newspapers that had a fashion column, increased their coverage of the shows held in New York by department stores, custom houses, and wholesale manufacturers; they began to feature American designers prominently, crediting them by name. Many of the names first mentioned belonged to designers who had been active and successful for many years before they became overnight sensations. As the designers themselves came to be well known, stores and retailers became less important.

Eleanor Lambert, a publicist who began to specialize in fashion in the late 1930s and whose 1940s clients included Norell, Adrian, and Trigère, was influential in spreading the news about American design. She sent press releases and photographs to newspapers around the country, making it easy for

almost any local paper to run articles about American fashion. In 1943 she organized the first of what would become semiannual press weeks in New York. She also played a major role during the 1940s in founding the Costume Institute, which eventually became part of the Metropolitan Museum of Art, New York, and which served to inspire local designers; the annual fashion awards, sponsored by Coty, given out by the Council of Fashion Critics; and the annual benefit fashion show for the March of Dimes. Benefit shows gave social cachet to an industry whose product was evolving into an art form.

Also influential were such fashion journalists as Lois Long, a champion of native styles, wholesale and custom-made, since she first began writing for the *New Yorker* in the mid-1920s, and Virginia Pope of the *New York Times*, who often ran profiles of American designers and in 1942 originated the annual show called "Fashions of the Times," which ten years later became the newspaper's fashion magazine supplement. Fashion editors, like Diana Vreeland and Carmel Snow of *Vogue* and Sally Kirkland at *Life*, supported American designers by showing their clothes and even commissioning special designs from them and helping them in organizing their businesses.

Magazines and newspapers lauded such generic components of American style as polo coats, shirtwaist dresses, and sweater sets as much as they described specific designer creations. Interestingly, attention was accorded to every level of fashion, from the most haute custom dress down to inexpensive mass-manufactured misses' dance frocks. The top rung of designers included such custom designers as Fira Benenson of Bonwit Teller, Sophie of Saks, Muriel King of Stein & Blaine, Wilson Folmar at Jay-Thorpe, Arthur Falkenstein, Mainbocher (newly arrived in New York after running a Paris couture house for a decade), Valentina, and Jean Schlumberger, who designed fashions for Chez Ninon before turning to jewelry. The custom department at Henri Bendel was run by Mr. Leone, whose staff of designers included Mabel McIlvain Downs; Bergdorf Goodman had Leslie Morris and Bernard Newman, among others; and Hattie Carnegie, Milgrim, and Herman Patrick Tappé also designed luxurious custom clothes.

More well known than the American couturiers were the top-of-the-line ready-to-wear designers, since their clothes were advertised and sold by name all over the country rather than just in their own salons and showrooms. This group in the 1940s included of Nettie Rosenstein, Maurice Rentner, who was also chairman of and spokesman for the Fashion Originators Guild, Philip Mangone, Trigère, Anthony Blotta, Bruno, Ceil Chapman, Harvey Berin, Jane Derby, Mme Eta, Jo Copeland for Pattullo, Norell, and, from California, Adrian, Irene, and Howard Greer, all three of whom had been involved with movie costume design. All were versatile designers who provided clothes for evening and for dressy daytime events in town.

Perhaps the most innovative of the new names in American fashion belonged to those who worked in the area of sports and play clothes. Tom Brigance at Lord & Taylor, Claire McCardell, Vera Maxwell, Clare Potter, Tina Leser, and Sydney Wragge for B. H. Wragge all worked within the new category of separates. Besides being moderately priced, their clothes, designed with very real women in mind, managed to be both practical and creative.

New York also boasted top accessory designers, such as Lilly Daché, G. Howard Hodge, John-Frederics, Florence Reichmann, Sally Victor, and Walter Florell for hats, Koret and Josef for pocketbooks, and costume jewelery designers like Miriam Haskell. Brooke Cadwallader, a fabric designer, issued each season limited-edition silk scarves screened with patriotic or historical themes; other fabric designers included Hope Skillman, who specialized in cottons, and, on the West Coast, Pola Stout, whose handwoven geometric woolens proved a source of inspiration to Adrian and Irene.

The war provided American designers with a chance to enjoy the limelight (the *New York Times*'s fashion show of 1944 had limelight as its theme—the clothes were made out of various chartreuse-colored materials), but, more important, the wartime hiatus freed Americans from having to compete with the French on French terms. Having no choice but to use mostly American fabrics and techniques, once considered a liability, they turned it into an asset. At the same time, being given specific limitations spurred them to be

The message to buy war savings bonds was hardly subliminal; even department store windows spread the word. This display shows variations on a wartime staple: the narrow dress with broad shoulders and narrow skirt, made interesting with a pleat or two or with embroidery or other ornamentation.

more inventive, and with everyone limited in the same way, competition to solve problems resulted in excellent design. In its August 16, 1943, issue, *Life* magazine compared "the first sizeable collection of French creations to reach the U.S. since the German occupation" with New York designs. The magazine found the French designs "vulgar exaggerations of famous silhouettes," the dresses brief but at the same time overly draped; rather than use simple fabrics sparingly, couturiers used loud ones to compensate for restrictions. *Life* blamed the sorry state of the couture on the French having to cater to German tastes. In contrast, the New York day and evening dresses were cited for being trim, figure-flattering, and even sirenish.

The regulation known as L-85, first announced in 1943, affected every kind of clothing made out of materials important for the war effort with the exception of wedding gowns, maternity clothes, infants' wear, clothes for children up to the age of four, religious vestments, and burial shrouds. One of L-85's purposes was to maintain, or freeze, the silhouette, because any significant change would have necessitated adjustments of machinery, technique, and extra labor. The regulations were directed at manufacturers, and the War Production Board issued variations throughout the period of shortages and government priority.

What to wear on a date with a man in uniform was a commonly asked question in the 1940s. Lord & Taylor dressed these two mannequins in one of the period's favorite solutions: the dinner, opera, or theater suit. Being long and dressy, they were considered formal, but being covered up, they were less formal than ball gowns. The Library, Fashion Institute of Technology, New York

The restrictions confined men to single-breasted, two-piece (rather than three-piece) suits and pants cut without pleats or cuffs. What was called the "fancy-back" jacket, popularized by Clark Gable, was banned, as were double-breasted dinner jackets. For the most part, it was not the restrictions that limited men's clothing production but the fact that the factories concentrated instead on making uniforms. Particularly as they were returning from the war, men looking for new clothes, even those who could afford whatever they wanted, often found that stores didn't have much stock.

The application of L-85 to women's clothing was necessarily more complicated. If made of wool or another material important to the war effort, dresses could have skirts that measured only up to seventy-two inches at the hem (which is actually fuller than the average gathered skirt today). This ruled out real dirndls, entailing narrow versions. Suit jackets were limited to twenty-five inches in length, which comes to just below the hip on the average woman, and pants could be only as wide as nineteen inches in circumference at the hem (the mid-1980s narrow pant leg averages around fourteen inches). The hem depth for skirts was not supposed to exceed two inches, and belts were also limited to two inches in width. On shirts and blouses, turned-back cuffs, double yokes, sashes, scarves, and hoods were banned and only one patch pocket allowed. Coats were not to have any back pleats. Fully pleated skirts were replaced by skirts with a couple of kick pleats. Narrow, long dresses usually featured slits for movement.

These regulations were not difficult to heed, and by 1943 designers found themselves using even less material than allowed. *Vogue*, on February 1, 1943, reported on the shoestring silhouette, writing, "No law compels us to wear clothes as narrow as these. L-85 allows for much more generous measurements. Voluntarily, a group of American designers have pledged themselves to use less fabric than L-85 allows—in order to save every yard. The British, who have felt the pinch of fabric shortages longer than we, practically live in slim coat dresses. They call them austerity fashions, but if this is austerity, let's have more of it."

Hollywood was not exempt from L-85, and both Irene and Edith Head felt that the limitations had strengthened costume design. When Edith Head visited Manhattan in 1944 she told the *New York Times* (February 1), "How well I remember the day when we would swirl fox skins around the hem of a secretary's dress, or put a white satin uniform on a trained nurse. Now we hold to stark realism." Although escapist movies, so popular in the Depression, continued to be made in the 1940s, most avoided out-and-out glamour, since it would not have been patriotic to revel in excess. Film designers, like the rest of Americans, made do with previously worn clothing, changing collars or other details so that moviegoers wouldn't recognize a given outfit. They did this both to reflect what was happening in real life and to set an example of simplicity and ingenuity. Typical 1940s films featured women wearing suits, sweaters and skirts or pants, or bathing suits. In a way, the sweater girl, as exemplified by the soldiers' favorite pinups Rita Hayworth and Lana Turner, was the 1940s answer to the platinum blonde in platinum fox and satin.

Not every article of clothing was made according to the limitations: there were plenty of full-skirted evening dresses, for example. The War Production Board's regulations protected materials needed for uniform production, making them scarce for other uses, and encouraged the manufacture of unneeded

1940

materials, including rayon net, taffeta, and faille, in order to keep existing manufacturers employed.

Wool, which went into winter uniforms and blankets for the several million–strong United States armed forces, was the most restricted fabric, with most wool production directed at the government. Even knitting for one's friends or relatives who were soldiers was regulated, with the Red Cross dictating who knit what—socks, scarves, or sweaters—for whom. Although American women were allowed to wear wool in the amounts dictated by L-85, they were encouraged to dress in wool blends, fabrics made out of recycled wool, and in rayon versions of the material. Rayon gabardine was the most prevalent wool substitute, and it was used for men's shirts and other clothes as well as for women's garments.

Since much of World War II was fought in the air, silk was another vital war material. It was used for parachutes and for gunpowder sacks, since it disintegrated in an explosion without jamming the mechanisms of heavy artillery. The survival maps carried by pilots in case of a crash landing in a strange country were printed on silk, since it withstood constant folding and dampness without losing legibility, and pilots wore silk scarves to keep their necks from chafing as they constantly turned around to look behind them. Little silk remained available for clothing, and women missed it for dresses, such underwear as slips, and, especially, stockings.

Nylon stockings, introduced for the first time in 1939, made a wonderful substitute, but nylon was also restricted since it, too, was used in making parachutes. Rayon stockings were devised, but at any given time the War Production Board allotted very small percentages of the national output of rayon yarn to hosiery mills. Cotton stockings, particularly of mesh, could be obtained, but women already wearing short skirts that showcased their legs found these less than flattering. Leg makeup became more than a gimmick: women used it and painted seams up the backs of their legs with eyebrow pencil. They darned what stockings they had, and J. C. Penney even offered a service that reknitted the holes of stockings. Articles appeared showing how a woman down to her last pair could wash them and immediately dry them by swinging them in the air around her head.

Cotton had its military uses, too, for summer uniforms, sandbags, and balloons. Fortunately for women, heavy cottons like velveteen and corduroy were plentiful, as they were produced by the automobile upholstery industry, which otherwise would have been somewhat idle, and these materials could replace wool for cool-weather wear.

Man-made dyes were available only in limited quantities since they were made from the same base substance needed in dynamite manufacture, and it was urged that women wear clothes of undyed materials (greige goods) as much as possible. Alcohol and glycerine, components in makeup, perfume, and soaps, were also recruited for the war effort, as were various plastics that had been used for cosmetics containers. Rubber went into airplane and jeep tires, making elastics for girdles, brassieres, and underpants scarce. Metal restrictions kept zippers, metal buttons, and trim to a minimum; corsets had to be laced rather than zipped up.

Even jewelry was affected by the war. Platinum was reserved for military purposes, so precious jewelry was made out of gold, usually in combinations of green, yellow, pink, and white, and set with large, semiprecious stones

By 1942 the War Production Board had issued its regulations as to how much material could go into a dress, skirt, jacket, blouse, or pair of pants, and American designers were busy trying to save even more fabric than was necessary as well as figuring out how to get around shortages of metal or leather. This 1942 ready-to-wear dress by Harvey Berin was made to look like a suit in the interest of saving fabric; the sleeves and skirt were made of rayon crepe, the more valuable wool fabric reserved for a vest effect. Rhinestone-set buttons (definitely not needed for the war effort) made the dress appropriate for a variety of occasions.

American ingenuity was tested and
strengthened by wartime restrictions and
scarcities. This 1946 coat by Connie
Adams, made of the best-quality cotton
mattress ticking rather than inferior wool
or another material so that it could sell
for around $17, is an example of honest
and witty American style at its best.
Photograph: Horst. Courtesy Vogue

Adrian, Hollywood costumer turned
ready-to-wear and custom designer, is
generally credited with devising the
broad-shouldered silhouette that proved
so compatible with wartime regulations.
This 1943 Adrian suit features a jacket of
yellow tweed with an interestingly shaped
collar of black velvet and a straight black
skirt. Combining several fabrics in one
ensemble was a device that saved material; a good-quality or rationed fabric
would be used with one not needed for the
war effort. Photograph: John Rawlings.
Courtesy the Edward C. Blum Design
Laboratory, Fashion Institute of
Technology, New York, and Vogue

like topaz, aquamarine, and amethyst. The white or base metal used for costume jewelry was replaced in much of the 1940s pieces with sterling silver, which was then plated with a lesser metal to prevent tarnishing. Silver jewelry other than costume became very popular, particularly Mexican pieces, with their bold designs, and there was also an increase in copper and brass handcrafted jewelry.

Because foot soldiers used up a pair of boots a month, fabrics filled in for leather when it came to pocketbooks and to shoes, which might sport soles of rope (as in espadrilles), cork, wood, or plastic. Order L-217 restricted the leather in women's shoes to six colors—black, navy, white, and three shades of brown—and it mandated that two colors of leather could be used in one style only if the sole was made of a nonrationed material. In 1943 the government removed Sam Browne belts (made of leather) from uniforms; military belts made of webbing sufficed. Not all of the restrictions lasted for the duration of the war, and not all of them stopped when it ended in 1945. Leather shortages lasted for a few years.

Many American women looking back at the 1940s barely remember most of the specific restrictions because, with the exception of shoes, which could be purchased only with a ration ticket, most of the problems of scarcities and limited use had already been solved in the garments that were available to buy. American designers were skillful at working with what they had, and they came up with ingenious solutions to making narrow clothes look interesting and full of movement and getting around the restrictions on using zippers or extra materials.

Claire McCardell fastened clothing with brass tabs and hooks instead of buttons or zippers, made dresses out of surplus cotton balloon cloth, and designed evening clothes with matching aprons for hostesses who did their own cooking. The wholesale designer Joset Walker specialized in drawstring-waisted dresses, which were easier than tailored ones for women to launder and iron. Vera Maxwell, known for her expertise with tweeds, designed a coat using only two and one-quarter yards of fabric, with no collar or revers, no overlap at the front, and absolutely straight lines. Adrian showed a Victory suit: its long, narrow jacket fastened at the waist with a self-fabric tie, and the skirt was made with a yoke of nonmatching, probably recycled material that did not show underneath the jacket. Tom Brigance designed the sleeveless sleeve, made of folds of fabric gathered at the shoulder. Fira Benenson put "income tax" pockets on jackets, so called because they were bottomless, since they ended at the jacket's hem; as they were cut in one with the jacket, they used less fabric. For women whose houses were cold due to lack of heating oil, Mainbocher provided evening sweaters, cardigans dressed up with embroidery or glitter. B. H. Wragge showed wrap dresses fastened with giant safety pins, and Karen Stark, designing for Harvey Berin, used sterling silver zippers on dresses. Other designers came up with bright dimout scarves, versions of coveralls or jumpsuits, dresses that were cut and draped so that they needed only two buttons. Most used cap sleeves, which saved almost a full yard of cloth.

Despite regulations, the wartime silhouette was actually varied. Movies of the period have fixed in many minds the silhouette first made famous by Adrian with its broad-shouldered, straight jacket and pencil skirt. Especially when accessorized with platform-soled shoes, towering high-crowned hats or

One of the many American styles that matured and flourished during the 1940s was a kind of town and country look that was handsome and tailored but didn't directly ape men's traditional sportswear. This 1944 striped dress by ready-to-wear designer Jo Copeland for Pattullo embodies this style, especially as shown here, with rugged leather accessories. Fabric gloves were an important war-related accessory, born of leather rationing. Photograph: Louise Dahl Wolfe. Courtesy the Edward C. Blum Design Laboratory, Fashion Institute of Technology, New York, and Harper's Bazaar

These two 1942 custom-made long dinner suits by Henri Bendel had plain bare dresses underneath, which could be worn with or without their glittery jackets. These display the typical large-scale, scrolling, and airy embroideries of the period. Photograph: John Rawlings. Courtesy the Edward C. Blum Design Laboratory, Fashion Institute of Technology, New York, and Vogue

turbans, hairstyles rolled above the forehead and filling a snood in back, bold jewelry, large, elongated pocketbooks, and purple red lipstick, this is remembered as the 1940s look. While influential—it was taken up by many designers, including Irene, Vera Maxwell, Philip Mangone, and Anthony Blotta—it was not the only silhouette. Equally popular was the dressmaker suit with a fitted, shorter jacket ending just at or just below the waist and a slightly flared skirt. This silhouette was typically worn with daintier accessories like pumps, graduated strings of pearls, silk lapel flowers, and softer hairstyles, such as the partially curled pageboy. For both the tailored and the more feminine styles, lingerie touches of white lace, eyelet, or organdy forming all sorts of collars, jabots, and cuffs were appealing, serving both to change the look of an ensemble and as an antidote to the uniforms worn by so many women.

Besides the tailored shirtwaist dress, often made of gabardine and worn all over the country, women could buy softer dresses of pliable synthetic jerseys, made with shirring and various drapery effects, and with peg-top skirts that narrowed toward the hem. Stores also carried the popular peasant look: drawstring necklines, small puffed sleeves, and gathered narrow skirts. Dinner dresses, typically more covered up than full evening regalia and therefore more suitable to a subdued social life, tended to be fluid and columnar and featured lots of drapery. They were often made of two colors of a fabric used together or a synthetic print. Although the concept of dressing down was important, with the category of afternoon-length semievening dress gaining ground, it was also important to keep the troops happy, so girls dancing with soldiers could justify full-skirted dresses of rayon taffeta or net, which were available throughout the war.

In the area of leisure clothes, pants were increasingly worn, in both long and long-shorts versions, and sportswear designers showed weekend wardrobes of interrelated pieces, such as jackets that could be worn with pants, skirts, or over bare long dresses for a dinner look and two-piece bathing suits that could be covered up with shorts or skirts for sports. The idea of separates, which many claimed to have originated, was developed most fully in the relatively new area of college clothes.

By the 1940s, girls planned and packed their freshman trunks as carefully as they later would hope chests; campus life dictated its own variety of clothes for specific occasions. Students favored polo coats for football games or on dates. To class they sported skirts and sweaters, wool or woollike dresses, jumpers, and, occasionally, suits. They best liked versatile suits, with skirts that could be worn on their own and jackets that looked well with other skirts. With classroom clothes they wore saddle shoes or loafers with short or knee socks or, if they were in a cold climate, stockings. Natural leather pumps or gillie shoes served for dressier occasions. Expected to dress for dinner every night, college students put on a suit, a skirt with a fancy sweater, or a dress. Dates required date dresses in wool, jersey, corduroy, or velveteen. Students located close to other schools or to military bases went to dances, for which they wore evening dresses made of synthetic silk and décolleté, or taffeta with a jersey bodice, or black velveteen and organdy in a jumper and blouse. Few college girls could carry off the long, draped dinner dress, considered the height of slinky sophistication. Even lounging around the dorm had its requirement: a bathrobe that was more like an at-home garment. Pants, includ-

Germaine Monteil, a fashion designer who also founded a cosmetics firm, made this Renaissance-inspired evening dress with brocade doublet in 1942 for a special exhibition held at the Metropolitan Museum of Art in which mannequins wearing contemporary clothes by New York fashion designers were scattered throughout the art galleries. Photograph: John Rawlings. Courtesy the Edward C. Blum Design Laboratory, Fashion Institute of Technology, New York, and Vogue

The columnar nature of the fluid long dresses of the 1940s lent itself perfectly to Greek influences, as in these two 1944 rayon crepe dresses by Mme Eta, one based on a toga and underdress, the other on a pleated chiton, inspired by the Metropolitan Museum of Art's exhibition "The Greek Revival in America." Photograph: John Rawlings. Courtesy the Edward C. Blum Design Laboratory, Fashion Institute of Technology, New York, and Vogue

ing blue jeans, served as casual wear and for sports.

A company that directed its designs at the student and whose clothes were worn in the country by youthful older women was B. H. Wragge. As early as the late 1930s this firm, run by Sydney Wragge, circumvented the common complaint about separates being hard to display and sell by planning carefully coordinated collections and providing editors and stores with brochures showing how the clothes worked together, how to promote them, how to highlight them in window or interior displays. Although this kind of promotional direction is common now, stores in the 1940s were grateful to be shown how to sell the concept of separate items of clothing.

Wragge tied each collection together with a theme, including wild game, American antiques, autumn foliage, and named his subtle, coordinating colors correspondingly, after birds, Williamsburg artifacts, plants. For the autumn foliage group, he commissioned artist Marcel Vertès to design prints, and he appliquéd brightly colored leaves on dresses. His jackets, skirts, vests, blouses, jumpers, shirtwaist dresses, and coats were made up, according to the theme, in colors of rayon gabardine, velveteen, corduroy, and jersey.

College girls aspired to collect as many Wragge pieces as they could, since being able to mix and match their clothes greatly simplified packing for a weekend off campus, which might include, besides a formal dance, an afternoon concert, a varsity game, and luncheons. Separates answered these needs, just as they did those of grown women who might be buying fewer clothes than usual due to shortages and wanted to be able to use each garment in as many ways as possible. This concept would become one of the most important elements of American ready-to-wear fashion, as it not only appeals to active lives but makes it easier for a woman to put together an individual ensemble that fits her figure and suits her needs.

After the war ended, with materials coming back into circulation, American designers began experimenting with more frivolous fashions. Skirts became fuller and were dropped from a hip yoke; coats were cut with much more cloth; dresses featured leg-of-mutton sleeves; and the draperies and peplums of the war years grew into side swags, tunics, panniers, and even bustles. The *New Yorker*'s Lois Long, dismayed when she saw New York designers abandoning their allegiance to simple, wearable clothes, urged them to return to what they knew best now that they had proved themselves. However, with men returning from the front, women wanted to greet their future husbands in the most alluring plumage they could afford. The postwar American woman wore higher, more spindly heeled shoes, sheerer stockings, wasp-waisted corsets, bras that produced a pointier, higher bust, shorter, curlier hair, and more delicate accessories.

In 1947 Christian Dior single-handedly restored the supremacy of the French couture with his controversial New Look. Although this silhouette, with its tiny waistline, longer hems, and full skirts, was not new—in fact, it had been on the American design scene throughout the war—it signaled the revival of the feminine silhouette for day. Women protested it, as they could not possibly have any of their new clothes remade to duplicate such an exaggerated style, and with rationing of fabric still going on in Europe, the materials to make the clothes were not even in full supply.

Besides inspiring ready-to-wear designers to experiment with the baroque styles prevalent in the couture, the New Look divided American women into several camps: those who continued to dress in the narrow, tailored silhouette advocated by Adrian and other designers; those who wore the more casual versions of sportswear; and those who chose to look as feminine and curvy as possible. Designers for this last group included Ceil Chapman, who offered flattering short (ballet-length), bouffant evening dresses, and Anne Fogarty, who, because she specialized in misses' or petites' sizes, made her full-skirted day and evening clothes with their separate crinoline underskirts available to teenagers and young-looking, small women.

The period during which the world was cut off from French fashion was actually not very long—the collections resumed in 1944 and continued to gain strength, culminating in the 1947 opening of Dior's new house. This means that the rise of American fashion—and New York as a fashion center—had more behind it than a few years of independence from Paris. What rendered New York so important was its demonstrated competence, skill, and ingenuity; the clothes it produced were stylish, appropriate for Americans, and well made even in the thousands. The difference that the war years made was that this was finally recognized. Ready-to-wear was no longer considered a necessary evil; it was modern, it was democratic, and New York had proved that it was stylish.

This 1949 gray wool jersey version of Claire McCardell's monastic, or tent, dress was narrowly pleated and wrapped around the waist with her signature spaghetti ties and sold for $45. The umbrella was from Uncle Sam's Umbrella Shop and the hat from John-Frederics. Photograph: Horst. Courtesy Vogue

Postwar fashions featured longer skirts, circular cuts, and such luxuries as this cropped bolero, which was designed not for versatility but simply to complete a single look. This soft-edged suit of 1947–48 was designed by Pauline Trigère.

Using undyed fabric helped the war effort because coal-based dyes were needed for explosives. This 1945 Hattie Carnegie evening dress featured a natural hand-loomed fabric and a jeweled belt. Photograph: John Rawlings. Courtesy the Edward C. Blum Design Laboratory, Fashion Institute of Technology, New York, and Vogue

Not every 1940s dress featured broad shoulders and skimpy lines. American designers proved ingenious at making narrow clothes that didn't look like any economies had been taken. This 1946 Traina-Norell after-five dress of rayon crepe demonstrates that the silhouette could be narrow yet curvy; bold, as in the tassel pattern, yet feminine, with its soft bertha collar. A Marcel Vertès mural forms the backdrop. Photograph: Horst. Courtesy Vogue

ADRIAN

In the spring of 1942 Adrian, already world-renowned for his movie costumes, opened his own fashion house in Beverly Hills, showing both ready-to-wear and custom-made clothes, as well as hats. In 1944 he won a Coty Award, and by 1946 he had brought out two perfumes, Saint and Sinner, which were followed by lipsticks, and in 1948 he opened an Adrian boutique in the recently merged Gunther Jaeckel store in New York, increasing his recognition on the East Coast.

Adrian was born Gilbert Adrian in Connecticut in 1903. He studied at the Parsons School of Design in New York and at its Paris campus before becoming a costume designer for revues and movies in New York and then for Metro-Goldwyn-Mayer in Hollywood.

Adrian's designs fall neatly into four categories: reedy, broad-shouldered tailored suits; floor-length, somewhat sober, beautifully draped dinner dresses; fairly elaborate afternoon or cocktail dresses; and lavish, entrance-making ball gowns. He was at his best in the first two categories, which displayed his talent for combining dramatic flair with subdued dignity. Most of his suits had long jackets that narrowed at the waist and slim skirts. Details like raglan sleeves and wrap fronts gave way, after the introduction of the L-85 regulations, to narrow sleeves and self-piping ties at the fronts of jackets to replace buttons. He was adept at using Pola Stout's inventive geometric woven fabrics, cutting jackets and skirts so that the stripe of a given material was repeated at the shoulder and skirt, contrasting with the solid field. For his dinner gowns, he often used fabrics printed with his own designs, based on animals, *trompe-l'oeil* effects, Greek or Etruscan motifs, or Americana patterns. Common characteristics of his afternoon and evening dresses were asymmetrical draperies, bustle effects, and such trimmings as silk flowers, jet passementerie, or fringe. *Life* magazine quoted Adrian's feelings about the New Look in its April 14, 1947, issue: "American women's clothes should be streamlined in the daytime, full of imagination at night. I do *not* like padded hips. To try and make women pad their hips in this day and age is a little like selling armor to a man." Adrian's sophisticated suits and extravagant ball gowns sold for between $145 and $1,200.

LARRY ALDRICH

Larry Aldrich was born in 1906, one of six children of Russian-Jewish immigrant parents. His intention to become a lawyer was sidetracked by a summer job working for a friend's dress business. In 1927 he founded his own manufacturing company, hiring designers to work for him until in 1933 he took over the designing himself. Typically, his clothes were not featured with his name until the 1940s.

Aldrich produced clean-looking clothes with no extraneous details. He conceded to the New Look only by using more fabric, as in pleated skirts. Prices ranged from $45 to $55 for a suit and around $70 for dresses. During the 1950s and 1960s they climbed to between $100 and $200.

American designers were inspired by clothes from all over the world. The tunic top of this 1943 Hattie Carnegie ready-to-wear two-piece ensemble was based on a Russian Cossack blouse and made in red crepe embroidered with red bugle beads. Sally Victor, a New York milliner, designed the accompanying mink hat and matching combination muff and pocketbook.

Peasant styles, popular for sportswear, were especially prevalent in the collections of California designers, such as Louella Ballerino, who made this serape-striped skirt and matching shawl.

These two evening dresses made by Adrian in 1948 feature painterly starfish prints and demure eyelet ruffles. Photograph: Louise Dahl Wolfe. Courtesy the Edward C. Blum Design Laboratory, Fashion Institute of Technology, New York, and Harper's Bazaar

LOUELLA BALLERINO

In high contrast to the somewhat austerely tailored silhouette of the war years was the important trend of peasant-inspired clothes, and one of the look's advocates was the California designer Louella Ballerino. After graduating from the University of Southern California with a degree in art and art history, Ballerino married and had two children. The stock market crash forced her to find work. At first she thought of making fashion sketches, several of which she had previously sold, but as the demand for them had lessened, she took a job at a custom dressmaking house and went to night school to study various aspects of fashion. Before long she was teaching fashion history at night school. At the same time, she worked in a shop where she occasionally sold her own designs, and in 1938 she went into business for herself.

Ballerino's first major success was a peasant dress of rough fabric crewel-embroidered with bright wool Tonga figures. Taking costume history as her major source of inspiration, she based her collections on styles and forms of decoration in Dutch, Aztec, Russian, Norwegian, Polish, Mayan, Chinese, Native American, and South American costume and textiles. Accordingly, she usually employed boldly patterned materials, such as large-scale prints and wide, bright stripes.

FIRA BENENSON

Fira Benenson had been in charge of Bonwit Teller's Salon de Couture since 1934, but it wasn't until 1940, when Paris became inaccessible, that she began designing. Up until then, her main duties had been to travel to France twice a year to select and purchase models and to oversee their construction back in Bonwit's workrooms. These authorized models were sold with the couturiers' labels in them, including those of Schiaparelli, Lanvin, and Chanel.

Benenson's experience with the couture went beyond her professional work. She had been dressed in Paris clothes since she was a young girl growing up in Russia, the daughter of an oil, real estate, and precious metals tycoon, whose huge house was located across from the Winter Palace. Grigori Benenson's family left Russia for England in 1920. Fira, by then a striking-looking woman in her early twenties, studied at the Sorbonne and hobnobbed with Misia Sert and the Polish writer and boulevardier Alfred Savoir. She briefly ran a dress shop in London before relocating with her father to New York. There he built up another real estate fortune, only to lose it in the aftermath of the stock market crash in what *Fortune* reported had been described as " 'New York's largest real-estate mortgage-foreclosure auction' " (October 1946, page 134).

At Bonwit's, Fira Benenson designed two collections annually, each of about seventy-five pieces averaging in price from $195 to $550. Her distinctive style was to enliven plain but luxurious fabrics not with obvious decorations but with beautifully restrained dressmaking details like shirring, tucking, and appliqué. In 1943 she worked with an L-85 regulated silhouette of natural shoulders, fitted waists, and circular skirts as wide as the fabric restrictions would allow.

In the spring of 1948 she opened her own salon at 37 West Fifty-seventh Street, and by the fall of that same year her ready-to-wear line was sold around the country. Both her made-to-order and her ready-to-wear collections were distinguished by her use of dressmaking details, flattering silhouettes, and, for evening, pretty, décolleté necklines.

Benenson's salon was still in operation in 1954, at least for ready-to-wear; it is not known how long her business lasted. She died in 1977.

HARVEY BERIN

Although he had begun his own business in 1921, after having worked after school for an uncle in the manufacturing business, Harvey Berin did not begin to be known by name for his clothes, which were designed by Karen Stark, until the 1940s, when American designs became prominent. Berin ran his business as a business, keeping a close eye on the quality of his product; he prided himself on being known for and on being able to deliver feminine clothes with excellent fit and construction. He admitted his allegiance to Paris, going there twice a year to see the collections of Christian Dior ("always news there"), Jacques Fath, Balenciaga, Lelong, and Patou. For the $1,500 admission price he would bring home a dress or a toile but would never copy it exactly; he always somewhat modified the designs. In the 1940s he

showed dresses with fitted—but not too fitted—waistlines, semifull skirts, and such details as scattered jet embroidery.

ANTHONY BLOTTA

Anthony Blotta was born in Italy around 1888 and studied at the Academy of Fine Arts in Rome before coming to New York, where he worked for a wholesale coat company from the age of nineteen. He started his own company in 1919. As was the case with most wholesale fashion manufacturers, Anthony Blotta did not begin to have his name mentioned in the press until the patriotic 1940s. In 1941 he won the Neiman-Marcus fashion award. His designs resemble those of Norell in their use of aspects of tailoring as decoration: unusually placed pockets and, especial-

This Anthony Blotta ready-to-wear suit shows how the New Look was absorbed into daytime clothes. The skirt is unabashedly luxurious, pleated all around, and the fitted jacket is accompanied by its own shawl. The Brooklyn Museum Library Collection, New York

ly, the ornamental use of plain buttons. His buttons were closely spaced, all the way down the front of a dress or sewn in arcs on either side of a front closure of a suit jacket. Although his wartime designs carried the favored broad shoulders, he avoided the boxy silhouette, instead showing dresses and coatdresses with narrow waists and slightly flared skirts and suits with short, curved-in jackets over slim skirts. He deployed a sophisticated color sense, combining black or brown with sky blue (a characteristic 1940s combination), navy with poppy, pale blue, or amber, and brown with green. In typical American fashion he dressed up wool for night, as in a pin-striped suit whose stripes were formed of lines of white sequins.

TOM BRIGANCE

Despite the fact that while fighting in World War II (he was decorated for bravery for his work in the Counter Intelligence Service) he was necessarily absent from the New York designing world from 1942 to 1947, Tom Brigance still managed to make quite an impact during the 1940s with his innovative sportswear designs. Born in 1913 in Waco, Texas, to an English mother and a French father, he studied at the Parsons School of Design and the National Academy of Art in New York and at the Sorbonne and the Académie de la Grande Chaumière in Paris. His first jobs were in Europe, selling sketches on a free-lance basis to French and English fashion houses and working in London designing for Jaeger and for Simpsons of Piccadilly. Back in New York in 1939, he became in-house designer for Lord & Taylor.

Almost immediately, he established a strong individual signature, primarily by avoiding the 1940s tendency toward austere tailoring. His play clothes were composed of wrapped tops that bared the midriff with trousers, shorts, skirts, and skirts with bloomers underneath, along with wrap play dresses and bathing suits. Brigance did much with soft sarong draping; he juxtaposed materials like synthetic jersey with cotton piqué or snappy stripes with sweet eyelet; and he used interesting prints, such as those designed by the French artist Marcel Vertès for 1942 bathing suits. In the *New Yorker*'s issue of January 11, 1947, Lois Long wrote, "It is evident that all those years in uniform did nothing to quench the spirit of Mr. Brigance." His first postwar collections included all manner of sports clothes and sundresses and, by 1948, at-home ensembles (like a midcalf skirt of taupe velveteen worn with a taupe linen shirt) and more tailored city clothes (like a silk shantung coatdress). Prices ranged from $22.95 for bathing suits to $210 for a coatdress.

BROOKE CADWALLADER

Brooke Cadwallader was one of America's most prominent textile designers. He specialized in signed, limited-edition scarves, usually depicting historical or current events. He also designed printed fabrics, which were used by Adrian, Hattie Carnegie, Nettie Rosenstein, Maurice Rentner, and Traina-Norell. According to Eleanor Lambert, his publicist, Brooke Cadwallader scarf collectors included the Duchess of Windsor, Mrs. Harrison Williams, Mrs. Byron Foy, Mrs. Gilbert Miller, Diana Vreeland, Dorothy Shaver, Janet Gaynor, Gene Tierney, and both Winston Churchill and his wife.

Cadwallader was born in the Philippines in 1908 and lived with his family in San Francisco before being sent to Phillips Academy in Andover, Massachusetts. After graduation he studied at the School of the Museum of Fine Arts in Boston. Then he returned to the Philippines, where he worked for his father's mining company for four years before moving to Paris to resume his study of painting. There he met his future wife, then the *directrice* of a top Paris scarf house, Maison Tilly, and it was at her urging that he applied his painting talent to scarf and textile design. He was an immediate success, his prints used by Schiaparelli, Balenciaga, Molyneux, and Paquin. When the Germans arrived in Paris, the Cadwalladers moved to New York, where they established a downtown design studio.

Cadwallader's success led him to segue into designing men's neckties, scarves, and silk robes for his own label, Bronzini, which he began in 1947. He disassociated himself from Bronzini in 1950. Part of the appeal of Cadwallader's scarves (made in quantities of 1,600) and his other designs lay in the high quality of the printing and the fact that he worked out special colors for each pattern, taking care never to repeat color combinations.

HATTIE CARNEGIE

During the 1940s Hattie Carnegie employed a thousand people, mostly in her ready-to-wear business. At her East Forty-ninth Street store, the first floor was given over to accessories, perfumes, and ready-to-wear clothes, from various Seventh Avenue manufacturers as well as her own. The second floor was the custom department, where her in-house designers during the 1940s included Jean Louis and Pauline Potter, who, when she married, became Pauline de Rothschild. Clients of the custom department during the war included the Duchess of Windsor, who ordered clothes while stationed in the Bahamas. Special clients had their own mannequins, made to their measure, in the custom workrooms. According to *Life* magazine of November 12, 1945, "to rate your own dummy at Hattie Carnegie's is probably the financial equivalent of supporting a race horse." Clearly the custom clothes, which included French models, were expensive, but the dress specially made by Carnegie for the chanteuse Hildegarde in 1940 stands out: embroidered with 75,000 real pearls, it was valued at $250,000 and toured the country before being auctioned off for charity.

Carnegie's ready-to-wear collections consisted of Hattie Carnegie Originals, which started at around $40 for a dress, Spectator Sports clothes, designed by Bruno, and hats, with the label Hatnegie, all of which were sold around the country as well as at her own store. At her Forty-eighth Street entrance, she had a boutique called the Jeune Fille Shop, where women of all ages looked for relatively inexpensive clothes with the Carnegie flair.

Hattie Carnegie was forever being quoted to the effect that the woman should wear the dress rather than vice versa, and she was justly renowned for her little black dresses and tasteful little suits. However, her clothes could be quite innovative. During the war she showed an evening outfit with a Romanian-style peasant blouse embroidered with gold paillettes rather than black and red cross-stitch, worn with a long, black velvet dirndl; an evening dress of black sequins made like a schoolgirl's jumper, worn with a Valenciennes lace–trimmed organdy blouse; flapper-style short evening dresses (above the ankle) covered with bead fringes, narrow but featuring waistlines; and suits of various herringbones and other tweeds sewn with beads and sequins. A Carnegie collection usually presented something for everyone: boxy suits as well as curvy ones with narrow or circular skirts, long dinner sheaths as well as full-blown ball gowns, simple little dresses that could be worn for years to come along with entrance-making ones. In 1948 Carnegie won a Coty Award.

CAROLYN MODES

The company Carolyn Modes expanded its ready-to-wear in the 1940s to include evening clothes, cocktail dresses and suits, and dressmaker suits. Prices climbed to $115 for a "Paris-inspired" coat in 1948. In 1949 the company ran advertisements stating, "Who is Carolyn? Carolyn is a famous fashion organization. Each month they survey all the important fashion creations. They select only the most outstanding in design and in value—to bear the famous Carolyn label of fashion approval." The ads skirt the issue of what the company did with its discoveries; it probably copied them inexpensively. However, the firm was associated with two designers during the decade: Lo Balbo and, curiously, Harvey Berin, who had his own ready-to-wear company at that time. In keeping with its higher prices and its forays into dressier clothes, Carolyn Modes featured on its dresses and ensembles more fussy details than it had in the past, as in its 1940 rayon dresses with elaborate shirring or scattered sequin motifs; a 1942 wool dinner dress with beaded collar and rhinestone buttons; and a 1944 rayon dress with six tiers of scallops at the skirt.

CEIL CHAPMAN

Ceil Chapman was one of the most popular American designers ever for the simple reason that her clothes were feminine, flattering, easy to wear, and suitable for almost all ages. Today they are sought after by antique-clothing wearers who couldn't care less about the French couture or museum-quality examples of fashion art.

Ceil Chapman was born on Staten Island, New York, in 1912. She married Samuel Chapman and during the 1930s worked in a clothing shop, where she met Thelma Furness and Gloria Vanderbilt. Together they started a dress business called Her Ladyship Gowns. After this enterprise failed, Chapman and her husband began their own ready-to-wear business in 1940. Besides designing clothes for the wholesale trade, Chapman costumed the musical *South Pacific* and made clothes for television, notably the weekly dress for Faye Emerson to wear on her program, which alone came out to 130 dresses in 126 weeks.

Chapman found her niche early on and stayed with it. Noting that there was a gap between day and evening clothes, she specialized in "late-day" dresses or ensembles. With their fitted bodices, full skirts, pretty décolletages, and ballet-length hems, they came to be identified with the New Look. She also made evening clothes.

Chapman rarely used printed materials, instead relying for decoration on effects like embroidery with sequins and beads, appliqué, and machine stitching, such as quilting and puckering, which she used to follow the shape of the body, with narrower, smaller patterns at the bodice widening in the skirt. These quilting and tucking details are somewhat reminiscent of Vionnet's experiments with fabric; that Chapman could mass-produce such garments and sell them fairly inexpensively is amazing. In the 1940s her price range was about $25 to $90, and in the 1950s her dresses rarely climbed above $200. Part of the reason for this is that she didn't scoff at using synthetic materials like rayon jersey, acetate taffeta, nylon marquisette, or chiffon.

During the war, Ceil Chapman avoided the ponderous heavy-shouldered look and worked with off-the-shoulder necklines in both formal designs, as in a 1944 organdy, full-skirted ball gown with piqué appliqué, and casual items, as in a 1945 dress of tiny gingham checks with a peasant-blouse bodice for a summer outdoor party. She could dress down postwar evening clothes, giving them a youthful look, as in evening dresses made to look like separates, with taffeta skirts and either jersey tops or pleated white shirtwaist bodices with puffed sleeves and round collars, or make them glamorous ball gowns, with intricately draped bod-

ices and skirts. Although Ceil Chapman worked often with black, she also made evening clothes in pretty, romantic colors. A group of 1948 ball gowns were made of white swiss muslin, apricot tulle, shell pink organdy, coral satin, bright navy satin, and cloud blue chiffon.

CHARLES COOPER

Toronto-born Charles Cooper had been designing for seventeen years when he was written up in a 1940 *Harper's Bazaar*. He worked by draping and cutting directly on one of his models or one of the replicas he had made of them, creating fluid 1940s designs. One group of 1942 dresses, made mostly of rayon crepe, featured unusual ways to wrap the waist using attached satin belts of piping. One dress had built into it two long, pointed ties that circled the waist.

JO COPELAND

In the 1940s Jo Copeland, the designer for Pattullo, began to be recognized for her work. The pictures of her that ran in the fashion press, which revealed her own good looks, were probably a great advertisement for her elegant designs. These relied little on either the wartime silhouette or the postwar New Look. Instead, Copeland designed throughout the decade in her own idiom of narrowly fitted clothes with short, waist-length jackets, skirts with side draperies or asymmetric cascading ruffles and, for informal evenings, hemlines above the ankle, and gala ball gowns made with trumpet-flaring skirts.

Copeland worked with pure silks and wools and, more often, in all the varieties of rayon and synthetics. Mostly she used extremely subtle forms of decoration, as in a 1941 dinner dress of copper jersey with sleeves of copper satin, but they could be bold, too: giant curly ostrich fronds of red bugle beads scattered over a red crepe evening dress of 1942 or a 1949 evening dress of white organdy painted with even more gigantic peacock feathers.

Although Copeland produced everything from hats to daytime clothes to grand evening gowns, her specialty was after-five clothes, for the theater, at-home dinners, or dances in the country. She liked suits for all occasions and made them in wool, faille, taffeta, printed crepe. She designed these either so they could be worn without a blouse or made the blouse so important that the blouse and skirt could work as an ensemble when the jacket was removed. An unusual ensemble was her 1948 dinner suit of dubonnet-colored jersey with a dyed-to-match mole jacket.

DOROTHY COX

Dorothy Cox trained as a portrait painter before she became a designer. In the 1940s she worked for McMullen, a ready-to-wear company known for shirtwaists. Most of her dresses had fitted bodices and soft skirts, and they were available in wool jersey, perhaps with a hood, in cotton fabrics designed by Hope Skillman, or in Moygashel linen, and were also made in silks and other dressy materials for evening. She designed suits that looked like two-piece dresses with the same bell-skirted silhouette. As a 1948 advertisement pointed out, her clothes were designed "not just for a famous few, but for Miss and Mrs. Average American."

Ready-to-wear designer Jo Copeland of Pattullo designed this 1948 evening suit of purple faille. The Library, Fashion Institute of Technology, New York

DAVID CRYSTAL

The firm of David Crystal produced such staples of American fashion as wool or cotton shirtwaist dresses and casual suits that sold in the $25 to $40 range. Town clothes were made in polished tweeds and plaids, and David Crystal also produced more casual turnouts in abstract rayon prints, consisting of shorts, wrap skirts, bare-midriff tops, and shawls.

LILLY DACHÉ

During the 1940s Lilly Daché opened a branch store in Chicago, introduced perfumes called Drifting and Dashing, published her autobiography *Talking Through My Hats*, and added dresses and accessories to her millinery designs. Daché's hats were more of-ten than not asymmetric: crowns and brims tilted to one side, and hats were trimmed with veils designed to hang down one side of the head, turn under the chin, and be pinned up with a brooch to the hat on the other side. When wool (for felt) was scarce, she used yarn, specifically mop yarn, and twine, and during the war she even made caps out of the gold epaulettes from uniforms. For summer, she made hats out of dress cottons, topstitching the brims to give them the proper shape. Her first clothing collection, for 1949, featured feminine clothes described as saucy.

DAVIDOW

Davidow, which grew out of the company Wm. H. Davidow & Sons, in existence since 1880, produced rather expensive (averaging $150) suits made of fine wool tweeds or gabardines and sporty dresses that fell exactly in between dressmaker town clothes and casual country clothes. Galanos worked there as a designer in the late 1940s.

JANE DERBY

In its issue of October 29, 1959, the *New York Times* described Jane Derby as a "small, fragile Virginian whose customers have always worn diamonds and hats" (page 32). Born Jeannette Barr in 1895 in Rockymount, Virginia, she worked as an apprentice designer during the Depression before opening her own retail establishment in New York in 1936. In 1938 she founded Jane Derby, Inc., which, except for the years during World War II, she ran until her death in 1965, when Oscar de la Renta took over the company.

Her prewar and postwar designs ran the gamut from coordinated four-piece town suits and full evening regalia to simple jersey day dresses and summer casual evening patio dresses. She imported materials from Bianchini and Abraham, two highly regarded French fabric houses, and her price range was $100 to $200. Most of her clothes reflected the fact that she was not a young designer: she paired her dresses with jackets or shawls; created soft silhouettes; employed flattering boat, or off-the-shoulder, necklines and delicate details, such as tiny, self-piping bows.

EISENBERG & SONS ORIGINALS

The Eisenberg & Sons wholesale fashion company was founded in Chicago in 1914 by Jonas Eisenberg. During the 1930s the company specialized in little black dresses in wool, silk, or synthetic silk and in dinner clothes, almost always ornamented with beautifully made costume jewelry, belt buckles, buttons, clips, or pins, and in embroidery simulating costume jewelry. The designer for the company, whose name appeared on the label, was Irma Kirby. The company was known for its jeweled embroideries and its "touches of white," usually in the form of collars and cuffs of *broderie anglaise*, white-embroidered muslin, and Valenciennes lace. In the mid-1930s, the Chicago store Carson Pirie Scott & Company advised Eisenberg to begin making costume jewelry that could be sold separately, as the pieces on the clothes were sometimes stolen. Most of the costume jewelry was made of large white or clear stones imported from D. Swarovski & Co., set in silver-tone metal pavé with smaller stones. The designs were more fluid and floral than Art Deco jewelry had been.

By 1941 Eisenberg costume jewelry, like the company's clothes, was sold in one major store in every major American city. The firm expanded its clothing range (which was priced at $39.95 to $89.95) from evening clothes to include linen summer dresses and tweed or other wool coats, dresses, and suits. In 1949 it initiated a line called Eisenberg Suburban, which concentrated on these more casual looks and included such sporty items of costume jewelry as Maltese crosses that could be worn in the daytime. Eisenberg & Sons Originals dresses continued to be made with its trademark rhinestone buttons or lacy white collars, while it also used more and more embroideries, especially passementerie and gilt chain-stitch designs sewn with occasional faceted stones. Throughout the decade its silhouette remained narrow, with peplums or bits of drapery for interest in the skirt, even after the New Look arrived. The company sold four perfumes, named Excitement, Startling, Stirring, and Enticing, as well as lipsticks and costume jewelry accessories, such as compacts. During the war, its costume jewelry was set in sterling silver since white metal had been commandeered by the government.

MME ETA

Although most known for her 1943 Grecian theme collection, featuring softly pleated chitonlike evening and dinner dresses embroidered in gold beads with classical motifs, Mme Eta also designed collections based on Cape Cod (1944) and the Middle Ages (winter 1945), including, for the last, a black rayon velvet dinner dress with a sequined almoner's pouch. Her clothes, available on a ready-to-wear basis at such stores as Lord & Taylor, were considered flattering to matronly figures.

Eta Valer Hentz was born in Budapest and educated at the Hungarian Royal State Academy of Industrial Arts. During the 1920s she was involved in a business partnership with Maurice Rentner for a company called Ren-Eta, and she started her own business in the late 1930s with Ann Sadowsky, who had previously worked with Jo Copeland.

ARTHUR FALKENSTEIN

Before the 1940s, Arthur Falkenstein had bought at the Paris collections and then duplicated the clothes to sell in his New York made-to-order house on West Fifty-eighth Street. By 1941, though, he was showing his own original designs, which tended toward the dramatic. He designed wool suits, coats, simple day and dinner dresses, on up to elaborate evening clothes. Passementerie was a favorite form of decoration. In 1942 he showed a prophetic coat: made of heavy, black wool twill lined in beige

wool, it swung out from the shoulders in a tent shape and ended above the knee. After the war this became a dominant style.

WILSON FOLMAR

In 1939 Wilson Folmar, head designer in the custom department at Jay-Thorpe, Inc., began designing ready-to-wear evening clothes under his own name for the manufacturer J. Rothenberg, and he was immediately recognized as one of the new important American designers. He specialized in dinner and evening clothes, frequently combining black lace and opaque black silk, although he also produced such daytime costumes as printed dresses with wool coats lined in a matching print.

Folmar was born in Troy, Alabama, on July 4, 1911. He painted as a child and studied architecture at Auburn University and the University of Alabama. In 1931 he quit school with the thought of traveling in Europe, but, stopping in New York, he began to study commercial art at the American Institute of Design. As it happened, his landlady was the mother of Maybelle Manning, proprietor of a custom dressmaking house on Madison Avenue, and through her he got a job working as a sketch artist for Manning. Gradually he began to design as well as to sketch, and in 1935 a dress he made for Tallulah Bankhead was spotted by a buyer of Jay-Thorpe. Offered a job as a designer there, Folmar accepted, and he became the head of the custom department by 1936.

Even while he participated in the war as a first lieutenant in the Air Force for five years, Folmar managed to keep his hand in at both of his jobs. He also designed the uniform for the Civil Service Women Employees; it featured pockets shaped like the United States shield. When he returned to New York in 1946 he continued to design for Jay-Thorpe, and he did ready-to-wear for another manufacturer, Ben Gam, until 1956; in 1957 he became the designer for Edward Abbott. He also worked for Maurice Rentner in the 1950s.

FOXBROWNIE

Foxbrownie (the name was hyphenated in fashion magazines but not in the company's advertisements) clothes, designed by Brownie, were expensive (prices were never mentioned), available on a ready-to-wear basis, and made from imported fabrics from the best houses. The company specialized in late-day and casual evening clothes: afternoon dresses of printed silk with matching gloves, full-skirted restaurant dresses with flattering above-the-table necklines, and floor-length dinner dresses made of draped silk crepe.

LOUISE BARNES GALLAGHER

Louise Barnes Gallagher continued in the 1940s to be associated with the sheer wool known as Gallagher mesh. Her ready-to-wear designs were fairly expensive; for example, a day-into-evening dress and matching jacket went for $155 in 1940. Lois Long described her clothes as patrician. These were tailored clothes, but they borrowed more from nineteenth-century men's tailoring than they did from contemporary man-tailored styles. Although Gallagher worked with the broad-shouldered silhouette, her lines were softer, with fitted bodices, narrow waists, and skirts arranged with some movement to the drapery. Gallagher typically dressed up a wool dress with silk taffeta bands, reminiscent of a tuxedo shawl collar, or dressed down a printed chiffon dress by pairing it with a natural linen, vaguely old-fashioned, many-buttoned vest.

HOWARD GREER

Howard Greer produced custom-made clothes in his Los Angeles store for such actresses as Kay Thompson, Greer Garson, Deanna Durbin, Gypsy Rose Lee, and Dinah Shore. For Greta Garbo he designed a complete wardrobe, for afternoon, cocktails, dinner, and grand evenings; in his autobiography, *Designing Male*, he claimed that the only time Garbo became enthusiastic about her new clothes was when they discussed the tweeds. In her book *Woman to Woman*, Gloria Vanderbilt recalled that she had gone to Greer for clothes because he also designed for her idol, Rita Hayworth. She wrote that he had a good sense of color and was expert at draping material. She also stated that he invented the tabletop neckline for dresses worn to restaurants, which focused attention on the pretty neckline rather than on the skirt, and had kept the natural round shoulder throughout the war.

Howard Greer was born in Nebraska and had worked as a sketch artist for Lucile in Chicago and New York before being drafted to serve in World War I. After the war, he kicked around Europe, writing a fashion column for *Theatre* magazine and selling fashion sketches to such couturiers as Poiret. When he returned to New York, he worked at the Hickson store, and then designed costumes for Famous Players-Lasky (later Paramount), which led to a job designing for Hollywood films. He opened his own house on Sunset Boulevard on December 27, 1927.

Greer designed mostly afternoon, late-day, and evening dresses. His ready-to-wear clothes sold in the $200 to $400 range, climbing as high as $650 in the 1950s. Whether full- or narrow-skirted, they usually featured a tightly swathed torso accentuated by either a bolero-shaped jacket or a bustlelike fullness in the back. Two examples of his little black dresses show his tendency to work with an unexpected twist: one featured a midriff section of salmon pink, the other a high, salmon pink collar tied in a bow at the back of the neck falling in streamers almost to the hem. Another dress from the same year, 1948, was made in obvious homage to his mentor, Lucile: black, with exaggerated dolman sleeves, it narrowed at the long skirt almost to a hobble, the hem banded with plush black fur.

JOSEPH HALPERT

The New York wholesale firm Joseph Halpert specialized in fairly inexpensive ($45 for a silk dress in 1943) dresses, suits, and coats. In the late 1940s the firm entered into an agreement with Parisian couturier Jacques Fath to produce his designs on a ready-to-wear basis in New York. This line included well-made and stylish suits and dresses in the late-day category, typically made of wool or matte-finish silk, enlivened with touches of velvet or satin.

ELIZABETH HAWES

Having retired from fashion designing in 1940, except to create a uniform for the Red Cross Volunteers in 1942, Elizabeth Hawes turned her attention to writing a column for an afternoon-evening newspaper called *PM*, writing more books *(It's Still Spinach, Men Can Have It, Anything but Love, a Complete Digest of the Rules for Feminine Behavior from Birth to Death)*, and acting as a union organizer for the automobile industry. To gain insight into the plight of women machine operators, she took a night job at an airplane plant, which resulted in a book called *Why Women Cry, of Wenches with Wrenches.*

In 1948 she reentered the fashion world, opening a shop on Madison Avenue at Seventy-first Street. Her first collection, which was covered by Lillian Hellman for "The Talk of the Town" section of the *New Yorker*, included fifty-one models, of which eighteen were copies of her own designs from the 1930s. The guests at the show participated in a contest to see who could correctly identify the new and the old models; three people tied for first place with thirteen right answers each. When she closed the shop in 1949, it marked the end of her professional involvement with fashion. Up until her death in 1971 she designed for herself and for her friends, specializing in hand-knitted separates.

IRENE

Irene Lentz, born in South Dakota in 1901 or 1907, used her first name professionally. She began designing in her own boutique on the campus of the University of Southern California, Los Angeles, in the 1930s. She next ran a boutique in Hollywood, and then became the head of the custom department at Bullocks-Wilshire in Los Angeles, where her clientele continued to be composed mostly of film stars. When Adrian left Metro-Goldwyn-Mayer in 1942, Irene took over as head costumer, a job she retained until 1949. In 1947 she established a ready-to-wear business that specialized in fairly high-priced (around $300 for a suit) tailored daytime ensembles and striking evening gowns. Most of her suits had the broad-shouldered jacket and slim skirt silhouette, the jacket narrow and long, using English worsteds and geometric woolen fabrics woven by Pola Stout. Irene's evening clothes were dramatic, with sweeping draperies and attention-grabbing trains, separate scarf panels, and lavish ornamentation, such as beading or embroidery.

ARTHUR JABLOW

Arthur Jablow was a New York manufacturer of ladylike suits, coats, and other daytime ensembles. His most typical suit silhouette featured a long, slightly fitted jacket and narrow skirt, and his clothes sold from $100 to $200.

154

CHARLES JAMES

In 1940 Charles James returned to New York after having spent almost a decade abroad and opened a couture house at 63 East Fifty-seventh Street. When cosmetics and skin cream mogul Elizabeth Arden decided to branch out into couture clothing, she hired James to design for her, as well as to oversee the installation of a custom department on the second floor of her Fifth Avenue building. James planned to have the entire floor reconstructed, with a salon, cutting and fitting rooms, and dressing rooms. Before the work was completed he showed his first collection for Arden in Chicago and as part of a benefit in New York. Both James and Arden were known for their fiery temperaments, and James was fired before he could produce another collection. In 1945 he reestablished his own business at 699 Madison Avenue, where his clothes were available on a made-to-order basis.

Throughout the 1940s James worked within his own particular vision of the silhouette. His often asymmetric, usually draped clothes were made in lustrous, weighty fabrics like heavy faille, slipper satin, and velvet, combining several different textured materials in the same color range in a single dress. One of his first designs to appear in the fashion magazines after his return to New York was an evening outfit of black faille; it had one trouser leg and one skirtlike leg folded over to the other side. James's evening clothes often featured unusual color combinations, such as apricot and eggplant used with black, shell pink with ginger, or orange and rose. Preferred evening wraps included sculptural coats in stiff, pale-colored materials and stoles of tulle.

KALMOUR

Kalmour was the label of a New York wholesale company called Kallman & Morris, Inc., which produced inexpensive ($20 to $50) evening clothes and costume jewelry during the 1940s. Although Kalmour offered narrow, long dinner dresses, usually of shirred rayon jersey, most of its evening clothes were full-skirted, made of varieties of tulle or net with names like Celanese rayon Marquisheer and decorated with sequin and gem embroideries. Kalmour costume jewelry included enameled metal brooches made in the shape of fairly large sprays of flowers, popular during the period, as well as other typically 1940s looks, such as brooch-shaped, gem-set pendants suspended from thick, coiled golden chokers.

MURIEL KING

Muriel King tried to retire from fashion design in 1940 but was soon back in business in a venture called d'Armand-King. Dur-

This 1945 Charles James evening or at-home dress, photographed in James's couture salon, featured sleeves both puffed and long. It is worn here by Mrs. William Woodward, Jr. Photograph: John Rawlings. Courtesy the Edward C. Blum Design Laboratory, Fashion Institute of Technology, New York

OPPOSITE
This 1948 Irene ball gown, typically dramatic in silhouette, juxtaposed coin-dotted pewter silk taffeta against a foamy white underskirt. Photograph: Louise Dahl Wolfe. Courtesy the Edward C. Blum Design Laboratory, Fashion Institute of Technology, New York, and Harper's Bazaar

ing the war she devised a wardrobe of coordinating pieces in "flight blue" for women aircraft workers, which were taken up by the companies Boeing, Lockheed, and Douglas for their employees. King free-lanced for Lord & Taylor as a designer and after the war became the head custom designer for Stein & Blaine. There she continued to create designs elegant in line and classic enough to wear for several seasons. She made coats, daytime suits, dresses, and evening clothes and also experimented with the concept of separates for night, designing a wardrobe of a two-piece, long, black velvet evening dress, a short black velvet theater suit, and a blouse. The long, bare, two-piece dress could be worn to a white-tie event, the long skirt with the jacket to a black-tie event, the long skirt and blouse to an informal dinner, and the short skirt and blouse to a restaurant. This notion took the sting out of buying an expensive evening dress that could only be worn a few times. By the 1950s Muriel King's designs for Stein & Blaine had come to be perceived as dignified, which, in the world of fashion, signifies the kiss of death. In 1957 she retired from fashion designing to concentrate on her painting; she died twenty years later.

TINA LESER

Tina Leser was born Christine Wetherill Shillard-Smith in 1910 to a Philadelphia stockbroker and his wife, a painter who had studied with James McNeill Whistler and would exhibit at the 1912 New York Armory Show. As a child Tina traveled with her parents to Europe, Africa, and Asia. At the age of twelve she lived for six months with the family of an Indian poet. After deciding to become an artist she studied painting, design, and sculpture at the Philadelphia Academy of Fine Arts, the School of Industrial Arts, also in Philadelphia, and the Sorbonne in Paris. In 1931 she married Curtin Leser and moved with him to Honolulu, where she opened a boutique selling her own designs for resort wear in 1935.

When she came to New York on a buying trip in 1940 she brought with her a playsuit she had made out of Philippine cotton shirting and, with the encouragement of both Carmel Snow of *Harper's Bazaar* and Edna Woolman Chase of *Vogue*, showed it to Saks Fifth Avenue, which ordered five hundred copies. She then, in 1941, started her own business in New York, closing her Honolulu boutique in 1942. In 1943 she dissolved her business to become associated with the firm of Edwin H. Foreman. She won both the Coty and the Neiman-Marcus fashion awards in 1945.

Almost all of Tina Leser's designs, whether as casual as her playsuits and bathing suits or dressy, were influenced by her keen appreciation for various Oriental and ethnic aesthetics. She used Tahitian and Mexican fabrics, Indian sari cloth, prints adapted from Japanese kimono silks, and styles such as djellabas, mandarin jackets, and sarongs. While most of her 1940s output fell into the category of sportswear, rarely did she employ traditional haberdashery. Instead she made outfits with shorts, brassiere tops, and loose jackets; narrow, long pants, bare-midriff blouses, and flyaway overskirts; bathing suits with bloomer or bustle-back bottoms; smocklike beach cover-ups; and full evening skirts paired with cropped, dolman-sleeve shrug jackets.

LILLI ANN

The Lilli Ann of San Francisco company, headed by Adolph Schumann, was founded around 1942. Jessica Daves, author of *Ready Made Miracle*, described it in 1967 as one of the three giants, in terms of annual production, of the West Coast, the others being Levi Strauss and Koret. During the 1940s Lilli Ann advertisements featured photographs by the great Hollywood photographer Hurell displaying dressmaker suits and what were called picture coats. These suits and coats, made primarily of European fabrics, had enough dressy details to qualify them for matinees and cocktail parties. Although Lilli Ann coats of the late 1940s reflected the influence of the New Look, being circular or cut with fitted waists and full, flaring skirts, the suits retained their earlier 1940s silhouette of long jacket, closely fitted through the torso, and narrow skirt.

CLAIRE McCARDELL

From her first collection (1941) for the newly reorganized company Townley Frocks, Inc., it was clear that Claire McCardell had crystallized her thinking about how clothes should look, and feel, on the body. Her dresses were soft rather than strident, like some of their contemporary counterparts, made with her favorite surplice neckline or in her monk silhouette, which was cut like a tent to be belted to the wearer's waist. McCardell showed cut-in shoulders, although Townley's staff informed store buyers that the clothes could be made with pads.

McCardell was the first designer to take the category of sportswear and make it answer to every possible need. Golf skirts and bathing suits were just as important to her as evening clothes, and she would no sooner have put a sequin on one of the late-day dresses than on a cycling ensemble. All of her designs, for whatever purpose, shared certain constants. Bathing suits were made with the same halter necklines, and out of the same fabrics, as her dresses, or with the same hoods she showed on tops to wear with pants. Wrapped or peasant-inspired tops showed up in bathing suits, all kinds of dresses, to wear with shorts. With the exception of her long dresses, meant for nighttime only, most of McCardell's dresses could have been worn anywhere to any kind of occasion. Jersey, denim, chambray, and taffeta were all treated to topstitching; spaghetti ties wrapped around the waists of playclothes as well as party clothes. Bathing suits, suit jackets, and late-day dresses all closed with little brass hooks. Wool was used for everything from jersey leotards to a wedding dress. Bare midriffs made shorts outfits, bathing suits, and beach dresses more casual and winter dresses more formal.

For the most part, McCardell's wartime and postwar looks presented little change. Even when working within the guidelines set by the government, using just 1¾ yards of jersey for a dress, McCardell managed to achieve a flowing look. Her predilection for natural shoulders along with her use of dirndl skirts predated the New Look, although she never made tightly fitted or rigidly constructed clothes. McCardell's specific wartime design contributions included a Civilian Defense uniform and the immensely popular $6.95 "popover" dress in 1942. Created in response to a request from *Harper's Bazaar* for an all-purpose housework style, the popover, made in topstitched denim with a wrap front, large patch pocket, and attached oven mitt, sold in the tens of thousands.

MAINBOCHER

In 1940 Mainbocher, fresh from his ten-year success running a couture house in Paris, opened up shop at 6 East Fifty-seventh Street in New York. Although he continued working with the finest materials (if they made the trip from England to America without being sunk to the bottom of the ocean) and workmanship he gave his New York Couture designs a practicality that was immediately discernible. Throughout the war, and long after, Mainbocher designed simple long or short black evening dresses that could be worn again and again with a change of accessories. His favorite quick-change devices were belts, to which he added swaggy half or whole aprons or full-blown overskirts in such materials in as tulle, lace, or lamé brocade. According to a 1940s invoice, these appendages were known as glamour belts. Also practical were his cashmere cardigan sweaters, which he imported from England and then either lined in silk to match the dress underneath, creating a polished costume less tailored than a dress and jacket, or embroidered with beads, metal, or passementerie, for a cozy yet formal evening look. Both versions were copied extensively and remained in fashion for decades.

One of Mainbocher's favorite devices was to use luxurious materials in casual new ways, and, conversely, to elevate humbler fabrics for ball gowns. Thus he designed lumber jackets in moire or lamé and evening dresses in eyelet or gingham, which he had specially woven for him in a glittery version by the American fabric company Galey & Lord. In 1940 Mainbocher teamed up with Warner to provide women with a wasp-waisted corset, which, after the more relaxed undergarments of the 1920s and 1930s caused a stir.

During the war (when his invoices were stamped with the information that his designs met with L-85 standards) he designed uniforms for the WAVES, the Women Marines, and the American Red Cross, and in 1948 he provided the Girl Scout troop leader with her lighter and brighter green covert cloth camp dress. During the 1940s he also costumed many Broadway plays, including Noel Coward's *Blithe Spirit* in 1941 and *One Touch of Venus* with Mary Martin in 1943. In 1948 he brought out a perfume blended from his favorite white flowers (the only color flower he ever had on display in his salon) called White Garden.

Mainbocher was born Main Rousseau Bocher in Chicago in 1891. When his father died, he was obliged to leave the University of Chicago after one year to go to work. His first job was answering complaints at Sears, Roebuck. He next studied art at the Chicago Academy of Fine Arts and in New York at the Art Students League. In 1911 he left New York for Europe, where he continued to draw, and he worked there as a commercial artist. During World War I he returned to New York, where he supplied fashion drawings to the wholesale company run by Edward L. Mayer. By 1917 he was serving as a sergeant major in the American Expeditionary Force Intelligence Corps.

When the war was over Mainbrocher remained in Europe, this time to study singing. After three years he took a job in Paris as a fashion artist for *Harper's Bazaar*, which he held for three years before becoming the fashion editor of French *Vogue*. When he decided, in 1929, that he should be designing rather than selecting clothes, he bought several dress forms and using cheesecloth, taught himself to cut and drape on them. He opened his Paris couture house at 12 Avenue George V in 1930. At the height of his success he employed three hundred and fifty people. When World War II threatened, he moved to New York and opened what became the city's finest and most exclusive couture house, with average 1940s prices of $185 for a blouse, $425 for a suit, $810 for a dress and cardigan, and $750 for an evening dress.

PHILIP MANGONE

Philip Mangone's company, which employed up to four hundred people as of 1945, specialized in suits, short coats, and coats, which sold for $100 to $200. Rarely did Mangone use any fiber other than wool, in fabrics that he designed himself or that were created by Pola Stout, except when designing for his subsidiary firm the Greco Blouse Company, which produced blouses that complemented his suits. Mangone was responsible for the uniform suit worn by the Women's Auxiliary Corps, and he often used military shapes and details after completing the commission. Although he worked with the softer dressmaker silhouette, most of his suits and coats featured the narrow, broad-shouldered look especially after 1947, when he responded to the New Look by designing garments with even broader shoulders, the suits with narrow jackets almost to the knees. Mangone liked capes and included one in every collection, and he was also fond of three-quarters and seven-eighths coats and toppers that went over suits. Another signature was his treatment of fur; he used silver fox or black fox bands on the hems of capes and coats, squirrel bellies for linings, and Persian lamb and nutria for trims.

VERA MAXWELL

Vera Maxwell was another of the American designers who were suddenly discovered by the fashion press in 1940. For some time she had been designing for herself when in the mid-1930s she was approached in Best & Co. by one of the store's buyers, who asked her where her jacket and skirt came from. The buyer, anxious for just such designs, encouraged Maxwell to work in fashion professionally, which she did, beginning at the wholesale houses of Adler & Adler, Max Milstein, and Glenhunt until starting her own firm called Vera Maxwell Originals, in 1947. Her 1930s designs concentrated on separates, such as a 1935 weekend wardrobe of related pieces and an alternative to the suit—a dress with a jacket. She had been born in New York in 1901, where she studied as a dancer and performed for the Metropolitan Opera Ballet before becoming a model for a wholesale firm in 1929, when he started making her own clothes.

Her specific contribution to the war effort was the coverall jumpsuit she devised for the women workers at Sperry Gyroscope, but even before the war she was designing a narrow look that economized on fabric. In 1940 she showed reefer suits, daytime costumes consisting of reed-slim coats with matching skirts and simple blouses. In 1942 she patterned a suit jacket after a lumberman's shirt with envelope patch pockets. Although she designed mostly tailored suits and coats or cape combinations, she also made casual sportswear with an ethnic or peasant look. Vera Maxwell playclothes of 1942 included shorts paired with simple tops and embroidered Peruvian jackets and striped cotton dirndls or shorts to be worn with jackets fastened by crocheted buttons. By 1946 some of her designs looked softer, with slightly full-skirted, pinch-waist coats, but she also continued working with her narrow, broad-shouldered silhouette.

GERMAINE MONTEIL

In 1935 Germaine Monteil was considered one of America's most innovative dress designers when she began to experiment with the sideline of cosmetics. By the end of the 1940s her skin preparations including balms, lotions, and night creams, cosmetics such as lipstick and powder, and such perfumes as Laughter and Nostalgia had absorbed her attention to the point that she ceased designing.

Her fairly expensive ready-to-wear clothes worked mostly for formal daytime occasions and dressed-down evenings. She made a specialty of dinner suits with floor-length skirts and pioneered the short evening dress with a ballet-length skirt. Her most typical silhouette had a flared, circular-cut skirt, an emphasized midriff, and a short, cropped jacket, although she also designed columnar long and short dresses. She frequently used prints, especially in rayon, and allover beading. Her suits featured the same kinds of feminine touches as her evening clothes; jackets as well as coats tied at the waist with self bows, and one suit was laced up the front with wide bands of fabric run through oversize grommets.

MONTE-SANO

Vincent Monte-Sano was a manufacturer of better coats and suits. Although it made ready-to-wear in the 1940s, the company had been founded as a custom-tailoring house in the 1920s, and aspects of handwork and finishing lingered. Monte-Sano's designs fell in between the strictly tailored and dressmaker categories; his principal signature, besides excellent construction, was interesting cut. Thus, a narrow coat might be made with full sleeves to give movement to the restricted wartime silhouette or cut as close to the figure as a sheath dress before it flared out at the knee. Suit jackets were predominantly long and curvy, with rounded revers and pockets. Prices started at above $100.

CARRIE MUNN

In 1942 Carrie Munn opened a shop at 640 Madison Avenue, where she sold both custom and ready-to-wear designs, specializing in evening wear, although she also designed for daytime.

Mildred Orrick, who designed this plaid cotton evening dress in 1947, got her start when she brought a design idea to Diana Vreeland, fashion editor at Harper's Bazaar. *Vreeland liked the concept of an ensemble based on leotards and suggested to Claire McCardell that she manufacture it since she had the production capacity. Following the success of this look, Orrick began designing under her own name. The thong sandals worn with the dress would never have become as popular as they did in the 1940s if stockings hadn't been so scarce. Photograph: Louise Dahl-Wolfe. Courtesy the Edward C. Blum Design Laboratory, Fashion Institute of Technology, New York, and* Harper's Bazaar

Her clothes were described as joyous; one of her dance dresses, which she christened Adorable, was made of black lace, net, and pink taffeta, with black bows for sleeves. Her clients loved it so much that she designed a new version of it every year. In 1949 she showed her version of a weekend wardrobe, built around a quilted black satin skirt. For Friday night it could be paired with a black and pink silk jersey short-sleeved top; on Saturday night it went over a striped balloon underskirt and with a black lace off-the-shoulder blouse; and for Sunday the designer suggested wearing it with a sweater.

NORMAN NORELL

In 1941 Norman Norell showed his first collection for the wholesale firm Traina-Norell. It was such a success that the first Coty Award, given out in 1943, went to Norell. He had been born Norman David Levinson in 1900 in Indiana. As a child he exhibited artistic tendencies, particularly at the age of twelve when he coped with the idea of a long convalescence by redecorating his room with burlap walls painted gold, gold curtains, black carpet, and red, round bed. At nineteen he went to New York to study art at the Parsons School of Design, returning home for the summer to open and run a tie-dyeing boutique. (Tie-dying, along with batik, was briefly popular during the 1920s.) The following September he switched to Pratt Institute in Brooklyn.

In 1922 he began a short-lived career in costume design, working at Astoria Studios on such projects as a Rudolph Valentino movie, along with Valentino's wife Natacha Rambova and Adrian, both of whom would also become dress designers. In 1924 Norell went to work for the wholesale fashion company of Charles Armour, where he stayed three and a half years before taking a designing job with Hattie Carnegie. Under her tutelage he began to curb his dramatic tendencies, but when he left it was after an argument over whether the sequined skirt he had designed for Gertrude Lawrence to wear in the musical play *Lady in the Dark* was too flashy.

As a designer under his own name, he developed his skill of perfectly balancing flashiness against simplicity, which became his greatest asset. His first great success was a sprightly black and white checked gingham shirtdress. During the 1940s his clothes, beautifully if not perfectly made, looked restrained, yet often forward-looking. From his first collection on these were certain signature elements that remained constant three decades of designing.

Norell's favorite collar had a pussycat bow, and he used it for suit blouses and shirtwaist dresses. He also showed weskit blouses with suits. He liked chesterfield collars in contrasting

colors for suit jackets and coats. He favored plain, round buttons, in black against beige, white against dark colors. He used sequins, but always in a solid pavé effect, for otherwise simple blouses and dresses. He liked wool for evening, and dressed it up with spare, décolleté silhouettes or with lace, sable, or jew-

Although Norman Norell was known for his influential pared-down designs, he was also capable of working in the very romantic vein that presaged the feminine 1950s. This 1948 Traina-Norell strapless dress of pin-tucked and embroidered organdy was worn over matching embroidery-trimmed trousers of pink satin. Photograph: John Rawlings. Courtesy the Edward C. Blum Design Laboratory, Fashion Institute of Technology, New York, and Vogue

eled buttons. His patterns were limited almost entirely to stripes, dots, and checks. He liked to work with shirtwaist or straight shapes, with covered up or bare bathing-suit necklines, but he also experimented with silhouette, showing a tunic coat or an overblouse, both belted at the natural waist, over slim skirts in 1944, bolero vests over curvy, slim long and short dresses in 1946, short jackets with pinched-in waists and over full skirts in 1947, swing coat shapes in different lengths in 1947, and both an Empire and a natural waistline in a single 1948 dress. His favorite materials were silk faille, wool jersey, and wool crepe, and besides black, he liked pale robin's-egg blue, bright orange, red, and beige. A day dress or coat might cost up to $200.

MILDRED ORRICK

Mildred Orrick, another of the talented sportswear designers of the 1940s, was born and reared in Virginia. When she moved to New York to study at Parsons School of Design, she boarded at the Three Arts Club, where her fellow student and friend Claire McCardell was also staying. After Parsons, Mildred Orrick worked for several years at the couture house of Natacha Rambova, where she served as sketch artist and model and designed for the theater, notably for a successful production of *Lysistrata*. During the 1930s she married, had the first two of three children, and worked sporadically, as a fashion illustrator for *Harper's Bazaar* and doing a little designing.

During World War II Mildred Orrick submitted an idea for leotard-based dressing to Diana Vreeland, then at *Harper's Bazaar*, who liked it so much that she arranged for Claire McCardell to oversee its production, which resulted in McCardell getting the credit. Next she went to work for another designer friend, Joset Walker, and in 1945 she was able to begin designing under her own name, for a company started by Janice Milan. Orrick was highly regarded for her polished, smart, innovative sportswear, which included sundresses, crisp shirtwaists, play clothes, and bathing suits, many in cotton in such dark shades as cinnamon, olive green, and brick red combined with black. One specialty was the floor-length sundress.

After the company disbanded, in the 1950s, Mildred Orrick worked anonymously, as a designer at Anne Fogarty and at Townley, where she supervised the collections during Claire McCardell's illness and after her death. At the end of the 1950s she switched over to Villager, where she designed for almost a decade.

MOLLIE PARNIS

By the 1940s the company known as Parnis-Livingston had moved to Seventh Avenue, and Mollie Parnis designs were known by her name alone. Although she had started out specializing in dresses, most of which fell into the day, afternoon, and late-day categories, she also designed suits. She kept prices moderate (in the $100 range) by using inexpensive materials, including man-made ones. Her 1940s clothes were feminine, with emphasized waistlines, the skirts becoming fuller as the decade progressed, and abundant dressmaker details, especially bows at the neck, at the back of cummerbund sashes, and down the backs of dresses.

PHELPS

With the tweeds and wool jerseys of the 1940s, the most appropriate accessories were Phelps pocketbooks and belts, which, since they were handmade, had a rough-hewn look that was suitable for country clothes. In 1940 William and Elizabeth Phelps, husband and wife, rented an 1843 cellar at Washington Square and set up shop making leather goods with a staff of four. They were an immediate success, winning a Coty Award in 1944, and they were responsible for popularizing the shoulder bag. Both their pocketbooks and belts, as well as combinations thereof—such as pouches suspended from belts—were made of heavy calfskin, polished by hand with mild soaps and waxes, and finished with eggs and milk. They were decorated with brass eagles, military insignia, old medals, and harness bits that a

This 1946 suit by Clare Potter contrasted a navy wool jacket with a coral red wool jersey skirt and topstitched belt with gilt metal disk fastening.

member of their staff found for the Phelpses in flea markets and junk shops. Their most famous design, a wide belt with oversize brass grommets and a rectangular buckle, was featured on the cover of *Life* magazine in 1945. In 1947 they moved their business to Pennsylvania, where they lived and worked, recruiting artisans from veterans' hospitals, in a cluster of old stone buildings that had once been a historic furnace.

CLARE POTTER

Clare Potter continued in the 1940s to be highly regarded for her ready-to-wear sports clothes, which were described by Virginia Pope, fashion editor of the *New York Times*, as both functional and alluring. Many of her pajama costumes or sun-backed dresses were dressy enough to wear at night, and an interesting ensemble that could go both ways was a 1941 pair of black satin shorts with a ruffled white blouse. Potter was famous for her pants, which, whether tailored or flowing, were guaranteed to be perfectly cut. Known also for her color sense, she liked to combine several contrasting hues in a single suit (jacket, blouse, belt, and skirt) or evening dress (bodice, cummerbund, and skirt), achieving a look that was both polished and insouciant. Her main 1940s silhouette was narrow and fluid, and she was credited with having launched the bathing suit with little bra and bloomer pants, the evening sweater (in 1940, before Mainbocher had had a chance to show his), the hand-knitted cardigan, and

the first sidesaddle drapery. Her clothes were reasonably priced; an entire ensemble could cost as little as $35, although another might climb to $100.

BEN REIG

Beginning in 1941, Omar Kiam was the name designer for the firm of Ben Reig, which had been founded in 1929. Kiam's 1940s designs were usually made with touches of fur, as in a civet (or rabbit) belt around the waist of a long, white crepe dinner dress, or a short leopard jacket paired with a beige silk dress. His clothes were elegant, different, especially from the prevailing broad-shouldered silhouette, and expensive; they sold for up to $300. Kiam was fond of using fabrics in either unexpected colors, like a sweeping 1948 ball gown in gray tulle, or color combinations, like pink fleece for the jacket of a black rayon crepe dress or fuchsia, green, and purple paisley for the midriff of a navy wool dress. In 1948 Kiam designed a line of costume jewelry for Ben Reig.

Nettie Rosenstein designed this ankle-grazing black silk surah evening dress in 1948 with triangular flyaway panels jutting from the shoulders and providing back interest in the skirt. While not as expensive as a custom-made dress, at $175 it was high-priced. Photograph: Horst. Courtesy Vogue

The New Look as interpreted for evening was not particularly new. Strapless long dresses with full skirts, like this 1947 summer evening style by Adele Simpson, had been in fashion since the end of the 1930s. Photograph: Louise Dahl Wolfe. Courtesy the Edward C. Blum Design Laboratory, Fashion Institute of Technology, New York, and Harper's Bazaar

NETTIE ROSENSTEIN

When Nettie Rosenstein is credited with having invented the little black dress, it is probably due to her early 1940s designs in black crepe and other supple materials that were made in daytime lengths but, by dint of dressy detailing and bare necklines, could be worn to most evening occasions. These, along with beautiful draping, were a Rosenstein specialty. Rosenstein and her fellow designer and sister-in-law Eva Rosencrans worked by draping the material directly on live models of medium size, resulting in clothes that were flattering to the average American woman, who needed and wanted to look as if she had a more prominent bustline and a smaller waist and hips. Besides day-into-evening dresses, Nettie Rosenstein also made suits, which featured interesting blouses, printed dresses with matching gloves, costume jewelry, including pieces made like stylized musical notes or enameled daisies, and pocketbooks.

In 1947, the year Nettie Rosenstein won the Coty Award, an advertisement showed a ball gown with a caption claiming that the designer had "squandered" pale blue satin. The dress was strapless, with a fitted bodice to below the waist, from which flowed a huge skirt of unpressed pleats.

CAROLYN SCHNURER

Carolyn Schnurer, a designer of inexpensive, creative play clothes, sportswear, and bathing suits, came to designing through an unusual route. She was a music and art teacher in the public school system when she made a suggestion for a pinafore design to a friend, the sportswear buyer at Best & Co. It proved successful, and the buyer urged her to design professionally. At first her clothes, made by the swimsuit company run by her husband and two partners called Burt Schnurer Cabana, were sold only through Best & Co. Eventually they could be found at Franklin Simon, and then Peck & Peck, as well as all over the country.

During the war, having successfully put forward the idea to a vice president at Franklin Simon that a trip to South America for inspiration would make a good promotion, she traveled to Peru, collecting native costumes and jewelry. Her collection based on South American themes, along with the native costumes, toured the United States, to be displayed in the best store in every major city.

After the war she formed the company Carolyn Schnurer with her husband. Despite the fact that space and equipment were in short supply—the first collection had to be made up in hotel rooms—the new venture was an immediate success. Her sportswear designs included beautifully cut, spare sundresses, with such cover-ups as little capes or shawls made out of fishnet, and dressmaker bathing suits in calico and other cottons with bandeaux and pleated skirts or shorts. In 1947 bikinis were the new swimwear sensation, named after the Bikini Island where the atom bomb had been tested, and Carolyn Schnurer's polka-dotted version was as brief as could possibly be. She also designed more formal clothes, such as vest, blouse, and skirt turnouts, velveteen suits, and date dresses. Her price range in the 1940s was $10 to $30.

ADELE SIMPSON

In 1942 Adele Simpson became the name designer for the firm Mary Lee, a ready-to-wear dress company she bought out in 1949, changing its name to her own. When she started at Mary Lee, she had been designing professionally for more than a decade, having begun when she graduated from Pratt Institute after completing the four-year program in two years. Beginning in 1927 she was the main designer for the firm Ben Gershel.

Adele Simpson's 1940s designs, priced at around $100, fell into the feminine category. The gently fitted suits were narrow at the waist, had flared skirts, and displayed touches of white, especially in *broderie anglaise*, at the throat. She also designed typically 1940s short, draped, day-into-evening dresses in rayon; long, reed-slim, strapless evening gowns; and full-skirted evening dresses in linen or cotton, one of her favorite materials. After the war she expanded the silhouette she worked with, giving suits peplums or tunic jackets, with matching shawls, and back or side panels to dresses and coats for movement. An unusual suit of 1948, made in black wool with a coral wool jersey blouse, had narrow breeches that buttoned below the knee underneath the pleated skirt.

SOPHIE OF SAKS

By the 1940s, the head custom designer of the Salon Moderne at Saks Fifth Avenue had dispensed with the professional name sophiegimbel and had come to be known simply as Sophie of Saks. During the war, the Salon Moderne sold only her designs. After the war, finding that her own clothes sold better than the renewed offerings from the French couture, Sophie made them the focus of the department. So highly regarded was she as one of America's top custom designers that in 1947 she became the first American fashion designer ever to appear on the cover of *Time* magazine. Along with Sophie, Saks Fifth Avenue also boasted another exclusive in-house designer, Tatiana Du Plessix, wife of artist and editor Alexander Liberman, whose department was custom millinery.

Sophie's 1940s custom designs usually fell into the formal category, whether for daytime or evening. She made fitted coats and suits that were known for their feminine shapes, although she was also a fan of the strong, padded shoulder line. While she lowered the hemlines of her clothes in 1948 in concession to the New Look, she maintained her narrow yet curvy silhouette. Her signatures were her color sense, her wonderful materials, which were always imported, bowknots, actual or embroidered, used as decorative devices, and experimental cuts. In 1945 she showed taffeta evening dresses with winged backs and in 1948 evening gowns with bustles or fishtail trains or made as fitted sheaths forming harem poufs below the knee. In 1949 she designed both low-waisted suits and dresses wrapped at the hips and flapper-inspired sequined chemise dresses. Always she provided her customers with classic ball gowns, bare-bodiced, full-skirted, and made with every kind of handwork.

PAULINE TRIGÈRE

In 1942 Pauline Trigère began designing on her own, with a small collection of just under a dozen dresses. By 1944 her ready-to-wear clothes had won notice from the press, and in 1949 she won her first of three Coty awards. Born in Paris to a dressmaker and a tailor, Trigère worked for the Paris couture house of Martial et Armand before coming to New York in 1937. Here she was hired by Ben Gershel, worked as an assistant to Travis Banton, and then designed for Hattie Carnegie. She left Hattie Carnegie in 1941.

Trigère has always worked by cutting material directly on a live model, resulting in clothes characterized by imaginative tailoring rather than fluid draperies (although she has made draped jersey dinner dresses.) Her clothes stood out during the 1940s in that she didn't rely on shirring and other prevalent techniques to

Pauline Trigère, whose 1946 scarf-tied suit is shown here, was one of the designers just starting out in the 1940s who was able to benefit from the new awareness and attitude toward American fashion. From a fairly humble beginning, selling a collection of a dozen pieces out of a suitcase, she soon became one of New York's most respected talents.

give interest or movement to a narrow dress, instead letting the cut stand on its own. That she had certain fortes was evident early on: her specialties were coats, wool dresses, sometimes for after-five, and evening dresses that were dramatic without being fussy. Her price range in the 1940s started at around $90.

Trigère's 1940s coats ran the gamut from cavalry officer's greatcoats to long Directoire redingotes in velvet for evening with frog closures to snappy, flared, waist-high jackets. Her wool dresses most often featured high necklines and such interesting cuts as a slightly barrel-shaped skirt, and the wool was sometimes dressed up for evening with elements of silk taffeta. Her evening clothes could be sophisticated, as in a long, narrow dress of gold and white lamé; romantic, as in a ballet-length dance dress with off-the-shoulder neckline in pink eyelet; or handsome, as in pale blue satin evening pajamas cut with a full skirt and a sailorlike bodice.

VALENTINA

In 1940 Valentina moved into the four-story building at 21 East Sixty-seventh Street that had just been vacated by Elizabeth Hawes. There she was in charge of sixty-five employees, although she bought all of her own fabrics, did all of the designing, supervised most client fittings, and acted as a salesperson as well as her own model—in-house, when she was demonstrating the dual purposes of many of her ensembles, and for the magazines, where she posed in her own designs for photographs and drawings. A Valentina dress in 1940 started at $250.

Valentina had very definite opinions about what constituted good taste, and among her pet peeves were wearing little prints simply because it was spring; silk flowers, except in the hair; and fur, unless it was sable. She scorned clothes that couldn't be worn for years or that were appropriate only for a single season or purpose. She also disliked high-heeled shoes and, along with Claire McCardell, promoted ballet slippers (which weren't rationed). In 1942 she appeared in an ad endorsing dark, opaque rayon stockings, which were easier to manufacture than sheer ones. She helped elongate the sometimes too abbreviated line of the 1940s, and her appearance at the new El Morocco club in 1941 in a short evening dress helped put over the idea of less formal evening clothes.

Valentina's 1940s daytime designs included simple silk or wool crepe dresses cut on the bias with a decided 1930s look, turnouts of pleated unbleached linens, and raw silk dresses and suits for not only summer but also fall, spring, and winter. Her evening clothes fell into three categories: beautifully draped long dresses, many with a medieval air and often in black, with a contrasting panel of another color; ballet-length, full-skirted dresses; and, especially toward the end of the decade, décolleté ball gowns in rich shades of damask or brocade.

JOSET WALKER

Despite the fact that Joset Walker was born in France and learned the fashion trade by working as a costume designer for Broadway productions and in Hollywood, her clothes were among the most casual and fresh-spirited available. Her particu-

Russian-born New York couturier Valentina often posed for photographs wearing her own designs. Here she has arranged a diamond bracelet over her heart-shaped, black velvet hat and pinned one of her signature Maltese crosses on the bodice of her off-the-shoulder black wool two-piece evening dress of 1943 so as to reveal its ice blue lining. Photograph: John Rawlings. Courtesy the Edward C. Blum Design Laboratory, Fashion Institute of Technology, New York, and Vogue

Prophetic fashions do not always have to be startling. This 1949 suit by Sydney Wragge of B. H. Wragge, one of the most popular labels in the 1940s, featured a new silhouette that would stay in style for more than a decade. The short, boxy jacket and slim skirt with back kick pleat were made in lightweight tweed, with a matching rayon faille blouse. The Library, Fashion Institute of Technology, New York

lar category was sports clothes, especially for outdoor activities such as cycling, swimming, and sunning. Rather than design several large collections annually, she put together small groups of clothes every two months. Her price range into the 1950s was $4 to $60, with most items hovering around $15. Her favorite fabric was cotton, and she used it in the late 1930s and early 1940s for peasant clothes inspired by her travels in Mexico and Guatemala. She made bloomers for cycling, ballet-length beach robes, ensembles composed of denim skirt, vest, and white T-shirt cropped above the waist, and bathing suits, as well as halter-necked, low-backed, or strapless sundresses in seersucker, cotton mull, and various prints that could also be worn at night.

B. H. WRAGGE

Many designers have claimed that they invented the concept of separates, but Sydney Wragge of B. H. Wragge was undeniably the best at presenting the public with interchangeable wardrobes. His ads usually featured several photographs rather than a single artistic one, and they depicted many of the different possibilities inherent in a group of shirts, skirts, pants, coats, and

jackets. Since the clothes were inexpensive (most retailed at between $5 and $25), customers could afford to buy several items to mix and match.

Wragge made appealing use of themes, particularly American ones. As the clothes themselves didn't change radically from season to season, and most new ones could work easily with those already in a customer's closet, the themes helped sell new styles. Basing a collection on American Harvest or the watercolor seascapes of artist Gordon Grant affected not the silhouettes of the clothes but the colors of the fabrics and the designs in Wragge's special prints. For the marine painting collection, prints (mostly in rayon) included a fish-bone, starfish, and mermaid flower pattern; colors were described as cove blue, lobster red, oilskin yellow, sea-foam green, cork tan, and shingle.

For his pleated, straight, or slightly dirndl skirts, well-tailored pants, narrow jackets, usually single-breasted, camp-style shirts, and simple dresses, Wragge used, in addition to rayon, tweeds, wool twill, cotton velvet, wool jersey, and silk surah. By the end of the decade he was relying less on the themes and experimenting more with the clothes themselves. He designed many two-piece dresses, some with decorative zippers, others with turtleneck tops, and jackets that were cap-sleeved or sleeveless, worn over long-sleeved shirts and dresses.

Summer evening dresses were often made like long sundresses, a new entity in the 1940s. This Maurice Rentner version of 1946 features a whimsical gypsy print highlighted with sequined embroidery and jeweled bands forming the single shoulder strap. Photograph: John Rawlings. Courtesy the Edward C. Blum Design Laboratory, Fashion Institute of Technology, New York, and Vogue

Sophie Gimbel, the in-house designer for the Salon Moderne at Saks Fifth Avenue, after the war resumed purchasing models from Paris to be copied in her workrooms. However, finding that her own designs sold much better, she cut back on Paris fashions and offered mostly Sophie Originals, along with her ready-to-wear lines. This Sophie Original short evening dress is from 1949. Photograph: Louise Dahl Wolfe. Courtesy the Edward C. Blum Design Laboratory, Fashion Institute of Technology, New York, and Harper's Bazaar

T H E   1 9 5 0 s

As men returned from the war
and resumed their old jobs, many women abandoned their responsible positions with relief. These were college-educated daughters of feisty suffragettes
and rebellious flappers, and, like every generation, they rejected many of
their parents' philosophies and achievements as they traded in their uniforms
for aprons. The biggest part of the population was newly wed, busy raising the
baby-boom generation and moving in record numbers to GI Bill houses in the
suburbs. While many women continued to work, inspiring a new magazine
called *Charm* aimed directly at career girls, having a good job became something of a glamorous anomaly. The stylish working woman occasionally sur-
faced in movies and in the novel medium of television, but even she seemed
to be biding her time until a beau proposed. More common, especially on
television, were pleasant, attractive, somewhat vapid housewives and moms.

Social life shifted to cookouts, casserole buffets, and, especially, cocktail
parties, which ended early enough so that the baby-sitter could be driven
home at a reasonable hour. Although many people think of the 1950s and the
strapless, floor-sweeping ball gown as synonymous, American women did not
go out dancing as much (the big-band era had dwindled to a close), so they
adopted the narrow-waisted New Look instead for shirtwaist dresses, for sun,
play, and swim clothes, for suits, short evening dresses, and cocktail ensembles. Although the 1950s seem in retrospect to have been a fairly dressy period, when women clad themselves in gloves, hat, pocketbook, stole, and
shoes just so, it was actually a time of increasing casualness, reflecting the
importance of family-oriented activities.

Attempts during the patriotic war years to define the American look had
proved difficult: all anyone could agree on was that the American woman had
bright, strong teeth and shiny hair; that she was taller, with longer feet than
her counterparts around the world; and that she strode instead of mincing her
steps. Besides her vitamin-fed mien, she might be gamine, sweet, sporty, tailored, sophisticated, or casual whatever she did or wherever she lived. Unlike
the European woman, who generally followed the latest style, she remained
true to her type, which the great variety of American clothes made possible.

The comeback of the couture resulted in fashions that promoted novelty,
luxury, and quality—and, above all, a feeling of Frenchness. The couturiers
did not aim to dress an American type, as they had in the 1920s, when their
clothes became simpler, more *sportif*, and almost relaxed. Christian Dior,
Pierre Balmain, Jean Dessès, Nina Ricci, Jacques Fath, and Balenciaga all
designed for a woman they pictured as a hothouse flower, who wanted to for-
get the war and dress as if it had never happened.

The French used fabric with abandon as they laced women into silhouettes
of their own devising: here a fitted torso with a clearly defined waist, there a
fitted torso with raised or lowered waistline. They played with fishtail trains,
sweeping asymmetric panels, trumpet skirts over skintight ones, a profusion
of embroideries, laces, jeweling, silk flowers, ribbons, and tulle, introducing

something new each season that the smart woman had to have.

American women followed the dictates of the couture in that they raised or lowered their hemlines according to the current *printemps-été* or *automne-hiver* mandate, and they adopted certain other novelties, but beyond that they dressed as they wanted to, according to their type, heeding etiquette as to what to wear when. Appropriateness was everything. Young marrieds and new mothers expressed the responsibilities of their positions by being as ladylike as possible: just leaving the house called for wearing a hat, going downtown shopping required gloves. Driving the children to school or doing housework in the fishbowl of a house with picture windows demanded a cotton shirtwaist dress in summer or a skirt with a sweater set in winter. Because of the growth of the suburbs, the distinction between town and country was all-important. Just as women needed separates that filled a variety of needs, they also clamored for tweeds that looked polished in the city and little black dresses that didn't look too sophisticated in exurbia. Day-into-evening clothes also satisfied the desire to be properly dressed at all times, accommodating the needs of both working girls meeting a date after five and housewives coming into the city for shopping and then the theater with covered-up daytime ensembles that looked bare when the jacket was removed.

As the couture became stronger it also became more international. The marriage and coronation of Queen Elizabeth elevated British couturiers in the eyes of the world, and the Italians galvanized their reputations by showing together at the Pitti Palace in Florence, thus attracting fashion buyers and editors from other countries. New York also had its couture, or custom designers, and the work of Mainbocher, Charles James, Castillo of Elizabeth Arden, Sophie of Saks, Leslie Morris of Bergdorf Goodman, as well as that from the special departments at Hattie Carnegie, Bergdorf Goodman, and Henri Bendel, was treated with as much respect as that of Fabiani and Simonetta, Fontana, and Capucci of Italy and Hartnell, Amies, and Stiebel of London.

However, the simpler custom clothes of the Americans, the conservative styles of the British, and the dashing looks of the Italians all occupied second place in the pages of magazines run by Francophiles. Such magazines as *Vogue* and *Harper's Bazaar* concentrated on couturier clothes, most likely because they were staffed, for the most part, by couturier-client types: women wealthy enough to have their clothes custom-made or elegant enough to be given them for free. The average American woman found the most realistic and affordable clothes, other than those featured in the occasional "Bargains" or "Finds" article, in the advertisements of *Vogue* and *Bazaar*. However, they did cover the New York collections, and they also ran special sections, like *Bazaar*'s Junior Bazaar, showing young styles, and *Vogue*'s Mrs. Exeter articles, which featured clothes for silver-haired ladies.

More than anything, the top fashion press strove for a ladylike mood. The photographer Horst P. Horst recalls that he almost gave up working with fashion in the 1950s, so stultified was he by such restrictions as never being able to pose a model sitting on the floor, standing with her feet more than eight inches apart, or showing her hands in any position other than clasped, preferably in the air near her face. Following the lead of department and specialty stores, ready-to-wear designers had begun, in the 1940s, to run full-page ads, often using the best photographers. By the 1950s, the most consistently

In sportswear more than in any other category, American designers were fond of exploiting ethnic or exotic influences. Carolyn Schnurer, who designed this ready-to-wear Bombay dress-shirt bathing suit and cover-up of white cotton sateen in 1951, was inspired by a trip to India. Photograph: Horst. Courtesy Vogue

This model, demonstrating the extras available in a 1955 Cadillac, was dressed as if for a gala party in the 1950s ubiquitous strapless tulle dress, filmy stole, pearl choker, and white gloves.

172

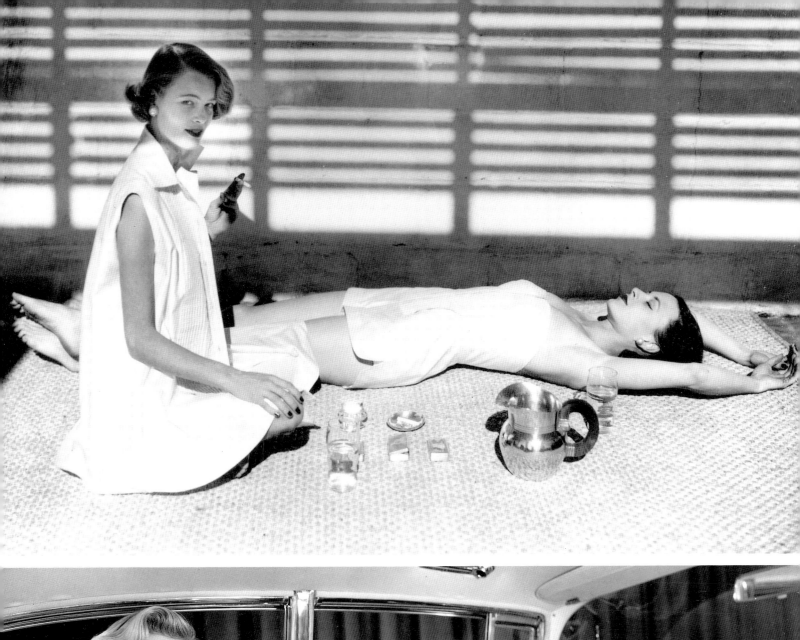

These two 1950s winter dresses were designed by Jane Derby (left) and Claire McCardell in wool jersey. The Jane Derby ensemble consists of separates: full skirt, blouse with neck-tying scarf, and tweed jacket. Claire McCardell's velvet yoked dress is a version of her 1938 monastic style, designed to flow from the shoulder, to be belted wherever the wearer wished.

Sundresses were among the most versatile of 1950s styles. They could be worn in the daytime to picnics or around the pool or at night to almost any nonformal event. Usually made of cotton, they ran the gamut from extremely simple and casual to innovative and elaborate. This 1954 Carolyn Schnurer example with separate bracelet sleeves, made in a cotton print named Aida, cost $18, thus offering versatility and a natural elegance at an affordable price—an American specialty. Photograph: John Rawlings. Courtesy the Edward C. Blum Design Laboratory, Fashion Institute of Technology, New York, and Vogue

elegant ads were those run by Modess; these invariably depicted beautiful women dressed in lavish creations by such designers as Charles James.

New York's importance, however, lay in the field of ready-to-wear. With its mind-boggling variety of wholesale designers and the quality of what they produced, New York was undeniably a style center. The War Production Board, among its many endeavors, had sponsored a nationwide measurement of one hundred thousand American women, and with these guidelines the industry devised standardized measurements in graduated sizes for all figure types. As a result, well-made and -designed ready-to-wear achieved an excellent fit, almost equal to that of custom-made clothes. American women no longer had to resort to numerous fittings, and designers no longer had to include a belt with every dress so that the wearer could fit it to herself.

By the 1950s the level now known as couture-calibre had emerged in ready-to-wear. The American woman aspired to be one of the few in her town to own an "Original," which meant a dress made perhaps in the hundreds distributed sparsely around the country. These were by such New York designers as Traina-Norell, Ceil Chapman, Nettie Rosenstein, Trigère, and Jo Copeland of Pattullo. Now that American fashion had become newsworthy, stores and fashion magazines discovered and promoted young designers. Among the new talents of the 1950s were Estévez, Scaasi, Sarmi, and Galanos, the last of whom began by working on the West Coast and became famous after he began to show his designs in New York.

American custom designers, especially those connected with stores, had been designing ready-to-wear clothes at least since the 1930s. In the 1950s Sophie of Saks began designing ready-to-wear; Fira Benenson left Bonwit Teller to design primarily ready-to-wear; and Charles James experimented, unhappily, with mass production. Mainbocher was the only New York couturier never to produce off-the-rack. New York hatmakers also began to manufacture less expensive lines that could be distributed all over the country: Lilly Daché, John-Frederics, Sally Victor, and Mr. John (formerly with John-Frederics) came out with Dachettes, John Frederics Charmers, Sally V, and Mr. John Juniors. Now that they knew the names of designers, American customers shopped specifically for the names they liked. Following their lead, the French were just beginning to use the cachet of their made-to-order designs to sell *prêt-à-porter*. Several were experimenting with such boutique lines, and a few had gone so far as to design ready-to-wear clothes to be made in America, notably Christian Dior-New York and Jacques Fath for Joseph Halpert in the late 1940s. That they had the clothes actually made in New York was an acknowledgment of the excellence of American workmanship.

Because there were so many types of American women and so many requirements across the country for different types of clothes, most American designers offered multiple silhouettes at any given time. The New Look silhouette of fitted bodice and big skirt dominated fashion, but it existed in tandem with a narrow, curvy style as well as a boxy look. In 1957 the sack dress threatened to depose the New Look. American women bought the waistless, straight dresses by the thousand, only to find out that men hated them. They then altered the dresses to fit more closely, as in the sheath silhouette. Gradually the sheath evolved into the prevailing style in the 1960s, although full-skirted dresses continued to be shown and worn, especially for summer and evening.

Nothing was dearer to the American woman's heart than an ensemble that could go from day to night or from town to country, such as this 1951 Hattie Carnegie costume, which juxtaposed tweed with velvet. The coat featured a variation on a Chesterfield collar and velvet cuffs that fastened with jeweled buttons. The camisole bodice and skirt underneath were formal enough to wear to the theater or El Morocco; with another blouse the skirt and coat could go to the office or a committee meeting. Photograph: Horst. Courtesy Vogue

Although some designers promoted knitted fabrics, especially for traveling wardrobes, most used crisp and full-bodied materials. Day fabrics included silk shantung, tie silk, sheer wools, and wool-and-silk mixtures. Evening looks favored paper taffetas, faille, moire, and heavy satin. Among prints, floral patterns, medium in scale, abounded; flower designs were also prevalent in brocades and warp-printed silks. Most printed patterns were expressionistic or blurry and painterly rather than hard-edged. Colors, usually either pastel or deep, tended to be subtle—taupe, rose, sapphire, moss green, olive, lilac.

Suits came in versions with jackets in straight, tailored styles, or so defined at the waist that they almost formed peplums, worn over narrow or full skirts. Both jackets and coats had fairly short sleeves, known as bracelet-length, in order to accommodate long gloves wrinkled at the wrist. Coats were fitted, coachman-style; cut to flare from the shoulder in a tent or swing shape; or straight, as in reefers and polos. Most 1950s wool suits, coats, and dresses featured dressmaker details, including appliqué, various kinds of tucking or trapunto, and braid.

The single greatest constant of dresses for all occasions was the ornamental neckline. Necklines of even bathing suits and sundresses might be cutout, perhaps scalloped; versions of halters and camisoles; or off-the-shoulder, with fabric in asymmetric or ruffled arrangements. Another typical 1950s element, dependent on the use of more fabric, was the dolman sleeve and cut-in shoulder line, which appeared in dresses as well as coats and jackets.

The cocktail dress, which could be worn to any informal event where men would be dressed in their business suits or in sports coats and flannel slacks or khakis (left over from war uniforms and a new look for men), was the most significant article in a woman's wardrobe. It could be a "little black dress" or a floral-toned, short, swishy evening gown; it could be a sundress, the dress that had been worn underneath a suit jacket all day, or any kind of plain dress, as long as it was embellished with the proper accessories.

The first and foremost accessory item was costume jewelry. Here, the matching set, or parure, prevailed, and it might consist of earrings, worn close to the ear and following the shape of the lobe, choker or bib necklace, bracelets, and brooch. Brooches were very 1950s; they were worn on coats, suit collars, to the side of an evening décolleté. As in precious jewelry, the most prevalent look was white: platinum or platinumlike metal set with rhinestones or diamonds, in floral and foliate shapes and motifs—a far cry from the geometric forms of 1930s and 1940s Art Deco and Art Moderne. The costume jewelry industry, still centered in Rhode Island, was considered one of America's top contributions to fashion. Here as elsewhere there were important names to consider: Miriam Haskell, Trifari, Coro, Richelieu. Dress designers, including Hattie Carnegie, Adele Simpson, Trigère, Nettie Rosenstein, and Scaasi, followed the lead of the Chicago-based ready-to-wear firm Eisenberg in making costume jewelry to complement their clothes.

Depending on how a specific cocktail dress looked, it could be given a lift with pearls, dull gold, or tinted rhinestones. It was considered very chic to combine tweeds and diamanté jewelry, indicating a level of sophistication to which not every American woman aspired. Cocktail clothes were further accessorized with hats: cartwheels of velvet, lace, or horsehair; little turbans or close-fitting caps of brocade, taffeta, or satin. Gloves were *de rigueur.* For

Tom Brigance designed this playsuit, slit to the waist at the sides, in 1957. Photograph: Louise Dahl Wolfe. Courtesy the Edward C. Blum Design Laboratory, Fashion Institute of Technology, New York, and Harper's Bazaar

night they were worn in every length, in materials ranging from kid to cotton to taffeta, and in every color of the rainbow, as well as in patterns to match the dress. Shoes were high-heeled—the highest in history—with rounded toes. Black suede opera pumps, a standard, could see one through the winter season. Other choices included evening sandals, for both summer and winter, which might be made from slipper satin and dyed to complement one's dress.

In direct response to the shortages of the war years, accessories placed high on the must-have list and could be found in great quantity and variety. A woman making a major purchase in the 1950s, such as a good suit, a coat, or a best dress, would visit the other departments in the store to choose appropriate shoes, hat, gloves, pocketbook, and scarf. Matching shoes and pocketbooks were worn mainly in black, brown, and blue as well as such new neutrals as beige, deep red, and cordovan. Magazines devoted double-page spreads to whole suites of accessories, all in a range of a single color, as in sapphire scarves, belts, shoes, and pocketbooks shown with aquamarine slips and other underwear, hats, stockings, gloves, and, of course, jewelry.

Crocodile, especially in brown, was what every woman really wanted, almost as much as she wanted a mink stole in one of the newly developed moon-lit-shaded breeds like lunarine. Pocketbooks looked bigger and more rounded than they had been in the 1940s. Most had short straps and were carried in the hand or worn over the arm. Shoulder bags, in heavy leathers, went with tweeds and other casual sports clothes.

Women wore hats in the daytime, even when sitting at their desks working. Although new styles were constantly being promoted, the same variety was available throughout the decade, from wide-brimmed, low-crowned hats worn back on the head to brimless caps, cloches, toques, flat turbans, and pillboxes that were perched on top of the coiffure. By 1959 and 1960, hats began to develop towering crowns, just as hair was growing more bouffant.

In the 1950s hairstyles were achieved by means of permanents and set in pin curls, resulting in softly waved pageboys or curlier shorter coifs. In keeping with the feminine mood, makeup became more elaborate: a pale base, powder, rouge to highlight high cheekbones, and eye makeup, which was fairly new. The eyes were painted to extend their shape with dark eyeliner turned up at the corners and deep color on the eyelid. Blondes with blue eyes wore sky blue eyeshadow, green-eyed women a blue green, and brown-eyed women amethyst, olive, or blue green.

Suburban living resulted in new versions of sportswear, designed less for active, specific sports like tennis, swimming, golf (although these had their wardrobes, too) and more for relaxing on the patio. Play clothes included sunsuits like those worn by children, sundresses, which could be quite ornate, shorts, and short pants, like the narrow-legged capris, toreadors, or pedal pushers. Narrow, long pants with a side zipper, a popular look, originated at the Jax of California boutique. For summer, a great variety of cotton fabrics were available—stripes and plaids, seersuckers, examples woven with ribbon or wallpaper stripes, and those with embroidered effects or eyelet details. Businessmen, when they weren't commuting in their gray flannel two-piece suits, white shirts, and skinny ties, were mixing martinis or manning the barbecue in madras sports jackets, shorts (which were such a fad that for a while they were even worn with coats and ties), short-sleeved sports shirts, polo shirts, or even Hawaiian shirts.

Because so much of the population was pregnant at any given time, and perhaps because Lucille Ball of the popular television series "I Love Lucy" dared to be pregnant on television, maternity clothes came out into the open, although in advertisements and editorial photographs they were always modeled on nonpregnant women. Most popular was the two-piece maternity ensemble consisting of smock top and narrow skirt. The skirts were made with either holes cut out at the abdomen or expandable panels. Some women got away with wearing sack dresses in their regular size, and the idea caught on and brought about the one-piece maternity dress.

For the most part, early television depicted a sanitized view of family life, with exaggeratedly middle-class housewives as the most prevalent female characters. Women wanting to emulate television fashions would have concentrated on the ball gowns and cocktail dresses worn by singers or those shown off by Loretta Young in the entrance scene to her series. The only clothing style directly attributable to television was that of cowboy clothes, specifically the 1955 fad for coonskin caps, worn by fans of "Davy Crockett."

The movies continued to present images of glamour, and in the 1950s film stars fell into the same categories as American women in terms of style, running the gamut from girl-next-door Doris Day to sexy Elizabeth Taylor. American women did not copy clothes from movies as they had in the 1930s, probably because they could more easily find desirable ready-to-wear items, now that they were openly written about and advertised. An exception,

James Galanos designed this ethereal confection of cotton tulle with a shirred bra bodice and short pouf skirt. By 1958 the hems of short evening dresses began inching up, even reaching the kneecap in a design by Scaasi. The shoes, by David Evins, show the late-1950s style of stiletto heels and pointed, elongated toes.

Short evening dresses, first introduced during World War II, became an American staple. This 1951 example of draped tulle and chiffon over white satin with strapless bodice and ballet-length tulle skirt and chiffon bustle was made by Charles James, New York's most inventive and mercurial couturier. Photograph: Horst. Courtesy Vogue

though, was the chiffon, wrap-front cocktail dress designed by Helen Rose for Elizabeth Taylor in *Cat on a Hot Tin Roof* in 1958. Helen Rose also designed a ready-to-wear version, which sold very well across the country.

Although the 1950s fad for cashmere or lambswool cardigans trimmed with fur collars, jeweled embroideries, bows, and appliqué had its genesis in Mainbocher's wartime evening sweaters, another 1950s folly came seemingly out of nowhere. As early as 1951 American girls and women were making felt circle skirts and decorating them with Christmas trees, 45 rpm records, popular sayings, and/or poodles made in fabric appliqués, rickrack, and braid.

With these and other full skirts with crinolines, teenagers wore bobby socks and saddle shoes and put their hair up in ponytails. They continued their 1940s habit of wearing jeans with the cuffs rolled up, cardigans buttoned backward, and man-size shirts. Rebellious teens who had fallen under the spell of James Dean or such rock and roll stars as Elvis Presley did their best to dress like hoods and their girls. Boys adopted sideburns, motorcycle jackets, and Brylcreem-enhanced hairstyles. Fast girls preferred long, tight skirts and tight sweaters. Most girls fought constantly with their parents for the right to wear Tangee or even darker lipstick, black dresses, or, to parties and proms, strapless dresses. Although they would have been loath to admit it, teenagers adhered to their own etiquette of dress, which differed from school to school but was every bit as rigid as that of their parents.

All in all, the 1950s was a decade of exaggerated normalcy. Men, home from the wars, went to work and set out to raise families, while women bent over backward fine-tuning the seasoning in their meat loaves, seeing to it that the children's faces were scrubbed, and making sure that they themselves looked pretty. Everything was just fine, and would stay that way until the baby-boom children came of age.

Despite the prevalence of the wasp-waisted, full-skirted New Look throughout the 1950s, plenty of other silhouettes abounded. As a straight dress that could be worn belted or not, the chemise dress was available throughout the decade, especially in 1957, when it made waves as the sack. This 1955 version of black broadcloth, offered by ready-to-wear designer Jeanne Campbell of Sportwhirl, winner of one of that year's Coty awards, features a cowl back. It sold for approximately $25.

This 1950 dress of navy wool jersey by ready-to-wear designer Anthony Blotta falls into the sheath category, which combined a narrow line with an emphasized waist. Wearing wool for after-five events was an elegant Americanism.

OPPOSITE
During the 1950s, fashions were used to sell everything from cars and major appliances to foods and cosmetics. Advertisers especially favored pairing pastel shades of dresses with pastel washing machines or, in this case, toilet paper. Sarmi designed the 1958 mint green ball gown in the exact same tint as Scott Paper's new product. Photograph: Horst

This 1950 evening dress by Leslie Morris, custom designer for Bergdorf Goodman, satisfied a particular 1950s desire: for wonderful at-home clothes that could be worn by hostesses entertaining in front of the fire or presiding over buffet dinners. It features a glove-sleeved bodice of black mousseline de soie and a full tartan plaid skirt. Photograph: Horst. Courtesy Vogue

ADOLFO

Adolfo was born Adolfo Sardiña in Havana in 1930 and went to Paris as a teenager to apprentice at the houses of Balenciaga and Chanel. In 1953 he left Bergdorf Goodman, where he was working in the millinery department, to become a designer at Emme, a custom millinery establishment at 26 East Fifty-sixth Street, which moved to 19 West Fifty-seventh Street in 1954. Throughout the 1950s he was well known as one of New York's premier milliners, and in 1955 he won his first Coty special award. His hat designs ranged from little caps just barely covering the crown to floppy beach cartwheels more than a yard in diameter. In 1954 he told Lois Long of the *New Yorker* that he wasn't designing pillboxes or Camembert-shaped hats, and in 1957 he showed varieties of cloches to go with the twenties-style sack dresses then being promoted.

ADRIAN

Adrian continued making his clean daytime suits and his increasingly wearable evening clothes, along with a line of men's shirts and ties, but his designing career ended abruptly after he experienced a heart attack while preparing his fall 1952 collection and was advised by his doctor to retire. He died in 1959.

LARRY ALDRICH

Larry Aldrich was described in a *New York Times* article (October 29, 1959) as "imperious, aloof and artistic," a "man with a sense of adventure and one who rarely fumbles." His clothes during the 1950s (designed from 1957 by Marie McCarthy) were, more than anything else, appropriate—for town, theater openings, private dinner parties, trips to museums rather than for the country. Throughout the decade he offered designs that reflected current styles without being slavish. Even in the beginning of the decade, when the fitted New Look was at its height, his clothes did not cling to the figure like wet cloth; his narrow-waisted, narrow-skirted suits and dresses were characterized by an easy fit and were less décolleté than most fifties clothes; clothes for evening, if not covered up, had jackets. Suits of taffeta, cocktail clothes of sheer wool, theater clothes of brocades or chiffon carried restrained decoration of self-fabric bands or flat or string bows.

GEOFFREY BEENE

Geoffrey Beene was born in Haynesville, Louisiana, in 1927. To live up to his family's expectations, he began medical studies to become a doctor, but soon quit to go to the University of Southern California. From there, he took a job at I. Magnin in Los Angeles, then studied in France at l'Ecole de la Chambre Syndicale de la Couture Parisienne and the Académie-Julian and in New York at the Traphagen School of Fashion. He worked for a year with Samuel Winston, a Seventh Avenue manufacturer, and then went to Harmay as assistant designer in 1950. Harmay fashions in the 1950s, ladylike and feminine, included tweed suit costumes with short jackets, sometimes bloused out at the back, and narrow pencil skirts, and finely tucked linen afternoon dresses, trimmed with bands of lace. Although Harmay credited Beene by name for his designs in its ads by 1957, it fired him when it judged that he went too far in his appreciation for the slightly easier-fitting look of the late-fifties chemise. He then went to work for Teal Traina.

HARVEY BERIN

The house advertisements and editorial copy carried the name of Karen Stark, the designer for Harvey Berin, but Harvey Berin had final say on all sketches. A typical Stark for Berin design was the gray wool dress or suit with a white collar (these seem to have been made in different versions every year). The *New York Times* wrote in October 28, 1959, "Buyers look to this man for pretty dresses that do not mean hair-raising prices. Mr. Berin does not disappoint his followers," and "Mr. Berin does not like skimpy, tight dresses that wrap around the body like a bandage" (page 32). Although the company showed the somewhat boxy silhouette in 1957, Berin clothes were more often defined at the waist, whether narrow or full-skirted, and carefully tailored.

For this beige wool dress from his resort collection of 1958–59, Larry Aldrich made the unfitted or sack silhouette more palatable by raising the waistline, dropping the shoulders, and giving the skirt a modified barrel shape. High waistlines signaled the beginning of the trend from the fitted bodice of the 1950s to the more unfitted look of the 1960s. Hat by Lilly Daché.

BILL BLASS

Indiana-born Bill Blass designed for various Seventh Avenue manufacturers, including David Crystal, both before and after World War II, during which he served in the army, but it wasn't until the mid-1950s that his name began to be mentioned in the press and in advertisements as head designer for the firm Anna Miller. In 1959 Anna Miller's company merged with that of her brother Maurice Rentner, one of the most respected personages in the New York fashion world, and Blass stayed on as head designer. Bill Blass's fondness for the glamorous styles of the 1930s (which, via the movies, had inspired him to become a designer in the first place) was already evident by 1959 in at-home clothes that featured halter necklines, glittery sequins, and floor-length culottes made in the style of beach pajamas. The average price for a daytime ensemble by 1960 was $300.

It was not unusual in the 1950s for bathing suits to look like abbreviated evening dresses. This Tom Brigance suit of 1954 features a print of scattered faceted jewels. The Brooklyn Museum Library Collection, New York

This 1959 red silk cocktail dress by Bill Blass for Maurice Rentner featured a sculptured silhouette and a tabletop, or decorative, neckline.

ANTHONY BLOTTA

Anthony Blotta continued in the 1950s to produce tailored dresses, dress and jacket ensembles, and suits and coats made either of wool dressed up for evening with interesting décolletages, glittery buttons, or collars and cuffs of fur or of traditional evening fabrics, like satin, tempered by a severe cut and lack of decoration.

TOM BRIGANCE

During the 1950s Brigance, who won the Coty in 1953, was exclusive designer at Frank Gallant, although he also designed for Fonde, Sportsmaker, Sinclair, and Gabar. His range expanded to include coats and suits as well as all manner of dresses, play clothes, and bathing suits. As ever, his sportswear was the most innovative. For casual evenings in 1951 he offered a corduroy pantsuit with pleated, cuffed trousers and cardigan jacket, the top consisting of a band of cotton twisted at the neck, covering the breasts, bare in a triangle at the midriff, and buttoning to the pants so as not to become disarranged. His bathing suits, which might be made from cotton velveteen, damask, piqué, or wool jersey, often had bloomer bottoms and strapless, halter, or one-shouldered bodices. At a time when patterned fabrics tended toward the misty and romantic, Brigance found and made use of bold, bright, crisp designs that looked forward to the 1960s.

DONALD BROOKS

Donald Brooks was born in New Haven, Connecticut, on January 10, 1928, and was educated at the Fine Arts School of Syracuse University and at Parsons School of Design, New York. During the mid-1950s he designed junior-size sportswear for a company called Darbury, and in 1959 he moved to Townley as designer, replacing the late Claire McCardell. In 1958 he won both a Coty special award and the American Fashion Critics Award for sportswear.

While Darbury's clothes were inexpensive (a spring coat retailed for $35 in 1956), Brooks managed to create designs that were neither cheap versions of higher-priced clothes nor junior versions of adult clothes. Instead, Brooks used materials like denim, cotton canvas, and bright floral cottons for raincoats and argyle plaid knits for casual, sporty dresses. At Townley, he began to experiment with more luxurious materials and to make more grown-up late-day and evening clothes.

GEORGE CARMEL

George Carmel designed for his company tailored clothes that sold during the 1950s for $150 to $400. He generally featured easy rather than rigid silhouettes, using textured materials like nubby wool, silk tweed, and extra wide—wale corduroy. With the last, he made in 1957 a bright red coat that was lined in curly lamb dyed pink.

HATTIE CARNEGIE

Hattie Carnegie advertisements during the 1950s usually featured a photograph of a model dressed in a suit or dress and jacket ensemble posed with the doorman at the entrance of her store, with the caption "from hat to hem," indicating that Carnegie could dress a woman in everything she needed except for shoes.

Carnegie was most famous for her suits, which, whether ready-to-wear or custom-made, typically had short, slightly boxy, slightly curvy jackets ending a few inches below the waist and straight skirts. They were made in pretty, bright-colored wools, some with unusual textures, like a glacé mohair that resembled silk, and were designed to be worn with the jacket closed, showing jewelry at the throat rather than the collar of a blouse. Many suits featured such dressmaker details as curved, stepped seams, shaped, cutaway hems, or trims like ball-fringe braid. Her evening clothes ran the gamut from ball gowns, many of which were custom versions of Paris designs, to at-home styles, sometimes incorporating evening pants, from summery linen dresses in pastels embroidered with beads and sequins or trimmed with silk to long, soft, fluid dresses of crepe or chiffon. After Hattie Carnegie's death in 1956, the store gradually lost its cachet. By the mid-1960s, many of its employees had left to start new businesses.

BONNIE CASHIN

Bonnie Cashin was born in California in 1915. While still in high school, she designed ballet costumes for a local troupe. When the troupe's manager was hired by the Roxy Theatre in New York, Cashin went along to design up to three sets of costumes a week for the theater's twenty-four showgirls. For a revue based on a fashion sequence, she designed street clothes, which caught the eye of Louis Adler of the wholesale firm Adler & Adler. He offered her a job and she accepted. For the next several years she designed both costumes and ready-to-wear.

In 1943 Bonnie Cashin left New York to become the costume designer at 20th Century-Fox in Hollywood. Over the next six years she costumed sixty movies, including *Claudia* in 1943, *Laura* and *A Tree Grows in Brooklyn* in 1944, and *Anna and the King of Siam* in 1946. Many of her films from 1947 to 1949 were codesigned with Charles LeMaire. In 1949 she returned to New York and her former job, designing for the sportswear house Adler & Adler. A year later, she won a Coty Award and the Neiman-Marcus fashion award. She remained with Adler & Adler until 1953, when she formed her own company in partnership with Philip Sills.

From the beginning of the 1950s, she aimed to make clothes that could be used in a variety of ways, reflecting the variety in the lives of active women. In 1950 Bonnie Cashin designs included casual floppy hats in velour or linen, simple sheath dresses that could be made gala with organza or other dressy aprons, and her purse-pocket raincoat (which she redesigned several times), so named for the roomy interior pocket it provided so that a woman wouldn't have to battle the rain with an umbrella and a pocketbook.

Cashin first used the phrase "layered dressing" in print in 1952. Her apron dresses fell into this category, as did her double

Sketched and designed by Bonnie Cashin for Adler & Adler, this 1950 summer shirtwaist was sprightly and fresh-looking. The Brooklyn Museum Library Collection, New York

coats: sleeveless coats and coats with sleeves that could be worn individually as well as together. She was fond of knits, knowing that they traveled well, and designed knitted dresses and jacket ensembles that could go anywhere. By 1956 she was making pants, coats, car coats, and apron skirts out of canvas duck trimmed with leather piping and pairing them with ribbed sweaters with turtlenecks, funnel necks, or hoods. In its issue of October 29, 1959, the *New York Times* described Cashin as working "like a hummingbird . . . capable of whipping up a poncho, an evening dress or a raincoat over a cup of coffee."

OLEG CASSINI

In 1950 Oleg Cassini, with the then-unprecedented sum of $100,000 from backers, established his own ready-to-wear company in New York, in May showing a collection of sixty-five pieces. The business was an immediate success, doing a reported $750,000 in sales in its first year.

Cassini was born in Paris on April 11, 1913, to noble Russian parents (his father was a count). The family lived in Paris, Russia, and Copenhagen before settling in Florence, where Cassini's mother established a successful couture house on the Via Tornabuoni. Cassini attended the English Catholic School, the University of Florence, and the city's Academy of Fine Arts. He got his first job for the house of Patou in Paris, working as one of six sketch artists. He then decided to open a small couture house of his own, called Cassini Studio, in Rome. Disturbed by conditions in Fascist Italy and troubled personally by a romantic scandal, he moved to New York in 1936.

In New York, Cassini interviewed for a job with Germaine Monteil, who told him he needed experience in ready-to-wear, and was hired, supposedly as a design assistant, by Jo Copeland for the business she ran with Ann Sadowsky. This short-lived position was followed by others with manufacturers such as William Bass as well as with a Mrs. Boulogne, whose husband had tried to build for her a fashion company. For a brief period in 1938, he established and ran Oleg, Inc., a small couture house on Madison Avenue between Fifty-ninth and Sixtieth streets. After a messy marriage and divorce, he decided to move to California.

Paramount Pictures hired him to replace Omar Kiam as one of Edith Head's design assistants. After leaving this job he married the actress Gene Tierney and occasionally designed costumes for some of her films, notably *The Razor's Edge*, which was set in the late 1920s and early 1930s. With partner Paul Portanova, he ran a company called Casanova (based on their two names) that sold ready-to-wear gabardine suits. After a decade in California he returned to New York, where he quickly found backing for a new venture.

Oleg Cassini's 1950s designs are characterized by an almost extreme femininity, with romantic fabrics, including taffeta, chiffon, cobweb lace, and point d'esprit, and minute waistlines, true for both narrow- and wide-skirted dresses as well as tailored suits. Cassini suits often made use of military details, like rows of braid and buttons, a leitmotif that he had been fond of since seeing his first design made into an actual ensemble in the 1930s.

Ceil Chapman's specialty was flattering, feminine day and evening clothes. This early-1950s short evening dress was made of tulle with a pattern of rosettes stitched into, rather than applied onto, the material. The Brooklyn Museum Library Collection, New York

CEIL CHAPMAN

Ceil Chapman remarried in the 1950s and became Mrs. Thomas Gillespie Rogers, Jr. She continued making her signature ball gowns and cocktail clothes, for the most part avoiding the hemline and silhouette vicissitudes of the time. Most of her dresses, whether floor-length or ankle-length or shorter, had fitted bodices, either strapless or more covered up, tiny waists, and full skirts, often poufed in places. Many came with stoles designed as part of an ensemble. Cotton and silk organdy were favored materials, as was reembroidered lace. One 1955 evening dress, *Vogue* (March 15) reported, had a baby blue silk organdy neckline "circling the bosom" and a white lace skirt caught up with blue bows in a "delicious turmoil." By 1956 and 1957 Ceil Chapman was working in a softer idiom, using varieties of chiffon for dresses with straight but swirling skirts and draped bodices with low V necklines. In both 1950 and 1959 Chapman designed variations on a favorite theme—dresses with flowing, black, high-waisted skirts and white silk organdy or chiffon blouses.

JO COPELAND

At Pattullo, Jo Copeland continued to design dressy daytime and evening ready-to-wear that was beautifully made and fairly expensive ($150 to $450). In this decade, however, her designs went beyond the idiom she had developed in the 1940s to encompass every variety of 1950s silhouette, in clothes that were boldly rather than delicately feminine. She made fitted sheath dresses and evening gowns with carved, petaled, uneven hemlines as well as one made from yards and yards of chiffon gently twisted into a halter neck and flowing skirt. Her suits included boxy, almost swing-shaped jackets, tiny, close boleros, or nipped-in-at-the-waist dressmaker jackets. She was a master of detail, putting an egg yolk yellow silk lining in a jacket, a multicolored Roman-striped silk collar on a wool dress, a wide, self-fringed faille scarf swinging from the belt of a narrow dress in panels. She rarely used prints, opting instead for the decorative effect of embroidery or trimmings of wide ribbons. In 1957 she designed a line of costume jewelry for Richelieu.

DAVID CRYSTAL

The David Crystal company continued in the 1950s to produce sportswear that was less sporty than clothes for actual sports although less formal than dressmaker suits or cocktail ensembles. The firm's two major mainstays were shirtwaist dresses, either narrow or with full skirts, and easily fitting cardigan-jacketed suits. In 1957 it produced a line with the label "A Christian Dior Junior designed for David Crystal" that was twice as expensive as its regular line, with suits or dresses selling for $100 to $145.

LILLY DACHÉ

In the 1950s, Lilly Daché branched out into two off-the-peg hat lines, called Mlle Lilly and Dachettes, and she also turned her attention increasingly to dressing her clients from head to toe. In a 1954 fashion show held in her penthouse, the models wore her little hats called "drop of a hats," her dresses and coats, stockings (complete with gold-tinged painted legs underneath), low-heeled shoes covered with printed fabric, and costume jewelry, and they were made up with her new pearlized face powder and coiffed according to her direction. Daché proved forward-thinking in realizing that hair would become as important as hats; the hairdresser Kenneth started out working for her in her salon. The Daché building on East Fifty-sixth Street functioned more as a boutique than as a specialty shop. Although the wares were luxurious and of the highest quality, the fripperies she offered for sale had a whimsical air about them, and they were displayed in amusing ways. In 1956 she published her *Glamour Book*, which perhaps inspired her to name her shampoo Glampoo.

DAVIDOW

Davidow specialized in suits rather than evening clothes, and its expertise resulted in beautifully made garments. A rounded lapel might be repeated in the curve of the cutaway hem of a jacket; pocket tabs might be so placed to create an effect as decorative as appliqué; a large plaid might be used to great effect with a smaller version; or a suit of tiny checks might be trimmed with simply a bias band of the check sewn around its edges.

JANE DERBY

Jane Derby's wholesale fashion company turned out feminine, fairly conservative clothes during the 1950s. Like most Americans, Derby appreciated the allure of combining day and evening materials, using tweeds with silk jacquard or ottoman. She was also fond of a modified peasant look of bodices with round yoke necklines and puffed sleeves. She preferred soft colors, finding it unnecessary to rely on black or navy for a smart effect; a 1957 evening dress of white silk featured a trainlike back panel of brown cobwebby lace.

ESTÉVEZ

In 1955 Luis Estévez began designing in his own name for a company called Grenelle. He was an immediate success, selling $3 million worth of medium-priced clothes ($40 and $50) the first year, and in 1956 he won a Coty Award. Born in Cuba in 1930, Luis Estévez attended prep school in this country. He was studying architecture in Havana when a summer job at Lord & Taylor led him into fashion. After attending the Traphagen School of Fashion, he worked for a manufacturer in New York and then worked in Paris for Patou.

Estévez has said that his wife inspired him to create his feminine and lively 1950s fashions. He told *Life* magazine in April 2, 1956, that "she likes her dresses to have sharp lines and to be as sexy as possible within the boundaries of good taste." He was known for his intricate necklines, which could be cut in at an-

This window display for the Lilly Daché boutique at the Plaza Hotel was typically 1950s in its airiness and whimsicality. By the late 1950s Lilly Daché, astutely sensing that the era of the hat would soon be over, accordingly began to concentrate less on millinery and more on accessories, such as the jeweled necklaces worn by the giraffe.

gles, twisted into halters, or unusually shaped Us or Vs. He used black and white freely, as well as the blurry floral prints popular at the time. Although he did some day clothes, he specialized in cocktail and evening dresses: these could have full, rustling skirts or very narrow lines with floating back panels. In the fall of 1959, he showed an African-inspired collection in a showroom decorated with a tent. From northern Africa he borrowed burnoose sleeves and attached hoods; his prints featured oversize palms, tigers among fern leaves, and zebra stripes.

ANNE FOGARTY

Anne Fogarty, née Whitney, was born in Pittsburgh in 1919. She gained her first experience with fashion reworking her sisters' hand-me-downs to suit her, and she remembered getting in trouble at the age of five for choosing to accessorize a pink dress with a red hair bow. She transferred out of college to study drama at the Carnegie Institute of Technology; later she realized she had wanted to be an actress in order to wear costumes. In pursuit of an acting career, she moved to New York, where she worked as a fitting model for Harvey Berin. At one of her lunchtime auditions she landed a job in summer stock, but when she came back to give notice, Berin persuaded her to think instead about becoming a designer, and he promised that his staff would help train her. When two of his designers left to work for Sheila Lynn, a fashion company, she went with them as a model, with the guarantee of a chance to design.

By then Fogarty knew that she wanted to design, although her next few jobs—as a fashion copywriter, a stylist for fashion shows, and in an advertising agency on its Cohama textile account—sidetracked her. At Cohama's suggestion, Youth Guild, a new fashion company specializing in teenage clothes, hired her as a designer in 1948. Her first designs, which were attributed in the fashion press to Anne Fogarty of Youth Guild, featured her version of the New Look—called the paper-doll silhouette—in

This 1950s Lord & Taylor window display celebrated the full-skirted and youthful dresses of Anne Fogarty, who was famous for her crinoline styles made in junior sizes. The Library, Fashion Institute of Technology, New York

corporating its close-fitting bodice and full-skirted silhouette into young-looking day and casual evening clothes. One 1948 dress—actually a black corduroy jumper, with scoop neckline and puffed sleeves over a pale blue poplin shirt—was the kind of thing a teenager could wear to lunch at her grandparents, on a date, or to a casual dance party. In 1950 she switched to the Margot dress company, where she designed for junior sizes.

These clothes earned for Anne Fogarty a Coty Award in 1951. Although inexpensive (well under $100 in most cases), they did not fit the category of sportswear, since she designed primarily dresses. And although they featured very fitted bodices and immense skirts, they were simple almost to an extreme (Fogarty rarely used any kind of trimming, especially silk flowers, which she despised) and made in casual materials such as tweed, flannel, denim (as early as 1951), and velveteen. The silhouette changed slightly in her 1954 Tea Cosy line; these dresses were fitted to the body from the neckline to below the waist before spilling out into a full skirt. Fogarty was most famous for her separate crinoline underskirts; to counter criticism that they might seem cumbersome, she was always explaining in articles how easy they were to move around in and to travel with. By 1956 Anne Fogarty was working with a narrow silhouette, such as fitted sheath dresses, as well as her still-popular paper-doll look.

In 1959 Fogarty published *Wife Dressing*, a book that offered such advice to wives as not to wear their hair in pin curls around their husbands, what to wear for every kind of occasion, and when not to fall for a bargain.

SEYMOUR FOX

Seymour Fox was one of the better ready-to-wear manufacturers of the 1950s, specializing in coats and dressmaker suits made of beautiful tweeds, wools, and fleeces. A 1951 tweed coat sold for $225. Excellent workmanship included curved seams, bound buttonholes, and bias self-fabric edging. Most of the Seymour Fox suits were made with long, narrow-waisted jackets and narrow, or pencil, skirts. Ads for the company in 1954 mentioned that it designed with the "custom-sized" customer in mind, which presumably meant that the clothes were cut to fit women with the kinds of figure flaws that usually required special tailoring. The company lasted into the 1970s.

GALANOS

In 1951 James Galanos opened his own fashion establishment, in a small shop on Beverly Drive in Los Angeles, with a small group of samples, or models. Although some stores and buyers recognized the Galanos quality, it wasn't until he began showing his collections in New York in 1953 that he achieved widespread recognition. In 1954 he won both the Coty and the Neiman-Marcus awards, and Lois Long predicted that he might become a "man of destiny."

Two years might not seem like a long time for a fashion designer to establish a reputation, but for Galanos it had been many more years than that before he established himself in his métier. He had been born in Philadelphia to Greek immigrant parents and reared in New Jersey. Early on he recognized his interest in fashion, and after high school he moved to New York, where he attended the Traphagen School of Fashion. While a student he sold his sketches to various fashion houses and had fruitless interviews with some of his idols, including Fira Benenson, the head custom designer at Bonwit Teller. He worked briefly in the fabric department at Hattie Carnegie.

An entrepreneur looking for a designer for a fashion business he wanted to start for his wife heard of Galanos through a Traphagen teacher and sent him out to California. When the business never happened, Galanos went to work for Jean Louis, head costume designer at Columbia Pictures, as a sketch artist. The businessman reentered the scene with an offer to send Galanos to Paris, where the young man ended up working as an unpaid design assistant for the couturier Robert Piguet. There he had the opportunity to see his designs realized as couturier dresses, and he stayed through several renewals of his student visa, finally returning to New York when he was offered a job by the ready-to-wear firm Davidow. However, Galanos found his fashion sense and talent at odds with the fairly conservative sportswear that Davidow featured, so he quit and went back to California, where Jean Louis suggested that he go into business for himself.

From the beginning Galanos distinguished himself by his virtuosity with fabrics. He worked in cotton, wool, silk, and linen, but his major 1950s signature was chiffon, from which he made dresses with fifty yards of skirt, collars with ten cutaway layers, narrow evening dresses with fishtail trains, and even layered chiffon wide-brimmed hats. He was equally adept at creating more sculptured silhouettes out of materials like matelassé brocades. His shapes included narrow sheaths, sacks cut with fluid drapery, and full, bell-skirted dresses. He experimented with the waistline, high, low, and natural, and he made suits with forward-looking long body jackets. The average price mentioned for his clothes in the 1950s was $400, then at the high end of the spectrum.

ELEANORA GARNETT

Eleanora Garnett clothes were available at her store in New York at 47 East Fifty-first Street as well as in Italy, where they were made on the Via di Villa Sacchetti in Rome. They were offered on a ready-to-wear basis, at mid-range prices ($145 for a silk cocktail dress in 1955), and tended to be somewhat feminine, as in a 1953 suit with a ruffled collar. They ran the gamut from suits on up to ball gowns, although full-skirted, ballet-length cocktail dresses seem to have been a specialty, and intricate detailing or workmanship, as in a dress with a thousand pleats or one made out of knitted lace, was a hallmark.

RUDI GERNREICH

In 1949 Rudi Gernreich, based in California and working as a free-lance fashion designer, signed on with George Carmel, a New York manufacturer. Three years later he went into partnership with William Bass, producing youthful, relaxed clothes that were especially popular at the influential West Coast boutique Jax. He began experimenting with knitted fabrics and worked in conjunction with the Westwood Knitting Mills. In 1959 he broke off with Bass and opened his own business in Los Angeles.

Gernreich was born in Vienna, Austria, in 1922, the son of a hosiery manufacturer. As a teenager he showed an interest in fashion, but his plans to study the couture in Paris fell apart when Hitler's rise to power led Rudi and his mother to immigrate to California in 1938. Gernreich attended Los Angeles City College and the Los Angeles Art Center School, but a performance of the Martha Graham Dance Company inspired him to become a modern dancer, as well as a costume designer, for the Lester Horton Dance Troupe. It now seems clear that much of his allegiance to freedom of movement, to a celebration of the body, as well as to leotard-based dressing, was formed during his six years of dancing professionally.

Gernreich's 1950s designs were composed of informal sportswear, day clothes, at-home clothes, and swimwear. He did not work within the rigidly constructed current silhouette, showing instead easily fitting clothes made out of wool, jersey, or other pliable materials, usually in solid colors or geometric stripes and checks. In 1952 he revived the 1920s and 1930s knitted wool maillot, which he went on to make in various versions for more than a decade. With their total lack of interior construction, these contrasted strongly with 1950s dressmaker bathing suits.

HOWARD GREER

Howard Greer's 1950s clothes were of the entrance-making variety, as befitted his Hollywood design background. He designed strapless, short dresses with full-skirted, sheer overdresses, and he wound chiffon in brilliant tones around the strapless bodices of his lamé or brocade evening gowns. Most of his designs were fitted throughout the body, except for jutting bustles or folded-over sash panels to vary the line. Greer retired in 1962.

PHILIP HULITAR

In 1949, after custom designing debutante, wedding, and maternity clothes for Bergdorf Goodman for fourteen years, Philip Hulitar established his own business, which included some day dresses but specialized in cocktail and evening clothes ranging in price from $100 to $200. In 1959 the *New York Times* wrote, "Dedicated to making beautiful women more beautiful, Mr. Hulitar is a man who has always loved the rustle of silk, the cling of chiffon and the drape of matte jersey. Women who want to show off good figures should let Mr. Hulitar help them." His clothes were both sexy and romantic. He often used the princess line, with a very flared skirt, as well as the sheath silhouette with separate overskirt in back, typically in black silk combined with black lace and floral prints. He liked silk cabbage roses as trimming as well as for whole shawls or shrugs to go with bare dresses.

IRENE

Irene of California (not to be confused with Irene of New York, the milliner) continued to design her ready-to-wear suits and evening clothes throughout the 1950s. Her daytime silhouette rarely changed: most of her suits were made with long, fitted jackets and long, narrow skirts. Imaginatively tailored, they did not have the exaggerated femininity of dressmaker suits; details like pieced sections of geometric fabrics ending in pointed panels were dramatic rather than fussy. Irene also used the long, fitted torso for ball gowns, which often featured large, bow-tied panels at the hips, asymmetric draperies or hemlines, strapless décolletages, and contrasting use of two luxurious fabrics in one design.

The narrow yet curvy suit silhouette was a favorite of the California-based designer Irene, whose 1957 striped wool version with stepped collar and decorative button tabs is shown here on Betty Furness.

New York couturier Charles James, frequently described as a sculptor of fashion, designed this 1950s short evening dress in his inimitable way: he carved the material to stand away from the figure in undulating curves. Photograph: Horst

ARTHUR JABLOW

David Kidd designed for Arthur Jablow, a New York wholesale firm, in the 1950s. The company produced elegant daytime dresses and suits and coats that were feminine without relying on overly decorative treatments. For example, a suit in a small shepherd's-check tweed had two black suede bows placed at the front closure; a simple white piqué dress featured a narrow skirt under a slightly belled tunic.

CHARLES JAMES

In 1950 Charles James won the Coty Award. He also began experimenting with different forms of ready-to-wear, which

strained his already inadequate business sense. So committed was he to maintaining both the individuality and the extraordinarily high quality of his couture clothes that he had trouble both watering down his designs for mass production and understanding its limitations. His solution was to sell original models to such department stores as Lord & Taylor and Saks Fifth Avenue, which treated them as they did originals from the Paris couture: as patterns from which to make copies. These usually sold for around $200, about one-sixth the cost of the custom model.

In 1955 James entered into a business arrangement with the blouse manufacturer Samuel Winston to produce a line of his clothes; this situation culminated in a lawsuit in which James claimed Samuel Winston, specifically its Roxanne division, was illegally pilfering his ideas. He lost the suit and became increasingly bitter about the fashion world, closing down his custom business in 1958. Although he designed a line of ready-to-wear for Korvettes in 1962, he spent the rest of his life documenting his old designs and producing an occasional custom dress for one of his faithful clients. He died in 1978.

Charles James's work of the 1950s was more varied than it had been before, perhaps because he was involved with ready-to-wear. While he continued to design outstanding and original evening clothes with sculptural forms and virtuoso cuts, his experiments with daytime suits, coats, and dresses especially revealed his inventiveness, so different were they from anything else then being designed or produced. Made in twills, tweeds, fleece, and other woolens, coats and suit jackets featured sleeves cut in one with the torso (or that were deep dolmans); collars lined to hold their shape standing up to frame the face; and cocoon shapes for coats and tulip forms for the skirts of the suits. Rarely was anything more than the cut needed for visual interest. James also designed, for the first time, maternity clothes, for Lane Bryant, and children's fashions.

LINDA KINOSHITA

A protégée of Charles James, Linda Kinoshita opened her own couture salon in the West Fifties in 1957. Although born in California, Kinoshita explored her heritage in Japan, studying painting, flower arranging, and music, and she often incorporated ancient Japanese clothing elements into her contemporary couturier clothes, made with the precision one would expect from someone who had been in charge of the James atelier. All of her designs were worked out in miniature on a small mannequin before being translated into patterns.

Kinoshita created short kimono jackets as suit elements or to go over dresses; necklines, like that of the kimono, that stood away from the nape of the neck; and at-home kimono costumes, such as the one she designed in apricot brocade with an obi of brown ribbons for Babe Paley, her most famous client. She was known for her inventiveness with materials: she used camel hair for evening coats to be paired with lace and satin. She also designed for the wholesale house Dynasty, which specialized in Oriental-style evening clothes, made of Japanese silks and Chinese brocades and manufactured in Hong Kong. Kinoshita continued designing into the 1960s.

ANNE KLEIN

Junior Sophisticates, formed in 1948 with Anne Klein as its designer, was aptly named. The clothes were made in petite, or junior, sizes, were medium-priced (generally $50 to $90, going as low as $6 for a nightgown), and they didn't talk down to young, small women. The New York Times of October 27, 1959, wrote that Anne Klein had made it "a downright blessing to be a junior size" and that she was "justly famous for well-behaved clothes that have a fresh air worldliness."

Anne Klein was born in Brooklyn in 1923 and started working at the age of fifteen as a free-lance fashion sketcher. She was a designer for a firm called Varden Petites before signing on with Junior Sophisticates.

A typical Anne Klein 1950s cocktail dress was made in wool rather than taffeta; an evening dress, in mink ice satin in lieu of baby blue tulle, was cut in an interesting shape, with a bloused back tunic and straight skirt rather than an off-the-shoulder neckline and a crinoline. Anne Klein worked with sheath shapes, sometimes with bloused bodices, and in 1958 she showed low-waisted dresses with pleated skirts as an alternative to the sack. Her suits and dress-and-jacket ensembles featured blazers cut like pea jackets, sometimes lined in rabbit fur for a grown-up touch.

TINA LESER

In keeping with her talent for borrowing nuances from other cultures, Tina Leser produced a line of Spanish-inspired clothes in 1950. The collection included black toreador pants, ending just below the knee, paired with frilly white blouses, and black velvet bullring suits, the skirts lined in red satin, and with black braid–trimmed gray wool cloaks. Other 1950s looks included dressed-up bathing suits made of changeable taffeta and dressed-down evening turnouts with narrow pants and contrasting blouses, as well as sundresses draped like Tahitian pareos. In 1953 she left Edwin H. Foreman and resumed running her own business.

CLAIRE McCARDELL

Claire McCardell designed with an allegiance to certain convictions: she believed that women's clothes should be versatile, comfortable, durable, flattering, and easy to care for. By remaining faithful to her own aesthetic rather than trying for novelty twice a year, she designed clothes that were timeless. If an idea was good, she stuck with it, using it over and over; if a woman loved one of her dresses she could wear it for decades.

One of her constants was the monastic dress, which could be full, perhaps pleated, or string-bean slim, as long as it didn't have a built-in waistline. Preferring that her customers determine where their own waistlines should be, McCardell provided them with tie sashes, often made of the bias piping one of her sewers christened spaghetti; with these, a dress could have one or two or even three waistlines. McCardell continued to make popover dresses, characterized by a wrap front, and by 1951 she

The main alternative to the constructed dressmaker bathing suit during the 1950s was a stretchy version of maillot, often made in wool. This 1950 bathing costume by Tina Leser consisted of a two-piece bathing suit with a gray wool bottom and a white calico bra under a torso-covering tube and bolero of fire-engine red. The bolero was sold separately for $13, and the suit, in three pieces, was available for $25. Photograph: Horst. Courtesy Vogue

had transformed the popover into a coat, a beach cover-up, and a hostess gown. Any of her designs, from bathing suits to evening turnouts, might feature her signature topstitching, pockets, and the brass tab closures she called work-clothes grippers. Used on the front of a dress, they gave the wearer the ability to make its neckline as high or as low as she deemed appropriate.

McCardell disliked pretentious fabrics, especially shoddy versions of fine ones. She favored honest fabrics like wool jersey, which she described in her 1956 book *What Shall I Wear?* as being "every bit as regal as velvet," corduroy, cottons in strong solid colors or plaids, and silk surah or taffeta in nondressy colors like orange, olive green, or khaki.

McCardell wrote in her book that "the clothes that go with active sports show up your background more than any other clothes," and she paid particular attention to comfort, appropriateness, and practicality in her sportswear. She knew that a woman had no chance of looking capable, and therefore graceful, if she couldn't move her arms freely enough to swing a golf club or tennis racket, and she abhorred the thought of women being too gussied up outdoors, especially sitting around the pool in lamé and lace. Although her own bathing suits could look like evening dresses, they at least looked like hers, with halter necks, sometimes hoods and sleeves, and wrapped waists, and she chose materials for them, such as wool jersey and heavy cotton, that held their shape after immersion in water. She designed knickers, shorts, and pants, and she made a specialty, as early as 1949, of short play dresses and skirts that presaged the 1960s mini.

In 1956 McCardell began designing a line of children's clothes called Baby McCardells; these looked just like what she designed for women. Sundresses were made with halters, bathing suits in the shapes of bubbles, party dresses had spaghetti ties, and there were even ballet slippers in diminutive sizes. McCardell's design career ended when she died in 1958.

MAINBOCHER

Although Mainbocher opened a department in his couture salon in 1950 called La Galerie, where clothes were made-to-order in standard sizes and available within a week, for the most part he concentrated on his couture, which revealed both his Parisian training and his American roots. His ball gowns tended to be simple and, because of their perfect cut and gorgeous materials, dramatic, and the rest of his clothes featured the luxury of practicality. He continued to make dresses that could do double duty by adding an overskirt, apron, jacket, or cardigan sweater. Suits could go for either day or evening. Mainbocher used mattress ticking for coats and gingham for couture summer shifts decorated with self bands, piping bows, and appliqué. He contrasted linen with taffeta and jersey with faille, and he used fur on the inside, rather than the outside, of wool coats. His suits, which featured primarily boxy jackets and narrow dirndl or straight skirts, fell into the dressmaker category, with their details, such as curved bands and inset seams, appliqués, and self bows, often mirrored in the construction of the accompanying blouse.

During the 1950s he designed the costumes for several Broadway plays, including *Call Me Madam*, with Ethel Merman, *Wonderful Town*, with Rosalind Russell, *The Sound of Music*, with Mary Martin, and *The Great Sebastians*, with Lynn Fontanne.

One of Claire McCardell's pet shapes for bathing suits and playsuits was the bubble, shown here in a calico version on Betty Furness, and she used it for both her adult and Baby McCardell collections.

In this 1957 custom-made evening dress, Mainbocher contrasted the restrained sliplike cut with a luxurious fabric of black velvet cut to a chiffon ground.

Mainbocher, designer of New York's most patrician, and expensive, custom-made clothes, tended to favor suits with slightly boxy jackets and dressmaker details. This 1959 daytime ensemble, made of wool in a soft shade of rose, was shaped gently to the body. Bracelet-length sleeves were popular in the 1950s since they could be worn with long gloves, crushed around the wrists, or with jewelry.

PHILIP MANGONE

Philip Mangone's most prevalent suit shape during the 1950s was lean, with a narrow skirt and a slim, nipped-in-the-waist jacket. Suits, made out of soft tweeds or checked or solid worsteds, were often accompanied by swing coats of various lengths in large-scale plaids. In the early 1950s Mangone played with the possibilities of scarves by cutting stoles in one with the top of a coat or running a scarf through a slot in the lapel of a suit. As he had since he first began his wholesale company in the 1910s, he stuck to suits and coats.

VERA MAXWELL

Vera Maxwell, while continuing to work with the category of coats and suits during the 1950s, also began to show more and more dress and coat ensembles for both summer and winter, as well as in floor-length versions for evening. A typical example featured a printed silk dress in a simple shape with a raw silk coat lined in the matching print. Her colors were warm and natural, with chamois paired with peach, coral with beige, rust with lime yellow. Prices ranged from $125 for a three-piece suit to $245 for a dress and coat costume.

This Vera Maxwell dress was formal enough for a summer dance yet made along simple, sundress lines from the rather humble fabric cotton eyelet.

MONTE-SANO & PRUZAN

Jacques Tiffeau was the primary designer, between 1952 and 1958, at Monte-Sano, which became Monte-Sano & Pruzan during the 1950s. Besides daytime coats and suits, the company also made evening coats, considered necessary items during the 1950s, and suits that were more like two-piece dresses. No single silhouette prevailed; coats were available in shapes that included swing, barrel, princess, coachman, and even a circle style with a dipping hem and high half-belt in back. Interesting suit looks included belted and boxy jacketed suits; one suit of 1959 had an oversize double-breasted blazer with short sleeves paired with a straight, just-below-the-knee-length skirt.

CARRIE MUNN

Throughout the 1950s Carrie Munn remained faithful to her favorite full-skirted, narrow-waisted silhouette. In the early part of the decade she was known for her decorated circle skirts, in felt, quilted materials, and corduroy, which were trimmed with passementerie, tassels, embroideries, or appliqué, and with these she advocated wearing simple jersey tops. Her suits had full, petticoat-widened skirts as well, and were decorated with grosgrain, braid, and bullion. Her prices started at $125 and went higher for custom-made designs. In the February 2, 1952, issue of the *New Yorker* Lois Long summed up her clothes as being "far too pert for real ingénues."

This casual evening costume, designed in 1953 by Carrie Munn, a New York designer who operated out of her own store, was named Magic Carpet and featured an asymmetric neckline and a flowery quilted skirt embroidered with sequins. Typically early-1950s accessories included the satin opera pumps and the rhinestone earrings, choker, and bracelets.

NORMAN NORELL

In the March 21, 1953, issue of the *New Yorker*, Lois Long credited Norell with being "the fustest with lines that will later show up with Paris labels." First there was his 1950 chemise dress, absolutely straight, with no seams bifurcating it anywhere, which

This Clare Potter afternoon dress of carnation-printed cotton broadcloth was photographed in 1953 for a special feature in Vogue *celebrating (in a tongue-in-chic manner) psychoanalysis. The copy directed that the best way to alter one's ego was to don a print frock. Marcel Vertès painted the backgrounds. Photograph: Horst. Courtesy* Vogue

he showed on mannequins wearing flattening bras. In 1951 he designed narrow dresses nipped in at the waist with flared, abbreviated spencer jackets, à la 1805. Then there was his 1952 Norfolk-jacketed suit with a low hip belt, and his equally straight 1955 pea-jacket suit. Also in 1955 he offered Empire-waisted evening dresses, and in 1958 he designed a dress described as a parachute chemise, which featured a high-waisted yet straight front and a bubble back.

Throughout the 1950s Norell honed his skill at combining day and evening elements. He showed lavishly full-skirted shirtwaist dresses in watered silk, or lace, or jersey combined with organdy. He paired satin-collared tweed jackets with satin ball gowns and made trench coats out of silk. He placed white collars and cuffs on daytime shirtwaists as well as taffeta evening dresses, and he also continued to design strict, décolleté dresses in various solid-colored wools.

He was famous for his sequined dresses, which, with their slithery, skinny silhouettes, earned the name mermaid dresses by 1952. And he was also capable of stepping out of a purely sophisticated mode, making full-skirted summer dresses in sprigged cotton with aprons, pantaloons, and even sailor collars.

MOLLIE PARNIS

Mollie Parnis's most famous customer during the 1950s was Mamie Eisenhower, and both made headlines in 1955 when the First Lady, dressed in a Mollie Parnis green and blue silk taffeta dress for a reception, shook hands with a woman in the receiving line wearing the exact same model. Mollie Parnis's two most prevalent looks during the 1950s were extremely full-skirted shirtwaist day and afternoon dresses and suits with straight skirts and short, boxy jackets. One of her competitors in the ladylike, moderately priced dress business was her sister Jerry Parnis, who also ran a wholesale house. A third sister, Peggy Parnis, designed lingerie for a company called Chevette.

GRETA PLATTRY

During the 1950s Greta Plattry was one of the New York ready-to-wear designers working in the same mold as Claire McCardell, Tina Leser, and Clare Potter, providing women of all ages with young and extremely inexpensive (at most $40) day clothes and sportswear. Her pet look was hand-knitted cardigans combined with cotton summer dresses or with full, unpressed pleated skirts for casual turnouts, but she also designed all kinds of sundresses, dressmaker bathing suits, cover-ups, playsuits, and pants and halter-top ensembles. She began designing in the 1940s, retired in 1960, and came out of retirement in 1966 to prepare special country and casual clothes for a division of Teal Traina.

CLARE POTTER

Clare Potter's 1950s designs were dressier than they had been previously, with evening separates, tailored day dresses, and casual suits taking the place of active sportswear. She was fond of materials like shantung and heavy linen, most often using them and other materials solid rather than patterned, adding homespun decorations such as ball fringe or braid. She continued designing into the early 1960s, when she founded a wholesale company in Nyack, New York.

BEN REIG

Omar Kiam continued to design for Ben Reig in the 1950s, stopping shortly before his death in 1954. His 1950 and 1951 designs included full-skirted suit-dresses, short evening dresses, and fitted suits and sheaths. Typically, he enlivened garments with a single striking detail, as in a smoke-ring scarf of fur shown with a tweed suit, a deep hem flounce on an otherwise narrow dress, or a band of horsehair that both acts as stiffening on a sheer overskirt and plays two forms of transparency against each other. The September 11, 1950, *Life* magazine described his work as one of "expensive elegance."

NETTIE ROSENSTEIN

The predominant silhouette at Nettie Rosenstein throughout the 1950s was full skirted and tiny waisted, which she and her sister-in-law Eva Rosencrans used for ball gowns, shirtwaists in evening fabrics, day dresses, and suits. Most of the ball gowns were accompanied by coordinating cloaks, stoles, and jackets trimmed with embroidery, beading, or fur.

Nettie Rosenstein had cultivated such excellent relationships with the great European fabric houses that they made exclusive materials for her, including such innovative fabrics as a cotton bunched and stitched to look three-dimensional, shantung organdy, and taffeta gauze. Lace, a favorite fabric, went on the sheer bodices of cocktail dresses or made up whole ball gowns. In 1957 Nettie Rosenstein made a rare foray into sportswear, with maillots made out of Lastex. She withdrew from the dress business in 1961 in order to concentrate on pocketbooks and other accessories, and Eva Rosencrans went to design for Ben Reig.

SCAASI

Scaasi ready-to-wear designs began to crop up in the fashion magazines in the mid-1950s, when he was still working as a freelance designer before starting his own company in 1956. Born Arnold Isaacs in Montreal in the early 1930s, he studied design in Canada and Paris before working as an apprentice at the house of Paquin. He moved to New York in 1951 and worked for just over two years with Charles James. When he began on his own, he used a reversed version of his last name.

Scaasi's early forte was evening clothes, which cost around $495 for a single dress. Both bold and lavish, evening dresses were made with dramatic, sweeping skirts and decorative tabletop necklines in fabrics like chiffon, brocade, slipper satin, and velvet. Rarely were any of his clothes trimmed, relying instead on cut and fabric for decoration. Patterned materials were large-scale, whether floral or abstract. A Scaasi specialty was matching evening coats, cut like floor-length cardigans and lined in the same fabric as the dress underneath. A particularly effective costume was his 1957 evening gown of white silk satin paired with a camel-hair long coat lined in the same satin.

In 1958 he showed a polka-dotted silk evening dress with a bubble hem ending just at the top of the knee. Although shorter

This late-1950s suit by Scaasi, with its sculpted cutaway jacket and reed-slim skirt, reveals the influence of Charles James, with whom Scaasi had apprenticed before starting out on his own.

skirts had been creeping into fashion for almost a decade via sports clothes and teenagers' wardrobes, this was the first example—not just in New York but anywhere—of a knee-baring formal evening dress.

CAROLYN SCHNURER

Although Carolyn Schnurer designed for the inexpensive mass market (at her peak, annual volume was $7 million a year, the average price for a dress around $30), she was capable of great innovation and quality. She even moonlighted, anonymously, as an evening dress designer for one of the best New York custom houses. Her 1950s designs for her own label included sundresses and summer party dresses in prints borrowed from French provincial cottons or other sources inspired by her travels and such casual winter evening looks as a sleeveless gray wool sheath dress that could be dressed up with rhinestones and fur and an ensemble of herringbone circle skirt lined in taffeta paired with a strapless, knitted wool tube top and matching cardigan. When she divorced her husband (and business partner) in the late 1950s, she quit fashion design and became a consultant, first for the fabric company J. P. Stevens and later for a fashion executive placement agency.

ADELE SIMPSON

Adele Simpson's specialties during the 1950s were dark, dressed-up cotton clothes for summer in town and dress and jacket ensembles for day, as well as for after-five. Her most formal clothes were short, softly draped evening dresses in chiffon, although by the end of the decade she was making long evening clothes as well. An ad of 1951 described her typical silhouette as having "a well defined waist and concave curved diaphragm." Except for the occasional boxy or swing-shaped jacket, most of Simpson's designs celebrated the curvy figure. Simpson was capable of using unusual materials, as in white denim for the cape jacket of a 1950 black linen summer dress, or velvet as a summer cover-up for a gingham dress, but her favorite materials were simply pretty ones: cottons, some of which were exclusive to her from the American firm Galey & Lord, chiffon, and silk tussah taffeta. By the end of the decade she was signing her name to costume jewelry as well as to clothes.

SOPHIE OF SAKS

During the 1950s Sophie of Saks designed ready-to-wear, known as Sophie Originals, which sold exclusively at Saks Fifth Avenue in the $100 to $500 range; custom clothes for the Salon Moderne, which carried the department label rather than her own name; furs; and, beginning in 1955, custom wedding dresses. For daytime her clothes were feminine; many of her suits were made in silk with matching blouses and jacket linings and might feature dressmaker details, such as curved patch pockets mirroring curved seams. Afternoon dresses as well as evening gowns might have a very wide oval neckline, often executed in a sheer material, a favorite of Sophie's. Although she made many full-skirted, narrow-waisted dresses, she also experimented with various other silhouettes, notably a princess line, which might use a bolero or other high-waisted effect. Sophie liked to look at museum cos-

tume collections for inspiration, and her new designs reflected the flavor of a period from the past without being theatrical, as in her 1955 line of narrow evening dresses inspired by but not aping those worn in the 1910s.

PAULINE TRIGÈRE

In the September 22, 1951, issue of the *New Yorker*, Lois Long wrote, "The utter femininity of Paulinè Trigère's graceful any-time-of-day-length dress suggests the Vionnet of old." Although Trigère's clothes were not always compared to those of Vionnet, they were often described in terms of sewing technique involved. Trigère was known by 1951 as a master of the princess cut, for dresses that had no obvious seams or gores, for clothes made with tucks rather than darts for shape, and for skirts eased out by means of widening panels rather than gathering.

A Trigère specialty was wool for evening. From it she fashioned a halter dress suspended from a gold metal neckband; a stark black dinner suit with leg-of-mutton sleeves; floor-length dramatic dresses with cutaway necklines; and, in 1959, a short, strapless columnar black dress with a single panel descending to the floor. Throughout the 1950s she favored the sheath silhouette with a flared below-the-knee trumpet skirt, which she made in what she called "intermission length," about ten inches from the floor. Another leitmotif was tunics; these were found in flared coats held out over narrow skirts, in evening dresses with cutaway overskirts, and in wool day dresses. Trigère's prices in the 1950s climbed as high as $315.

Designed by Eva Rosencrans for Nettie Rosenstein's 1958–59 resort collection, this cocktail or short evening dress, of silk surah printed in green and gold in a blurry floral pattern, was made with a butterfly bodice over a slim skirt gathered into a back panel and accessorized by a Nettie Rosenstein necklace. The dress retailed for about $185.

Pauline Trigère's skill with the scissors is evident in this black poult-de-soie short evening dress from her 1959 Collage collection.

Hannah Troy, a ready-to-wear designer, was responsible for this late-1950s date dress, made of floral printed ottoman with a wide cowl neckline, cap sleeves, and full skirt, which sold for the moderate price of $90. Photographed at the Brooklyn Botanic Garden, the dress was accessorized by a Marvella necklace and Fiorentina pumps.

HANNAH TROY

Although Hannah Troy began her business in 1937, it was not until the early 1950s that her work appeared regularly in the fashion magazines. She was known for her adaptations rather than original designs, but the couturiers whose models she bought to copy were Italian rather than French. So supportive was she of the fledgling Italian fashion industry that the country honored her with its Order of Merit in 1954.

Being small herself, she made clothes for women under 5'4" in both regular and petite sizes, working in the categories of formal evening and day wear. Her short evening dresses, little black dresses, daytime shirtwaists and sheaths, and day and theater suits had minimal decoration, except for a bow or two, and small-scale patterns, most often checks or stripes. Ready-to-wear, they ranged in price from around $50 to $250. During the late 1950s her designer was George Samen, and in the 1960s the clothes were designed by Murray Neiman.

VALENTINA

Valentina was known for couture clothes that managed to look effortless in spite of all the careful workmanship and wonderful materials. In 1951 *Vogue* opined in its February 1 issue that Valentina never "makes a thing that isn't as timeless as a pair of kid gloves."

Valentina's suits were soft, with circular skirts and unfitted but not boxy jackets. She often paired wool jersey blouses with skirts and jackets of grosgrain, raw silk, or pongee. She made evening wraps out of horse-blanket wool and lined her wool clothes with failles and taffetas. She liked ensembles or even dresses that were convertible; she made short and long ball gowns with removable aprons or trained overskirts and showed traveling costumes that, upon arrival in a resort, could be peeled down to shorts and shirt by taking off the coat and skirt. In 1950 she brought out a perfume called My Own. In 1957 she closed her couture house, coming out of retirement in 1964 to costume Margaret Leighton as an aging actress in the play *The Chinese Prime Minister*, providing her with mouth-watering clothes, including silk or wool jersey at-home dresses and a silk ottoman traveling suit worn with a chin-tied hat, always one of her favorite looks.

B. H. WRAGGE

During the 1950s Sydney Wragge of B. H. Wragge designed less for a college-age client and more for a sophisticated wife; his advertisements began to feature the caption "D.E.'s (or C.R.'s or J.G.'s) wife wears B.H. Wragge." Wragge's clothes suited the town more than the country, although they had the salt-air tinge of waterside resorts. Linen was a favorite fabric, and he used it, beginning in 1950, for skinny sheath dresses, sometimes paired with natural pongee coats. As early as 1950 he showed an absolutely straight dress, in gray flannel, buttoning down the front with rhinestones, that could be worn belted, and in 1955 he designed an unfitted linen dress that presaged not only the 1957 sack dress but also the 1960s chemise dress. He produced perfectly cut pants and showed them with sleeveless jersey tops or hand-knitted, cowl-necked sweaters, and he had a special way with shorts, particularly as parts of ensembles. In 1956 he designed a white linen jacket and shorts, with a row of medals parading across the left breast, and in 1957 he made a shorts suit with cropped cardigan jacket in beige and gray checked silk woven with gold Lurex. His prices during the 1950s stayed as low as $9 but climbed as high as $69.95.

BEN ZUCKERMAN

In 1950 Ben Zuckerman started his own company, after having previously been involved as a partner in the firms Zuckerman & Kraus and Zuckerman & Hoffman. He had immigrated to New York as a child from Romania and began working in the garment industry as a teenager. During the 1950s he won three Coty awards, landing him in the Hall of Fame.

Ben Zuckerman's specialty was coats and suits, made for day in bright and interestingly textured woolens with sculptural shapes and highlighted seams and for evening with glittery buttons and linings to match his silk or lamé blouses and dresses. The clothes sold for $150 to $300. At the beginning of the 1950s his suits were extremely curvy, although paired with slim skirts, and made with rounded lapels, cutaway oval hems on jackets, and arc closures. As the decade progressed, his shapes grew away from the body; he showed flared seven-eighths-length coats with straight skirts, coats with semifitted fronts and unfitted backs, and dresses with boxy jackets.

B. H. Wragge designed this sporty checkerboard dress with dolman sleeves, slightly blouson bodice, and narrow skirt in 1959. The Library, Fashion Institute of Technology, New York

Throughout the 1950s scarves and stoles were important accessories. This 1959 wool dress by B. H. Wragge gained versatility from its stole, which could be arranged in different ways with different jewelry. The Library, Fashion Institute of Technology, New York

Ben Zuckerman, a ready-to-wear manufacturer of coats and suits, was known for his superb and exacting cut, as shown in this 1958 geranium tweed with a sculptural shape. Photograph: Louise Dahl Wolfe. Courtesy the Edward C. Blum Design Laboratory, Fashion Institute of Technology, New York, and Harper's Bazaar

It was never truer that there is power in numbers than in the 1960s, when, by the end of the decade, fully a third of the American population was under voting age yet managed to make its voice heard. It was an unsettling time in which to grow up: American pride in its accomplishment at landing a man on the moon was tempered by the lingering shock of the assassinations of John F. Kennedy, Martin Luther King, Jr., and Robert Kennedy. Race riots had shaken the country, and the Vietnam War kept escalating. For a generation that had started kindergarten in schools equipped with fallout shelters in the event of nuclear attack, the violence in the world was terrifying. Hundreds of thousands strong, the young marched for peace, demonstrated for racial equality, conducted sit-ins, communed at music festivals. They united to rebel against their parents' generation, the one that had gotten the world into such a sorry state.

The operative word for the entire ten years, and into the next decade, was *youth*. The influence of this huge sector of the population was inescapable, and as the youths themselves changed, so did the meanings associated with the word. For the first part of the decade *youth* implied—at least in the world of fashion—freshness, charm, simplicity, and ease. These associations continued to hold, although, as the decade wore on, the idea of youth became ever more mock innocent as it simultaneously began to signify being hip, up to or ahead of the moment, in, with-it. By the late 1960s it meant antiestablishment, rebellious, experimental, even weird.

Reigning over the first youthful phase was the First Lady, Jacqueline Kennedy. She wielded as powerful and widespread an influence over fashion as had the Gibson Girl, and for much the same reasons: she was beautiful, charismatic, and young, and her style was fairly simple and therefore easy to copy.

Jackie Kennedy managed to combine a nonstuffy spirit with ladylike elegance. Her clothes, whether made by Oleg Cassini, her main costumer, Chez Ninon, Gustave Tassell, or Donald Brooks, shared certain characteristics. Most of her dresses, for both day and evening, were sleeveless and had no defined waistline. Her dresses, coats, and suits came not in patterns but in solid colors, clear tones of apricot, candy pink, sky blue, grass green, yellow, beige, white, or cream. Her clothes rarely featured much detail; a dress was usually cut with an overblouse, a suit had a boxy jacket, and buttons, the most frequent ornaments, were large and made to match the dress.

She kept her accessories to a minimum. She wore little jewelry—a necklace, perhaps of pearls, or a brooch and earrings. White gloves, in varying lengths, accompanied every ensemble, and she carried a small envelope pocketbook covered in fabric to match her clothes. She favored low-heeled, plain shoes. Following her example, American women began to go hatless, wearing instead little nonhat items such as fabric-covered hair bands and bows at the back of the head as well as her signature pillboxes. Women also stopped putting their hair up in pin curls and, instead, rolled it on big curlers and teased or back-combed it for volume.

The First Lady's appearance was so simple and pared down that it looked young, and women greeted it as liberating, since it released them from the exaggerated femininity of the 1950s, especially the unrelenting and uncomfortable fit. Females of all ages took to wearing her kind of shift dresses and simple accessories, and in no time at all the look that had first appeared as refreshingly young had become the mainstay of the establishment.

On May 10, 1963, Bill Cunningham, writing a column for *Women's Wear Daily*, reported on what socialites were wearing in New York: "Here is the code: pastel suit—unbuttoned—chain-handled tiny alligator bag—gold bracelets—natural colored gloves—two strand necklaces—no hat—low-heeled shoes and no fur after March 1. If you don't stick to this code, you're definitely O U T." This was the style associated with women who dressed at Mainbocher or wore Norell, and within a few years it was already beginning to be perceived as boring or conservative. Women continued to dress simply for day, but they began to be much more elaborate and experimental for evening.

Traditionally, women enter into a phase of more ornate style after they have been married for a while and their families are complete. At that time, they usually have more money to spend on themselves, as their husbands are beginning to reach the top of the ladder in their business or profession, and their post-pregnancy figures have stabilized. They seek to offset the creeping appearance of crow's-feet and gray hairs by wearing more expensive clothes, bigger jewels, and flattering furs. And so in the 1960s the parents of the baby-boom generation dressed up more, bound for much more formal parties than those they had attended in the barbecue 1950s.

Chief among the formal evening events were charity balls, which proliferated madly during the 1960s, and, because parties for a good cause are open to anyone proven adept at check writing, the boundaries of society expanded and its doings burgeoned. The number of gossip columns multiplied in order to report on all the action, and the relationship among fashion, status, and celebrity grew so close that they began to merge. All you had to do to get invited to the party was offer to underwrite it; all you had to do to get your name in one of the columns was wear something newsworthy.

By 1964 evening clothes sported beads, glitter, deep décolletés, feathers, and sumptuous materials. The *maquillage* included false eyelashes and intricate eye makeup; the hair, styled especially for night, was pinned up with false braids and looped hairpieces and adorned with jewels and feathers. No one seemed to mind if the price of her new dress was mentioned in the press, so Eugenia Sheppard of the *New York Herald Tribune* or Suzy of the *New York Journal-American* or Ruth Preston of the *New York Post* described each new notable five-thousand-dollar evening coat, beaded dresses so laden with jewels that they were called floor-length tiaras, and new necklaces down to every last stone.

Fashion was definitely becoming more outrageous, which could take the form of fantasy materials and details or the display of more and more skin. Already in 1964 women wore see-through blouses to openings, and some of the three thousand women who bought Rudi Gernreich's topless bathing suit must have worn it. Skirts were also on the rise. In Paris, Courrèges gave his imprimatur to the mini, showing it for evening sewn with sequins and paired with short boots. Actually, above-the-knee-length skirts had already been around. Scaasi showed a knee-baring evening dress as early as 1958, and the

Although Hattie Carnegie had died, her luxurious specialty shop kept going, purveying the same kind of formal, elegant clothes, like this ice blue ball gown overlaid with black lace apron panels, as it had when she was alive. The tumultuous 1960s proved disastrous for old-line custom dressmaking establishments; many, like Carnegie, closed by the end of the decade. The Brooklyn Museum Library Collection, New York

American fashion magazines like *Seventeen* and *Mademoiselle* aimed specifically at teenagers had presented many skirts of shorter lengths in the early 1960s. American women had gotten used to short summer skirts during the 1950s, offered by both Claire McCardell and Norell, and in the early 1960s had worn the little cotton shifts made by the highly successful Lilly Pulitzer of Palm Beach with bare, suntanned legs. Knees are much in evidence in many early-1960s photographs of women in their play clothes.

The short skirt wasn't merely a hem length, it was a silhouette, characterized by a body-skimming fit with no accent on breasts, waist, or hips, and it was incorporated into all three of the mid-1960s directions in fashion. It was used for the simple, grown-up-but-youthful conservative style, for the mock-innocent baby-doll look, and for the wacky and with-it boutique designs.

In the first category, the short shift dress, along with coat and dress ensembles and suits, was made in heavy materials like cotton brocade, double-knit wools, two fabrics bonded together. For evening these dresses might be beaded all over or just around the neck in a necklace effect. Both day and evening looks employed simple lines, usually enlivened by sculptural seam construction, which might be curved or geometric. Clothes such as these, designed by Adele Simpson, Ben Zuckerman, Harvey Berin, Shannon Rodgers for Jerry Silverman, Larry Aldrich, Malcolm Starr, and Mollie Parnis, were accessorized with bold costume jewelry, made in the manner of Kenneth Jay Lane (a costume jewelry designer who often copied the jewelry worn by famous people) after David Webb (the hottest designer of precious jewelry in the 1960s): large brooches in Maltese or domed shapes and animalier bracelets and earrings in enameled metals and set with cabochon sham turquoise, coral, or amethysts amid rhinestones. With the decline of hats, hair had become an accessory, teased and lacquered into a bouffant shape if short or worn in a lion's mane if long.

The baby-doll look was quite literal: it featured very short skirts, high waistlines, puffed sleeves, Peter Pan collars, jumper or apron effects, lots of laces and ruffles, and sometimes even bloomers. Such styles, designed by Geoffrey Beene, Chester Weinberg, and Bill Blass, were accessorized by elaborate doe-eye makeup, spiky eyelashes, rosy cheeks, and pale, frosted lips, with hair worn in ringlets around the face. Legs were clad in lacy, pale stockings and feet in Mary Jane shoes. Jewelry might include a ribbon worn as a choker.

Funky, with-it clothes, influenced by Op art and Pop art, began to appear in 1961, when Junior Sophisticates showed a Mondrian-print shift dress (four years before Yves Saint Laurent presented his). Companies like Bandbox Junior Petites or Crazy Horse made fifteen-dollar dresses printed with *trompe-l'oeil* checked vests, pocket watches, or neckties and hip-hugger belts. Prints, a major characteristic of this type of clothes, were freewheeling, kaleidoscopic, and psychedelic. Patterns, whether geometric or swirling florals, tended to be linear or hard-edged, outlined with black. Accessories for these clothes included chain belts, wide-strapped watches with humorous dials, little wire-rimmed granny glasses, and jewelry made out of Lucite or other plastic. Women wore stockings in patterns to match the dress or of fishnet or grid mesh and low-heeled shoes in brightly colored patent leather with ornaments of tortoiseshell or Lucite at the squared toe. There were also boots of every description, ranging in height from ankle-grazing to thigh-high and

A popular style during the early 1960s, perhaps because it was worn so often by Jackie Kennedy, was the overblouse dress. This one, offered by ready-to-wear designer Mollie Parnis in 1960, was made of cherry red and gold acetate and Orlon brocade and sold for $185. Vendome made the costume jewelry earrings. Photograph: Leobruno-Bodi. Courtesy Vogue

205

B. H. Wragge designed this sporty version of the two-piece overblouse dress in 1964–65. By this time, both hairstyles and hats—when they were worn, which was increasingly infrequent—had grown in size. The Library, Fashion Institute of Technology, New York

Op and Pop art both influenced fashion, as well as the way clothes were presented and displayed. This 1960s window at Saks Fifth Avenue featured a ladylike, boxy jacketed suit from Originala, one of the better Seventh Avenue coat and suit manufacturers, posed on an invisible turbaned mannequin against an Op art painting. The Library, Fashion Institute of Technology, New York

made of suede, calf, python, or fabric decorated with appliqué. The boutique patron parted her hair in the middle and wore it long, if necessary, ironing it to achieve the desired degree of straightness. She painted her eyes with black eyeliner, above and below the lid, sometimes adding a line of white above the eye, and painted on eyelashes below. Shimmery white, pale pink, and even blue lipstick made the lips recede and the eyes stand out even further.

Such kicky clothes came from the boutiques, which by 1966 had managed to depose once and for all the conviction that creativity in fashion filters down from the couture into ready-to-wear. Although the couture is sometimes described as a laboratory for fashion, 1960s boutiques were actual laboratories. These hole-in-the-wall shops functioned as hangouts, and ideas sprang from the air as the owner-designers sat around chatting with friends. While they sold some inexpensive ready-to-wear from the Seventh Avenue firms that specialized in misses' (teenagers') sizes and styles, much of the stock was made in-house, using such techniques as rudimentary sewing, hand-painting, tie-dyeing, batik, lacing together leathers with thongs, and applying studs and grommets, macramé, crochet, and glue-on appliqué.

Whereas fashion magazines had previously served to instruct their readers in the nuances of propriety, during the 1960s they switched to urging their readers to keep up to date, to lose their inhibitions, and to be experimental. *Vogue*, as well as other periodicals, allotted pages each month or fortnight to coverage of the boutique scene, both in New York and Los Angeles as well as in London, Paris, and Rome. With Diana Vreeland at the helm, *Vogue* itself operated somewhat as a boutique. Under her direction such stylists and designers as Giorgio di Sant' Angelo created special makeup and body paint, hairstyles, clothing, body covering, and jewelry and accessories effects, usually for a particular photo shoot, which meant they didn't actually exist for readers to purchase. However, these creative concoctions mirrored the spirit and the do-it-yourself aspect of the boutiques, and as such they inspired designers both in ready-to-wear and in the couture. In fact, 1960s fashions more probably emanated from the boutique scene than from the street.

In New York, boutiques were scattered around the Fifties and Sixties between Second and Sixth avenues, as well as throughout Greenwich Village. In a May 1967 article for *Harper's Bazaar*, Thomas Isbell divided boutiques into four categories according to décor: those with architectural space-age, hard-edged surfaces and blinking lights; those with nostalgic Victorian and Edwardian stained glass, bead curtains, and curlicue furniture enameled in bright colors; those with India bedspreads on the walls, incised brass tray tables, and hookahs; and those that combined all three styles.

At boutiques like Paraphernalia, Tiger Morse's Teeny Weeny, Serendipity, Splendiferous, and Abracadabra, fashions could appear in a twinkling of an eye. The semiannual collections, or clothes made according to season, couldn't keep up with the pace established by the little shops, where new clothes showed up all the time. Department stores, which, after all, were based on the idea of groupings of boutiques, or departments, strove to make their own boutiques more up to the moment. Bergdorf Goodman started its Bigi department, aimed at young customers, and also gave its milliner Halston his own boutique for the young-minded couture client. Bonwit Teller established its S'fari shop, which sold imported clothes as well as the more interesting American designs by such new talents as Giorgio di Sant' Angelo.

For those customers who didn't desire the latest thing, there was always Peck & Peck and Best & Co., two stores that did very well catering to a conservative clientele.

Boutique fashions included dresses and pants for men made out of strips of plastic set with battery-operated lights; skirts fashioned from counterfeit dollar bills; do-it-yourself dresses of plastic and metal rings; paper and Mylar minis, jumpsuits, and underwear. Boutique sportswear ran to ribbed T-shirts called poorboys, batik or tie-dyed bikinis, clothes made out of leather or suede sewn together with thongs and usually fringed, and low-slung, flared-leg pants. Bell-bottoms, first described by *Vogue* in 1965 as *"patte d'éléphant"* pants, featured a leg tightly fitted at the thigh and flaring below the knee. By the end of the decade this look had entered general circulation in the form of jeans made accordingly.

Other offerings included glittery nail polish, body makeup, plastic decals for faces, legs, and midriffs, as well as accessories for interiors: psychedelic posters, preferably for black light, beanbag chairs, molded plastic stacking

Boutiques, where new fashions showed up almost every day, enlivened 1960s fashion. The best known was Paraphernalia, which opened in New York in 1965 and within a year had branches all over the country. Among its in-house designers was Betsey Johnson, shown here in 1967 with model Twiggy, the 1960s ideal of beauty, both wearing Betsey Johnson designs. Photograph: Howell Conant. Courtesy Life *Magazine*

chairs and Parsons tables in jelly-bean colors, clear plastic blow-up chairs and pillows, paper flowers, and soda bottles that had been heat-stretched into distorted shapes. These stores were patronized not only by teenagers but also by socialites who had fallen under the spell of throwaway chic—buying something for twenty dollars as a lark and tossing it out when the next fad came along.

By 1968 the groovy set had discovered new places to shop: antique clothing stores, army-navy outlets, and ethnic emporiums. At antique stores, women hunted for fringed shawls, lacy blouses, long, velvet coats and dresses from the 1930s; men for ornate old military jackets, antique vests, frock coats to wear with jeans. Army-navy stores became the source for jeans, work shirts, and jeans jackets that might then be personalized with patchwork, embroidery, metal studs. Ethnic stores provided all kinds of gently priced antiestablishment looks like crinkly tie-dyed tunic shirts, Indian block-printed or mirror-embroidered clothes, Mexican wedding dresses and fringed shawls, and such jewelry as trade-bead necklaces, elephant's-hair bracelets, and silvery white metal necklaces and rings hung with miniature bells.

All of these types of stores were enormously influential, both in establishing a preference for men and women assembling their own individual eclectic looks and in furnishing Seventh Avenue with ideas. Donald Brooks and other designers used black and white in gigantic stripes, chevrons, ziggurats, and checkerboards to enliven otherwise simple dresses and coats. To them, the more graphic a pattern, the better it was, and windowpane plaids, spiraling circles, and positive-negative effects often showed up in their work. Bill Blass and Geoffrey Beene both worked with zingy pinstripes for gangster turnouts. Even the most conservative designers adapted the look of peasant blouses, dirndl skirts, bolero vests, and fringed shawls, and they put them together in evening ensembles featuring several different glittering brocades, paisley silks, or eye-popping prints. Ethnic inspirations also included variations on the forms of caftans, burnooses, and dhoti pants, which are wrapped like a diaper but hang low between the legs, with slits for the feet.

The long skirt first showed up in 1965, in one of Chester Weinberg's collections. Next came Jacques Tiffeau's 1966 version, and then Galanos's below-the-knee-length dresses of 1967. By 1968 the midi dress was featured in almost every collection. With its fitted bodice, long sleeves, and full skirt ending just below the knee, it was an extension of both the peasant-ethnic and the baby-doll styles. Boutiques also prompted designers to experiment with culottes, knickers, and other pants variations, and they influenced fur design, inspiring the concept of fun furs—dresses and even jumpsuits made from mink or sable; mini coats in bright colors of patchwork; and coats in which the skins were used horizontally in contrasting shades.

The freedom of expression encouraged by the idea that anything goes went hand in hand with the actual freedom of the clothes themselves in how they felt and were worn. Although seminudity or nudity captured a good deal of attention, breast-baring styles were nowhere near as freeing as the more prosaic innovations of the "no-bra" bra and pantyhose. Rudi Gernreich introduced his bra in 1964, which was designed not to mold the breasts into a specific shape but merely to cover them comfortably; he was also instrumental in developing tights into pantyhose. In the space of a few years, women went from wearing uplift bras, girdles (even thin women, since nice girls didn't jiggle), stockings, ever more difficult to cope with as hemlines rose, slips, and, of course, underpants, to wearing light-as-air bras and bikini underwear, plus the occasional half-slip. They didn't need underwear that imposed a shape upon them, since clothes skimmed the body. As tights evolved into pantyhose, available in meshes as sheer as stockings as well as in enticing lace patterns, grids, or printed designs, they also became more affordable, and women stopped worrying about having to throw them away when a single leg was snagged or had a run. Pantyhose and, to a lesser extent, bodystockings, along with the stretchy little bras, guaranteed that a woman in a shift dress and flat shoes was not encumbered in any way. Whether she was dancing the watusi or going to work, her clothes freed her.

Eyelet ruffles decorate this Chester Weinberg 1969–70 midi version of the baby-doll look. The skirt was made of lavender printed polished cotton; the "pearl"-centered earrings and ring were designed by Robert Originals and the ankle-strap shoes by David Evins.

ADOLFO

Adolfo, who had been the milliner at Emme during the 1950s, opened his own salon at 22 East Fifty-sixth Street in 1962. Having brushed up on dressmaking techniques with a fellow Cuban designer, Anna Maria Berrero, who herself had learned by working in Paris, Adolfo began showing clothes of his own design accompanied by his hats. At first he kept his clothes simple to offset the decorative nature of his millinery: an early offering was his 1962 off-white, suede sheath dress with a low waist. As the 1960s progressed and voluminous hairstyles obviated the need for hats, Adolfo's clothes became more elaborate and his hats simpler. His most popular hats for the period were his oversize fur berets and his fairly mannish classic straw fedoras. His late-sixties fashion designs included Renaissance-inspired concoctions for his special client Gloria Vanderbilt Cooper, harem-pant evening and at-home turnouts, opulent peasant looks consisting of brocade dirndls, vests, and bishop-sleeved blouses, and the first of his more casual knitted ensembles for day.

ADRI

Adrienne Steckling, born in Saint Joseph, Missouri, educated at the Washington University School of Fine Arts, Saint Louis, and at Parsons School of Design, New York, worked as a designer for B. H. Wragge from 1960 to 1967 before designing for her own division, Clothes Circuit, at Anne Fogarty, Inc. Her name also appeared in the late 1960s as Adri for Collector's Items. She worked most often in various forms of natural and synthetic mixtures of jersey, creating extremely simple and fluid designs; her short little dresses tended to be soft, with V necks, wrapped fronts, and high waists, and in solid colors.

LARRY ALDRICH

By 1968 Marie McCarthy's name was appearing in the company's ads along with that of Larry Aldrich. Aldrich designs for the period continued to be practical, as in dinner dresses with jackets that looked like suits with floor-length hems, often made of daytime materials such as wool or wool jersey combined with glittery trims, and sequined skirts or tops. By 1966 the company was well known for its all-beaded mini dresses. It also produced some softer evening looks, using such fabrics as chiffon with ruffled necklines or drawstring peasant-blouse necklines. Typically, Aldrich's designs absorbed current fashion without translating it literally. Two styles from 1969 that allude to the wildness of clothes for the end of the 1960s in a restrained way are a bare-midriff ensemble composed of separate black linen sleeveless top and matching short dirndl and a harem-pant ensemble with turtleneck top and full trousers of brightly printed Qiana designed by Julian Tomchin. In 1972 Aldrich disbanded his company to concentrate on the Aldrich Museum of Contemporary Art in Ridgefield, Connecticut, and to establish the Soho Center for Visual Artists in New York.

RONALD AMEY

Ronald Amey of Burke-Amey designed some of the most original clothes of the 1960s. Born in Arizona in 1932, he studied design for one semester at Chouinard in Los Angeles, worked in Los Angeles for a small fashion establishment, and then enlisted in the Air Force during the Korean War, serving as an electronics instructor. At a military base in New Mexico he began an informal fashion business with Joseph Burke, a fellow serviceman; their clientele consisted of the army base wives.

After his discharge, Amey moved to New York, where he briefly attended Parsons School of Design, then got himself hired at—and fired from—six different fashion companies. In 1959, at the age of twenty-seven, he founded Burke-Amey with Burke as a partner, at 16 West Fifty-seventh Street. At its height, Burke-Amey had forty employees and made all of its clothing on the premises, selling its garments from $130 to $1,200 in stores around the country.

In 1970 Amey bought out his partner and founded Ronald Amey, Inc. Like many top-of-the-line fashion businesses in the early 1970s, the new venture did not succeed. Prior to his death

Geoffrey Beene was adept at combining
the youthful baby-doll look with sophisticated tailoring and dramatic use of black
and white cotton cloqué. This side-col-
lared dress was designed in 1969.

As kids discovered at boutiques that specialized in Indian and Mexican imports,
ethnic clothes were exotically made, fun
to wear, and satisfactorily anti-establish-
ment. As designers soon caught on, peasant, gypsy, and various ethnic looks
abounded. This 1969 evening dress with
matching kerchief was designed by Geoffrey Beene in his signature braid-trimmed
style.

in 1986, Ronald Amey had been involved for three years in designing on a free-lance basis for Aurura Ruffolo, Inc.

The *New York Times* found Ronald Amey's first collection in
1959 too wild and innovative; at his second collection, it noted
that he seemed to have calmed down. But it was for his innovative and bold design that Amey became known, particularly for
his use of dramatic prints on which he often collaborated with
fabric designer Tzaims Luksus. Amey used interesting materials, including white lace embroidered with black raffia for the
bolero of an otherwise simple 1963 white silk evening dress; gigantic blanket-plaid wools for 1969 mini dresses; and, in the
early 1970s, appliqué or beading to create swirling motifs
against plain, fluid dresses. At a time when fairly stiff clothing
that got its sculptured effects from thick materials was in vogue,
Amey produced soft and flowing designs.

GEOFFREY BEENE

After working for Teal Traina as a designer, receiving credit on
the labels and in editorial copy, Geoffrey Beene started out on
his own in 1963. The new venture was an instant success, and
within a year Beene had won his first Coty Award as well as the

Neiman-Marcus fashion award.

Beene's designs, in keeping with the mood of the decade, were
more youthful than they had been for Harmay in the more wom-
anly 1950s. However, his look was more innocent and school-
girlish than rebelliously antiestablishment. His clothes fell primarily into three categories: very simple clothes, such as little
wool day dresses or floor-length jersey dinner dresses; sweet
high-waisted dresses and ensembles based on jumpers or vests
over blouses; and obviously witty looks, such as his all-
sequined, floor-length football jerseys, his gangster-moll pinstripes, or his dress decorated with the comic-strip character the
Little King. As he would in the 1980s, he worked with a variety
of hemlines, making daytime wool mini dresses or short sequined
evening dresses with feather hems; floor-length ball gowns or fluid dinner dresses; and below-the-knee-length looks as well, for
both day and evening.

HARVEY BERIN

During the 1960s, when most designers were experimenting with
all the newly developed synthetics and wilder- and wilder-look-
ing designs, Harvey Berin (by Karen Stark) remained loyal to

Oversize paillettes, a 1960s favorite, sewn to apricot chiffon composed this 1965 strapless, tubular evening dress by Donald Brooks.

sheer wools, laces, velvets, and various kinds of silks and to silhouettes modified from current trends, as befitted a company
whose clientele included past and present First Ladies Mamie
Eisenhower, Bess Truman and daughter Margaret, Pat Nixon,
Lady Bird Johnson and daughters Lynda Bird and Lucy Baines.
As Harvey Berin put it, his designs had to be acceptable to "Fifth
Avenue as well as Des Moines," and as such the company tended
to design for grown-up women whose lives required theater suits,
cocktail clothes, and dressy daytime ensembles. Berin preferred
the quality of Italian over Austrian crystals and rhinestones for
embroideries. Harvey Berin closed his business in 1970, la-
menting that competition from Hong Kong had changed Seventh
Avenue.

MR. BLACKWELL

Mr. Blackwell, of California, was a former child actor born in
Brooklyn who became well known primarily for his annual fashion critique, "The Worst-Dressed List," which displayed a fondness for diatribe. Ironically, Blackwell's own designs were on the
flashy side. His dresses, primarily for late day, were usually
black, enlivened by detailed leopard bodices and gigantic white
organdy sleeves. They retailed for $100 to $300. Blackwell often
appeared in his advertisements.

BILL BLASS

From the moment he joined Maurice Rentner, Bill Blass became
one of America's most popular designers. His clothes weren't ter-
ribly expensive, falling mostly in the $100 to $300 range, and,
while falling between conservative and wild, were hardly middle-
of-the-road. Blass designed suits, jacket and dress ensembles,
pantsuits, little day dresses, casual and dressier evening looks,
and bathing suits. His skirts rarely climbed high above the knee,
but when they did it was for evening rather than for day. In 1967,
the same year he took over the company, he began designing
clothes for men, which, like his women's fashions, reflected all
of the going novelties without slavishly aping them. Among his
first men's designs was a casual version of black tie, pairing a
brown velvet dinner jacket and black wool pants with a light
braid down the sides.

In 1965 Blass ran an ad picturing himself and a model, both
dressed in houndstooth-check suits (hers with a skirt), and the
caption, "Who needs Paris when you can steal from yourself?"
Many of his women's designs incorporated aspects of men's tailoring, notably the double-breasted, notched-lapel blazer, which
he often showed as a sleeveless bodice to a dress. Tailored, daytime effects were prominent for evening, as in his 1960 spaghet-
ti-strapped dress in black sheer wool, with glacé kid tie belt; his
1961 double-breasted, notched-lapel vest and long skirt interpreted in fluttery pink chiffon; his 1965 paillette-covered shirt
worn with narrow silk trousers; and his 1966 bright silver nylon
trench coat. Another specialty for evening was frothy short dresses in lace. Unlike most 1960s designers, Blass rarely used beads
or sequins; when he did, it was to achieve the effect of a glittery
fabric, with the sequins pavé instead of embroidered in a pattern. From 1960 on Blass designed his own particular versions of
unmatched suits, as in a turnout of camel-hair jacket, chestnut

*Many designers, including Jo Copeland, who offered this evening ensem-
ble of a heavy white silk coat over a black silk cocktail dress in 1968,
knew that their customers felt uncomfortable in extremely youthful fashions and therefore worked with hemlines that just grazed the top of the
knee.*

*Bill Blass designed this textured silk sheath dress with square armholes
and chain belt, a favorite 1960s accessory, in 1968.*

Anne Fogarty was fond of the Empire waistline combined with a low, curved neckline and short, puffed sleeves, and she used it often for evening dresses, as well as for this 1969 point d'esprit wedding dress, which sold for $160.

This romantic version of the 1968 midi dress was made in self-embroidered silk organza with a deep eyelet hem, emphasized waistline, and full bell sleeves by Wilson Folmar, a ready-to-wear designer who had formerly been associated with Jay-Thorpe.

velvet blouse with sleeves slightly longer than those of the jacket, and gray flannel skirt.

ANTHONY BLOTTA

Anthony Blotta's 1960s designs reflect the sculptural and somewhat rigid look of much of the decade's fashions as well as the increasingly casual air of the period. His dresses took the form of an overblouse and straight skirt, which might be made in charcoal wool; a T-shirt shape outlined with topstitching; or a chemise, blouson in the back, with bows at the shoulders, made of chiffon. Blotta died in 1971.

TOM BRIGANCE

Brigance continued to be one of the most important designers of bathing suits in the 1960s, producing designs that stood out because they did not depend on bareness for their interest. His two-piece suits might have striking, covered-up bodices, with asymmetric necklines and matching asymmetric cover-ups; maillots might have triangles cut out at the sides of the waist or softly draped halter necklines.

ELLEN BROOKE

Ellen Brooke worked for the Irish Export Board, acquainting herself with that country's native cottage industries and advising them on the possibilities of export, before starting her own fashion business, designing top-notch ready-to-wear in the late 1950s. Typical products of Ellen Brooke for Sportswear Couture included evening pajama ensembles with tunic tops and flaring pants and turnouts of vest, skirt, and blouse, which might be dressed up with a broadtail vest or a lacy jabot blouse.

DONALD BROOKS

Donald Brooks continued to design for Townley, winning his second Coty Award in 1963, until he opened his own company in 1965. During the decade he designed costumes for the theater, television, and the movies, winning a New York Drama Critics Award in 1963 for *No Strings* and gaining nominations for Oscars in costume design for *The Cardinal* in 1963, *The Third Day* in 1965, *Star!* in 1968, and *Darling Lili* in 1970.

Townley gave Donald Brooks the opportunity to create more

Rudi Gernreich collaborated with hosiery manufacturers and with Capezio shoes in order to present a total head-to-toe look. This giraffe-print costume of 1966 consisted of a stenciled calfskin seven-eighths-length coat, short matching skirt, printed turtleneck top, helmet, and Capezio tights and shoes. Photograph: Neal Barr. Courtesy Harper's Bazaar

elegant designs from higher quality fabrics than he had previously worked with, and he turned out evening clothes as well as dress and jacket or coat ensembles and other dressed-up daytime looks, all of which ranged in price from $200 to $300. It wasn't until he established his own label, however, that a true Donald Brooks signature emerged, characterized by very bold geometric or other patterns, striking, high-contrast colors, and interesting details, including uneven or handkerchief hems, dhoti-caftan combinations, and hoods on evening dresses. Typical creations were suits or dress and coat turnouts in heavy wool patterned with ziggurats, Op art squares and circles, pony skin amoebic shapes, or hand-span stripes used on the bias for diagonal and chevron looks as well as evening dresses made of wool embroidered with sequins or bugle beads in geometric designs. His costumes for *Star!*, a film biography of Gertrude Lawrence featuring Julie Andrews in the lead, spawned a special 1968 line of clothes that, like those in the film, borrowed elements of 1920s and 1930s fashion without slavishly imitating the period. Such elements included rhinestone embroideries, fringed chemise dresses, and a printed silk fabric made with an overscale plaid of blown-up Art Deco diamond bracelets. For 1969 he made hippie-inspired turnouts with peasant blouses, ruffled skirts and underskirts, and cummerbund sashes made in different printed fabrics as well as little black dresses and long black dresses sewn with ten-millimeter sham pearls.

BOB BUGNAND

A Parisian designer who worked in this country, Bob Bugnand designed ready-to-wear for a firm called Sam Friedlander. He also showed his custom clothes here, which were then made up in Paris, supposedly in only three weeks. A typical Bugnand design was an evening dress with a bodice resembling a sleeveless, double-breasted blazer, with notched rever buttoning in front; he specialized in the bead-encrusted evening look popular during the decade.

STEPHEN BURROWS

Stephen Burrows, who was born in Newark, New Jersey, in 1943, studied at the Philadelphia College of Art and at the Fashion Institute of Technology in New York. Designing first for Allen & Cole at 150 East Fifty-fourth Street and then for a boutique called O' that he opened with a friend from the Fashion Institute named Roz Rubinstein, he was one of the influential young free spirits of the late 1960s. Among his early designs were Native American– and/or cowboy-inspired unisex clothing made of suedes and leathers patched together with leather thongs and dripping with fringes. Stephen Burrows himself was photographed for *Vogue* in 1969 wearing calf-length pants, slave bracelets, and a jersey shirt under a jersey tunic, belted over the pants at the waist. He made his jersey designs for both men and women to fit like second skins, a harbinger of the narrow 1970s look, and he often used different fabrics sewn together in a kind of abstract patchwork, as in a jersey shirt with plaid jersey sleeves. In 1969 he became an in-house designer at Henri Bendel, where he had a boutique called Stephen Burrows' World.

BONNIE CASHIN

Bonnie Cashin continued working in her singular style in the 1960s; since it was already based on a casual, busy attitude, it did not have to be adjusted to reflect what was in the air. She most often used wool and leather, the latter to form piping on a garment of another material as well as in whole coats, vests, skirts, tunics, and dresses. All of her clothes of this period have an easy fit, some of them bloused, which contrasted with the stiff or sculptural effects in favor. Her skirts rarely climbed much above the knee, although she did show tunics that could be worn in lieu of minis with woolly tights. Since her typical client was on the go, constantly hopping in and out of cars, onto bicycles, or simply striding to and fro, she showed such practical alternatives to short skirts as shorts, culottes, and bloomers. Like her skirts, these were shown not with blouses but with ribbed sweaters, often turtlenecked. Her glove designs for Crescendoe featured topstitched fingers hand-stitched in contrasting colors. In keeping with her materials, her colors were natural and earthy, with an occasional strong yellow or red surfacing among her russets, taupes, sands, and moss greens.

OLEG CASSINI

In 1961 Oleg Cassini was one of several designers (Sarmi and Norman Norell were others) asked to submit sketches from upcoming collections to the new First Lady, Jackie Kennedy. According to his autobiography, Cassini designed a special group of dresses that he thought would particularly suit her, and then proceeded to present her with an ultimatum: she could wear his clothes only if she wore only his clothes. For his part, he would costume her completely for her new role, making her wardrobe organization much easier. The first two things of his she wore were a wool coat with a mink pillbox and muff, at the swearing-in ceremonies, and an evening dress of heavy white satin ornamented solely by a self-fabric rosette, at the Inaugural Ball.

His designing changed almost overnight. Although the clothes he made for the First Lady were exclusive and not part of his usual ready-to-wear collections, his overall look changed from that of decorative femininity to one of simplicity and an easy, not-too-fitted fit. Boxy jacket suits were ornamented only by self-covered buttons and came with sleeveless jersey shell blouses; evening and cocktail dresses were cut in straight lines, with low-waisted blouson bodices. By September 1963 his renown enabled him to branch out into swimwear, foundations, sportswear, furs, costume jewelry, hosiery, gloves, handbags, men's cravats, sport shirts, sweaters, and clothes for "young America." In the mid-1960s he disbanded his top ready-to-wear line and since then has been involved only in licensing arrangements.

CEIL CHAPMAN

While she made some full-skirted ball gowns in the 1960s, for the most part Ceil Chapman worked with an easier, straighter silhouette, using soft materials like jersey and chiffon for flowing, halter-necked dresses with saronglike skirts. She also used more beading, primarily in an allover abstract pattern of densely sewn, short bugle beads, which she made into theater suits and sheath dresses. In response to the youth craze, Ceil Chapman designed pajama ensembles for evening as well as dresses that ended in palazzo pants, and she also began to work with large-scale prints, combining stripes with paisleys. In 1969 her jeweled embroideries took the form of false necklaces, bibs, and wide midriffs, looks that were popular by the end of the decade.

CHARLES COOPER

By the 1960s, Charles Cooper for Cooper Couture had established itself as a California design entity. Despite its name, it featured ready-made clothes, which, at $100 to $300, were not the most expensive ready-to-wear. Cooper specialized in clean, bright colors, like orange and mint green, and in peppy prints, perhaps of black and white. Like most American designers of the period, he used wool fabrics for cocktail and evening clothes, as in a salt-and-pepper tweed evening dress or a pantsuit sprinkled with rhinestones or a tweed coat amusingly decorated with speckled guinea fowl feathers that echo the variegated quality of the tweed.

JO COPELAND

Most of Jo Copeland's designs for Pattullo in the 1960s fall into the category of dress-and-jacket ensemble, which she dressed up or down for night or day. Day versions, made of wool, might have an interesting detail such as a narrow, tiered skirt or an elaborate cummerbund treatment designed to peep out under the jacket. For night she combined wool with diamanté buttons and fur, or she made long dresses and jackets out of brocades or cut velvet woven in a plaid or moiré pattern. Rather than show mini dresses, she offered evening pantsuits, floor-length casual evening looks, and versions of the high-waisted, full-skirted, below-the-knee-length evening dresses that formed an alternative for older women. She closed her business in 1970, and she died in 1982.

VICTOR COSTA

Victor Costa, who had been working as a bridal designer in New York for some time, was hired in 1965 by the firm Suzy Perette, a company known for its close copies of French couturier clothes. It was Victor Costa's job to go to the Paris collections, pick out the dresses that would become the fashion "Fords," and copy them in this country, where they sold for as little as $40. At the time, unabashed knock-offs of couture clothes, like those sold by Ohrbach's, were at the height of their popularity.

Born in Houston, Texas, in 1935, Costa grew up with an interest in fashion. When he was ten, he designed paper-doll outfits, which he sold to his friends at school. After he attended Pratt Institute in Brooklyn and l'Ecole de la Chambre Syndicale de la Couture Parisienne, he moved to New York, where he sold sketches to such designers as Ceil Chapman, Oleg Cassini, Herbert Sondheim, and Philip Hulitar before working for the bridal companies Pandora and the Bride's World.

DAVID CRYSTAL

In 1968 David Crystal, a company known for its somewhat sedate wool dresses and suits, became associated with Lacoste and began making shirtdresses that were long versions of the alligator-adorned T-shirt. The David Crystal Chemises Lacoste, from a waffle-knitted polyester (Dacron) double knit that came in solid colors or patterns, primarily stripes, took the form of dresses, tunics for pants turnouts, and even tunic bathing suits.

LILLY DACHÉ

Hats were becoming extinct during the 1960s. Although Lilly Daché added numerous nonhat attractions to her millinery establishment, including a beauty parlor and an art gallery, and sold stockings, wigs, costume jewelry, cosmetics, and men's neckties and accessories, she didn't ignore her first love. She unfettered her invention in cartwheels, lampshades, poufs of feathers, organdy coifs, upturned buckets, pillboxes almost the size of actual pillboxes, and space-age helmets of black grid mesh, sometimes to wild effect. When she closed her business in 1968,

one of her most loyal clients, Loretta Young, showed up to buy the last thirty hats. Although Lilly Daché retired, she found it hard to resist offering her daughter, Suzanne Daché, suggestions when she, too, became a hatmaker, during the early 1970s.

DAVIDOW

By the 1960s, the firm of Davidow had become known for its Chanel-like suits with trims of woolly braid or blouses that matched the jacket's lining. According to Jessica Daves, Davidow suits had a cachet all their own; she described them in her book *Ready Made Miracle* (page 92) as "tweedy, aristocratic" clothes that would never go out of fashion.

OSCAR DE LA RENTA

In 1962 Oscar de la Renta went to work designing for Elizabeth Arden's fashion salon, replacing Sarmi, her most recent designer. He had been born in 1932 in the Dominican Republic, had studied to be a painter there and in Spain, and had worked, as a sideline, sketching clothes for Balenciaga's Eisa branch in Ma-

One of the consequences of the youth-quake was the vogue for an extremely young, even babyish mien, achieved by lavish eye makeup, sometimes with the kind of painted-on lashes a doll might sport, pale lips, elaborate curly mane of hair, and little, high-waisted baby dresses. This 1969 short evening dress by Oscar de la Renta was made of large-scale cotton piqué trimmed with bands of rhinestones and shown with chandelier earrings by Kenneth Jay Lane.

drid. Next came a job as an assistant designer to Antonio del Castillo at the house of Lanvin in Paris. Having become interested in ready-to-wear, which he was designing for Lanvin, he decided to move to New York, and shortly after beginning with Arden he became known as someone to watch. In 1965 he became the designer for Jane Derby, and when she died, he took over the company, giving it his own name.

Oscar de la Renta's day clothes showed the influence of Balenciaga and his evening clothes that of Castillo. Coats and suits made in pale, textured mohairs, double-faced wools or thick cotton matelassé were cut with curving shapes, collars that stood away from the neck, and highlighted seams that emphasized the gently fitting cuts. Evening clothes ran the gamut from softly fluid, long chiffon dresses to opulent ball gowns with fitted, V-necked bodices and full, long skirts.

By 1966 de la Renta was taking the most amusing aspects of youthquake fashions and incorporating them into his couture-calibre evening turnouts, such as harem pajamas with beaded cuffs, tunics paired with sequined knickers or mini pants, and bare-midriff pants with matching long coats in ikat-patterned silks. In 1968 he showed a group of evening clothes made of black crepe, with embroideries of gold galloon worked with crystal beads and pearl drops. Some were conventional, with the embroidery edging V necklines, others featured the transparent openwork for whole bodices, and two were made with low-slung skirts, baring the navel, with either a bare-breasted vest-necklace or a long-sleeved black top ending in galloon border midbreast. In 1969 his hippie-inspired styles included daytime turnouts with fringed ponchos combined with skirts or pants and fringed evening vests embroidered with words like *peace*, *groovy*, and *dig it* in rhinestones and beads.

JANE DERBY

Jane Derby continued to make traditional and flattering clothes in the 1960s, specializing in evening and late-day garments, including moderately bare silk dresses with matching waist-length jackets. Her clothes were softer than most 1960s designs; she often used jersey or chiffon in dresses that featured minute tucks and gathers. A 1962 dress of a stiff fabric, perhaps cotton piqué, was softened by a ruffle along the boat neck. When Derby died in 1965, Oscar de la Renta, her new designer, took over the business.

ESTÉVEZ

Luis Estévez continued in the 1960s to make sexy short and long evening dresses, mostly as fitted sheaths, some with lace overlay. He also created less fitted clothes, as in a group of 1961 barrel-shaped ottoman coats, and he often offered a dress in two versions, one with a bouffant skirt and one with a narrow skirt. His necklines remained a focal point; one in particular was cut out in the shape of daisy petals, leaving the fabric looking like the spokes of a wheel. In 1967 his horizontally tucked evening shirt for men made a splash. Late-1960s creations included evening jumpsuits. Estévez moved in 1968 to California, where he continued to design as Estévez for Neal and for various other companies, but never on as big a scale as in the 1960s. By the 1980s he was known mainly for his couture.

ANNE FOGARTY

Anne Fogarty, who established her own business in 1962, branched out considerably in the 1960s, designing in misses' and regular sizes pants and blouses to be worn together, pantsuits, long dresses (most of her 1950s evening dresses had been ballet-length), minis, caftans and djellabas, suits with boxy jackets, and mini dresses with separate bloomers or pantaloons. Her new favorite silhouette, which she used again and again during the decade, was the Empire, with a very high waist, low scooped neckline, tiny puffed sleeves, and long, narrow skirt. These dresses were made in cotton organdy, silk surah, acetate taffeta, cotton eyelet, or allover paillettes. Her lines included A. F. Boutique, Clothes Circuit, and Collector's Items. She closed her business in the 1970s and died in New York in 1980.

WILSON FOLMAR

By 1964 Wilson Folmar had left Edward Abbott and gone into business for himself, with Larry Aldrich as a silent partner, calling the new firm Wilson Folmar, Inc. In addition to a line of medium-to-high-priced ($150 to $1,500) ready-to-wear cocktail and evening clothes in mostly simple shapes and lavish fabrics, ornamented with braids, crystal embroideries, and fabric bows, Folmar designed a less expensive line for younger customers under the name Folmar Fantasy. Folmar went out of business in 1972. In 1978 the Montgomery Museum of Fine Arts in his home state of Alabama held a retrospective of his design work.

GALANOS

Galanos not only remained true to his own vision during the 1960s, ignoring many of the current fixations with hem length and exaggerated youthfulness, he also showed remarkable range within his own work. No one designed more beautifully made soft, supple, chiffon dresses than he; at the same time, he carved strict, pure day and evening clothes out of wool. His beaded embroideries were the most intricate and complex of the decade, his unadorned clothes the sparest. Mainbocher, the only other designer whose work approached the quality of Galanos's, was a couturier who dressed a primarily East Coast establishment in a luxurious yet refined way. Galanos, located on the West Coast, worked within the category of top-notch ready-to-wear, with dresses starting at $295 or $395. While clearly aimed at the women who could afford them, they managed to elude being confined to a single image. A woman in a Galanos dress could be any age. However, since the clothes were not made to order, she had to have a good figure, as well as a sense of daring.

Although Galanos designed mini dresses, primarily with a natural waistline, most of his evening clothes were long, and most of his day clothes grazed the top of the knee. If another length was appropriate for a style he used it, and accordingly showed the midi-length dress, in 1967, a year before it hit Seventh Avenue. As an alternative to short skirts he offered varieties of pants, ranging from a casual 1967 turnout of mid-calf white shorts paired with a black tank top to luxurious pantsuits and pajama costumes. He also experimented with bareness, showing jumpsuits of lace lined in beige marquisette, outfits of flowing pajamas with bra tops and cover-ups, evening dresses with cutaway backs and sides. Constantly searching for unusual fabrics, Galanos came up with raffia-embroidered lace, prints by artist Raoul Dufy and fabric designer Ken Scott, hand-painted silks, and Op art patterns. He was famous for his layered chiffon dresses, which played strict tailoring against the soft flow of the material; he made these in solid-colored and cut-velvet chiffons as well as those printed with animal-skin patterns. Even the simplest Galanos dress featured considerable dressmaker technique, such as smocking, tucking, flat piping, and embroideries.

RUDI GERNREICH

Rudi Gernreich's name became a household word when, to his amazement, the California designer sold three thousand of his topless bathing suits in 1964. The suit, which was awkward-looking, was not influential in and of itself since women who were sunbathing and swimming topless were doing so in their bikini bottoms. Gernreich continued to design articles of cloth-

Rudi Gernreich, the influential and avant-garde California designer, liked to work with knits and to liberate the body. He used clear vinyl strips for his black wool bikini made in 1968 for Harmon Knitwear. His 1968 mini, made of hot pink wool knit inset with clear vinyl for Harmon Knitwear, came with matching knee socks and bikini underpants. Modeling both outfits was Peggy Moffitt, Gernreich's muse. Photographs: William Claxton

ing intended to chisel away at the national prudery, but relatively few women could overcome the very basic notion that bodies, especially imperfect ones, should be covered. Those who felt differently relished Gernreich's see-through blouses and mini dresses inset with clear vinyl strips.

Besides his experiments with partial nudity, Gernreich designed less controversial clothes that were freewheeling and spirited, both in their look and their construction. He worked often with knits, including many synthetic ones, making them in dots, stripes, checkerboard, and other Op art patterns, in black and white or such colors as orange, hot pink, lime green, and purple. He regularly designed low-waisted and other easily fitted bathing suits as well as dresses. He experimented with hosiery, designing socks, stockings, and tights intended to be part of a total look, either matching or contrasting with bloomer dresses, shorts, and chemises. His forays into Oriental costume resulted in obi-wrapped knit dresses and bathing suits and in variations on the dhoti diaper-wrap look for short as well as long dresses.

Gernreich's line of clothes retailed for up to $500, and a line he made for Harmon Knitwear sold in the $40 to $125 range. Layne Nielson designed the accessories that were shown with Gernreich's clothes; these included shower cap–shaped hats and earrings made of large artificial flowers or yard-long pheasant feathers. In 1969, two years after he made the cover of *Time* magazine and one year after he was inducted into the Coty Hall of Fame, Rudi Gernreich took a leave of absence from fashion; he later returned to designing, but worked on a more sporadic basis.

GEORGE HALLEY

In 1966 George Halley, who was born in Ohio and had worked for Charles James, Jo Copeland of Pattullo, and Jane Derby, started his own fashion business with his wife, Claudia, who had been one of Norell's favorite models. From the beginning he was hailed as a great talent. The November 1966 issue of *Vogue* showed his black jersey caftan jumpsuit with gold embroidery and an evening turnout of black sequined pants and white ruffled blouse, which had been photographed by Richard Avedon, with the caption, "These brilliances from the imagination of George Halley, a new exhilaration—pyjamas cut with great clarity of line and an eye for the true hang of cloth." In 1968 Halley won a Coty Award. Most of his designs featured simple shapes, like the high-waisted, full-skirted, long evening dress, but were interpreted in creative and romantic materials, such as cut velvet in a bold floral pattern, organdy printed with immense rhinestone-centered flowers, and patterned chiffon overlaid with flat coq feathers printed to match the silk underneath.

HALSTON

Roy Halston Frowick was born in 1932 in Des Moines, Iowa. He attended Indiana University and, briefly, the Art Institute of Chicago. While in Chicago he sold hats he had designed and made himself in a beauty parlor, where he was discovered by Lilly Daché, who hired him to work for her in New York. In 1958 he moved to Bergdorf Goodman, where he designed custom millinery; in 1966 he was put in charge of his own in-store boutique, which gave him the opportunity to design clothes as well. After ten years he left Bergdorf's to start his own ready-to-wear business, selling his clothes and accessories to stores around the country and in New York in a boutique at Bloomingdale's.

In terms of design, Halston did an immediate about-face once he was on his own. He stopped making such fantastical head ornaments as organdy hair-dryer bonnets, fringed lampshades, and jeweled, mirrored, or flowered hoods, helmets, and coifs, and instead began designing the kind of radically simple clothes that would characterize the 1970s. From the beginning he worked with several fabrics and styles continuously, refining them season after season. Most of his early turnouts employed the long, narrow silhouette that would supplant the 1960s baby-doll look; his ensembles featured skinny trousers, close-to-the-body tunics, jackets, and coats, wrap fronts for dresses and coats, long

mufflers, pliable materials like wool jersey and velvet, and, for pattern, fabrics that had been tie-dyed. In 1969 he won his second Coty Award (the first had been for millinery in 1962).

PHILIP HULITAR

Philip Hulitar continued designing his shapely, feminine, and sophisticated evening clothes up until his retirement in 1964. His below-the-knee-length and fitted floor-length cocktail dresses were made most often in chiffon, black lace, black crepe, or brocades and featured flattering bateau, one-shoulder, halter, or strapless necklines. The curvy sheath silhouette was given emphasis by means of trains and separate floating panels.

IRENE

Although Irene died in 1962, her company continued under the design direction of Hubert Latimer. Latimer left in 1970 to become the first American designer for Christian Dior–New York; in 1973 he went to work for Mollie Parnis; later, he became a free-lance designer.

Even in 1960 Irene was still producing her favorite type of suit with a long, fitted jacket and a narrow skirt. Her evening clothes tended toward the dramatic, with bold contrasts of materials, décolleté bodices, and asymmetric details. Latimer's designs for Irene were more casual and modern; they concentrated on pantsuits rather than tailored skirt suits and above-the-knee, dressed-down evening dresses.

ARTHUR JABLOW

Arthur Jablow ready-to-wear, still designed in the 1960s by David Kidd, turned out clothes typical of Seventh Avenue's fascination with and dependence on Balenciaga in the 1960s. Suits had boxy jackets and were made in thick materials like wide-wale corduroy or bouclé tweed, and coats and dresses were made with highlighted seams in sculptural cuts. Prices went just over $200.

JEAN LOUIS

In 1961 Jean Louis left Columbia Pictures, where he had been designing costumes since 1943, and started his own couture business in Los Angeles, which eventually offered ready-to-wear. Born Jean Louis Berthault in Paris in 1907, he had worked as a sketch artist for the couture house of Drecoll before immigrating to New York, where he designed for Hattie Carnegie during the late 1930s and early 1940s. He continued to work in films after starting his own business; his movie projects, which numbered well over a hundred, included *Gilda* (1946), *Born Yesterday* (1950), *Pal Joey* (1957), *Judgment at Nuremberg* (1961), *Thoroughly Modern Millie*, and *Guess Who's Coming to Dinner* (both 1967).

Aside from his movie designs of the 1960s, Jean Louis created dramatic daytime ensembles of coats and dresses or suits and luxurious evening gowns, pajamas, and cocktail dresses, typically using beautiful fabrics, with trimmings of fur borders and beaded embroideries. He continued designing ready-to-wear un-

til 1988, when he retired, except to make the occasional dress for
a long-time client.

BETSEY JOHNSON

The most important designer to emerge from the boutique scene
was Betsey Johnson, who started at Paraphernalia in 1965. In
1966 French actress Anouk Aimée, shopping in New York at
Paraphernalia, compared Betsey Johnson favorably to Chanel.
Tens of thousands of the dress that British actress Julie Christie
bought from her (with ten-inch-long pointed white collar) were
sold around the country. Johnson's other designs included leath-

*This heavy black Bianchini silk dress with its stand-out full
skirt was one of Charles Kleibacker's best-selling styles in
1968. It was accessorized for this photograph with chandelier
earrings by Kenneth Jay Lane.*

*Silk poppies or daisies adorn the softly draped strapless bodices
of these two chiffon evening dresses designed in 1968 by
George Halley.*

er dresses with grommets down the center, what she called noise dresses, with hems of jangling grommets or shower curtain rings, flared minis made out of cotton and synthetic blend football jersey, sweaters and other clothes made with huge industrial zippers, kit or do-it-yourself plastic dresses that came with decals and appliqués for the client to arrange to her satisfaction, and fluorescent bikini underpants for both men and women, sold packaged in tennis ball cans in sets of three.

Betsey Johnson was born in Wethersfield, Connecticut, in 1942, and spent a year at Pratt Institute in New York before transferring to Syracuse University, where she was elected Phi Beta Kappa and graduated magna cum laude with a degree in art in 1964. She went to work at *Mademoiselle* magazine, where she had been a guest editor during college, and, after making sweaters for her editor friends there, was encouraged to think about designing. Next came the job at Paraphernalia, where she made all of her own patterns and samples. (She had sewn since she was a child, making doll clothes out of sequined and glitter materials.) She left Paraphernalia after just two years, joined up with two friends to start a boutique called Betsey, Bunky and Nini on East Fifty-third Street, free-lanced as a shoe designer, and, from 1969, became the designer for a company called Alley Cat.

NORMA KAMALI

In 1967 Norma and Eddie Kamali opened a boutique at 229 East Fifty-third Street. Then working for Northwest Orient Airlines, Norma Kamali could fly cheaply enough to Europe to go to London or Paris almost every weekend. The Kamali shop was therefore at first stocked with imports primarily from swinging London, although Kamali began to supplement the stock with her own designs. Norma Kamali, born Norma Arraez in Manhattan, grew up making her own clothes and wanting to be an artist. Toward that end, she attended and graduated from Fashion Institute of Technology in New York.

KASPER

Herbert Kasper was born in New York. He attended New York University until he left to serve in World War II. While he was stationed in Germany, he participated in army shows, both as a performer and as a costume designer. When he returned to New York he switched to Parsons School of Design, where one of his student project designs was bought by the milliner Mr. John. Kasper spent his junior year abroad, working in Paris as a free-lance assistant designer with Jacques Fath, Christian Dior, and Marcel Rochas and sending fashion sketches to Mr. John in New York. When he left Europe he found work designing for the Seventh Avenue firm Arnold & Fox. Lord & Taylor liked his work, and when it decided to promote him as a young American designer suggested that he use his last name only. Kasper for Arnold & Fox designs included medium-priced ($50 for a dress) day dresses and short, summer evening dresses with bodices fitted down to the hip and full skirts. In 1965 Kasper joined the firm of Leslie Fay, begun after the war by Fred Pomerantz, which went public in 1962. (Today, the company, run by John Pomerantz, is one of the largest fashion businesses in the country.)

At $50 to $300, Kasper's designs for Joan Leslie, a line of Leslie Fay, were medium-priced and aimed at a specific market: ladies who wanted wearable, flattering clothes that paid little heed to the youthquake. Although Kasper made use of an occasional floral print, his most common patterns were plaids; these he made up into coat and dress ensembles and suits with variations on the Eisenhower-type jacket or the pea coat. Most of the evening clothes were covered up and restrained; a perfectly plain long dress might be enlivened by fabric woven with glistening threads or with a necklace of beads and braid embroidered around the neck. Almost all of Kasper's short dresses ended just above the knee. In 1968 Kasper joined the movement toward a longer, covered-up evening dress with a dirndl skirt.

BUD KILPATRICK

Bud Kilpatrick was a California ready-to-wear designer whose 1960s clothes were inventive and extremely luxurious, usually made with European fabrics. Suits and coats were meticulously tailored, with kimono sleeves or interestingly placed tab pockets or self scarves. Evening clothes were both restrained and creative, as in his 1963 long dress with boat neck, slightly Empire bodice of black and white houndstooth wool, and long, full skirt of black silk, paired with a floor-length houndstooth coat.

CHARLES KLEIBACKER

In 1963 Charles Kleibacker, generally regarded as a master of the bias cut, went into business for himself at 26 West Seventy-sixth Street. Although he soon expanded into larger quarters at 23 West Seventy-third Street, his business never grew large, primarily due to the difficulties of producing bias-cut clothing. Dissatisfied with the quality of workmanship available through contractors, Kleibacker preferred to keep his operation small enough for him to supervise the entire process of construction.

Kleibacker's beautifully made, off-the-rack designs, sold at Bergdorf Goodman and Henri Bendel, were characterized by a fluidity unusual in the 1960s and simple-looking draperies resulting from the intricate cut. Most of his dresses were made in solid colors, especially black or beige, from imported materials, including four-ply silk crepe, silk jersey, or taffeta.

Charles Kleibacker was born in Alabama and graduated from the University of Notre Dame with a degree in journalism. He worked as a newspaper writer in Alabama before attending New York University, where he studied retailing. Next he worked as a fashion advertising copywriter, for Gimbel's and then DePinna. A job with the entertainer Hildegarde took him to Paris for six months, where Hildegarde patronized her favorite couturiers. Seeing couture clothes up close, especially a collection of designs by Madeleine Vionnet (by then retired), made Kleibacker realize that he wanted to design. He found a job working for Antonio del Castillo, who was then at Lanvin. In 1958 Kleibacker returned to New York, where he was hired as an assistant designer under Eva Rosencrans at Nettie Rosenstein; when Rosenstein stopped making clothes to concentrate on accessories, Kleibacker left to start his own company.

Anne Klein was known for her fun, young clothes. This 1967 at-home dress juxtaposed giraffe spots with black and white stripes, bifurcated by a curvy orange zigzag. Her 1964 jumpsuit with palazzo legs, made of kaleidoscopic patterned cotton with matching hat, was intended as patio pajamas or for at-home. It is shown with costume jewelry by Vogue and shoes by David Evins. For her 1964 suit for Junior Sophisticates, Anne Klein paired a white cotton cord jacket with a one-piece dress of navy and pimento red cotton, shown with a chain belt and a hat by Sally Victor.

ANNE KLEIN

As the head of her own fashion house by 1963, Anne Klein began working with the concept of separates dressing for both day and evening. Although she made dresses, she shaped them more like elongated turtleneck sweaters or T-shirts rather than the boxy, stiff chemises prevalent at the time. She preferred warm colors, with shades of beige and brown predominating, and she liked to pair traditional evening fabrics with daytime ones for casual nighttime turnouts. Blazers and weskits in brown cotton velvet were shown with high-necked blouses with jabot or stock-tied collars and kilts, trousers, shorts, or knickers in plaid, herring-bone, or tweedy wool. She kept her price range in the 1960s reasonable, from $50 to $100 except for the leather coats she designed for Mallory, which averaged $200. To keep prices low, she worked with varieties of man-made fabrics, especially for blouses and dresses. In 1969 she won her second Coty Award.

JOHN KLOSS

John Kloss had originally studied architecture and worked on Wall Street before turning to fashion, studying at Traphagen School of Fashion, New York, and working for couturier Bob Bugnand. In 1959 he started designing on his own. His early-1960s designs tended to be sculptural, as in a 1963 evening dress of heavy white cotton ottoman. By 1968, when his at-home clothes began to be featured in a boutique at Henri Bendel, he was working with fluid matte jersey for such unusual loungewear items as glittery leotards or pajamas and dresses made with rows of tiny buttons and button loops that could be fastened as low or as high as the wearer wanted. His nightgowns were more fluttery, made in various sheer nylons with lettuce-edged tiers.

TINA LESER

In the 1960s Tina Leser concentrated less on sportswear and more on dresses and at-home clothes that, in keeping with the mood of the decade, could see a woman through any possible evening occasion. Her dresses ranged from low-waisted, full-skirted, short summer cottons to long T-shirt shapes made out of interesting materials, such as a geometric openwork eyelet. At-home items included beach dresses, cut in a straight line with slits to the knee and appliquéd with African masks at the neckline, pajama ensembles with Turkish vests, and dresses patterned after djellabas. Among the fabrics she used were such Oriental favorites as sari silk, as well as glittery organzas printed with flowers or embroidered with braid and jewels. Leser continued to design into the early 1970s.

MAINBOCHER

In the 1960s Mainbocher's couture designs were sometimes accused of being staid. However, his elegant clients appreciated the subtle allure of daring to wear one of his plain, long wool coats when all those around them arrayed themselves in feathers, furs, and glitter. Among Mainbocher's designs that shaped the

establishment look for the first half of the decade were his boxy-jacketed suits with sleeveless blouses; his four-seam sheath dress with a back zipper; and his accessories look, which could be pared down to just a bow-tied hair band, low-heeled shoes in black crocodile, calf, or silk, and pocketbooks made to match the fabric of the ensemble. With a Mainbocher dress and jacket ensemble, which could cost as much as $2,450 in 1967, one wore good jewelry.

Most of Mainbocher's designs were simple in shape and luxurious of fabric. Besides the boxy suits he offered dresses made to look like a sleeveless blouse attached to a slightly full dirndl skirt, worn with a jacket or cardigan, short evening dresses with flattering dinner-table necklines, long dresses and coats, and, throughout the decade, fluid, bias-cut evening clothes that reflected his 1930s Paris designs and presaged the dominant style of the 1970s. By the end of the decade Mainbocher bowed to some of the youthquake influence by providing his more up-to-the-moment clients with bloomer or pants evening costumes. For those not quite ready to take the pants plunge, he showed his with slit-front overskirts.

Mainbocher continued to design clothes that could be changed around with the addition or removal of an apron or, in the case of a blouse, of a separate ruffled collar. Many of his evening clothes were made of damask, which can combine a bold-scale pattern with subtle coloring; other favored materials included surah, wool bouclé, mohair, or challis, reembroidered lace, and heavy silk crepe. He continued to use fur linings, and made whole costumes out of velvet-thin broadtail. He retired in 1971 and died in 1976.

VERA MAXWELL

Vera Maxwell's 1960s designs were aimed at conservative women who appreciated the occasional interesting material or color but on the whole favored simple silhouettes and thigh-covering skirts. Although she designed suits, most of her work was composed of easily shaped sheath and overblouse dresses made in raw silk, Indian silk, cotton mull, or gingham. A 1963 design featured a black rayon, linen, and cotton tank top and a narrow dirndl skirt of natural-color fishnet crochet.

MONTE-SANO & PRUZAN

Monte-Sano & Pruzan continued during the 1960s to produce expensive (around $325 for a suit) well-made suits and coats that were mass-manufactured but hand-finished. A specialty of the house was short-sleeved suits; their jackets might be short and curved, belted and with dolman sleeves, or blouson, all usually paired with straight skirts. As the decade progressed, Monte-Sano & Pruzan fabrics grew bolder, including large-scale tweeds, bright plaid double-faced wools, and patterned heavy cottons. The company also experimented with the day-into-evening category, making tweed dress and jacket ensembles with jeweled buttons and a low evening neckline on the dress, black dresses that could work for both day and night, and suits softened by large silk scarves arranged around wide necklines.

JOHN MOORE

John Moore, who started his own company in 1964, produced clothes that were both elegant and full of verve. He specialized in evening and dressed-up day clothes, priced at around $500 for a jersey dress. He worked directly with material on a dressmaker form, since he believed that that method gave him more depth than he could get from just drawing on paper. He designed Lady Bird Johnson's evening gown for the Inaugural Ball.

John Moore was born in Texas in 1928, and he grew up studying art and music before attending Trinity University, the University of Texas, and finally Parsons School of Design, New York, from which he graduated. While he was still at Parsons, his work gained the notice of Eleanor Lambert, who often included his designs in fashion shows she helped organize. After Elizabeth Arden hired him and, almost immediately, fired him, he went to work for Jane Derby, designing for her in the year that she won a Coty Award. In 1951 he moved to Matty Talmack, where he was also responsible for the firm winning a Coty. He ran his own business for a little over ten years before deciding to return to Texas, to the town of Alice, to run an antiques business.

NORMAN NORELL

Following the retirement of his partner, Anthony Traina, Norell took over his wholesale house in 1960, renaming it Norman Norell, Inc. He continued designing up until his death in 1972, when the house hired Gustave Tassell to continue working in the Norell manner for five years.

Norell's 1960s designs are characterized by avant-garde experimentation within the confines of classic American style, tempered by the highest-quality workmanship to be found anywhere in the ready-to-wear industry. While he charged high prices for his clothes, day suits or coats costing well over $1,000, Norell worked hard to maintain control, having everything made in a single factory and keeping annual production around the manageable amount of $2 million.

In 1960 Norell made waves with his culotte walking suit, which combined cropped pants with a tailored jacket. In 1961 he

came out with the first evening jumpsuit, which ended in midcalf knickers and was made out of apple green velvet cut to satin with a matching floor-length sleeveless coat edged at the hem with a band of sable. In 1963 Norell showed his first daytime pantsuits, made with tailored trousers, double-breasted cape jacket, and wool jersey shirt. He continued experimenting with pants and by 1965 was showing them for evening, in his signature sequins, and also in a pajama version of silk with one black and one white leg, with a tunic top slashed diagonally across in black and white to match. He augmented his sequined dresses, which in the 1960s were supple, floor-length T-shirts of jersey hand sewn with flat sequins, with rhinestone embroideries. To preserve the shapes of the sequined dresses, Norell clients kept them in boxes or drawers, much as they would rolled-up Fortunys. His day clothes became more relaxed, with blouson shapes and shifts

made of skirt, shirt, and vest, usually in three different materials, or made with shirttail tunics over straight skirts. He avoided the prevalent stiff look for evening as well, showing gently shaped, long kimono dresses and varieties of shirtwaists, including new versions of his 1950s organdy sailor dresses.

In 1968 Norell showed midi-length, floor-length, and above-the-knee-length dresses, all with silhouettes adjusted accordingly, and he continued showing below-the-knee, wide-belted shirtwaist dresses for day and evening, coats in the same silhouette over pants, just-above-the-ankle-length dinner dresses, and his long sequined dresses throughout the hemline controversy of the early 1970s. After Norell's death, Tassell worked with many of the Norell signatures, exchanging pavé bugle beads for sequins in simple designs. In 1973 a Gustave Tassell for the House of Norell bugle-beaded slip dress and cardigan retailed for $5,250.

MOLLIE PARNIS

In the 1960s Mollie Parnis continued to dress First Ladies, including Lady Bird Johnson and Pat Nixon. Typical offerings included shirtwaist dresses, dress and jacket ensembles, shifts, overblouse chemises, and suits with short, boxy jackets. She was fond of patterned fabrics, and these became more geometric and bolder in palette as the decade progressed. By 1966 she was providing those clients of hers who wanted to look more stylish with harem-bottomed evening pajamas, jumpsuits with bead-embroidered necklace necklines, dresses with very low V necks, and mini dresses paired, for propriety, with pants.

BEN REIG

In 1961 Eva Rosencrans left Nettie Rosenstein, who was abandoning the dress business in order to concentrate on accessories, and became the designer for Ben Reig, who had begun his wholesale fashion house in 1929 and whose main designer during the 1940s and early 1950s had been Omar Kiam.

Eva Rosencrans's designs for Ben Reig included suits and dress and coat ensembles for day, short evening dresses and long ones paired with long brocade coats, and pantsuits for evening. Prices were not inexpensive; a tweed suit with matching shawl lined with nutria was $895 in 1963. For the most part the clothes were luxurious in their simplicity; an evening dress of black silk was classic, cut with a fluid skirt and fitted bodice with twisted halter neckline. Short evening dresses were made of wonderful materials, such as lace, and, rather than featuring the ubiquitous 1960s beading, were shaped like tents or had fitted torsos with dropped waistlines to give them interest.

SHANNON RODGERS

In 1959 Jerry Silverman started a ready-to-wear dress company with Shannon Rodgers as its designer, with the label Shannon Rodgers for Jerry Silverman. Jerry Silverman was a graduate of Harvard Law School who had worked as a lawyer; after World War II, during which he served in the army, he became business manager of a fashion company called Martini, which specialized in outright copies and adaptations of Paris dresses. There he met designer Shannon Rodgers, who had started out with a degree in architecture from Western Reserve in his native Ohio and designed costumes in Hollywood before serving in the navy during the war.

In his first trips to the Paris collections, which Shannon Rodgers later described, he learned a valuable lesson; never to use every idea from a single couture dress. Instead, he came to absorb details, later choosing exactly which new shape or decoration would work on a simple American dress. The designs of Shannon Rodgers for Jerry Silverman tended to be simple, highlighted by a single interesting detail: a trapunto pattern, a scroll or braid, an asymmetric back neckline. Although the company made many sculptured late-1960s sheaths, it also showed gently fitted dresses and suits with blouson bodices.

The Jerry Silverman company lasted through the 1970s; in 1983 Jerry Silverman and Shannon Rodgers founded both the School of Design and Merchandising and the accompanying costume collection of the Kent State University Museum. In 1983 Jerry Silverman died; Shannon Rodgers has continued to serve as the museum's curator.

GIORGIO DI SANT' ANGELO

Giorgio di Sant' Angelo personified the exuberance of the last half of the 1960s. He wanted to wean women from the boxy dress with a zipper up its back, and he succeeded. He didn't simply design clothes, he ornamented the body, wrapping model Verushka in collages of various fabrics, painting a flower around one of Twiggy's eyes, glueing uncut emeralds around the eye of another model. He made bikinis from cascades of gold chains, a

face-framing tiara of Lucite with giant rhinestones dangling within its geometric cutouts, and scattered flower appliqués on bare legs. His jewelry surrounded the upper arm or the calf, and his clothes ranged from very bare and spare, as in leotards or beaten brass breastplates, to covered up and layered, as in full-sleeved peasant blouses worn with multiples of ruffled, beribboned skirts. He experimented with stretch fabrics, found the sheer velvet he wanted from a manufacturer of coffin linings, and also recognized the appeal of cotton and leather. He decorated clothes with found objects, such as old braids and ribbons, feathers, and knotted cords, and he also developed his own materials, working out new ones with DuPont and redyeing, reembroidering, and mixing others.

Giorgio di Sant' Angelo was born in Florence, reared in Italy and Argentina. He studied industrial design and ceramics before coming to America in 1962 to work at the studios of Walt Disney. After a few weeks, he left that job to travel around America, ending up in New York, where he designed textiles. He also showed a group of Lucite and black and white plastic jewelry, which gained the notice of first Catherine de Montezemolo, and then Diana Vreeland at *Vogue*. While becoming a fashion designer, he worked often for *Vogue* as a stylist. He founded his own ready-to-wear business in 1966.

SARMI

Ferdinando Sarmi, also known by his title Count Sarmi, opened a high-quality ready-to-wear company in New York in 1959, and in 1960 he won a Coty Award. He had been born in Ravenna, Italy, and studied law before turning to couture as a designer for the Italian house of Fabiani. Carmel Snow, editor at *Harper's Bazaar*, discovered his work at the 1951 Pitti Palace shows and recommended him to Elizabeth Arden, who was looking for a new

couturier for her fashion salon. Sarmi stayed eight years at Elizabeth Arden, who was not the easiest person to work for. At one point, according to her biographers Alfred Allan Lewis and Constance Woodworth, she went through Sarmi's collection with her scissors, cutting off all of his signature bows because, she complained, it was bad enough to have to share credit with him by having his label on the inside of the clothes; she really didn't like having it on the outside as well. One of Arden's clients, Pat Nixon, wore a Sarmi for Elizabeth Arden dress to the Inaugural Ball in 1957.

Although Sarmi designed perfectly suitable day clothes, his specialty was grand evening dresses, which he mostly made full-skirted to take advantage of such opulent materials as cellophane-embroidered lace, glittering brocades, and damask. He worked with chiffon for simple, narrow, toga-style dresses, as well as for more lavish ones trimmed with bodices of silk gardenias. Although he refrained from using exaggeratedly young styles, some of his fabric choices were daring: he made evening blouses of ermine, suits of lacquered ciré, and dresses of the biggest, boldest Op art prints ever seen. His prices climbed into the thousands. In 1972 he reorganized his business, calling it Ferdinando Sarmi, but it closed down shortly thereafter.

SCAASI

In 1963 Scaasi abruptly stopped designing his two ready-to-wear women's lines, his children's clothes for Kate Greenaway, his costume jewelry, and his men's sweaters and took a sabbatical before starting up again, this time to concentrate solely on custom-made clothes. Although he produced the occasional daytime suit and even a knitwear line and a line of pocketbooks in 1969, he focused on entrance-making ball gowns and short evening dresses. These were made of marvelous materials like an allover crushed, aluminum-colored cellophane, sheer black silk scattered with silver dollar–size sequins, or white net embroidered with whorls in silver bugle beads. He also made considerably more demure paper-doll short dresses in strictly cut white piqué or densely sewn ruffles of embroidered organdy and scalloped silk. He usually used simple yet striking shapes: sheer dresses were cut like tents over narrow underdresses, ball gowns were

designed with asymmetric hems sweeping diagonally from one knee to the other ankle. He also showed evening pants made entirely out of such unusual materials as alligator, guinea hen feathers, and silk flowers. In 1969, giving a nod to the ethnic craze, he showed a group of full-skirted, floor-length dresses concocted out of sari silk.

ADELE SIMPSON

Adele Simpson provided her 1960s customers with moderately priced (usually around $200 for a suit or dress) simple clothes, some of them modified versions of the more extreme trends. She was at her best when not trying for a hip look, as when she designed maillot-bare long dresses of black or white crepe and short dresses with schoolgirl white collar and cuffs. Her predominant daytime offerings were three- or four-piece suit ensembles, usually of thin wools in sherbet shades, with printed silk blouses and jacket or coat linings. In 1967 she started an ad campaign titled "Little Lady with Big Ideas," in which she posed next to different towering models wearing her more adventurous styles, like bare-midriff palazzo pants for evening in freewheeling prints. Simpson herself was always depicted wearing a shirt chemise with patch pockets either at the chest or hip.

SOPHIE OF SAKS

In 1960 René Bouché sketched Claudette Colbert for *Vogue* in the Sophie ready-to-wear tweed suit and jeweled ball gown specially designed for her upcoming film *Parrish*. In a sense, the two costumes typified Sophie's designs; the suit was classic, simple, and ladylike, the evening dress feminine and luxurious with its bead-embroidered bodice. Sophie's ready-to-wear, which sold for up to $1,000, and her custom-made clothes shared many constants: her individual color sense, which led her to use such unusual nighttime shades as taupe, gray, or chocolate brown; her bead embroideries, most often stylized floral allover patterns; her use of transparency, as in lace or sheer silk, for evening bodices; and her favorite bows, usually made in fabric and sewn to dresses for decoration. Besides bead-encrusted evening styles, she also excelled in long, softly draped chiffon dresses. In general, her clothes were cut with much more fluidity than the typically 1960s boxy silhouette. Although Sophie was known for her allegiance to flattering, somewhat conservative styles, she was also capable of playing with various youthquake aspects, as in her 1968 evening pajamas of geranium silk with cossack tunic top. In 1969, the year she announced her retirement, she showed a line of gypsy dresses made in Indian embroidered organdies or in boldly patterned chiffon with butterfly sleeves. Sophie Gimbel died in 1981.

MALCOLM STARR

A specialist in the field of beaded evening dresses, so popular during the 1960s, the company of Malcolm Starr, whose designer was Elinor Simmons, made daytime dress and coat ensembles and evening dresses of softly draped chiffon or silk and/or rayon crepe, but earned its reputation with its simple shifts, pajamas,

and long dresses embroidered (in Hong Kong) with allover lattice or scrolling patterns in beads, sequins, and brilliants. The beads were sewn, often in three-dimensional clusters, on net, organza, satin, and even linen, and they formed a pale palette, as in aquamarine with silver, rose with gold. Most dresses cost around $200. Uncommonly, the designs also sold in Europe.

STAVROPOULOS

George Stavropoulos was a couturier in his native Athens when he met and married an American woman and followed her back to New York. Here he opened a fashion house, predominately ready-to-wear, in 1961, and by 1962 he was hailed as a bright young maverick. When Lady Bird Johnson sat for her official White House portrait, she wore a dress by Stavropoulos.

All of his 1960s designs featured soft rather than stiff shapes: day coats made of wool fell in fluid folds; wool dresses had wrapped fronts and slightly puffed sleeves; evening clothes resembled simple togas. From the very beginning, he revealed a special talent with chiffon. Playing with it on a dressmaker's form, he made dresses with subtle draperies falling in bias folds. Convinced that hemlines should not change according to fashion, he did not participate in the short skirt or hemline controversy, keeping his just at the top of the knee.

GUSTAVE TASSELL

Gustave Tassell, winner of a 1961 Coty Award, was originally from Philadelphia but worked out of Los Angeles. He had his own factory and could therefore keep his operation small, prices

Allover beaded dresses, not unlike those made in the 1920s, were a 1960s evening staple, and one of the names best known for them was Elinor Simmons, who designed for Malcolm Starr. She made the 1967 beaded lace shirt with matching shorts underneath shown here.

Jacques Tiffeau, a talented New York ready-to-wear designer, was responsible for this tweed, leather, and wool knit shorts suit, which appeared on the cover of Harper's Bazaar in 1969. Accessories included a knitted snood, an item that would soon become a minor fad, by Emme, tights by Hanes, and David Webb gold twisted bangle bracelet. Photograph: Neal Barr. Courtesy Harper's Bazaar

relatively low, and quality top-notch. He also had a showroom in New York. Using such fabrics as silk and linen brocade, *peau d'ange*, and quilted cotton damask, he designed controlled, simple, and elegant clothes that sold in the $200 to $500 range. Typical designs spanning the decade included a spare, long, white dress of chiffon topped with a camisole; an afternoon shirtwaist of white piqué with crew neckline, short sleeves, bound buttonholes, and amethyst-jeweled buttons; a tweed day dress fitted to below the waist and having a trumpet skirt; white crepe columnar evening dresses with toga draperies in bottle green or azure wool; an ensemble of red shorts and white blouse forming a short jumpsuit with red jacket; and a turnout of black jersey pants, white linen blazer, chrome yellow silk jersey blouse, and green suede belt.

Tassell had grown up wanting to become an artist, and toward that end he studied at the Philadelphia Academy of Art and then moved to New York. During a job dressing windows at Hattie Carnegie, he became entranced by the world of high fashion. He took a position working for the wholesale house of Elfreda Fox and eventually returned to Philadelphia, where, out of a town house, he designed custom clothes. The retailer Nan Duskin arranged for him to try out as a designer with Hattie Carnegie. He showed her two dresses, which she liked, and she asked him to design a third. It sold well, and he was hired. However, dissatisfied, he decided to move to Paris in 1955, where he worked as a sketch artist for Geneviève Fath, who was then managing the couture house of her late husband, Jacques Fath, and then he free-lanced, selling sketches to various couture houses. In Paris he met fellow Philadelphian James Galanos, who encouraged him to try designing on his own in California, which he started doing in the very late 1950s.

In 1972 Tassell was hired by the house of Norell to take the place of the late designer, so he moved to New York and designed in the Norell tradition for five years. When the company closed down its fashion operations, Tassell started again on his own, on a small scale. Eventually he returned to Los Angeles, where he has produced small collections that private clients can order by size.

JACQUES TIFFEAU

Jacques Tiffeau, for Tiffeau & Busch, designed some of the most streamlined and beautifully cut clothes, young in flavor but restrained, of the 1960s. Originally from the Loire Valley in France, Tiffeau had worked as a tailor there before moving to New York and becoming a pattern maker at the firm of Monte-Sano & Pruzan. Eventually he designed for the company, and in 1958, after six years there, he left to start his own company, with Max Pruzan's daughter Beverly Busch, called Tiffeau & Busch.

The majority of Jacques Tiffeau's coats, suits, and dresses were made in heavy woolens and cottons, set into sculptural shapes by curved and geometric seams. He used wide-wale corduroy, windowpane-plaid double wools, cotton piqué, and silk matelassé for suits, which sometimes featured such quirky elements as short sleeves, Western-style shirt yokes, shorts under slit skirts, and matching leg sleeves to wear over boots. Tiffeau cut jackets to flare out at the back like sails and collars to look like folded paper. He was fond of squared armholes and very cut-in necklines.

In 1966 he showed longer skirts; unlike those that would be prevalent by 1968, his were A-line, like the midis of the early 1970s. Most of his skirts, however, were short; by the end of the decade they were thigh-high, especially in little, high-waisted, soft jersey dresses. In the late 1960s he reorganized his company, dropping the Busch and adding his first name, but the new venture did not last long. He retired during the 1970s to teach fashion design in Paris, returning to New York briefly to design for Originala coats and for the Blassport division of Bill Blass.

PAULINE TRIGÈRE

Pauline Trigère's 1960s clothes could be dazzlingly innovative, as in her white wool pantsuit worn with a rhinestone bra underneath the open jacket instead of a blouse, or classic in her own vein, as in perfectly cut dresses that rarely climbed above the knee. She continued to specialize in wool for evening, combining charcoal jersey with white paper taffeta, black wool crepe with rhinestone bands, and tweed with fox fur. She favored a narrow silhouette, often with a flared skirt below the knees, and wide, circular-cut short capes. She mitered striped and plaid materials so that they formed new patterns in jackets, coats, and blouses. She also started working with softer, more delicate materials as well, making flowered organza mini dresses with matching underpants and trimmed with appliquéd silk flowers. Keeping her business small enough so that she could oversee production, she made around a thousand garments a year, which sold at an average price of $300.

CHESTER WEINBERG

Although he did not found his own company until 1971, Chester Weinberg was highly regarded for his innovative fashions during the last half of the 1960s. In 1965 he showed the first longer skirts; tailored and A-line, they ended below the knee and were meant for daytime wear. Except for the occasional silk jersey bathing suit, Weinberg designed mostly evening clothes and informal daytime ensembles, which could include anything from caftans, jumpsuits, slash-hemmed, one-shouldered dresses, and ball gowns to culotte suits and little jersey dresses with smocking and white collars and cuffs. Gigantic prints in bright colors appeared frequently. Weinberg liked both the jumper-and-blouse style and the vest over a dress or blouse, and he showed both in such different versions as broadtail with challis, quilted silk with jersey, and metallic lace with patterned lamé. An unusual evening ensemble was a black-sequined mini jumpsuit over a Pierrot-collared blouse of dark green silk chiffon.

During the 1970s Chester Weinberg ran his own business, and his designs calmed down to accommodate the flavor of the new decade. He closed his house in 1975 in order to free-lance and teach fashion design, and he died in 1985.

B. H. WRAGGE

Sydney Wragge's 1960s clothes for B. H. Wragge managed to be consistently innovative without trying too hard to be young. His cut was easy, and he often used the paper-bag waistline or smocking for dresses and overblouses with a gentle fit. When he used patterned fabrics they tended to be bold, as in giraffes printed all over a silk suit or a single huge Japanese brushstroke character splashed across the midriff of a linen sheath. He also liked vivid colors: black and white jackets were lined in tangerine, apricot was trimmed with white. Dresses as well as pants and shorts were made with overblouses, and a specialty was strictly tailored, sleeveless chiffon blouses shown over lumpy tweed or pin-tucked straight skirts, creating a relaxed version of a dress. He also continued to make simple linen dresses, often with cut-in necklines or cutouts at the back.

Wragge also designed evening dresses while remaining true to a sportswear aesthetic, especially in a 1961 long dress of black wool with square neck and self belt paired with a gold Lurex cable-knitted cardigan sweater. His pants might be cut jodhpur style, for a flowing look, or stovepipe, as part of a pantsuit, and in 1969 he designed a white linen and organza pants turnout with a sheer midriff panel on the tunic top and sheer legs ending in opaque linen cuffs. He designed shorts turnouts and even shorts

jumpsuits. His prices climbed as high as $225 for an evening ensemble. In 1971 he closed his business, and in 1978 he died.

BEN ZUCKERMAN

Until he closed down his business in 1968, Ben Zuckerman enjoyed a reputation for meticulous tailoring and high fashion injected into the otherwise conservative category of coats and suits. He was fond of dressing up pale, ice cream–toned wool dresses or dress and coat ensembles with jeweled buttons, patterned silk linings, and such fur elements as an ocelot blouse, and he also took formal fabrics and made them into strictly tailored clothes, as in a charcoal silk theater suit with pin-tucked jacket or a skirt with overblouse cut like a shirt, with bound buttonholes and covered buttons, in flowery apricot organza. His best coats, in such favored fabrics as bold tweeds and pebbly and fuzzy wools, were cut like modified bubbles with both curved and geometric seams.

Op art inspired the geometric pattern of this 1966 strapless voile evening dress and stole by Tiffeau & Busch, which sold for $245. The Library, Fashion Institute of Technology, New York

Pauline Trigère sculpted this 1961 evening coat from black wool plush and designed the pattern of meandering lines of rhinestones to be graduated.

Practical dress and coat or jacket ensembles were popular during the 1960s. This splatter-printed silk dress, with matching lined cardigan three-quarter coat, was designed by B. H. Wragge in 1962. The Library, Fashion Institute of Technology, New York

he year 1970 was the fiftieth anniversary of the ratification of the Nineteenth Amendment, which had given women the right to vote, and interest in feminism abounded. With wider acceptance of birth control, women took charge of their own destinies; many of them went straight from college into the workplace, postponing marriage and children in favor of establishing their careers. Whereas 1960s women of all ages contrived to look as much as possible like little girls, 1970s women aimed to look not necessarily older, and not necessarily more masculine, but, rather, more serious.

The 1970s woman intent on proving herself avoided giving any indication that her appearance concerned her, since admitting she cared about her looks was tantamount to confessing that she was either vain or frivolous or both. Grooming became covert: hair had to look as if nothing had been done to it—despite the fact that it may have been sun-streaked in a salon and carefully blown-dry; makeup had to look natural—even though it took just as long to apply sheer foundations, blush, and lipsticks and to carefully smudge eye crayons. Fashion became simpler, both in terms of how it looked and in that fewer garments were required to meet a variety of needs, and at the same time more complicated. Although separates look carefree, putting them together to create an ensemble is more difficult than slipping on a dress.

The same year that women were celebrating their independence, designers united to introduce the midi skirt. Actually more of a new silhouette than simply a length, it was very narrow, paired with skinny sweaters or jackets. It differed from the midi dress, introduced two years earlier, in being offered not as an alternative for evening but as the dominant daytime style. Most women reacted negatively to the midi, claiming that it was cumbersome and harder to wear than the mini; that it was dowdy and would make them look older than they wanted to look; and that designers had no business trying to inflict their own ideas on women. While many women purchased and wore the midi skirt, many more vetoed and rejected it. Some continued to wear minis, and even donned the extremely short hot pants when they were introduced in 1971, but most took to wearing pants. All the top American designers, including Bill Blass, John Anthony, and Oscar de la Renta, showed pants as a staple.

Wearing pants was not in and of itself new. A nineteenth-century diarist, Thomas P. Cope, reported in 1843 seeing the actress Fanny Kemble wearing full male regalia, including trousers and a man's hat, for fishing. Amelia Bloomer's circa 1850 pantaloon ensemble, although it was considered shocking and horribly unfeminine, came into use for various hardy sports. As the thinking of what constituted feminine and unfeminine behavior changed, primarily in the area of physical activities such as shooting, bicycling, and riding astride rather than sidesaddle, pants came to be viewed as necessary evils. Before the phenomenon of indoor plumbing became a commonplace reality in the nineteenth century, wearing pants, especially throughout the day or evening, would not have been practical for women.

In the twentieth century pants continued to surface in various guises and continued to enjoy a shocking or avant-garde reputation. The bifurcated skirts, for evening mostly, introduced in Paris in the 1910s were harder rather than easier to wear than skirts, since they were part of an elaborately constructed one-piece dress that fastened across the shoulder, down the side, and around the waist with hooks and eyes. By the 1920s women regularly wore jodhpurs for riding. It wasn't until the late 1920s that the first real breakthrough for pants occurred, in the form of beach pajamas. So popular as to be a major and fairly long-lived fad, they were worn for daytime lounging as well as for casual evening occasions. Pajama costumes were not strictly tailored: they flowed like long dresses, giving a feminine appearance.

Man-tailored trousers emerged in the 1930s, worn to greatest effect by such actresses as Katharine Hepburn, Greta Garbo, and Marlene Dietrich, mostly for daytime. They set an example that would be followed extensively during World War II, when women wore pants to work in factories or gardens and to get around the stocking shortage. Although in the 1950s women reacted to such masculine looks popular during the war by adopting an exaggerated femininity, pants abounded, usually in fairly sexy, form-fitting, and ankle-revealing varieties. During the 1960s jeans began to be worn in great quantities. In the same decade the first designer pantsuits, seen as a glamorous alternative to the occasional skirt ensemble, appeared.

In the 1970s women went several steps further: they put on pants instead of skirts to go to work, to school, to restaurants, and out at night. Dress codes relaxed considerably, and only private clubs continued to ban trousers, as some of them still do. The pantsuit of the 1970s, usually made with matching trousers and tailored jacket or tunic and accessorized with low-heeled or stack-heeled pumps or boots, shoulder bag, scarf, gold jewelry, and perhaps even a fedora, was worn to prove a point. It indicated that women had rejected the midi skirt (and, in the case of older women across the country, the midi's alternative of a mini); that they were militant in ignoring the various social conventions regarding what was proper for a woman to wear when; and, last but not least, they were simply showing who was wearing the pants.

The concept of equality between the sexes led several designers, notably Rudi Gernreich, to experiment with unisex clothes, but the problem with these usually contrived styles was that they did not appeal to men, who wouldn't wear them, and therefore they lost their point. Outside of high fashion, the sexes dressed remarkably similarly. Wearing a man's clothes indicated that a woman was one of the guys, and, of course, it was always fun, and part of a remaining rebellious spirit, to confuse the old folks, who claimed they couldn't tell the difference between boys with long hair and girls in jeans.

For the first time in history, young women came of age having never worn a skirt, except perhaps for the very occasional visit with the grandparents. Young people wore jeans, preferably straight-legged, button-fly, and nicely faded, rather than the 1960s version, which was tattered and covered with embroidery and patches. Stores selling secondhand jeans cropped up all over the country, until designers eventually figured out how to make jeans that were already faded or worn in. Other options for students of both sexes were army fatigues, sailor pants with many-buttoned plackets, and painters' pants. Men and women wore pea jackets, windbreakers, down jackets and vests, turtleneck sweaters, and pullovers. Both also wore the heavy-soled Frye

In 1972 President Nixon visited China, sparking off interest in Chinese culture and inspiring such fashions as these Donald Brooks winter peony–patterned silk pajamas and Mu Gee clogs by David Evins. Photograph: Alberto Rizzo. Courtesy Harper's Bazaar

boots, clogs, Cork-ease sandals with beige suede wedge platforms of varying heights, ergonomic Earth shoes, espadrilles, and, by the end of the decade, cowboy boots and Adidas.

In the early 1970s, many continued to wear 1960s styles. The ethnic-peasant-eclectic-hippie look was still in full swing, and although it was based on batiks and tie-dyes, mismatched patterns, fringes and tatters and feathers, rings on the fingers and bells on the toes, it left a legacy of concepts that worked successfully for the increasingly tailored look. First, the importance of assembling one's own costume as opposed to wearing an accepted uniform provided a foundation for the renewed notion of separates dressing. Then, Eastern gauzes and rayons, so different from the boxy 1960s look, fostered a feeling for *flou*, or softness, which carried into the 1970s fluid, as opposed to tailored, clothes. Last, the end of the 1960s introduced the earthy, natural look, and from the very beginning of the 1970s models were depicted with long hair blowing in the wind of an electric fan, with glowing tanned skin imperceptibly made up with just a little blush, mascara, and lip gloss. Although the sexual revolution was a 1960s phenomenon, its 1970s continuation mandated a natural look for women who didn't plan to stay at arm's length and wanted soft, clean hair and makeup that would not rub off on someone else's face or clothes. This remained the major look for years.

The new concern for ecology brought with it a greater appreciation for anything natural. Orlon, drip-dry cotton-polyester blends, and Qiana began to be replaced by wool, cotton, and silk. The bright, swirling colors and patterns of the 1960s were eventually replaced by softer, blurrier designs, often with a hand-painted look, small prints, and a more subdued palette of paler tones. At the opening of the 1970s, colors were still bright, and outfits often made use of several solid and printed fabrics in *Yellow Submarine*–intense hues combined with either patchwork or layering. Around 1973 the Beige Decade began in earnest: colors suitable to the newly appreciated natural fibers included not only beige but peanut, sand, taupe, khaki, olive drab, and brick red. All neutral colors, they worked well for separates dressing, based on the concept of mixing and matching a variety of pieces. Interiors came to be done in neutrals like white, off-white, and beige as well. The natural style called for earth-toned, textured cottons in upholstery, for unstained woods, as in butcher block, and for plenty of green, growing plants, and busy women preferred maintenance-free, minimally decorated apartments and houses.

As designers realized that they had to offer the kinds of clothing that women wanted to wear, even at the loss of their own freedom to experiment, they began to design tailored clothes based directly on those worn by men. The single most important article of clothing in a woman's 1970s wardrobe was the blazer, and the single most common example was single-breasted, one-buttoned, and cut with medium wide, notched lapels. Shirts, also man-tailored, were made in chambrays, oxford cloth, or striped shirtings. Although both wrap and lightly gathered dirndl skirts were available, fly-front ones with buttoning side tab pocket were most prevalent. For summer, women wore blazers with either shirts or T-shirts, pants or skirts, and espadrilles; for winter, blazers and skirts in tweeds or gabardine with versions of the stack-heeled Gucci pumps known in some circles as Gucci loafers.

Calvin Klein and Ralph Lauren, the new stars on the ready-to-wear fashion horizon, both presented versions of menswear for women, Klein's more relaxed and Lauren's more precise. As the decade wore on, female versions of men's clothes looked further into the past, running to old-fashioned band-collared shirts like those that were formerly attached with separate collars, formal pleated-front shirts, and shirts with wing collars.

Whether clothes were man-tailored, softly flowing, or knitted, the 1970s fit was close to the body. An overall narrowness was more important than a minuscule waistline, and the ideal body, as exemplified by the decade's top model, Lauren Hutton, was slim and willowy. It was very important that the ideal figure be a natural one, achieved not by means of corsetry but by dieting and exercise. Working out brought with it the trend of wearing leotards, which were paired with jeans or wrap skirts, and clothes like T-shirts and shrunken sweaters worn as snug as leotards. Almost all clothes were cut close to the body, especially through the torso, with high and tight armholes and narrow sleeves. As the decade wore on, pants became more fitted, so that by the end of the 1970s women had to lie down in order to zip up their jeans. Some women began to unbutton their shirts to show off their narrow, firm bodies and braless breasts (and designers placed the buttons accordingly), and this was the first sporty, or daytime, low décolletage ever seen. Those who could carry it off wore blazers without shirts.

The simplicity of 1970s fashion had the same effect on American designers as the sporty styles of the 1920s had had on the Paris couturiers. Try as they might, 1970s designers could not force elaborate styles on women, who wanted easy-to-wear clothes that were versatile enough so that they decided when and where to wear what. Faced with the monotony of turning out yet another

The women's liberation movement in-spired Rudi Gernreich to accessorize his spring 1971 collection of separates for Harmon Knitwear with such military/militant accessories as toy rifles, riding boots, dog tags, combat watches, and avi-ator sunglasses. Modeled here by Peggy Moffitt is his white polyester double-knit jacket and cocoa shorts and desert hood. Photograph: William Claxton

The archetypal 1970s silhouette was lean and rangy, with clothes cut close to the body, especially through the torso. Louis Dell'Olio followed this line in his 1973 turnout of plaid blazer, grid plaid shirt, and flared-leg pants. The Library, Fash-ion Institute of Technology, New York

blazer, pair of trousers, man-tailored shirt, T-shirt, cardigan, shirtdress, or halter-necked evening dress and the pressure of having to compete with all the other designers producing the same type of things, Seventh Avenue began to concentrate on image rather than on the actual designs. American design-ers saw to it that their faces (and antics) became well known by managing to be in the right place at the right time to be snapped by the paparazzi, and they showcased their life-styles, hoping that consumer awareness of their good looks and good taste would boost sales. They increased their advertising, and thereby their leverage with fashion magazines and department stores, and they resorted to placing logos, initials, and even their entire names on their clothes. In short, the label went from the inside to the outside of the clothes.

Department stores entered a new era. Saks Fifth Avenue and Bergdorf Goodman closed down their by-now obsolete couture or custom departments, and all stores phased out their formerly huge millinery salons. Department stores filled with expensive, moderate, and lower-priced sportswear, all fairly much alike, divided their selling floors into designer boutique areas, shuf-fling them around as one designer became hotter than another. Bloom-ingdale's succeeded in selling itself as a place to see and be seen and modernized the idea of shopping as a leisure activity, particularly on week-ends, and Henri Bendel also proved adjustable by making the transformation from old-school couture establishment to a store capable of discovering and nurturing such talents as Stephen Burrows, John Kloss, Joan Vass, and Mary McFadden. Fashion students and fledgling designers waited in line outside the store on Friday mornings, when Geraldine Stutz, the director, reserved time to look at whatever was new and interesting. However, many of New York's formerly great stores, such as Hattie Carnegie and Jay-Thorpe, vanished.

Reflecting the new casualness of the 1970s, nightlife turned considerably less formal. Instead of going to charity balls, people went to discos like Studio 54. Although gaining admission to a disco might require attention-getting garb, no particular formula applied. Disco wear ranged from skin-tight jeans to a bare outfit with lots of body glitter to a campy getup. Women who didn't feel comfortable with the idea of wearing intentionally feminine clothes that signified traditional thinking about women's roles often opted for antique clothing. Somehow, an Edwardian lace blouse or camisole (especially when worn with jeans), a 1940s printed rayon dress, even a 1930s evening dress or 1950s cocktail dress didn't carry the same message as their contemporary counterparts. Antique clothing boutiques could be found all over Manhattan, and in the 1970s they were still well stocked and affordable.

For the most part, black tie on an invitation was something to ignore. In the 1979 movie *Manhattan*, Diane Keaton accompanies Woody Allen to a formal opening; although he and many of the other men are wearing dinner jackets, she is dressed in a blazer over a dark silk below-the-knee-length dress, the kind of ensemble most women wore to work and then out to a party afterward. Hollywood films of the 1970s reflected the prevalence of the casual and natu-ral style, and the actresses themselves played down the notion that part of their job was to set an example of glamour. Diane Keaton, Candice Bergen, Ali MacGraw, and Meryl Streep posed for publicity pictures and sat for inter-views wearing jeans, sweaters, blazers, and the occasional silk blouse.

What evening clothes that were made were definitely subdued. For most of the decade a 1930s influence reigned, expressed in bias cuts, in bareness,

A far more pragmatic solution to the problem of hem lengths than short shorts was pants. Long a part of both high and young fashion, trousers in the 1970s were adopted by women of all ages across the country to wear for all sorts of occasions. Whereas earlier pants looks had often been based on flowing pajamas or paired with mini dress tunic tops, 1970s pantsuits were deliberately masculine, with blazers and notched lapels, pinstripes, cuffs, and sometimes pleats, and worn with man-tailored shirts and even fedoras. Masculine tailoring also crept into skirt suits, which gradually overtook pantsuits for business wear as the decade progressed. Bill Blass designed the three turnouts pictured here in 1971.

This 1973 Calvin Klein ensemble of brown and beige cashmere reveals the softer side of pants dressing.

In 1972 Chester Weinberg topped his long, swirling black jersey dresses with smock jackets in yellow silk taffeta or bright green mohair. Photograph: Bill King. Courtesy Harper's Bazaar

particularly low V necks and backless backs, and in fluid materials like chiffon, matte jersey, and crepe de chine. Dresses like these were made by Scott Barrie, Stephen Burrows, John Kloss, and, above all, Halston, whose halter-necked, wrapped, backless designs in either knee- or floor-length were immensely popular. Even when embroidered in sequins, few evening dresses featured patterns. Further examples of the fluid look were pajama ensembles, often worn with wrapped jackets, floor-length T-shirts in matte jersey, and floor-length cashmere sweaters. Some shone in bright colors like red or electric blue, and black was beginning to creep back into the evening scene, but white, beige, pastels, and earth tones predominated in formal clothes of the 1970s, as in day clothes.

In 1975 the miniskirt finally went out of circulation, and designers as well as fashion writers were sanguine that women would start buying more dresses and skirts. Dresses for daytime usually featured gently blousing bodices, drawstring waists, and easy pull-over-the-head fit. One of the constants of the entire decade was the wrap front, used for jackets and tie-belt bathrobe coats as well as for dresses like Diane von Furstenberg's wildly popular 1972 example in cotton jersey. Another important dress of the decade, Clovis Ruffin's slightly flared, knee-length, matte jersey T-shirt with scoop neck and cap sleeves, was copied by the thousands.

The lean looks of both the tailored and the softer fluid clothes discouraged the use of all but minimal accessories. The thirties nostalgia at the beginning of the decade contributed longer muffler scarves and knitted beret-cloches.

Simple pieces made out of real materials replaced the funky plastic or ethnic jewelry of the late 1960s and early 1970s. For day or night, most women wanted a pair of diamond stud earrings or small gold wire hoops, a gold chain or two or three, and a cuff bracelet of ivory, cinnabar, or brass. Elsa Peretti, who began designing for Halston, came to the forefront with her diamonds by the yard, thin gold chains sprinkled with occasional collet-set diamonds, her ivory-and-coral tooth pendants, her organic bean-shaped bottles on a cord, and her belts of leather run through a molded silver or gold free-form loop. It was infinitely preferable to wear no jewelry at all than to wear anything fake.

The preference for real and natural materials extended to leather, and women took great care selecting shoes, boots, shoulder bags, and briefcases in tan, brown, and burgundy calf. They also wore leather watchbands, with gold-rimmed, white-enameled dial watches. For summer, women found straw baskets or beach totes to use as pocketbooks. In keeping with the color and look of straw they wore webbing belts and espadrilles. Summer also necessitated the wearing of sunglasses. At the beginning of the decade large tortoiseshell-framed dark glasses vied with the sportier wire-rimmed aviator style. By mid-decade, round tortoiseshell preppy glasses had taken the lead.

By the end of the 1970s, the style of man-tailored separates evolved into the preppy look and became much more regimented. Whereas women forging wholly new careers in the early 1970s may have felt free to dress like mavericks, particularly by wearing pants rather than skirts, women in the late 1970s following them into the workplace, who faced much more competition, fell under the spell of doing everything by the book. The specific book was John T. Molloy's *Dress for Success*, which, along with countless articles, counseled women intent on climbing the ladder to adopt a suitable uniform, just as men had. Pants were out. Big businesses instructed their female employees to wear them only if they wanted to remain secretaries. The dress-for-success look was available at moderate prices, since by the time it entered the vernacular most high-fashion designers had moved on to less tailored styles. The suggested uniform consisted of a skirt suit, a shirt with a floppy bow tie, low-heeled shoes, flesh-toned stockings, and inconspicuous jewelry. Subdued colors and materials, such as navy or gray flannel and pin-striped cottons, predominated.

For leisure, the preppy look could be blindingly bright. Such staples as Shetland sweaters, boat shoes, sailing slickers, rugby shirts, and polo pullovers were available in shades of watermelon, emerald, life-jacket orange, yellow, and royal blue. Styles first introduced by such designers as Ralph Lauren were watered down and offered in a medium-price range in mail-order catalogues as well as in the career sections of stores. This look continues to be the most prevalent 1980s alternative to high or extreme fashion.

Man-tailored separates evolved not only into the preppy look but also into a style defined as classics with a twist. This direction in fashion was led by such new designers as Perry Ellis, who showed his dimple-sleeved sweaters, broad-shouldered, boxy cardigans, cropped pants, and culotte minis in the last two years of the decade. While retaining an aesthetic for natural fibers and colors, he played with proportion, leading the way to a renewed interest in novelty. Women who had achieved success could afford to be adventuresome in their wardrobes, and more creative fashion would be a harbinger of the 1980s.

ADOLFO

Adolfo's premier medium during the 1970s, in keeping with the decade's close-fitting, body-conscious silhouette, was knits, specifically a closely worked crochet of silk and wool. With this material he designed long, skinny, halter-necked dresses with cardigans, other casual evening clothes, and daytime turnouts consisting of jackets, vests, skirts, or pants with soft silk blouses. The knitted materials had lacy or pointelle patterns or geometric designs. With his first little suits for Gloria Vanderbilt Cooper in 1967, Adolfo began working in a Chanel idiom, and by 1973 he was concentrating on his own version of the Chanel look, in knitted suits with braid details and deluxe buttons. In its September issue, *Vogue* wrote, "Coco's Paris apartment, the wit, the charm, the laughter bouncing off coromandel screens. Adolfo recalls it all with his wool bouclé suit, mint green, touched with silvery metallic embued with all the elegant Chanelisms."

In the early 1970s Adolfo began to perfect what became his primary signature look: knitted versions of the Chanel suit, made in bouclé yarns with tweedy effects and trimmed with braids or fabrics matching the coordinating blouses underneath. Drawing: Richard Ely. Collection of Society of Illustrators Museum of American Illustration. Gift of the artist

ADRI

In 1971 Adri was honored, along with Claire McCardell, with a fashion exhibition at the Smithsonian Institution, Washington, D.C. Until 1974 she designed a line of clothes and accessories known as Adri that was produced by various manufacturers. In 1975 she formed Adri Clotheslab, Inc. Her designs included separates put together in ensembles, which she continued to make in various kinds of synthetic jerseys at the beginning of the decade, later in the 1970s turning to natural fibers, such as unbleached linen.

Dresses of the late 1970s were typically easy, such as this 1977 Scott Barrie overblouse dress of raw silk (left), shown with Barbara Bolan pocketbook, and the blouson example in loosely woven silk and wool by Geoffrey Beene for his Beene Bag line. Photograph: © Barbara Bordnick

JOHN ANTHONY

In 1971, John Anthony formed his own company on Seventh Avenue. Born in New York City, educated at the Academy of Fine Arts in Rome and at the Fashion Institute of Technology in New York, he had worked for nine years as a designer of low-priced sportswear for Devonbrook and for three years designing for Adolphe Zelinka, leaving when the company was disbanded. Within a year of opening his own ready-to-wear company, he had won a Coty Award for designs that in many ways epitomized the 1970s. John Anthony's wrap coats and blazer suits with either slightly flared skirts or fairly wide-legged trousers were made most often in solid color materials, although he did use an occasional check or other geometric pattern. His expert tailoring gave way to softer, more relaxed, and more fluid designs toward the end of the decade, as in pajama turnouts with soft silk shirt jackets or simple little evening dresses with halter necklines and fluttering skirts.

SCOTT BARRIE

Scott Barrie, who had been born in Philadelphia, educated at the Philadelphia Museum College of Art and at the New York Mayer School of Fashion Design, worked as a designer for the Allen Cole boutique before starting his own business in 1969. Out of materials like Acrilan, Celanese acetate knit, Jasco matte jersey, and Lurex he made simple ensembles of pull-on T-shirts with pants, little wrap mini dresses, simple décolleté shirt-tunic dresses laced down the front with cords of chains, long halter dresses, and elasticized, pull-on, strapless jumpsuits. His wilder designs included bare-midriff or smoking pants turnouts in bold, large-scale, bright patterns.

GEOFFREY BEENE

During an era when most women's clothing was based on that of men and the fit, especially in the torso, had a shrunken air, Geoffrey Beene began to experiment with his own ideal of a relaxed, easy fit, and he rejected such mannish elements as blazers, pleated trousers, and man-tailored shirts in favor of elements he would make his own: jumpsuits, flowing pajamas with pull-on blouses, chemise shirtdresses, and strapless, tubular dresses. All through the 1970s—certainly before Yves Saint Laurent debuted his 1976–77 peasant-look collection—Beene based both evening and daytime looks on full-skirted dirndls, by 1975 sewn into waistbands with narrow cartridge pleats, paired with peasant blouses, shawls, and capes.

In terms of style, the 1960s continued into the first few years of the 1970s; correspondingly, Beene was still working with his somewhat demure looks of little wool dresses with white collars and cuffs, high-waisted dress and long cardigan coat ensembles, and long evening dresses with contrasting built-in boleros trimmed with braid. For these he used less heavy worsted and more mohair-softened wools, along with crepe de chine. Besides his so-called couture line (it was actually ready-to-wear), which could run as high as $950 for a 1973 sapphire silk evening dress embroidered on the upper back with a Japanese fan, he designed

lower-priced lines called Beene Bazaar, Beene Boutique, and, eventually, Beene Bag. Beene Bag designs resembled his couture line in style but made creative use of cheaper fabrics with their own integrity, like seersucker, mattress ticking, or unbleached muslin.

BILL BLASS

The mainstay of Bill Blass clothes throughout the 1970s was the blazer, which was usually single-breasted with a one-button closure, cut very narrow with high small armholes and skinny sleeves, and with fairly wide lapels. He showed such jackets with pants (most of his suits for the decade were pantsuits), with just-below-the-knee-length A-line skirts, and in evening materials as part of dinner or theater turnouts. Just as the decade began, he designed longer-hemmed dresses with slightly raised waistlines and gathered skirts ending below the knees, but these were soon displaced by trousers, which Blass dressed up by pair-

This 1970 evening dress by Geoffrey Beene for Beene Bazaar combined several of the designer's favorite looks: the mix of different patterns, an Empire waist, and a bolero jacket (not shown). Jewelry by Robert Originals.

The blazer was the single most important article in the wardrobe of the 1970s woman. Here, Bill Blass uses a blazer as a jacket for a 1971 pantsuit and, elongated, as an entire coat.

These two Donald Brooks summer evening dresses of 1970 made the midi length more palatable with skin-revealing slits and bare backs. Made in floral-printed cotton broadcloth, they are shown with costume jewelry by Robert Originals and sandals by Donald Brooks for Palizzio.

ing them with fur-trimmed wrap coats and cardigan sweaters. His evening clothes were typically long and fluid, sometimes cut on the bias in a direct 1930s style. In 1975 he announced that women across the country had asked him for clothes to wear to cocktail parties and then on to dinner; the cocktail dress, which had disappeared from the scene when pants took over, was then revived. His prices rose in the 1970s, although they did not reach 1980s heights, and he introduced Blassport, a less expensive line. He also designed under licensee arrangements luggage, shoes, sheets, cars, scarves, and furs and continued his menswear lines.

DONALD BROOKS

In 1970 Donald Brooks won his third Coty Award, and in 1971 he introduced a boutique collection. In 1973 he disbanded his business but continued various licensing arrangements, including designing loungewear for Maidenform, which was advertised in 1973 as costing from $9.50 to $24.00. His theatrical costume work earned him an Obie award in 1976 for a production of *The Tempest*, and he was also involved with his alma mater, Parsons School of Design, as a consultant and instructor.

Brooks's designs for the first three years of the 1970s were softer than they had been in the 1960s and encompassed the current predilections for ethnic looks, with bare midriffs, peasant-shaped clothes made in fabrics with prints borrowed from Navaho rugs or batik patterns, as well as the sinuous, pared-down look of bias-cut, long slip evening dresses, sometimes ornamented with bias-cut cascading ruffles.

STEPHEN BURROWS

Stephen Burrows' World at Henri Bendel was one of the most obviously in spots of the early 1970s. His clothes were appealingly unserious in the way they explored—and rejected—much of what was considered absolutely necessary in clothing construction. Instead of buttons, Burrows used snaps or laced cords. Instead of hiding machine-stitched seams on the inside of a garment, he exposed them and even flaunted them, using eye-catching colors and some of the alternative stitches on a sewing machine, like closely spaced zigzag, widely spaced zigzag, or edge binding, which, when applied to stretchy materials like jersey, produced the signature Burrows rippling lettuce effect. He worked with different fabrics in the same garment, such as leathers and suedes with synthetic jerseys, and he pieced them together to form yet another commentary on traditional sewing methods, creating a modern ornamental patchwork. Some of his clothes were made in Bendel's Fifty-seventh Street workrooms, in sizes 1, 2, 3, and 4, unusual for the time, but common now. In 1973 Stephen Burrows opened his own business and won a Coty "Winnie" Award, and in 1974 he won a Coty for at-home wear.

BONNIE CASHIN

In 1970, when skirt lengths became controversial again, this time because they were getting longer, Bonnie Cashin defended her longer styles in an advertisement: "I call my long things Sun-day clothes. They're for special occasions, like Sunday brunches with lots of Bloody Marys, tooting around the country side, antiquing—or for the Off Off Broadway scene." Even more than she had in the 1960s, Cashin worked with several lengths, experimenting with and fine-tuning proportions. She designed narrow, short dresses and high-waisted, fuller long ones; she showed long skirts unbuttoned over trousers, tunics over leggings, pants that were flared, narrow, or stovepipe that brushed the top of the shoe, grazed the ankle, or stopped just below the knee. In 1972 she founded the Knittery, which specialized in sweaters with a handmade look knitted from hand-spun wools.

Bonnie Cashin left active designing to concentrate on philanthropic activities, but two of her designs lived on in the 1980s. One is a red poplin raincoat, trimmed with khaki flat piping and fastened with her signature brass toggles, made exclusively for Orvis. The other, made in many versions after her original prototype, is the Coach leather pocketbook, made in heavy, matte-finish leather and usually featuring more of the brass catches.

LIZ CLAIBORNE

In 1976 Liz Claiborne, a veteran Seventh Avenue designer, started her own business in partnership with her husband, Art Ortenberg. From the beginning her special niche was working clothes for women who did not have to or chose not to wear suits to work. This was at the height of the dress-for-success tyranny, and Claiborne's increasingly casual, separates-based working wardrobes, which sold in a medium-price range, were immediately successful.

Liz Claiborne is from a New Orleans family, but since her father worked in Brussels she grew up in Europe, where she studied art at the Fine Arts School and Painters Studio in Belgium and at the Nice Academy. She had always wanted to be a fashion designer, and winning the *Harper's Bazaar* Jacques Heim design contest in 1949 cemented her ambitions. Her first fashion job was as a model sketcher for Tina Leser, where she worked for two years before moving to Omar Kiam for Ben Reig, where she was a design assistant. Starting in 1960 she designed for Youth Guild, a division of Jonathan Logan, where she remained for sixteen years.

VICTOR COSTA

In 1973 Victor Costa left Suzy Perette and returned to Texas, this time to Dallas, to begin his own company, which he did by buying into a firm called Ann Murray. He produced a small collection of his own designs, which he sold in New York, and within a year was successful enough to buy out Ann Murray, changing its name to his own. He continued to produce his own versions of French and American designer clothes, always with the idea that high fashion should be available in an affordable price bracket (around $100 for a party dress) and always concentrating on evening wear.

OSCAR DE LA RENTA

Although Oscar de la Renta made lots of safari-jacketed suits and floating dresses in caftan, butterfly-wing, or sarong shapes,

he also continued throughout the 1970s working with his signature silhouette of flounced, long skirt, cummerbund waist, fitted bodice, and full, ruffled-cuff sleeves for dresses made out of paper taffeta (an unusual fabric in the 1970s), chiffon, and velvet and decorated with ribbons and embroideries. While he used subtle and pale tones, such as coral peach and amethyst, he preferred bright and sunny colors, especially in his patterned fabrics that were reminiscent of Persian rugs and Chinese porcelains.

By 1972 the company had three main divisions, described in an ad as "a little something that's very expensive, a little something that's a little expensive and a little something that's Something!" The most expensive line started at around $500, and the Something! line, usually under $100, was composed of crinkled gauze beachwear and jeans appliquéd with chintz and gingham, with matching jeans jackets.

PERRY ELLIS

In the early 1970s, as the age of Aquarius was petering out, there was a faction of students and women who were both young and conservative and who wore neither Op art minis nor stiff little Courrèges-type frocks. Their idea of fashion heaven was exactly coordinated separates from Ladybug, Pappagallo, Talbot's, and, especially, John Meyer of Norwich, a company that had been founded by Arlene and John Meyer, whose designer from 1967 to 1974 was Perry Ellis. Derisively dismissed by the more fashionable, John Meyer's cable-knit sweaters, matching knee socks, Peter Pan–collar blouses, and pleated skirts or soft dirndls held more than first met the eye. This was the real preppy look, soon to be revived as a fashion fad, and Perry Ellis was responsible for its subtlest expression. The kilts might be a muted blend of heathery, grayed shades, mirrored by the knit of the sweaters and socks, and the blouses of linen, in Liberty prints, as well as in solid shades of cotton. The experimentations with proportions and the wit of the later Perry Ellis were not yet evident, but the quality of the clothes gave signs of his talent.

Perry Ellis was born in Portsmouth, Virginia, and he graduated from the College of William and Mary with a bachelor's degree in business and then from New York University with a master's in retailing. In 1963 he was hired by Miller & Rhoads, a conservative Virginia department store with twelve branches, as the sportswear buyer for all the stores, and John Meyer of Norwich was one of his biggest sources. As buyers often do, he suggested changes that could be made in the clothes; when these were implemented, they proved successful. In 1967 he was offered a job as merchandiser at the company, which turned into a design job. When John Meyer died in 1974, Ellis took a job with Manhattan Industries assisting Vera Neumann, who signs her scarves and other textile paintings Vera, in transforming her fabric paintings into clothes. In order to work with better-quality materials, he began designing a line of his own for Manhattan Industries under the label Portfolio.

Two years later, in the fall of 1980, Perry Ellis launched his own label. He was an immediate success, and from the beginning established himself as a designer of separates made of wonderful natural fabrics in sure colors, whether vibrant or pale, and interesting proportions. As at John Meyer, sweaters remained

Bonnie Cashin designed this turnout of piping-trimmed knicker jumpsuit and matching coat in 1972. Photograph: Bill King. Courtesy Harper's Bazaar

This Stephen Burrows 1973 evening dress and cape, shown on model Beverly Johnson, epitomizes the 1970s narrow, body-revealing silhouette. It was made in matte jersey with the designer's signature machine-stitched lettucelike edging. Photograph: Francesco Scavullo

By the end of the decade, designers such as Perry Ellis, bright new talent of the fashion world, had begun playing more with construction and shape and proportion. This 1979 ensemble featured a raspberry wool melon-sleeved seven-eighths coat, belted and worn over a mustard turtleneck and a mauve circular-cut knee-length skirt.

Photo by Francesco Scavullo

253

important to him; he often retained the cables of the Meyer sweaters but made the new ones of rougher wools, gave them details like his dimple shoulders, and designed either a shrunken or oversize fit. His clientele was more adventurous than the customers for John Meyer or Miller & Rhoads.

GALANOS

During the 1970s Galanos worked primarily with his long, narrow, and supple silhouette for dresses shaped like skinny caftans, overblouses and long skirts, or slips, as well as those with one-shoulder or plunging halter necklines. Fabrics for these ranged from bead-embroidered wool to printed sheer silks and hammered satins. Increasingly, he used a kind of tucking and smocking combination, as well as shirred piping and trapunto embroideries. His daytime clothes might be casual, as in a fluid dress with its skirt slit to reveal hot pants or a soft trouser ensemble, or formal, as in skirt-and-coat suits trimmed with fur. A group of 1970 evening dresses were made with prints based on the figures of warriors on antique Greek vases. Their perfect workmanship and wonderful materials made Galanos clothes expensive, to the extent that prices were rarely mentioned in magazines, but one 1973 bugle-beaded evening dress featured on the cover of *Vogue* cost $2,400.

RUDI GERNREICH

The ideal of equality between the sexes in the 1970s prompted Rudi Gernreich to show a collection of military-safari clothes for women accessorized with dog tags and toy machine guns and to dress men and women alike in floor-length caftans, one-piece maillots, unitards, jumpsuits, and his 1974 thong, which would later surface in the form of the 1980s thigh-revealing bathing suit. Similarly, he introduced Y-front underwear for women, which Calvin Klein popularized in the 1980s. He dabbled in such projects as designing home furnishings and developing a line of his own gourmet soups. His last accomplishment was his pubikini, photographed by Helmut Newton, intended to showcase the last taboo: a woman's pubic hair, which was shaped and painted bright green. He died shortly thereafter, in April 1985.

HALSTON

In the 1970s, fashion took two opposite forms: the man-tailored style versus the soft, unconstructed, pared-down look. Halston was firmly in charge of the latter. In 1972 he expanded his couture operations at 813 Madison Avenue, where he began to sell fairly inexpensive ready-to-wear on the ground floor, more expensive off-the-rack clothes on the floor above, and custom-made offerings on an even higher floor. The ready-to-wear lines were also available in stores around the country. At a time when the couture was grinding to a halt, and many of the best American designers were either retiring, fed up with the world of fashion, or dying out, Halston had become a star, visible at society events and, after it opened in 1977, Studio 54, then the hot spot of New York nightlife.

Halston's clientele, while receptive to the special experience of buying made-to-order clothes, demanded that their clothes be modern, casual, and easy to wear. Halston obliged them with such signature items as his floor-length, close-fitting cashmere sweater sets in pale colors; caftans and variations of djellabas in sheer, floating chiffon, sometimes tie-dyed, with optional matching bras; bare-backed, halter-necked evening dresses in matte jersey or chiffon; Ultrasuede shirtdresses and wrap coats; short shorts or long pants to be worn with tunics, turtlenecks, wrap jackets, coats, or capes; and, in addition, the sculptural, free-form jewelry, made from silver, gold, ivory, ebony, and black cowhide, by Halston's former model Elsa Peretti. In 1975 Elsa Peretti designed the teardrop bottles for Halston's perfume. By 1976 Halston was showing strapless long dresses like sarongs, tied above the breasts, as well as his floating long dresses with an asymmetric V neckline. In 1978 he moved his offices into Olympic Tower, on Fifth Avenue at Fifty-first Street.

A big look for evening during the casual 1970s was the caftan, here interpreted in a dolman-sleeved, flowing yet narrow version by Halston. Drawing: Richard Ely. The Frances Neady Collection, The Library, Fashion Institute of Technology, New York

CATHY HARDWICK

Cathy Hardwick began her business, first called Cathy Hardwick 'n' Friends, in New York in 1972. Previously she had worked as a free-lance designer after getting her start making silk bikinis and running a boutique in San Francisco, where she had moved as a teenager from her native Korea. In the 1970s she concentrated on lively separates, in an affordable price range, which she designed not only to work well together but also to coordinate with pieces from her previous collections.

BETSEY JOHNSON

As the designer for Alley Cat, Betsey Johnson made inexpensive (usually well under $100) young clothes that were much more humorous and spirited than most of the going modes. She used bright-colored fabrics, prints she had designed herself, and jacquard knits for sweaters in patterns she had worked out on machines, putting them into clothes that were modern and comfortable but with a vintage air. Her designs included the first post—hip hugger, high-waisted, pleated and cuffed trousers; long prairie dresses cut princess style and fastening down the front with braid attached with snaps or hooks and eyes; and 1940s- and 1950s-style sundresses.

Betsey Johnson left Alley Cat around the time that she had her baby Lulu in 1975, and her interests turned briefly to designing maternity and children's clothes, as well as patterns for Butterick. In 1978 she formed her own company, and she dedicated her first collection to Claire McCardell. Based primarily on the concept of stretchy body wear, the clothes related both to Johnson's original ambition to be a dancer and her open mind about technology. The fabrics included spandex or Lycra and cotton blends, and the separate pieces, which could be worn in various combinations, included bathing suits and bodysuits, leggings and pants, off-the-shoulder tops, and flared, gored skirts. Compared to all the tailored menswear styles of the 1970s, these clothes, while still separates, looked fresh and appealing.

NORMA KAMALI

In 1971 Norma Kamali quit her airline job to work full time in the boutique she ran with her husband on East Fifty-third Street. She began to concentrate on producing her own clothes rather than importing, and her early designs, such as a black strapless jersey dress with matching long mitts and a floating peignoir-type evening coat of patterned sheer silk trimmed with ostrich feathers, combined a Hollywood flair with a feeling for the kinds of clothes found in antique clothing stores. In 1974 the Kamali boutique relocated to 787 Madison Avenue, on the second floor, and Norma Kamali began to work with more sophisticated tailoring for more grown-up styles that included beautifully cut suits and fluttery silk afternoon dresses. In 1978, having divorced her husband, she opened her own boutique, called OMO, after On My Own, on West Fifty-sixth Street.

KASPER

In 1971 Kasper began to design a lower-priced line of casual separates, called Kasper for J. L. Sport, in addition to his regular line for Joan Leslie, which was composed of suits, dresses, and evening ensembles. His clothes for both lines fell in between the

Wool jersey, a fabric well suited to fluid, easy silhouettes, was used by Cathy Hardwick for these drawstring-waisted and towel-necked dresses and separates from her fall-winter collection of 1978–79.

Many aspects of the 1930s were revived during the 1970s. Charles Kleibacker, master of the bias cut, designed this flowing, sinuous evening dress made of eighteen yards of silk crepe de chine in 1974.

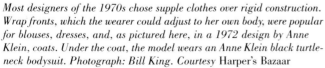

Most designers of the 1970s chose supple clothes over rigid construction. Wrap fronts, which the wearer could adjust to her own body, were popular for blouses, dresses, and, as pictured here, in a 1972 design by Anne Klein, coats. Under the coat, the model wears an Anne Klein black turtle-neck bodysuit. Photograph: Bill King. Courtesy Harper's Bazaar

Calvin Klein designed this luxuriously simple, straw-colored silk shirt-dress with snakeskin belt in 1973.

John Kloss brought the same easy construction to his dresses that he used for his lingerie and nightgowns. This 1976 knee-length dress of green Golden Touch Enka featured a low, square décolletage with adjustable drawstring.

1970s opposing schools of soft and unconstructed versus man-tailored. Kasper jackets were usually cardigans instead of blazers, his pants tended to be full and flowing, and his dresses were often made out of jersey fabrics with halter necklines and other references to 1930s fashion.

CHARLES KLEIBACKER

During the 1970s fashion caught up with Charles Kleibacker; the look he had pioneered of soft, imaginatively cut clothes that followed the body but did not impose a shape on it had become important. But whereas most designers used supple fabrics and cuts with a minimum of construction, Kleibacker continued to experiment with the intricate bias cut, keeping his operation small and selling only what his technicians could produce. In 1984 he moved to Ohio to become the designer-in-residence for the Department of Textiles and Clothing at the School of Home Economics as well as the curator of Historic Costume at Ohio State University.

ANNE KLEIN

In the 1970s Anne Klein continued to design classical separates, like hacking jackets, ruffled blouses, and kilts, knickers, or trousers, but she also worked with such modern ideas as bodysuits to be worn with zippered miniskirts and jumpsuits as well as clothes that reflected the current ethnic craze, like djellabas made in Indian printed cotton. By 1972 she was using as her trademark her astrological sign of a lion's face. When she died in 1974, her twenty-five-year-old assistant designer Donna Karan took over. *Vogue* noted in its coverage of Karan's first collection that her clothes tended toward the soft and sensuous while keeping the renowned Anne Klein tailoring and sophistication. Donna Karan hired her best friend from Parsons School of Design, Louis Dell'Olio, to work with her, and they became codesigners for the label. Together they produced appealingly casual separates, such as suede jeans to be paired with silky shirts, informal suits of short-sleeved blazer, circular skirt, and tank top, and wide-leg pants in jersey or raw silk as a basis for evening turnouts.

CALVIN KLEIN

Calvin Klein graduated from the Fashion Institute of Technology in 1962 at the age of twenty and then worked for five years for the Seventh Avenue manufacturer Dan Millstein. When he started his own business in 1968, he concentrated at first on coats, and by 1969 had landed one on the cover of *Vogue*. As of 1971 he had begun to experiment with sportswear, designing coatdresses, often in knits, hot-pants turnouts, jumpsuits, and classic blazer pantsuits that all shared certain constants of man-tailoring, notably in the way shirts, jackets, and pants were cut and in the use of topstitching. He did not neglect coats; these were available in a range from very casual, made in poplin lined with gingham, to dressier, in tweeds, to almost formal, in suede trimmed with fox.

In 1973, the year he won the first of three consecutive Coty awards, Calvin Klein emerged as a top designer who had his finger on the pulse of American women. Having learned, while touring the country, that women were becoming more name-conscious and wanted to be able to buy all their clothes from a single designer, he worked with the concept of wardrobes of interrelated pieces. One such grouping, all in the favorite 1970s color of beige, was composed of silk evening pants, tank top, shirt jacket, daytime trousers, cardigan sweater, polo shirt, and coat. With various combinations of these items a woman could be dressed for any occasion.

Although Klein designed dresses, like his 1973 strapless tube of black matte jersey, most of his evening looks remained fairly casual. Two-piece dresses were made in silk charmeuse in lustrous pale tones or in crepe de chine printed with foulards in daytime tones of beige and burgundy or navy and brown. Often these dresses featured wrapped blouses, whose décolletage the wearer could adjust to suit her preference. The pieces that wrapped were held in place by a soft suede belt edged with brass beading or by wider cummerbunds of woven webbing.

By 1975 Calvin Klein had become a celebrity, and he changed his somewhat homespun earlier image (a 1973 advertisement quoted him as saying about his new collection, "I made a lot of things that go with things") for a more glamorous one. His advertisements began to feature photographs by Chris Von Wangenheim, Deborah Turbeville, and Guy Bourdin, who shot a 1976 ad that showed a Calvin Klein silk blouse on a wire hanger, with the label visible at the back of the neck, hanging next to a mirror in which a nude woman was reflected. More and more, Calvin Klein was trading on the idea that the appeal of his clothes, simple as they were, lay in the attitude of the wearer, who affected their look by how far she unbuttoned her shirt or what she wore—or didn't wear—underneath her silk slide of a dress or her Calvin Klein jeans (his 1980 television ads starring Brooke Shields would be notorious).

JOHN KLOSS

John Kloss was known in the 1970s primarily for his innovations in the area of lingerie. Most successful was the novel bra he designed for Lily of France, which was made out of a stretchy, sheer, glittery, and earth-toned material that Kloss discovered in the Lily archives. The bra was both seamless and underwired, which made it perfect for women who really needed the support of a bra but wanted to look as braless as everyone else. John Kloss nightgowns, like the bras, did not rely on lacy trimmings for their interest; made from mostly solid-colored nylons in non-boudoir colors like lemon or taupe, they were cut like sophisticated evening dresses. Kloss sportswear was also simply cut and made of soft fabrics, like matte jersey and crepe de chine.

By the end of the 1970s, Kloss's various licensing arrangements began to go awry. Although he continued to design, his business problems grew, and in 1987 he committed suicide.

RALPH LAUREN

At a time when clothes had become increasingly casual and the divisions between day and evening, work and play had blurred, Ralph Lauren managed to revalidate the almost completely dormant idea of formal country clothes. Tweeds had formerly belonged to a category all their own, reflecting the fact that living in

Clovis Ruffin offered this white acrylic pleated tent dress in 1973, which was worn with the then-popular platform-soled pumps and a scarf around the neck.

Mary McFadden's earliest designs made use of hand-painted China silk, as in this 1975 one-shouldered, diagonal-hemmed, floaty short evening dress with Chinese button fastening.

the country had its full share of social conventions. Suburban development during the 1950s had created the need for clothes that could go from town to country easily, but by the 1960s country clothes meant cast-offs and jeans. Drawing on images of English country house life, and working much in the manner of such 1930s designers as Vera Maxwell and Helen Cookman, Lauren began to make clothes for women that looked just like the hacking jackets, shooting togs, and other sportswear classically worn by men. That he copied the clothes so literally, and that they were immensely popular, caused a stir.

Lauren was born in 1939 in the Bronx, and studied business at City College of New York before working at Alexander's, Brooks Brothers, and as a salesman for a necktie company. Ralph Lauren began his menswear company, Polo, in 1967 with the inspired idea of a wide, luxury necktie, which appealed to a generation of men who might never before have worn one. Bolstered by the success of his menswear, in 1971 he began designing for women with a line of man-tailored shirts. By 1972 he had expanded his women's-wear line to include Shetland sweaters, walking shorts and trousers, trench coats, and even pajamas and bathrobes, all made exactly like men's clothes, down to the French cuffs, interior pockets in jackets, fly-front skirts, and piping trim on the pajamas. The tailoring was based not on contemporary traditional clothing then being sold in stores like Brooks Brothers but on the styles available decades earlier: shirts with the round neckbands formerly used with detachable collars or with contrasting white rounded collars and cuffs; gray flannel mixed with tattersall checks and argyle in ensembles reminiscent of those in old photographs of school teams; and a fit close to the body, in the style of the 1930s, rather than boxy. Lauren even forbade the use of modern wool and cotton blends.

In 1974 Ralph Lauren costumed the male characters in the film *The Great Gatsby*. Women as well as men who saw the movie wanted to dress in the same kind of elegant, nostalgic, ice-cream shades of linen. Even more influential was the 1977 movie *Annie Hall*, in which the title character, played by Diane Keaton, wore imaginatively assembled menswear elements like tortoiseshell glasses, vests, oversize tuxedo shirts, hacking jackets, and fedoras. Although Ralph Lauren adapted items of male black tie for women, he did not produce evening clothes; for night, a Ralph Lauren client might combine velvet pants with a lace-trimmed shirt and tweed jacket. For the most part, Lauren's 1970s clothes were made to wear to work, for spectator sports, or for actual sports.

MARY McFADDEN

Before Mary McFadden designed her first group of three tunic ensembles, which were bought by Geraldine Stutz for Henri Bendel in 1973, she was often depicted in the pages of *Vogue*, where she was special projects editor. At a time when the applied arts of India, China, and Africa had aroused great interest, Mary McFadden set an example for *Vogue* readers to follow. The magazine showed her New York apartment and her house in Africa, where she lived for most of the 1960s, as well as McFadden herself: in a traditional Romanian wedding dress embroidered in scarlet, fuchsia, emerald, and gold, which she wore in lieu of a ball gown; in a braid-trimmed burlap weskit from the Electric

Circus boutique on St. Mark's Place, which she wore backward over black velvet Saint Laurent Rive Gauche trousers; and, hailing a cab for work, in an almost floor-length suede coat, her head adorned with scarves and African necklaces.

Mary McFadden was born in New York, reared in the South and on Long Island, and attended Foxcroft before studying in Paris at the Traphagen School of Fashion and Columbia University, where she majored in sociology. She worked for Christian Dior-New York and, after moving to Africa, for African *Vogue* and the *Rand Daily Mail*. She began designing almost by accident. She had often had clothes made to her own specifications from interesting fabrics she had found in her travels, and when *Vogue* wanted to show her tunic ensembles, and then Bendel wanted to sell them, she had to produce them. Her business started in a basement in 1973; by 1976 she had established Mary McFadden Inc. Her first designs included one-shouldered satin charmeuse robes, Chinese quilted vests, and fencing jackets paired with soft chiffon pants. In 1974 she showed a three-tiered dress, each tier dipping in back, of cream-colored, narrowly pleated silk. Within a year she had perfected the pleating process, using man-made silk, and began designing dresses in the Fortuny style and combining the pleated garments with silks that had been hand-painted and/or quilted in patterns based on Oriental, African, and even Viennese motifs. To fasten her clothes she used thick cords knotted with beaten brass openwork plaques.

VERA MAXWELL

Vera Maxwell contributed two innovations to 1970s fashion. The first was her discovery, in 1971, of Ultrasuede, which, when made into gently shaped coats, suits, and dresses, proved to be a round-the-year and around-the-country staple for women who wanted clothes that could go anywhere. In 1974 Vera Maxwell designed her first Speed Suit, which was really just a dress with a stretchy knit top, elasticized waist, and gathered skirt that could be pulled on over the head in a matter of seconds. She included Speed Suits, in long and short versions, in every collection up until her retirement in 1985.

ALBERT NIPON

In 1972, noticing that the birthrate was falling off, Albert Nipon and his wife Pearl decided to branch out from designing and producing their successful maternity line, Ma Mère, and go into manufacturing nonmaternity dresses. The Albert Nipon company, started in 1973, was run by Albert, with Pearl acting as the lead designer, and it was based in both Philadelphia, where both had been born, and New York.

Although known as a pants period, the 1970s spawned numerous successful dress designers, including Diane von Furstenberg and the Nipons. What Albert Nipon produced was what Pearl herself liked to wear: comfortable, feminine, moderately priced dresses in classic shapes with many dressmaking details like tucks, fagoting, and topstitching. A typical Albert Nipon dress might have been made in a bright, striped cotton stitched so that the stripes were close together in the bodice and open in the unpressed pleated skirt. In order to maintain control of their fairly

Pavé sequins were as ornate as the casual 1970s got. Norman Norell designed this 1972 camel-hair evening suit with paillette-lined jacket and blouse, modeled by Anjelica Huston and shown with a Van Cleef & Arpels necklace of coral, tiger-eye, and diamonds. Photograph: Alberto Rizzo. Courtesy Harper's Bazaar

detailed construction, the Nipons didn't hire out to contractors; instead, they imported the necessary machines so that they could supervise all the work.

MOLLIE PARNIS

In the 1970s, Mollie Parnis continued her association with the White House, being one of the designers favored by both Betty Ford and Rosalyn Carter. Her 1970s designs featured soft jersey day dresses with the new below-the-knee-length hem, suits with Eisenhower-type jackets, knit day dresses, jersey evening gowns shaped like slips or made with halter necklines, flowing lines, and accompanied by cardigan jackets. Her Boutique line, begun in 1970, was designed by Morty Sussman, and Hubert Latimer, who had designed for Irene, Charles Cooper, and Christian Dior-New York, was in charge of her couture, or higher-priced division.

CLOVIS RUFFIN

In 1972 Clovis Ruffin, who had been designing for various boutiques, founded his own company, Ruffinwear. He was an immediate success, and he won a Coty Award for inexpensive young clothes. Although he used such patterned fabrics as jersey printed with light bulbs or flamingos, he excelled with simple, easy-to-wear jersey and Lurex knit clothes, which the wearer could make as dressy as she wanted. His most successful design was a scoop-necked, gored T-shirt dress with a flared skirt.

GIORGIO DI SANT'ANGELO

As the 1970s opened, Giorgio di Sant' Angelo's designs moved in two different directions. In one, he experimented with leotards, bodysuits, and other stretch-knit items that formed the basis for an easy way to dress. The other was his Old West hippie look of patchwork dresses with lace-up fronts and eyelet ruffled skirts in mixed patterns, Western-style shirts and jeans made in various colors of fabric sewn together with embroideries and other trimming, clothes made out of unfinished leather skins laced together with thongs and sewn with scattered fringes, and bright red, turquoise, black, and white Navaho rug prints.

As the decade wore on, and women became more serious about paring down, Giorgio di Sant' Angelo continued working with innovative stretchy knit clothes, such as bodysuits made with sheer panels that could be worn as evening tops with wrap skirts, a beach wardrobe of white matte stretch-fabric bikini, wrap top, and tie skirt, all in a matching bag, and an all-in-one stretch tube dress with Doctor Denton feet that fell in graceful folds when the model was standing still but could stretch in any direction.

SCAASI

With the exception of Halston, Scaasi was New York's only couturier during the 1970s. His one hundred private clients were women who didn't want to bother putting together what he termed "bits and pieces," so they continued to come to him for formal clothes to wear to city luncheons, the races, and private parties. While he offered some trendy designs, such as the variations of hot pants he showed for evening at the beginning of the decade, he mostly created luxurious, shapely clothes that reflected his own vision of how women should look rather than the current fluid and narrow silhouette. He made sable-lined raincoats and hand-painted crepe de chine versions of caftans. He used only bugle beads, costlier than sequins, for embroideries. His specialty was sophisticated evening dresses, usually with small waists and full skirts, made of various imported embroidered organdies. For the March 21, 1977, issue of the *New York Post*, Scaasi told Eugenia Sheppard that it was "fun to be using more shape again." The times had caught up with him, the general mood again receptive to constructed, sculptural clothes made on the grand scale.

ADELE SIMPSON

Adele Simpson continued in the 1970s to produce daytime clothes, particularly suits, and evening dresses. Her suits were narrow, often with long shirt-jackets and pleated skirts. A model shown in 1973 was an almost exact copy of one of her 1951 designs, made in black and white checked wool with a matching long, fringed scarf. Her evening clothes were long and narrow, in keeping with the 1970s preferred silhouette, but might be Edwardian rather than 1930s in feel, as in a long, black, patterned silk dress with leg-of-mutton sleeves. She used jersey for night, for long dresses with matching cardigans sprinkled with rhinestones as well as for the halter bodices of dresses with piqué skirts. Her prices rose as high as $500 in the 1970s.

STAVROPOULOS

During the 1970s Stavropoulos clothes were right in keeping with the mood of the time; his narrow, often bias-cut, and bare long dresses exemplified the prevalent silhouette. He worked with black chiffon for pure halter-necked slips of dresses and jumpsuits with camisole bodices, and he layered different colors of chiffon for dresses that changed hue as their wearers moved across the dance floor. He incorporated movement into his clothes as an important element; bias ruffles rippled down the length of dresses, and attached scarves and shawls floated behind the wearer.

PAULINE TRIGÈRE

Trigère's signature wool evening looks during the 1970s included floor-length evening suits and long dresses, bared or covered up, some trimmed with rhinestone embroidery. She continued to specialize in coats (which sold for as much as $1,350) and designed capes to be worn alone or with coordinating suits. She worked more frequently with silk chiffon, usually printed in a bold pattern, and layered the fabric in order to play the transparency of sleeves, bodices, and matching long coats or overdresses against opaque slips. An interesting evening turnout was composed of black, high-waisted rayon shorts and an embroidered white cotton poet's blouse bodysuit.

261

KOOS VAN DEN AKKER

In 1970, after two years in this country operating a curbside boutique in front of Lincoln Center, Koos van den Akker opened a shop on Columbus Avenue. He moved next to West Seventy-second Street and, finally, in 1975, to Madison Avenue. He had been born in The Hague, where he studied at the Royal Academy of Art. He served in the military, then went to Paris, where he worked as an assistant at Christian Dior, and returned to Holland, where he ran a boutique in The Hague for three years. While seeing the movie *Breakfast at Tiffany's*, he fell in love with the idea of living in New York City, so he immigrated here in 1968.

His first designs were little shift dresses, which he stayed up all night sewing in his hotel room and sold the next day on the street for $30. Entranced by the huge variety of interesting and inexpensive fabrics in New York's stores, he began to work with collage, using patchworks of materials in his designs. Naturally, he was right in sync with the early 1970s taste for eclecticism in dress, and as the decade wore on, he continued to experiment with fabric collage, using the resulting patterns for useful jackets that could be worn with anything, as well as for suits, coats, and dresses.

DIANE VON FURSTENBERG

Born Diane Halfin in Brussels in 1946, she studied in England, Spain, and Switzerland before marrying Egon Von Furstenberg and moving to New York. For six years during the 1970s, Diane Von Furstenberg supplied women who were torn between wearing minis or pants with a practical, comfortable, flattering alternative: the wrap dress, in a moderate length, made of Italian fine cotton jersey, usually printed in a bright floral or geometric pattern against white. Before the fad played itself out, her company had sold more than 300,000 models at around $70 each, just expensive enough to act as status symbols; in addition, there were innumerable copies.

In 1977 Diane Von Furstenberg reorganized the company to deal solely with licensees and perfume. In 1984 she took over a space on Fifth Avenue across from Grand Army Plaza, had the exterior and interior designed by the architect Michael Graves, and launched a couture house selling made-to-order clothes in the $500 to $5,000 range, divided into the categories Smart Lunch, Vernissage, Party, Hostess, and Gala. The couture house closed down in 1988, and since then Diane Von Furstenberg has concentrated on plans, long bruited, to bring the wrap dress back, finally doing so in 1989.

By 1977, when this photograph appeared in the New York Times Magazine Fashions of the Times, *the natural look had come to mean earthy tones of sand, brick or clay red, and browns and easy, relaxed silhouettes in crinkly or handwoven-looking cottons and linens. Cinnamon Wear made the bloused red cotton dress (right) and the wrap and tie cotton dress (left); the drawstring blouson dress was designed by Gil Aimbez for Genre. Photograph:* © Barbara Bordnick

OPPOSITE

The 1970s saw the emergence of the cult of the body. Not only were jogging and other forms of exercise healthy, they also produced the beneficial side effect of leaner, fitter figures, which were shown off to their best advantage by variations on leotard dressing. Shown here are 1971 Giorgio di Sant' Angelo vibrant-hued two-piece stretch suits. Photograph: Alberto Rizzo. Courtesy Harper's Bazaar

263

Design in the 1980s can be summed up with a single word: exaggeration. Fashions, whether oversize or shrunken, crumpled or tailored, pastel or neon, short or long, sexy or mannish, bare or covered, sophisticated or innocent, have been taken to extremes. Along with their clothes, women's bodies, by the end of a decade obsessed with fitness, have grown more rococo: breasts are bigger, shoulders broader, arms and legs more muscular; even faces feature silicone-enlarged cheekbones and pouty, fuller lips.

Demographically, the baby-boom generation continued to wield great influence over what was designed and produced, and as these men and women have transformed themselves from rebels into yuppies, their tastes have become more luxurious and their appetite for new sensations more intense. Having reached top-level executive positions, they've found having and spending money acceptable and pleasurable; having started families, they've deemed comfortable surroundings crucial; and having begun to enter middle age, they've cast their sights backward in a nostalgia for the past that knows no bounds, whether it manifests itself in an attempt to recapture former elegant standards or a fascination with kitsch.

The latest technology, when it came to their cars, computers, microwave ovens, compact-disc players, and videocassette recorders, was everything. Otherwise, the baby boomers have proved sybaritic. They ate for amusement rather than sustenance, causing trends in food to wax and wane. At home they have rejected minimalism in favor of an eclecticism that celebrates the past. Revivals ranged from Victorian excess to Art Deco geometrics and 1950s organic forms. Revivals of revivals included Greek, Gothic, and Pompeian. The craving for tradition manifested itself in several versions: American rustic and English country house as well as a mood in architecture and interior design that recalls children's-book illustrations. Around the country houses sprouted verandas and cupolas; interiors were furnished with overstuffed chairs and sofas in mattress ticking or Laura Ashley sprigs; plates and knives and spoons and forks were scaled for Papa Bear rather than for Goldilocks.

In fashion, just about every style since the crinoline has resurfaced. This one decade has seen nineteenth-century bustles and crinolines; turn-of-the-century camisoles and petticoats; 1910s long hobble skirts under flared peplum tunics; Jazz Age drop-waisted chemises, bias-cut slinks, and wittily escapist Depression-era looks; World War II large shoulders and abundant shirring; 1950s Merry Widow bustiers, toreador pants, and off-the-shoulder stoles; and sheath dresses and day-glo minis from the 1960s. Revivals from the early 1970s include the happy face as a decorative motif and the renewed appeal of ethnic fabrics and garments.

With their spending capacity, the baby boomers have fueled grown-up rather than youthful fashion fads. Most high-school students, at least in New York, have dressed down in the 1980s, wearing jeans, thrift-shop overcoats, men's undershirts, and dark glasses for a look of deliberately uncool cool

(exceptions include their experimental punk-style haircuts and wearing of multiple earrings). Although a sense of how to put clothes together still tends to emanate from the street, and, even more, from the new phenomenon of MTV, the most intense trends of the decade, such as Hermès scarves and Kelly bags, Chanel suits, quilted pocketbooks, and gold chains strung with baroque pearls, have trickled down into inexpensive fashion from Fifty-seventh Street. The baby boomers, who came of age rebelling against the establishment, finally discovered status symbols and, inspired by the strong mid-1980s dollar, went after European ones especially.

The 1970s predilection for things natural escalated to suit the intensified tastes of the 1980s. Four-ply cashmere supplanted wool, linen became preferable to cotton, and silk jacquard to crepe de chine. Consumers chose jewelry of large semiprecious stones set in heavy metal; a Rolex instead of a tank watch; tennis bracelets in lieu of diamonds by the yard. Glossy leather in tones of brown or burgundy has been replaced by alligator, lizard, snake, or eelskin in forest green, electric blue, hot pink, red, yellow, and purple, for accessories or, even better, for garments of all types. Just-blown-dry 1970s hairstyles have become elaborately tousled, held in place by mousse or gel.

As an accompanying trend, the plain has been eclipsed by the ornamental. Solid-colored materials in earth tones have given way to cabbage roses, animal prints, polka dots, paisleys, tartans, and brocades; forms of decoration include tassels, chains, bows, and ribbons, as well as a wealth of beads and sequins. Whereas all one needed in the 1970s to be perfectly dressed were a pair of jeans, a shirt, sunglasses, shoes, and a watch, this decade's ensembles have been accompanied by hats and gloves, chosen for fun rather than propriety, any of a welter of new hair ornaments, scarves and shawls, costume jewelry parures, oversize belts, patterned stockings, and whimsical shoes. As accessories became more important, fashion designers turned their attention to offering total looks. Clothes by Perry Ellis, Ralph Lauren, Geoffrey Beene, Donna Karan, Anne Klein, Adrienne Vittadini, and Calvin Klein can be worn with complementary shoes, pocketbooks, or costume jewelry. At the same time, accessories specialists have proliferated.

Makeup became more elaborate, too, with darker, often outlined lips, bold eyeshadow, and, as awareness of sun damage on skin increased, pale, powdered skin. Businesswomen paid for lessons showing them how to apply cosmetics, and as makeup became more visible, so did its accoutrements:

compacts and lipsticks were pulled out from pocketbooks for touch-ups at the restaurant table.

The January 1981 inauguration of President Reagan heralded the return of formality and ostentation in society as well as in dress. Proms returned, more color coordinated and carefully planned than ever; weddings proliferated and were celebrated at night in tents or museum galleries rather than at dawn on the beach. Coming-out parties resumed, along with charity balls and private black-tie dinners. For such events women have decked themselves out in ball gowns with huge, billowing skirts, trains, and elaborate draperies and, as of the mid-decade, short evening dresses, less formal styles that were popular with Americans in the 1940s, 1950s, and 1960s. Designers such as Bill Blass, Galanos, Oscar de la Renta, and Adolfo, all favorites with Nancy Reagan, along with Carolina Herrera, Mary McFadden, Scaasi, Bob Mackie, and Carolyne Roehm, all contributed to the decorative air at parties. Victor Costa gained a following of women who wanted to look extravagant and lavish on a relative shoestring.

Although glamour has definitely been in the air, in the social columns, and on television shows like the immensely popular "Dynasty," not everyone jumped into a ball gown or dinner jacket the second the decade started. Out of the 1970s spirit of being unconventional came the new category on an invitation called creative black tie. This meant that men wore tennis shoes or cowboy boots instead of patent-leather pumps; jeans, safari shorts, or even boxer shorts with dinner jackets. They skipped the dinner suit altogether, or accessorized it with various imaginatively patterned and colored bow ties, cummerbunds, braces, vests, and socks. Women used creative black tie as an excuse not to dress up, or as an impetus to step out of their images for the evening, perhaps in something costumey. Those who simply wanted a more glamorous version of their day look for evening took advantage of evening sportswear created by such designers as Calvin Klein, Ralph Lauren, Gloria Sachs, and John Anthony.

Women stopped being afraid that if they looked decorative and even deliberately alluring they would not be taken seriously. Almost as quickly as the working costume developed into a standardized uniform across the country of blazer, skirt, man-tailored shirt, and foulard or grosgrain bow tie, there emerged a more individual look that visually separated the women from the girls, or at least the women who wanted to project a powerful image from those who wanted to play it safe. "Power dressing" still rested largely on suits and dresses, but more and more it also included pants, and it managed to be both more masculine and more feminine than the 1970s dress-for-success style.

Masculine aspects of the new business clothes included bold tailoring, larger shoulders, and men's fabrics used in interesting combinations. Donna Karan, designing directly for the woman executive, was influential in introducing such feminine characteristics as curvier shapes highlighted by wide belts and softer draping. Brighter and more contrasting colors, higher heels and shorter skirts, and signature accessories like scarves, eye-catching jewelry, even fragrance and lavish underwear became the signatures of self-possessed career women. In fields like the law, where a professional image can affect the welfare of other people, women, as well as men, dressed more conservatively. Catering specifically to businesswomen have been new stores like Streets & Co. and Alcott & Andrews, as well as enlarged women's de-

Stephen Sprouse helped pave the way for a 1960s renaissance, designing such nostalgic fashions as this neon pink, Nehru-collared reversible coat of 1985 shown over his black silk jersey sleeveless T-shirt and short wool gabardine skirt. Photograph: Bill King

For the first time, the working woman had several images, ranging from conservative to stylish, with underlying connotations of menial to powerful. At the highest level, menswear detailing was appropriate only when it had dash, as in this Oscar de la Renta pinstripe suit from 1985 of navy and white wool, with navy silk blouse, which sold for $1,355. Photograph: Bill King

Perry Ellis showed this simple yet influential silhouette in 1982. Such oversize, boxy-cut jackets would reign over fashion for years to come, paired with either very long pleated skirts, as shown here, or narrow, short, tighter ones later in the decade. Photograph: Erica Lennard

Although the preppy look has always been an important part of mainstream American style, remaining popular decade after decade, in the late 1970s and early 1980s it became such high fashion as to constitute a major fad. Ralph Lauren, whose 1980 ensemble of tweed, lace, linen, and velvet is shown here, is the style's most haute *practitioner.*

partments of men's stores. Designers like Liz Claiborne and Mary Anne Restivo have tried to strike a balance between the appropriate and the fashionable.

To offset the tension of high-powered jobs and to keep competitively in shape, women exercised even more, and, in doing so, influenced fashion. In the August 10, 1978, issue of the *Soho Weekly News*, Annie Flanders (who later founded *Details* magazine) wrote that Betsey Johnson had come up with the "revolutionary new looks that zoom us right into the '80s." The clothes, from Betsey Johnson's first collection under her own label for her own company, were made primarily out of spandex and spandex blends and proved just the ticket for women who, now that they were in shape, didn't want their bodies hidden by "baggy big tops, business suits, tents." Betsey Johnson's collection spawned a host of imitators and sparked the phenomenon of clothes made to look like exercise gear, as well as the exercise gear itself worn as street clothes. In 1980 Norma Kamali contributed in her own way to the new style with her collection of kicky minis, leggings, and big-shoulder tops made out of gray, pink, or striped sweatshirt fleece, which were widely popular.

Exercise clothing worn on the street included jogging suits, stirrup pants, Lycra tights in lieu of pants, and bicycle shorts, along with tank tops, ripped sweatshirts sliding off the shoulder, running shoes, and headbands. Exercise clothes themselves, worn outside or inside studios, became much more highly designed: there were newly developed shimmery Lycras, used in bare-midriff tops, cropped tights, and bodysuits in patterns and bright, contrasting colors, as well as cotton-Lycra blends in which cotton was the dominant note. All the materials used for aerobics gear could also be used for swimwear.

It's not hard to understand why 1980s women have complained that they were too busy to shop. Buying through the mail or over the telephone or availing oneself of the services of professional shoppers or consultants became an acceptable if not preferable alternative to braving the stores. Many department stores, as well as mail-order houses, followed the lead of Neiman-Marcus and Horchow by upping the quality of what they offer. Stores have found that they can target a specific sector of the population through direct mail marketing, and ever since Bloomingdale's published its lingerie catalogue photographed by Helmut Newton in 1976, catalogues have been better designed and have even begun to offer editorial content. For a lot of people, catalogues perform the job that fashion magazines once did, since the magazines, beginning in the nineteenth-century and continuing into the 1930s, used to offer shopping services that filled orders and even shipped the merchandise across the country to readers. Catalogues can also serve to clarify current fashions for women who find the top magazines puzzling in their presentations, elitist in their attitudes, and fantasy-prone in their selections.

Besides being too busy to shop, women have claimed that they just hate it. It is true that shopping has changed from being a pleasure, something of an excursion, to a duty that is increasingly harder to perform. The Manhattan real estate boom in the 1980s acted to break up what was formerly a large, concentrated core of fashion on and off Fifth and Madison avenues. Smaller stores could no longer afford to rent space close to the big flagships, and except on Madison Avenue, shopping is no longer a matter of strolling along from store to store. Manhattan residents or visitors looking for something new or interesting have to take the time to check out Soho and Tribeca, parts of

Women in the 1970s who would have looked aghast at feathers, flowers, bows, and ruffles wallowed in them in the 1980s. Large floral prints, sexy silhouettes, feminine necklines, and accessories such as seen in this 1989 Victor Costa dress were ubiquitous.

Leather was popular not just for shoes and briefcases but also for skirts, pants, coats, bustiers, dresses, and other articles of clothing. In 1987 Cathy Hardwick offered these two ensembles based on knee-grazing leather skirts combined with cotton or challis shirts and Shetland coats. Photograph: David Hartman

PREVIOUS PAGE
Among the many fashions revived from the past were crinolines. For this evening ensemble of 1985, Calvin Klein modernized a full silk skirt with its eyelet-edged underskirt by pairing it with an off-the-shoulder T-shirt. Photograph: Sheila Metzner. Courtesy Vogue

Greenwich Village, Chelsea, and the Flatiron district downtown and the Upper West Side, upper Madison, and Lexington Avenue. Of all the shopping areas in New York, the one most reminiscent of the days of yore is Park Avenue in the high Fifties and low Sixties. Sara Fredericks and Martha operate in the tradition of former luxury stores like Hattie Carnegie, and Helene Arpels, Mario of Florence, and Susan Bennis/Warren Edwards head accessories stores that are almost like galleries. An area that is regaining the luster it had a century ago is lower Fifth Avenue. Most areas are populated with a variety of stores, ranging from chain boutiques to boutiques aimed at a specific clientele, whether preppy, avant-garde, or casual.

Finding out about these stores by word of mouth takes time, and many women are as intimidated by small stores with no one in them as they are by the ultraglamorous specialty shop. But they are also put off by the department stores, which have not easily made the transition from palazzos of merchandise and special services with a singular image to buildings arranged with

With the rise in importance of accessories, designers turned to providing their clients with "total looks." Robert Lee Morris, who often collaborated with Donna Karan, designed these various-sized and -shaped beads in 1987, worn in typical bold profusion. Photograph: Klaus Laubmayer

boutiques offering something for everyone. In department stores women have to have a fine-tuned sense of direction in order to find the spot where they saw something they liked on their last visit. They also worry about pickpockets and have to cope with trying on clothes that have been attached with bulky antitheft devices or not being able to try on clothes at all if they have been grouped together on a rack connected by locked-up coils of wire.

In an effort to accommodate the older baby boomer, stores such as Bloomingdale's, on its fourth floor, Barney's, in its new women's building, and Bergdorf Goodman, in its entirely renovated building, have come up with reorganizations that promote a feeling of space and calm luxury, with carefully edited offerings arranged either by designer or according to categories, including business clothes, new young designers just becoming well known, or one-of-a-kind evening clothes. Department stores have also become more involved in producing and selling their own private labels. Although this category of clothing has existed since the days when department stores and specialty shops had large in-house design staffs, it has become more important in the wake of higher prices and customer dissatisfaction, as a way for the stores to answer their clients' specific needs and, in doing so, to cement their identity. Of all the New York department stores, the one that has most steadfastly maintained its image has been Lord & Taylor, which copyrighted the term *the American look* in 1945 and has been promoting it ever since. Lord & Taylor not only applauds contemporary American fashion, it also refers in its ads and promotions to the American fashion tradition of the past, mentioning its early discoveries in ads and even reviving Claire McCardell's "popover" dress in 1981.

The designer's manipulation of image is a 1980s continuation of a 1970s phenomenon. When American fashion designers first began to be famous, their celebrity boosted sales. In the 1980s their images have been their most

carefully designed product. In order to have complete control, they have taken out multipage spreads in fashion magazines and established their own stores or departments within stores. Their images serve to sell not just their most expensive clothes but also their auxiliary lines of perfumes, cosmetics, hosiery, and accessories. The autonomy of the designer has resulted in magazines coming to look more and more alike, as the editorial copy mirrors the contents of the ads, as well as the department stores seeming more and more similar.

Selling an image is expensive. It requires not only advertising but also special events that will garner publicity. It has come to be such an expected part of the fashion industry that new designers have to choose between slowly finding their way, growing gradually, or, with backing, trying to make an immediate big splash. Even as late as the 1970s, designers like Mary McFadden and Fabrice could launch themselves by making a tiny collection and selling it to a single store. The 1980s have been typified by the career of Stephen Sprouse, who got his fashion business going to a roar of attention, went bankrupt, started up again with new and better backing, and went out of business again.

Learning lessons from Sprouse and from David Cameron, who briefly blazed on the fashion scene in the mid-1980s, are such new designers as Isaac Mizrahi, who, from the dizzying heights of his own instant stardom, has repeatedly insisted that he hopes to be able to keep his business at a manageable size. Other designers, such as Zoran, work somewhat in the manner of Norell, who deliberately kept his own business from growing beyond $2 million in annual production in order to maintain quality control. Designers who remain small (at least in comparison to some of the giant empires) can also follow their own aesthetic without having to worry as much about being reined in by investors. Such a group includes Charlotte Neuville, Angel Estrada, Carmella Pomodoro, Isabel Toledo, Tom and Linda Platt, Michael Kors, Mary Jane Marcasiano, and Geoffry Gertz. Unfortunately for the consumer, it is not always easy to find out about or keep track of new, smaller designers. Despite the fact that new fashion magazines, each trying to fill a new void, are constantly appearing, actual fashion reporting, for which consumers seem nostalgic, is hard to come by.

There is a problem with the images created by the bigger advertisers as well, and that is that they create a chasm between fantasy and reality. The fantasy is that the clothes will change one's life; the reality is that image doesn't make up for high prices and poor quality. Designers whose clothes sold for hundreds of dollars in the 1970s began to use more luxurious fabrics and intricate workmanship and consequently upped their prices considerably. The notion of investment dressing, highly promoted early in the decade, backfired. The concept was supposed to justify tenfold increases in price at all levels. But since women who wore the most expensive clothes didn't need to concern themselves with the shelf life of a ball gown or luncheon dress, as they would be replacing it the following season to stay in style, it was the women who wore moderate-priced clothes who began to feel they were being bamboozled. They knew that these high-priced clothes described as investments did not last, as actual investments should. They wondered why they had to pay so much for machine-stitched hems, skimpy seams, fabrics that didn't launder well, or clothes sewn together with plastic thread that got

The opulence of the 1980s has called for grand fashions set in equally grand environments. Carolyne Roehm, shown here in her own design of velvet skirt, trapunto-stitched satin bustier, and evening coat in her apartment, set a gilded standard. Photograph: Skrebneski

scratchy after being melted by an iron or came out in a single yank, making a hem fall in seconds. They also complained about fit, especially in the wake of clothes available only in one-size-fits-all or small, medium, and large. The sad thing is that American clothes in the middle-to-lower price ranges, which were always so well made, can no longer be made in America. Rising labor costs forced manufacturers to work with plants in the Orient and elsewhere, and only the more expensive designers can afford to pay American workers.

There has also been a chasm in the 1980s between fashion featured by the press or in the stores and the clothes women actually wear. Most women adopt modified versions of what is currently fashionable; in the 1980s they endorsed such standards as boxy jackets, oversize sweaters and cardigans, silk blouses, copies of alligator-skin accessories or expensive precious or costume jewelry. When in 1987—in an echo of the midi skirt controversy of the 1970s—the industry unilaterally decided to revive the short skirt, women, horrified by such dictatorial methods, registered their dismay with a resounding rejection. Business dropped off noticeably, and stores and designers had to retrench and concentrate on what they thought women would want. The problem is that women want to wear whatever they feel like wearing. One outgrowth of feminism has been that women dress individually, usually but not always within the current variety of styles. Very few women ever replace their wardrobes all at once; most buy new pieces to replace worn-out ones, and they want to make sure that these go with what they already have. The transition from the fitted 1970s silhouette to the 1980s looser, boxier one took place gradually over a period of years.

Providing women with what they want has given impetus to two new directions in fashion. One is the return, on varying scales, of the couture house. With prices of ready-to-wear so high, some designers have figured that they may as well be making clothes to order, and the American client, famous for her dislike of fittings and having to wait for a dress to be made, has curbed her impatience in exchange for personal attention and a personalized dress. New York custom houses range from hole-in-the-wall studios or storefronts, run by designers who don't want to bother with mass production or who don't want to have to assemble the capital it takes to produce a full-fledged collection, to luxurious couturiers. The custom establishments sprinkled around New York may function like Anita Pagliaro, who designs wedding and evening dresses, or Lee Anderson, who provides her private clients with similar or different versions of her ready-to-wear clothes. Ready-to-wear designers like Carolyne Roehm and Adolfo operate couture departments. Former ready-to-wear designers like Donald Brooks, Jackie Rogers, and John Anthony prefer the smaller, more intimate scale of working directly with their clients. Donald Brooks, as well as the milliner Mr. John and newcomer to fashion Christophe de Menil, run their couture operations out of their homes. And then there is Scaasi, who celebrated twenty-five years as a couturier in 1989: his designs became so popular that he revived his ready-to-wear line.

The other direction in fashion is a movement toward increasing mechanization and advances in technology. Clothes in the 1980s have been sold via vending machines, and stores are increasingly turning to computers to answer questions about merchandise formerly handled by salespeople. Computers also help women see how they will look with a new haircut or different cosmetics. Technology, which has already provided women with man-made fi-

Embroidery, especially beaded, helped to feed the new appetite for luxury. Bill Blass designed this 1985 sequined and beaded bolero, which accompanied a slender black silk dress. It was worn with evening gloves and a jeweled minaudière by Judith Leiber. Photograph: Sheila Metzner

Scaasi used a print of enormous zinnias and asters for this pouf-skirted, off-the-shoulder evening dress of around 1986 made for his boutique line. Photograph: Gideon Lewin

Women at the top of the ladder could afford to emphasize their femininity. Donna Karan's executive woman was typically clad in sensual sarong skirts, showing lots of leg, shape-revealing sweaters, and attention-getting jewelry or accessories such as this wide, shaped belt.

Sailor clothes, long a source for American style, provided the inspiration for these classic cotton separates shown by Perry Ellis for spring 1989. Photograph: Richard Dunkley. Courtesy Lear's

bers, pantyhose, natural fiber and Lycra blends, is used by many designers to achieve new knitted and woven materials. A combination of the computer program that shows a woman how she might look after a face-lift and that which sends instructions to a machine via computer graphics to produce a new sweater design will result in women being able to look at themselves on-screen, try on a suit or dress that is still only in the sample or design stage, adjust it according to her preferences in color, lapel width, skirt length, or other variables, and then order it to be made.

People looking alike is a thing of the past, not the future. In their quest for independence, American women have at times embraced uniforms, like the shirtwaist and skirt, the little black dress, the business suit, and the pantsuit, but always with an eye to making it their own, whether within rigid parameters (the 1950s) or relaxed ones (the 1960s). Always they have insisted on the right to have their own style, as opposed to being slaves to fashion. Fashion implicitly means novelty and change, and American women have demonstrated that, while they like novelty, they abhor change unless it has a reason behind it, as in the case of the New Look. If it is meaningless, merely a whimsy of designers, like the midi skirt or the 1980s miniskirt, they reject it. The 1980s have established, firmly, that variety is the most important aspect of fashion. That simplicity is in the air does not mean that variety has no place. American style was founded on the idea of exploring the wealth of potential within the limitations of simplicity.

ADOLFO

In the 1980s, Adolfo has been operating out of a Fifty-seventh Street salon offering custom-made clothes and designing an exclusive line of ready-to-wear for Saks Fifth Avenue, although other stores also carry his ready-to-wear clothes. As befitted a dressy decade, his designs included full-scale ball gowns as well as sari-narrow evening dresses and Chanel-style knitted suits, trimmed with braid and appliqué for day, embroidered with gilt and jewels for night. His simple chemise-shaped knit bouclé dresses were often decorated with geometric patterns, knitted in or with contrasting bands in bright colors. Adolfo won a Coty Award in 1982.

ADRI

Adri, whose Adri Clotheslab, Inc., manufactures her designs in Italy, has continued in the 1980s to work with separates made in bold and natural fabrics, concentrating on black, white, beige, and bold primary colors and with an easy, easy-fitting cut.

LEE ANDERSON

Lee Anderson, who grew up in northern California, was educated at the University of San Francisco and the Traphagen School of Fashion, New York. In the 1980s she operated a small custom house at 23 East Sixty-seventh Street, the same block where Valentina and Elizabeth Hawes once had fashion establishments. Working with her has been Jeffrey Moss, whose hat designs are sold wholesale as well as made-to-order. Their designs are characterized by an allegiance to the past, both in terms of workmanship and style; they use beautiful materials that are often whimsical, an easy fit, and such touches of interest as piqué collars and silk-flower boutonnieres.

JOHN ANTHONY

John Anthony's early-eighties clothing was luxurious—tailored, as it had been in the 1970s, but interpreted in opulent materials, like wool trimmed with fur or silk embroidered overall in intricately beaded geometric patterns. Anthony quit Seventh Avenue in 1984 and took two years off. In 1986 he opened an atelier at 60 East Sixty-sixth Street, where he has designed smaller collections, averaging around thirty made-to-measure pieces (ordered individually by size rather than fit on a single figure; in between couture and ready-to-wear). Despite the salon's smaller scale, the pace is hectic; John Anthony exposed a nerve when he divined that women wanted individual attention when they were buying higher-priced clothes, like his crocodile-skin bustier, softly draped jersey and silk evening dresses, and double-faced wool cocoon coats.

One of the favorite evening silhouettes of the 1980s was the bustier-topped short evening dress, shown here in a taffeta version by John Anthony from 1988.

Adolfo, whose forte is knits, made this patterned evening sweater in 1983.

Adri's knit experiments included these various skirt and pant silhouettes.

GEOFFREY BEENE

The one subject Geoffrey Beene returns to again and again in interviews is fabric, and in the opulent 1980s, it has been the most important aspect of his work. He either creates his own or combs the world for unusual materials, and in putting together different textures, weights, moods, colors, and patterns, he never comes up with an effect for its own sake.

He has remained true to his major silhouettes—the soft, caftan- or chemiselike dress, the slim column, and the voluminously skirted look—using them also for pants and jumpsuits, with a variety of hemlines for all times and all occasions. Beene has become bolder with his earlier leitmotifs of bands of braid, scalloped lace, beading, appliqué, and trapunto. On other designs, these would be trimmings, but in Beene's hands they become a major part of the whole. In the 1960s and 1970s he repeatedly experimented with variations on the vest or bolero theme, usually set into a dress. In the 1980s this bolero evolved into a curved fencing jacket shape, which Beene explored by playing sheer materials against opaque ones, setting the form into the midriff of dresses and jumpsuits and also using it as an actual separate jacket with cutaway hem in various lengths, from above the

breasts to below the waist.

One of the key characteristics of American fashion has always been the blurring of the distinction between day and evening; Beene has played with this theme by juxtaposing metallics with gray flannel, houndstooth with warp-printed floral taffetas, lace with blanket-plaid wool. Sometimes his best ideas can be seen on the inside of the garment, such as cuffs turned back to reveal a use of fabric that ties the whole ensemble together.

BILL BLASS

In keeping with the fact that one of his customers, Nancy Reagan, was the new First Lady, as well as with the opulence of the era, Bill Blass created more ornate and luxurious designs in the 1980s. He used materials like panne velvet, satin, and taffeta, cashmere and sable, and, especially, he began to use beads—for *trompe-l'oeil* sashes, leopard-patterned skirts, over an entire blouse or skirt as solid bugle beads in subtle ombré pink to white, and with sequined embroidery to form whole pictures, in fact, paintings, on evening jackets. His treatment of fabric became more elaborate, from lush poufs and cascades to the difficult-to-execute dresses made entirely of diagonal tucking. He used colors both bright—orange, emerald, hot pink, yellow—and subtle, even old-fashioned, as in an evening coat of American beauty pink, a color not seen since the 1960s, paired with just the right pale sky blue, another 1960s color. His blazers gave way to jackets of all shapes, which he typically mixed in suits with different materials, and he also continued to borrow sporty, daytime elements for night, as in his long, cashmere, twin sweater sets paired with matching silk satin or lace bouffant long skirts or his jeweled red, white, and blue tennis sweaters.

DONALD BROOKS

In 1982 Donald Brooks won an Emmy for a television special called "The Letter," starring Lee Remick. He also designed Claudette Colbert's costumes for the television production of *The Two Mrs. Grenvilles*. By 1983 he was designing sportswear under licensing arrangements, and in 1986 he introduced a new line of primarily ready-to-wear evening clothes, which he showed in his East Seventieth Street town house to great acclaim. For most of the 1980s, however, he concentrated on custom-made clothes available privately by appointment only.

LIZ CLAIBORNE

Designing based on market research as to what working women need and want has proved enormously successful for Liz Claiborne's ready-to-wear company. It went public in 1981, with shares sold on the open market, and it generated sales of $550 million in 1985. Liz Claiborne specializes in sportswear and dresses for the workplace; her busy customers don't have time to

Bill Blass has proven adept at giving new life to American classics, such as the sweater set of the 1940s and 1950s, interpreted here for evening in wool and cashmere and paired with taffeta or satin skirts in 1984.

shop and want to be able to go straight to that department in a department store that will have their kind of clothes. To further help them she has branched out into play clothes and leisure wear. In 1988 *Business Week* reported that the company was returning to New York for production, renovating Chinatown factories, and ordering fabrics from American mills. In 1989, Claiborne announced her retirement and said that her company would continue.

VICTOR COSTA

Victor Costa has become somewhat infamous in the 1980s for his very close versions or recognizable-from-across-the-room designs taken from the best of French and American designers. His price range is almost ludicrously low when compared to the cost of the clothes he "adapts"; one Costa dress, made in imitation of a model by Karl Lagerfeld for Chanel, reputedly sold for exactly one-hundredth of the price of the original. Using American fabrics and trimmings, Costa produces his clothes in his own factories, where he trains local workers in the art of sewing. Rarely are his designs, whether his own or copies, subdued; most are bright and spirited, with boldly patterned materials and high-contrast details. As a Southerner, he knows the value of cotton, and some of his best designs make use of wonderful cotton prints for dressy, warm-weather clothes.

OSCAR DE LA RENTA

Oscar de la Renta's favorite color in the 1980s could be called *black with:* black with hot or shell pink, black with emerald or lime green, black with turquoise, lemon, or orange, and opaque black with sheer black. His clothes have feminine touches of ruffles, lace, bows, jeweled buttons, appliqué, and passementerie and, often, elaborate bead embroideries, sometimes in such *trompe-l'oeil* effects as a dress made with a beaded fringed shawl wrapped around the hips or a jacket with a three-dimensional parrot perched on one shoulder. His evening clothes, for the most part, were narrower than those of the 1960s and 1970s, and long dresses were made with asymmetric draperies, drawing them closer to the body. Beaded jackets, many in bolero shapes, became a keynote, usually paired with simple dresses or evening skirts and blouses. Most of his daytime clothes consisted of suits and pantsuits made in coordinated different fabrics, such as plaids with stripes or floral prints, stripes with dots.

PERRY ELLIS

Perry Ellis had a real talent for carrying out a theme: his Sonia Delauney collection for winter 1986 featured stained-glass colors in geometric patterns worked out in tinted furs, knitted cotton or wool, bugle-bead embroideries, and printed silks. His spring 1986 collection was inspired by his own appreciation of Chinese export ceramics, from which he borrowed a blue and white dragon for a sweater, Canton plum blossoms for socks or neckties. While it is easy to appreciate the intellectual play that went into unifying hundreds of garments, it is clear that Ellis did his best work in designing the pieces that went together into a single en-

semble. He had an almost emotional sense of where to crop a pair of pants or a sweater; which shade of beige to pair with which icy blue; how to make a man's blazer feminine and insouciant for a woman. Against these Perry Ellis separates, other 1980s clothes often seem contrived.

For this 1980 turnout, Perry Ellis combined a long, hand-knitted pullover with short, flippy culottes.

Since his death in 1986, the Perry Ellis collections have been designed by Jed Krascella and Patricia Pastor, and since 1987 by Patricia Pastor, whom Perry Ellis hired when he began his Portfolio line in 1976. She continued to use design themes (oval dots or egg shapes in spring 1987, scallops in winter of 1988) and to incorporate many of Perry Ellis's philosophies about proportion, color, and fabric. In 1988 Marc Jacobs replaced Patricia Pastor as head designer.

ESPRIT

Esprit de Corp., founded in 1970 by husband-and-wife team Susie and Doug Tompkins, has enjoyed a tremendous success by cashing in on trends quickly and opposing the 1980s dictum of investment dressing. Marketing its clothes by advertisements featuring "real people," including many Esprit employees, the company supported the concept of individual personality in clothing, offering several different lines for men, women, and children that sell in more than six thousand stores around the world. The clothes focus on peppy separates in bright colors or black and white, designed to be worn in a variety of mix and match or clash configurations. As befits a company aimed primarily at a young consumer, prices are low, usually well under $100. When the Tompkinses divorced in 1989 Susie, the designing half of the team, left the company.

FABRICE

In 1979 Fabrice, a Haitian-born New York designer, experienced his first real success with a silk blouse that he had had embroidered in beads by Haitian seamstresses. His timing was perfect, because the 1980s proved receptive to the luxury and glamour of beaded dresses, and Fabrice proved able to transform a look that had been popular in the 1920s and 1960s into something modern. His graffitilike drawings of winding lines, lightning bolts, astral bodies, and other doodles float in space on a ground of silk, silk chiffon, cotton denim, even wool. He designs these patterns in New York and sends them and the materials to Haiti, where they are interpreted in beads, crystals, jets, and pearls. The materials are made into dresses and various separates in his New York loft.

Fabrice, known for his abstract beaded patterns, here has applied his free-form graffitilike embroideries to a white denim strapless mini dress with matching jacket from 1986.

Fabrice trained as a fabric designer at the Fashion Institute of Technology in New York and worked for two fabric houses before starting his own business selling hand-painted silk dresses in the mid-1970s. His first clothing designs were simple; dresses were fairly straight and either long or short, and the beaded designs took an upper hand. If the beaded pattern had a jagged or scalloped edge, so did the dress. If the pattern of embroidery was asymmetric, the dress was asymmetric. Around the time he began making menswear, in 1985, his women's clothes became more structured; he began using stiffer materials in dresses, "smokings," and suits. Sometimes he even made clothes that were devoid of beading. He also began to paint directly on fabrics like silk taffeta, reviving his mid-1970s technique. Fabrice won a Coty Award in 1981.

GALANOS

When Nancy Reagan chose a Galanos evening dress for the 1981 Inaugural Ball, the California-based couture-calibre designer became much more well known. Typically, he did not change his routine, which consists of designing personal and perfectionist collections of clothes and showing them twice a year in New York. His clothes run high, usually between $3,000 and $10,000, and are aimed very specifically at the echelon of women who can afford them. His simple, tailored day clothes, whether dresses, pantsuits, or suits, are appropriate for charity luncheons, board meetings, or gallery hopping, and his evening clothes are formal, yet modern. Although he works with many silhouettes, including chemises and poufs, most of his designs are broad in the shoulder, narrow at the hip, and long of line.

Galanos is particularly known for his beading, which is done by hand in his atelier and worked out in the round, usually circling the body and following its curves. Among his most acclaimed 1980s styles were pearl-beaded, floor-length evening sweaters. His fabrics, for which he culls Europe, are often worked in combinations, with a single dress formed of bead-embroidered top, printed, draped midsection, and a skirt of a different pattern, usually all in the same scale and color range. Galanos's clothes are exquisitely made, inside and out; he is well versed in the vocabulary of sewing technique, which leads him to use such effects as tucking and smocking, which are almost dying out. In 1989 he returned to a former favorite material, chiffon, using it in his inimitable tailored or flowing way.

SANDRA GARRATT

Sandra Garratt's line of interchangeable knitted items of clothing has spawned a number of imitations. The idea first came to her in 1974, when she was preparing a graduation-year design project for the Fashion Institute of Design and Merchandising in Los Angeles. After graduation, she worked with Mary McFadden, Halston, and Zoran, and in 1977 she revived her graduation-project idea and started a company in Dallas called Units. After legal disputes, she left Units and founded Multiples in 1986. Multiples comprises knitted clothes made in one roomy size that can be fitted to the body by means of knitted tubes worn around the midriff, hips, or waist. They come in basic, useful colors and are sold by "stylists" instead of salespeople, since customers have to be shown the potential uses of each garment.

HALSTON

Halston's early-1980s designs included expensive—ranging into the thousands of dollars—all-beaded, abstract-patterned, narrow long and short dresses, as well as variations on his bias-cut toga dresses, casual daytime turnouts, and the occasional ruffly dress in a stiff material like organza. From 1982, when he agreed to design a line of reasonably priced clothes and accessories for J. C. Penney, his business began to go sour. Bergdorf Goodman refused to carry his higher-priced line on the grounds that the J. C. Penney association had served to dissipate his cachet. Then the company that owned Halston Enterprises was taken over, followed by several more takeovers, until Halston lost legal control over his own name. His attempts to renegotiate for the right to design custom and higher-priced ready-to-wear clothes under his own label failed, and although his name continues to be used by Penney's, his only actual designs have been private commissions and ballet costumes for the Martha Graham Dance Company.

Along with short skirts, stirrup pants, cut and worn very closely fitted, brought focus to the legs in the mid-1980s. This suit, with a cropped swing jacket and high-waisted narrow trousers in wool knit, was designed in 1987 by Cathy Hardwick, and sold for about $148. Photograph: David Hartman

For these 1988 evening ensembles of black with fuchsia or emerald, Carolina Herrera achieved a bold, sculpted silhouette by means of narrow lines and broad shoulders dimpled high at the top of the sleeve.

CATHY HARDWICK

Cathy Hardwick, whose reasonably priced ($100 to $300), casual, young evening clothes, peppy skirt suits and pantsuits, and separates can be described as classics with a twist, usually in the color, proportion, or fabric, built her business to an annual volume of $20 million, yet in 1988 she declared bankruptcy.

CAROLINA HERRERA

In 1981 Carolina Herrera, long an internationally known beauty and a fixture on best-dressed and most-elegant lists, started a couture-calibre clothing business in New York. She later began designing a more affordable line called CH, as well as furs, wedding dresses, and a perfume. Her most renowned design was the clover-scattered organdy wedding dress she made for Caroline Kennedy. Herrera's clothes, bold, strictly tailored, and sculptural of silhouette, reflect her Latin roots (she is Venezuelan). While she uses the most sumptuous of materials, she keeps decorations spare; most often she relies on the shape of a dress or suit, contrasts of material, and curved, petaled sleeves or skirts for a strong impact.

MARC JACOBS

Marc Jacobs, who was born in New York in 1963, won two Golden Thimble awards from Parsons School of Design when he graduated in 1984. He then began his own company, which featured clothes that were typically humorous, such as sequined tank dresses with hands encircling the waist and little mini dresses painted with gigantic flower-power posies. Many of his designs refer to traditional American textiles and fashions, such as his gingham dresses, which he updated by making in stretchy materials; his takeoff on an Adrian suit appliquéd with houndstooth tulips (Adrian himself was referring to Pennsylvania Dutch motifs); and a lavishly beaded evening jacket patterned after a patchwork quilt. In 1988 Jacobs was hired by Perry Ellis as the company's head designer.

BETSEY JOHNSON

Betsey Johnson has continued in the 1980s working with spandex and Lycra and cotton blends, making peppy, inexpensive clothes that often refer to her own design history. She has revived her Paraphernalia-era minis, fluorescent colors, and motorcycle-jacket zippers, and has even recycled some of her 1970s prints. Her patterns, whether flora or fauna, are cheerful, and she accessorized cabbage roses or fish clothing with striped Raggedy Ann stockings. She has also remained true to her favorite silhouettes, including the flared, or flip, skirt first shown in 1965, the prairie princess silhouette, fitted and then flared, and the fitted, drop-waisted look. Her most prevalent neckline has been off-the-shoulder in a wide, shallow curve or strapless, paired with glove sleeves.

Using stretch lace and point d'esprit in bridal white, neon colors, or black, she has produced clothes that are as casual as T-shirts, especially when made to pull on over the head, but also formal, in a tongue-in-cheek takeoff on 1980s opulence. Her exuberant aesthetic has extended to her handwritten and drawn graphics for postcards and catalogues and to the boutique-revival décor of her many stores.

NORMA KAMALI

In 1980 Norma Kamali suddenly became a household word when her collection of sweats, or separates made out of sweatshirt fleece, produced by Jones Apparel Group, took off. The clothes were sprightly and easy to wear, and although they sold by the tens of thousands at affordable prices, they were also widely copied. Made in gray, pink, or striped fleece for day and in black and Lurex for evening, the clothes included kicky short pull-on skirts, leggings, tops with shoulder pads, and long, flared skirts. In 1986 Kamali stopped working with outside licensees (such as the Jones Apparel Group) and was planning to control all of her own production when she was thwarted by the International Ladies Garment Workers Union, which protested her action. Kamali then decided to concentrate on designing only what she could produce, and sell, in her West Fifty-sixth Street store building, with the exception of a licensed line of bathing suits. She transformed her recently opened Soho shop into a furniture and interior accessories boutique.

Despite the fact that Kamali is so closely associated with the sweats look, as well as with her quilted down coats, she actually makes her clothes in a wide range of styles, from tailored business suits to formal ball gowns with trains, with special emphasis on the updated reference to the past. Her favorite period seems to be the 1940s, and her shirred, draped siren dresses and bathing suits are often shown with snoods and platform shoes. From the 1930s she borrowed the bias cut for long, slinky vamp dresses, and from the 1950s she has revived the shirtwaist dress, making hers with fitted torso and broad shoulders, in fabrics as diverse as eyelet, printed rayon, crushed velvet, and even Battenberg lace tablecloth fabric.

DONNA KARAN

In May 1985 Donna Karan, formerly of Anne Klein, presented her first independent collection; even before the show was over it was a smash hit. The clothes, designed by Karan for successful women like herself, struck a nerve: they filled the wardrobe needs of female tycoons and gave a boost to women still working their way up the corporate ladder. The Donna Karan look has been built on thoughtfully designed separates—her bodysuit-blouses keep a woman from having to worry about her shirt riding up; her coats are cut roomily enough to fit over suits and other bulky clothes; her skirts are draped into sarong shapes to soften the silhouette. Her experiments with stretchy versions of wool crepe, twill, cashmere, and lace have proved a boon to travelers.

From the beginning, Karan insisted that her clothes be shown with all of her accessories in the stores, both to cement the total image she desired to project and to help women too busy to shop for individual components. Several of her accessories have become ubiquitous: the extraopaque pantyhose, the wide belt with

its huge C buckle, and the triple strand of matte-finish beads by Robert Lee Morris, which ushered in a taste for both nonshiny metals and oversize graduated beads.

In 1988 Karan debuted her DKNY line, which, at just under $100 on up to $700, is at least half the price of her more deluxe line. Aimed at a woman's weekend needs, it included denim skirts, jumpsuits, pants, jackets, cotton T-shirts sold in packages of three, and other basics.

KASPER

During the 1980s Kasper's designs for Joan Leslie and J. L. Sport included daytime and nighttime sweater dressing as well as short and long evening dresses made with modified versions of the decade's favored bows, poufs, and swags of fabric.

PAT KERR

The popularity of antique clothing in the 1980s, particularly the frothy lace-trimmed dresses, petticoats, and camisoles known as Edwardian whites, spawned a whole category of clothing made of various lace patchworks with such romantic bygone elements as high collars, gigot sleeves, pointed waists, and ankle-length skirts. The most extravagant dresses in this mood have been made by Pat Kerr. A collector of rare and antique laces, in 1979 Kerr brought a group of the dresses she had made from antique pieces to Neiman-Marcus, where they were bought on the spot. Since then she has specialized in dressing brides, bridesmaids, flower girls, and ring bearers in mixtures of Honiton, Carrickmacross, Brussels, and point de venise combined with tulle and various pale fabrics edged with very narrow satin ribbons. From antique jet-embroidered panels, Alençon, and point d'esprit she fashioned lavish black evening dresses. She has found most of her vintage laces and materials at auctions in Europe and has them made into clothes in Memphis, where she lives part of the year. Prices for her one-of-a-kind dresses climb to $25,000 and beyond.

ANNE KLEIN

Under the design direction of Louis Dell'Olio and Donna Karan, Anne Klein grew into a much higher-quality fashion company, with clothes made out of cashmere, silk satin, and allover sequined embroidery selling in the four-figure range. In 1982, the company initiated Anne Klein II, which featured many of the same styles, slightly adjusted in terms of workmanship and made out of less expensive materials.

Dell'Olio and Karan typically worked with separates, designing boldly shaped blazers and other jackets and coats; blouses, cashmere or angora knit sweaters, and cardigans; long, flared skirts or short, straight ones; and trousers in strong, solid colors that could be combined any number of ways for day and evening. In 1985 the company showed a pale pink cashmere blazer, which was also made in pale pink wool for Anne Klein II. Cut along classic but strong lines and made in a surprising color that could be worn with most neutrals, it turned out to be one of the quintessential mid-1980s garments, and it was still being copied in the late 1980s.

The beauty of American style is that the most common of items, like a T-shirt, can be elevated to the most sophisticated of fashions, as in this 1987 wool jersey dress by Calvin Klein.

In 1985 Donna Karan left the company to start her own label, and Louis Dell'Olio stayed on at Anne Klein as head designer. The closeness of their working relationship is apparent from the fact that since parting ways, neither's aesthetic has changed appreciably. In fact, their separate collections often reveal that they are still thinking along the same lines. At the same time, both have been remarkably successful on their own. Under Louis Dell'Olio, Anne Klein grew by 50 percent in three years; he is in charge of both lines as well as all of the accessories, bathing suits, and furs. Like Donna Karan, Dell'Olio grew up on Long Island and attended Parsons School of Design. He worked for Norman Norell, Dominic Rompollo at Teal Traina, at Traina Boutique, and at Originala before joining Karan at Anne Klein.

CALVIN KLEIN

In 1983, when Calvin Klein told Charlotte Curtis of the *New York Times* that he admired the painter Georgia O'Keeffe because "she has pared down, simplified, gotten to the essence," Curtis noted that he was describing his own design aesthetic as well. Although many designers are credited with having a sixth sense when it comes to providing women with what they want, Calvin Klein is the one most often cited as knowing what women want before they know it themselves. Although this can take unusual turns, as when he correctly guessed that thousands of women would lap up man-tailored designer underwear, his prescience mostly consists of refusing to depart from the simple essentials. Calvin Klein's clothes of the 1980s have included camp shirts, sweater sets, turtlenecks, pantsuits, chemise dresses, wrap, polo, reefer, or pea coats, blazers with and without collars, long, flared and short, straight skirts. To these traditional American separates, he has imparted timely nuances.

At a time when women dressed up more, Klein responded by expanding his self-imposed limits to produce a "couture" collection of ready-to-wear evening clothes for women who don't want to change their simple style just because they're going to a party. His embroidered satin coats, taffeta full skirts and blouses, skinny short or long dresses in satin or lace were tempered by his typical use of subtle colors: lace in mink ice or pale camel, taffeta in taupe or ashes of rose, satin in pewter or palest peridot. Several of his evening looks became ubiquitous: the low-cut, all-over lace slip dress, the black jersey tube trimmed at the top with a band of black satin, and the strapless gold mesh tube, and they owe their popularity to the fact that Calvin Klein understands that the essence of modernity is insouciance.

MICHAEL KORS

One of the ablest practitioners of separates designing is Michael Kors, who left the Fashion Institute of Technology after one semester to take a sales job in a Fifty-seventh Street boutique that eventually turned into a designing job. His collections of ready-to-wear, beginning with his first under his own label in 1981, and priced as low as $100 but usually higher, have been mostly made in solid rather than patterned materials, including wool jersey melton, cashmere, lamé, silk, and cotton jersey in black, white, gray, or camel, as well as a few of the colors of the moment. His shapes are pure and basic; skirts are short and straight or long and circular; jackets, tunics, and coats are oversize, with broad shoulders. He never adds any extraneous detail; he eschews even accessories, except for belts.

RALPH LAUREN

By the end of the 1980s, Ralph Lauren successfully enlarged his range to include ballroom as well as mudroom. While he continued to produce all manner of what he called his roughwear, sportswear, and town wear, he expanded his evening offerings considerably, running the gamut from floor-length cashmere sweaters to strapless crepe de chine ballet-length dresses to full-blown ball gowns in muted satins.

In 1983 he introduced his first housewares collection, and his designs for sheets, towels, and tableware were so integrated with his fashion aesthetic that the housewares resembled his clothes, and his clothes began to look like his furnishings designs. All were assembled together in his first New York store, in the Rhinelander Mansion on Madison Avenue at Seventy-second Street, which he renovated. Concha belts inspired flatware patterns, Navaho blankets were transformed into sweaters, faded chambray work shirting became ruffled bed sheets, and carpet-bag brocades made evening coats.

Ralph Lauren has continued to borrow styles from the past, freshening them up by assigning old styles new roles. He has put classic men's engine-turned belt buckles on shoes, transformed bathrobes into velvet evening dresses, and changed polo coats into terry bathrobes. He uses old school ties as a basis for blazers and argyle for beaded evening sweaters as well as socks. Pin-striped trousers have become an evening ensemble when paired with a strapless top, triple strand of pearls, and a cartwheel hat.

MARY McFADDEN

In the 1980s Mary McFadden continued working with her more than twenty varieties of pleated silken fabrics, combining them with elements of hand-painted and/or channel-quilted China silk, macramé, intricate bead embroidery, and gilt lace, or simply using them for opulent T-shirts. Her designs, while still primarily columnar, became both more closely shaped to the body, with occasional cutouts featuring slivers of skin, and away from it, with built-out sleeves and skirts, in fabrics like organza or taffeta. Many of her designs were asymmetric, juxtaposing different colors and textures. Often she based her collections on a theme culled from history or various cultures; these became the source of her colors and patterns. While her clothes were ready-to-wear, they were made in her workrooms in New York, often with many elements, especially embroideries, done by hand.

BOB MACKIE

In 1982 Bob Mackie founded his deluxe ready-to-wear fashion company in New York, after having worked in California, where he was born, as a costume designer for more than two decades. Upon graduating from the Chouinard Art Institute in Los Angeles with a degree in costume design, he worked as a sketch artist for

Ralph Lauren, whose early-1980s ensemble is shown here, is prone to taking one article of clothing, like a blazer, and changing it into another, in this case a cardigan.

Jean Louis and then Edith Head. In 1963 he teamed up with Ray Aghayan to design for television's "The Bell Telephone Hour," which was followed by an eleven-year stint at "The Carol Burnett Show," where the costumes ran the gamut from exaggeratedly dowdy housedresses to takeoffs on clothes from Hollywood's golden age and the truly glamorous dresses worn by Carol Burnett as she chatted with her audience. Beginning in 1971, Bob Mackie found his greatest muse ever in Cher, whom he dressed for her every role on "The Sonny and Cher Comedy Hour." Since then his designs for her, usually very bare and very beaded, have been impossible to miss.

About a decade before starting his New York company, Mackie experimented with typically 1970s low-key matte jersey dresses and other styles, but that ready-to-wear venture did not last long. His 1980s designs, which can cost as much as $15,000, are much more in keeping with his theatrical background. Most are evening clothes, and most are long, made with bare expanses of sheer material strategically embroidered with swaths of beads, although he also works with nonbeaded fabrics for beautifully cut, long, narrow dresses and ball gowns. In the typical American tradition of blurring day and evening boundaries, he designed in 1988 a turnout of mini dress and jacket made to look like denim but completely covered with densely sewn bugle beads highlighted by topstitching. All of his clothes are made in New York.

ISAAC MIZRAHI

From the moment he showed his first collection in 1988, it was clear that Isaac Mizrahi would be the overnight sensation of the end of the decade. Although simple and refreshingly casual, Mizrahi's designs have a depth based on a reverence for the best American fashions of the past but, at the same time, are also grounded in innovation. He might use elements of American sportswear like jean skirts, playsuits, duffle coats, or camp shirts tied at the rib cage; classic fabrics like canvas, poplin, piqué, and gingham; he might even deliberately borrow such looks from American fashion history as Norell's Empire waistline, Geoffrey Beene's paper-bag waistbands, and Halston's sarong shapes, but the results are novel and stimulating.

Mizrahi grew up in New York, where his father worked in the children's clothing industry and his mother was a clotheshorse who wore Norell as well as French couture designs from Saks Fifth Avenue's Salon Moderne. He attended the High School of the Performing Arts and then Parsons School of Design, working for Perry Ellis during his last year of school as well as for two years after graduation. Before starting his own company he also worked for Jeffrey Banks and Calvin Klein.

ALBERT NIPON

Although Albert and Pearl Nipon continued to produce dresses that featured tucking and fagoting, white collars and cuffs, and sheer bodices of silk or lace with self slips underneath, their overall style became more glamorous and sophisticated, in keeping with the mood of the 1980s. Albert Nipon Couture (actually expensive ready-to-wear) included sequined evening dresses, mostly short, and the Executive line offered suits and dresses in

authoritative wools, bright colors, and stylish silhouettes. The company also produced lesser-priced lines of separates and more casual styles. Following Albert Nipon's jail sentence in 1985 for tax evasion, the company suffered a temporary falling off of its accounts.

MOLLIE PARNIS

In 1984, after just over fifty years as a designer and manufacturer of ladylike day and evening clothes, specializing in dresses, Mollie Parnis closed her business, only to start up the following year with a new Mollie Parnis At-Home division of the lingerie company Chevette, originally begun by her sister Peggy. The At-Home clothes included dressy bathrobes made in silk and dressed-down evening clothes, such as caftans, for entertaining.

Isaac Mizrahi drew and designed this 1989 gingham check wool shirt jacket and bicolored evening dress.

MARY ANN RESTIVO

In 1980, sensing that an important market in clothes for businesswomen existed, Mary Ann Restivo started her own company, offering tailored dresses, separates, and sports clothes. Born in New Jersey in 1940, she grew up wanting to design clothes; she made dresses for her dolls and accompanied her father, who ran a local boutique, on shopping trips to New York. She studied at the Fashion Institute of Technology in New York, and during the

1960s she designed young, boutique-type ready-to-wear for various labels, including Something Special. During the 1970s she worked primarily for a blouse company.

Although medium-priced and aimed at a practical-minded clientele, her clothes usually incorporate elements of high style, especially in silhouette. Restivo was one of the more successful designers when it came to selling short skirts. Her clothes are made to wear not only to the office but also for going out at night; her tailored separates in printed silk can be worn year round to work and to play. Other favorite fabrics include wool jersey, gabardine, and crepe.

This lineup of Mary Ann Restivo 1988 dresses reveals the popular broad-shouldered, knee-baring silhouette interpreted for day and for work. The Library, Fashion Institute of Technology, New York

CAROLYNE ROEHM

In 1984 Carolyne Roehm started her own deluxe ready-to-wear company, which proved to be an instant hit. The designer was born in Missouri, graduated from Washington University in Saint Louis, and worked for Sears, Roebuck as a designer before spending ten years at Oscar de la Renta, where she designed for various licensees, including his Miss O line. Since beginning her own company, Carolyne Roehm has produced lavish evening dresses and separates, formal day clothes, and, since 1988, an actual couture line that is custom-made for individual clients.

Most of Roehm's designs are fitted close to the body, often cut to reveal slivers of skin. Even at their narrowest, however, the clothes have featured swathed bands of drapery. Her evening clothes have ranged from severe long dresses in the style of John Singer Sargent's *Madame X* to pouf-skirted minis and almost casual cashmere sweaters paired with reversible long skirts. Many of her evening clothes are decorated with embroideries from the French firm of Lesage; these resemble three-dimensional pieces of jewelry.

GLORIA SACHS

After graduating from Skidmore College, Gloria Sachs studied textile design at the Cranbrook Academy of Art. Later, she stud-

ied at the atelier of Fernand Léger in Paris and with Italian architects Gio Ponti and Franco Albini. She worked as an in-house designer at Saks Fifth Avenue before beginning her own company in 1970. Her 1970s designs consisted of separates, such as pleated skirts, man-tailored shirts, and coats, made in matching fabrics. In the 1980s she has continued making uncoordinated suits and polished ensembles of sweaters with skirts or pants, all worked out in her original fabrics.

While most of her patterns are standard classics, such as plaids, dots, foulards, and paisleys, she stamps them as her own by carefully working out unusual color combinations, making tartans look fresh in brilliant yellow silk and paisleys subtle all in shades of gray. She works closely with the mills that produce her fabrics, which has enabled her to experiment with new techniques. Her foulard prints, which she first used in 1974, were made by an English mill previously involved in producing necktie silks, and from it she drew a much more supple rendition of her small patterns on crepe de chine than she would have gotten from ribbed silk or silk surah. When using a paisley, she starts out with an antique paisley pattern, such as might originally have been used for a mid-nineteenth-century shawl, and plays with the different screens involved in the printing process, removing some and adding others to achieve the updated, subtle look she wants. Cashmere sweaters, in solid colors with stripes around the neck and waistband or hem or, alternatively, with bead embroideries, are produced in her own mill in Scotland.

FERNANDO SANCHEZ

Although Fernando Sanchez has designed furs and luxurious ready-to-wear day and evening clothes, he is most known for what Bernadine Morris of the *New York Times* has described as loungewear separates. These are interchangeable camisoles, pajama pants, overshirts, short and long wrap bathrobes, and nightdresses made in elegant yet comfortable fabrics and styles that may be as appropriate for dining rooms as bedrooms. His signatures are fan-shaped lace motifs applied to the necklines of nightgowns and camisoles, a moiré-patterned synthetic satin with a brushed-flannel texture on the inside, and exterior seams machine-stitched in contrasting colors.

Sanchez was born in Spain and studied at l'Ecole de la Chambre Syndicale de la Couture Parisienne. He won the International Wool Secretariat Competition in 1954 before being hired by the house of Dior. He also designed fur for Revillon before starting his own company in 1974.

GIORGIO DI SANT' ANGELO

Suddenly Giorgio di Sant' Angelo became popular again in the mid-1980s, when his versatile wrap stretch pieces of clothing, unique materials, colors, and patterns provided an antidote to overly tailored or dressy styles. His fabrics especially have influenced other designers. He has continued to develop his own, using man-made fibers to give new properties to natural ones, as in sheer silk that can stretch indefinitely. Most of his clothes have been made in his downtown loft, although he has contracted out some items, and he has designed a bathing suit line for a licen-

see. He has often taken several dyes to hand paint or marbleize different materials in vibrant, bold colors or blurry soft ones, combining them in ensembles of bodysuits, tights, and floating shirts and skirts that play the different properties of one material against the next. He has even designed whole ensembles out of the same piece, a stretchy tube, which he used variously as a bodice, a bandeau, a skirt, or a twisted cummerbund. A 1986 evening dress featured a stretchy black skirt with a white lacy bertha collar and a taffeta pouf at the hem. The stretchy midsection could be telescoped, making the dress short and poufed. A sideline has been his work with lace, which he uses for sheer, stretchy biker's shorts, poet-blouse bodysuits, and romantic dresses of cotton or linen inset with sheer bands of Valenciennes.

SCAASI

Scaasi enjoyed a renewed reputation once the opulent 1980s got under way. His couture operations began to boom again, and, as demand for his entrance-making ball gowns, short evening dresses, and lunch-in-town ensembles grew, he decided the time was right to launch his first ready-to-wear line in decades. Scaasi Boutique debuted in 1984. Although the Scaasi Boutique evening clothes, which were priced around $1,000, were necessarily simpler than his couture designs, which typically start at $5,000, the two categories share certain constants.

Colors are bright, and used in unusual combinations like hot pink and orange, mauve and green, yellow and purple. Prints, primarily dots and florals, are usually multicolored. Rather than using added decorations, Scaasi instead finds European fabrics that have built-in surface interest, as in allover petaled organdy flowers or silk applied with diamanté traceries. It is the shape of the clothes that stands out, as befits a designer who trained with Charles James. Scaasi's dresses most often feature long, fitted torsos, skirts in the shapes of trumpets or poufs or both (which he calls brioches), and a special signature is necklines that stand away from the dress, as in petaled collars that frame the face, crumb-catcher panels standing away from a strapless bodice, or off-the-shoulder portrait collars. Since few of Scaasi's dresses are made to fit under (or be hidden by) a fur coat, he has devised evening stoles of one color of silk satin or taffeta faced with another, or long, full cardigan coats in a silk lined to match the dress.

SHAMASK

Born in Amsterdam, Ronaldus Shamask moved as a teenager with his parents to Australia, where he worked in window display. Later, he went to London to be a fashion illustrator and then moved to Buffalo, New York, where he designed costumes and sets for a multimedia performing company. In 1978, he and a partner, Murray Moss, founded a company and shop in New York called Moss on Madison Avenue. Shamask's early designs

Giorgio di Sant' Angelo, who has often worked directly with textile manufacturers and mills, has continuously perfected new stretch materials to wrap around the body in almost infinite variations. Shown here is a version of his body dressing from 1988.

explored the nature of construction; experimenting with how seams form shapes, he highlighted those seams to create a look often called architectural. As the 1980s progressed, his work became more fluid; he cut clothes so that they fell around the bodice, and the seams and construction became less obvious as he mixed colors and patterns of fabric in a single garment. His palette has remained subtle, running mainly to shades of gray, taupe, and beige, along with black, white, and red, and he has used linen, cashmere, angora, and cotton for interestingly shaped blazers, shirts, high-waisted skirts, and pants.

ADELE SIMPSON

During its fourth decade, the Adele Simpson company has been overseen by Joan Simpson Raines, daughter of the original founder, with Donald Hobson and then Wayne Kastning working on the design staff. The clothes, which range in price from $400 to $1,000, have included coats, suits, day dresses, and afternoon dresses, as well as all kinds of evening clothes, ranging from glittery pants ensembles to shirtwaists interpreted for night

This 1983 Adele Simpson dress of black and white dotted silk chiffon trimmed with ruffles is an example of the softer, more romantic, short evening look.

in changeable taffeta or crepe de chine to strapless ball gowns. The shapes of the clothes have tended to be classic; besides shirtwaists, Adele Simpson has been known for chemises and tunic dresses, as well as for decorative portrait necklines, beautiful fabrics, and a restrained use of bead embroidery.

WILLI SMITH

In 1983 Willi Smith won a Coty Award. He had been designing since the very late 1960s as a free-lancer, for a company called Digits, and then, beginning in 1976, under his own label, Willi Wear. Born in Philadelphia in 1948, he attended the Philadelphia College of Art before moving to New York to study at Parsons School of Design. In 1985 he created the uniforms worn by the workers draping the Pont Neuf in Paris for Christo's artwork, and in 1987 he designed the suits worn by Edwin Schlossberg and his groomsmen at his wedding to Caroline Kennedy. After

Willi Smith's death in 1987, the company continued to function, and it opened its first store, on lower Fifth Avenue, with interiors in a sylvan mode designed by the architectural group SITE Projects Inc.

Willi Smith's moderately priced clothes tended to be exuberant, unfitted, and youthful. He designed most often in the category of separates, making slouchy blazers, long, full dirndls, oversize shirts, dhoti pants, and tank tops. His evening clothes were peppy, such as mid-1980s pouf-skirted dresses with slits in the skirt as high as the waist or with racing-back necklines.

STEPHEN SPROUSE

Stephen Sprouse, the decade's most notorious success/failure story, was born in 1953 in Indiana, and at the age of twelve he sent drawings of his leopard-print jumpsuits to fellow Indianians Norman Norell and Bill Blass for review. After three months at the Rhode Island School of Design, he moved to New York and worked for Halston, yet another designer from Indiana. He later worked briefly for Bill Blass. During the late 1970s he designed clothes for his downstairs neighbor Debbie Harry, of the rock group Blondie. In 1983 he showed his first collection under his own label and was an instant hit. He went out of business in 1985, staged a comeback in 1987 with a new store in Soho and new backing, and went out of business again in 1988.

Sprouse designed several lines, from a "couture" line that featured garments costing in the thousands of dollars down to a line called SS, priced at around $100 for simple items. His clothes were inspired by the late 1960s and by 1970s punk rock style, and he also collaborated with Andy Warhol and Keith Haring on prints. Working primarily with simple shapes—motorcycle jackets, tank mini dresses, blazers, trench coats, and jeans—Sprouse made clothes that, with their day-glo palette, graffiti prints, oversize paillettes, and pavé safety pins, could be recognized from across a crowded club dance floor.

STAVROPOULOS

Stavropoulos clothes, while ready-to-wear, are intricately made. Zippers are sewn in by hand, often on the diagonal or in some other unusual way to accommodate the fall of drapery in a dress; chiffon is used in layer upon layer, creating effects of both transparency and opaqueness; ribbons are woven together in a lattice that forms a bodice or floats among the folds of a skirt. Feeling that muslin is too stiff for the kind of effect he wants, Stavropoulos has worked directly with his materials on a dressmaker's form; he has often made a dress from a single piece of cloth. Besides chiffon he uses imported woven laces, silk jersey, all-over embroidered organdy, and lamé velvets. The average collection numbers around ninety pieces, and prices range from $2,000 to $7,500.

PAULINE TRIGÈRE

At a time when more and more clothing has been made oversize to fit every size, Pauline Trigère's meticulously cut and crafted clothes stand out. Her 1980s designs have included dresses fitted to the figure by means of soft, inverted tucks, ensembles made out of positive-negative stripes, worked vertically and horizontally, plaid coats cut on the bias, and dresses made of striped materials with the stripes sewn together for a close fit in the waist and let out for fullness above or below in skirt or bodice. She has continued to specialize in evening dresses carved out of beautiful materials, like brocade, lace, or gazar, as well as wool dresses and daytime suits and pantsuits. The coats she designs for the firm of Abe Schrader sell for about a tenth of her regular ready-to-wear, for which prices have gone as high as $5,000. In 1985 she revived her 1967 rhinestone bra to wear under suit jackets for evening.

KOOS VAN DEN AKKER

Koos van den Akker Couture, which is actually both ready-to-wear and one-of-a-kind, is entirely produced in New York and sold out of the designer's upstairs boutique on Madison Avenue, as well as in other stores. All of Koos van den Akker's clothes are made from his collages, which combine such diverse materials as short- or long-haired fur, glittering brocades, lamés, reembroidered lace, jacquards, and cottons in outlined, appliquéd, and sometimes quilted, swirling abstract patterns. Most often the shapes of the clothes are simple, as in cardigan coats, dirndl skirts, caftan-shaped dresses, and drop-waisted chemises. His appliqué-edged cardigan suits were the most beautiful takeoffs on Chanel of the decade. During the 1980s van den Akker branched out into licensed summer dresses, sweaters (which were worn by Bill Cosby), furs, pocketbooks, and even upholstery.

The downtown fashion designer in the 1989 movie Slaves of New York *was based on Stephen Sprouse, whose 1988 collection was filmed for the fashion show sequence, including this "Glab Flack" T-shirt and cotton denim skirt and a sequined rock sticker men's jacket.*

Koos van den Akker, whether making luxurious coats, as shown in this 1988 example, men's sweaters, or seats for antique chairs, works in the medium of collage.

JOAN VASS

Joan Vass graduated from Vassar, and, before she designed a small collection of hand-knitted mufflers and hats and sold them at Henri Bendel in 1975, had worked as an art book editor, as an assistant curator at the Museum of Modern Art, New York, and as a columnist for *Art in America*. Within two years she began her own company, and in the 1980s she has been responsible for both Joan Vass, NY, a line of hand-knitted clothes made cottage industry–style in and around New York, and Joan Vass, USA, a lesser-priced licensed line consisting mostly of knits produced in South Carolina.

Her clothes have a quality of integrity; there are no extraneous decorations, no shoulder pads. She concentrates on easy shapes and beautiful natural fibers and colors; she displays the printed selvages of fabrics on the outside seams of skirts, implying that if the fabric is wonderful, there is nothing to hide. She has designed dresses, most shaped like pullovers, but specializes in separates: oversize cardigans and slouchy pullovers, various dirndl and flared skirts, leggings and other pants. Her favorite pattern is the stripe.

ADRIENNE VITTADINI

More than any other contemporary designer, Adrienne Vittadini works in the tradition of the great American sportswear designers of the late 1940s and 1950s. Like Claire McCardell, Tina Leser, Carolyn Schnurer, and their peers, Vittadini creates clothes for leisure and active sports, as well as more formal clothes that, like the sportswear, are relaxed and feminine, not based on men's tailoring. Inspired by comfort and technology, Vittadini applies the same thinking to bathing suits that she does to sleepwear and party clothes. Besides designing everything with the same standards, she designs across the board using the exact same materials and shapes. She has realized that if a woman likes natural fibers, she will want to swim in them, sleep in them, and play tennis in them, as well as wear them to work. The only difference in her designs is that the glittery ones are for parties, the brightest prints for leisure, and the more subdued colors for the office.

Working with new developments in computer-driven machinery as they come up, she has designed textiles simultaneously with clothes, creating a variety of knits. Some incorporate beads or sequins, some are made with sheer panels, some have dense, flat embroidery, built-in passementerie, textures reminiscent of woven materials like ottoman, and also flat patterns, which Vittadini borrows from paintings, antique textiles, and, sometimes, tongue-in-cheek, from current fads. She makes these into dresses, two-piece suits, pullovers, pull-on pants and skirts, and other easily related separates.

Born in Hungary, Vittadini moved to America with her family as a young girl. Having become interested in art, she attended the Philadelphia College of Art. After graduating she became an apprentice at the Paris house of Louis Feraud and worked briefly for Pucci in Italy. In New York, she designed knits for the fashion companies Warnaco and Kimberly before developing her own line at Kimberly called Avanzara, which soon led to her own company.

ZORAN

Zoran, whose full name is Ladicorbic Zoran, moved to New York in 1972 from Yugoslavia, where he had originally trained as an architect. He did odd jobs, including working for a boutique, before starting his own business in 1976. Fashion's minimalist master, he has based his wardrobes of ready-to-wear separates on the principles that clothes should fit easily, that buttons and other closures are unnecessary, and that solid colors, especially black, white, cream, and gray, are all anyone really needs. Although he began selling his clothes in the late 1970s, in the more opulent 1980s he has remained faithful to these tenets while working with increasingly luxurious materials, such as pavé sequins, satin, taffeta, silk gabardine, and cashmere, as well as cotton piqué, cotton knit, and double-faced wool. He experiments with proportion, showing cropped pants and pullovers, elongated tanks, and jackets in three-quarter- and seven-eighths-lengths, but his pieces work together in any configuration. Besides jackets, coats, pullovers, tank tops, and pull-on pants, he has also designed tank dresses, sarong skirts, and caftans.

One of the most popular and longest-lasting silhouettes of the 1980s was the 1920s-inspired drop-waisted chemise, shown here in a 1987 red cotton knit version by Adrienne Vittadini. It was priced around $100.

Typical of Adrienne Vittadini's experiments with the capabilities of knitting machines is this three-dimensional cable-knit sweater from 1986.

BIBLIOGRAPHY

Allen, Frederick Lewis. *Only Yesterday: An Informal History of the 1920s.* New York: Harper & Row, 1931.

Anspach, Katharine. *The Why of Fashion.* Ames, Iowa: Iowa State University Press, 1967.

Arnold, Pauline, and Percival White. *Clothes and Cloth: America's Apparel Business.* New York: Holiday House, 1961.

Bailey, Margaret J. *Those Glorious Glamour Years: The Great Hollywood Designs of the 1930s.* Secaucus, N.J.: Citadel Press, 1982.

Ballard, Bettina. *In My Fashion.* New York: David McKay, 1967.

Bender, Marylin. *The Beautiful People.* New York: Coward-McCann, 1967.

Bendure, Zelma, and Gladys Pfeiffer. *America's Fabrics.* New York: MacMillan, 1946.

Berch, Bettina. *Radical by Design: The Life and Style of Elizabeth Hawes, Fashion Designer, Union Organizer, Best-selling Author.* New York: E. P. Dutton, 1988.

Birmingham, Nan Tillson. *Store: A Memoir of America's Great Department Stores.* New York: G. P. Putnam's Sons, 1978.

Brady, James. *Superchic.* Boston: Little, Brown, 1974.

Carter, Ernestine. *Magic Names of Fashion.* Englewood Cliffs, N.J.: Prentice-Hall, 1980.

Cassini, Oleg. *In My Own Fashion: An Autobiography.* New York: Simon and Schuster, 1987.

Castle, Irene. *Castles in the Air.* Garden City, N.Y.: Doubleday, 1958.

Chase, Edna Woolman and Ilka. *Always in Vogue.* Garden City, N.Y.: Doubleday, 1954.

Chierichetti, David. *Hollywood Costume Design.* New York: Harmony Books, 1976.

Coleman, Elizabeth Ann. *The Genius of Charles James.* New York: Holt, Rinehart and Winston, 1982.

Crawford, M. D. C. *The Ways of Fashion.* New York: G. P. Putnam's Sons, 1941.

Daché, Lilly. *Talking Through My Hats.* New York: Coward-McCann, 1946.

Daves, Jessica. *Ready-Made Miracle.* New York: G. P. Putnam's Sons, 1967.

Dexter, Elisabeth Anthony. *Career Women of America 1776–1840.* Clifton, N.J.: Augustus M. Kelley, 1972.

Diamonstein, Barbaralee. *Fashion: The Inside Story.* New York: Rizzoli, 1985.

Dutton, William S. *Du Pont: One Hundred and Forty Years.* New York: Charles Scribner's Sons, 1942.

Earnest, Ernest. *The American Eve in Fact and Fiction, 1775–1914.* Urbana, Ill.: University of Illinois Press, 1974.

Ellman, Barbara. *The World of Fashion Jewelry.* Highland Park, Ill.: Aunt Louise Imports, 1986.

Fashion Institute of Technology. *All-American: A Sportswear Tradition.* New York: Fashion Institute of Technology, 1985 (exhibition catalogue).

Fitz-Gibbon, Bernice. *Macy's, Gimbel's and Me.* New York: Simon and Schuster, 1951.

Fogarty, Anne. *Wife Dressing: The Fine Art of Being a Well-dressed Wife.* New York: Julian Messer, 1959.

Footner, Hubert. *New York: City of Cities.* Philadelphia: J. B. Lippincott, 1937.

Fraser, Kennedy. *The Fashionable Mind: Reflections on Fashion 1970–1981.* New York: Alfred A. Knopf, 1981.

Gallagher, Louise Barnes. *Frills and Thrills: The Career of a Young Fashion Designer.* New York: Dodd, Mead & Company, 1940.

Greer, Howard. *Designing Male.* New York: G. P. Putnam's Sons, 1949.

Hawes, Elizabeth. *Fashion Is Spinach.* New York: Random House, 1938.

———. *It's Still Spinach.* Boston: Little, Brown, 1954.

Head, Edith, and Jane Kesmore Ardmore. *The Dress Doctor.* Boston: Little, Brown, 1959.

Head, Edith, and Paddy Calistro. *Edith Head's Hollywood.* New York: E. P. Dutton, 1983.

Hendrickson, Robert. *The Grand Emporiums: The Illustrated History of America's Great Department Stores.* New York: Stein and Day, 1979.

Herndon, Booton. *Bergdorf's on the Plaza: The Story of Bergdorf Goodman and a Half Century of American Fashion.* New York: Alfred A. Knopf, 1956.

Houck, Catherine. *The Fashion Encyclopedia.* New York: St. Martin's Press, 1982.

Jansen, Oliver. *The Revolt of American Women: A Pictorial History of the Century of Change from Bloomers to Bikinis—from Feminism to Freud.* New York: Harcourt, Brace and Company, 1952.

John Wanamaker. *Golden Book of the Wanamaker Stores: Jubilee Year 1861–1911.* Philadelphia: John Wanamaker, 1911.

Kelly, Katie. *The Wonderful World of Women's Wear Daily.* New York: Saturday Review Press, 1972.

Kidwell, Claudia, and Margaret C. Christman. *Suiting Everyone: The Democraticization of Clothing in America.* Washington, D.C.: Smithsonian Institution Press, 1974.

LaVine, Robert W. *In a Glamorous Fashion: The Fabulous Years of Hollywood Costume Design.* New York: Charles Scribner's Sons, 1980.

Lee, Sarah Tomerlin, ed. *American Fashion: The Lives and Lines of Adrian, Mainbocher, McCardell, Norell, Trigère.* New York: Quadrangle, 1975.

Lesse, Elizabeth. *Costume Design in the Movies.* New York: Frederick Ungar, 1977.

Lewis, Alfred Allan, and Constance Woodworth. *Miss Elizabeth Arden: An Unretouched Portrait.* New York: Coward, McCann and Geoghegan, 1972.

Ley, Sandra. *Fashion for Everyone: The Story of Ready-to-wear, 1870's–1970's.* New York: Charles Scribner's Sons, 1975.

Lockwood, Charles. *Manhattan Moves Uptown: An Illustrated History.* Boston: Houghton Mifflin, 1976.

McCardell, Claire. *What Shall I Wear? The What, Where, When and How Much of Fashion.* New York: Simon and Schuster, 1956.

McClellan, Elisabeth. *Historic Dress in America 1607–1870.* New York: Arno Press, 1977.

McDowell, Colin. *McDowell's Directory of Twentieth Century Fashion.*

Englewood Cliffs, N.J.: Prentice-Hall, 1985.

Melinkoff, Ellen. *What We Wore: An Offbeat Social History of Women's Clothing 1950 to 1980*. New York: Quill, 1984.

Montgomery Museum of Fine Arts. *American Fashion Designs by Wilson Folmar*. Montgomery, Ala.: Montgomery Museum of Fine Arts, 1978 (exhibition catalogue).

Milbank, Caroline Rennolds. *Couture: The Great Designers*. New York: Stewart, Tabori & Chang, 1985.

Nevins, Allan. *The Emergence of Modern America 1865–1878: A History of American Life*. Vol. 13. New York: MacMillan Company, 1927.

O'Hara, Georgina. *The Encyclopaedia of Fashion*. New York: Harry N. Abrams, 1986.

Rogers, Agnes. *Women Are Here to Stay*. New York: Harper & Brothers, 1949.

Ross, Ishbel. *Crusades and Crinolines: The Life and Times of Ellen Curtis Demorest and William Jennings Demorest*. New York: Harper & Row, 1963.

Snow, Carmel, with Mary Louise Aswell. *The World of Carmel Snow*. New York: McGraw-Hill, 1962.

Stegemeyer, Anne. *Who's Who in Fashion*. New York: Fairchild Publications, 1980.

Stern, Robert A. M., Gregory Gilmartin, and John Montague Massengale. *New York 1900: Metropolitan Architecture and Urbanism 1890–1915*. New York: Rizzoli, 1983.

Watkins, Josephine Ellis. *Fairchild's Who's Who in Fashion*. New York: Fairchild Publications, 1975.

Wendt, Lloyd, and Herman Kogan. *Give the Lady What She Wants! The Story of Marshall Field & Company*. Chicago: Rand McNally, 1952.

White, Norval. *New York: A Physical History*. New York: Atheneum, 1987.

Williams, Beryl. *Young Faces in Fashion*. Philadelphia: J. B. Lippincott, 1976.

PHOTOCREDITS

Numbers refer to pages on which illustrations appear.

Page 2, above: photograph by Ted Croner; below: Gordon Parks, *Life* Magazine © 1958 Time Inc.; 6: Copyright © 1962 by The Condé Nast Publications, Inc.; 9: Copyright © 1960 (renewed 1988) by The Condé Nast Publications, Inc.; 11 above: The Bettmann Archive; below: photograph by Ted Croner; 12 left: © 1989 All World Photos, Westport, Conn.; right: Courtesy Eleanor Lambert; 13: Copyright © 1944 (renewed 1972) by The Condé Nast Publications, Inc.; 14 above: Courtesy Betsy Pickering Kaiser; below: Courtesy Eleanor Lambert; 15: Courtesy Bill Blass; 20: photograph by Ted Croner; 25 above: The Bettmann Archive; below, 30 above, 32 left, 34, 38, 40, 41: photograph by Ted Croner; 49: All World Photos, Westport, Conn.; 51: photograph by Ted Croner; 54 above: All World Photos, Westport, Conn.; below: The Bettmann Archive; 55 above: All World Photos, Westport, Conn.; below: The Bettmann Archive; 57: UPI/Bettmann Newsphotos; 59: photograph by Ted Croner; 60: All World Photos, Westport, Conn.; 61 right: The Bettmann Archive; 63, 65 right: photograph by Ted Croner; 67: The Bettmann Archive; 68–71 above: All World Photos, Westport, Conn.; 71 below: The Bettman Archive; 73 above: All World Photos, Westport, Conn.; 73 below: photograph by Ted Croner; 74: All World Photos, Westport, Conn.; 75: photograph by Ted Croner; 77 above: All World Photos, Westport, Conn.; 77 below: photograph by Ted Croner; 78: The Bettmann Archive; 81: All World Photos, Westport, Conn.; 82: The Bettmann Archive; 84, 85: photograph by Ted Croner; 87, 88, 91: The Bettmann Archive; 93: photograph by Ted Croner; 94 above: photograph by Irving Browning; 97, 99: All World Photos, Westport, Conn.; 101: photograph by Ted Croner; 102: The Bettmann Archive; 103: photograph by Ted Allan/MGM, courtesy Betty Furness; 104: Copyright © 1938 (renewed 1967) by The Condé Nast Publications, Inc.; 106: All World Photos, Westport, Conn.; 107: Copyright © 1939 (renewed 1967) by The Condé Nast Publications, Inc.; 108: All World Photos, Westport, Conn.; 110–11: photograph by Ted Croner; 113: All World Photos, Westport, Conn.; 114: Courtesy Saks Fifth Avenue; 118: photograph by Ted Croner; 119: The Bettmann Archive; 122–27: photograph by Ted Croner; 131: Copyright © 1943 (renewed 1961) by The Condé Nast Publications, Inc.; 133 above: Courtesy Sandy Schreier; 135: photograph by Ted Croner; 136: Courtesy Eleanor Lambert; 137 above: Copyright © 1946 (renewed 1964) by The Condé Nast Publications, Inc.; below: Copyright © 1943 (renewed 1976) by The Condé Nast Publications, Inc.; 138 below: photograph by Ted Croner; 140 below: Copyright © 1944 (renewed 1972) by The Condé Nast Publications, Inc.; 142 above: Copyright © 1942 (renewed 1970) by The Condé Nast Publications, Inc.; below: Copyright © 1944 (renewed 1976) by The Condé Nast Publications, Inc.; 143 above: Copyright © 1949 (renewed 1977) by The Condé Nast Publications, Inc.; below: Courtesy Eleanor Lambert; 144: Copyright © 1945 (renewed 1973) by The Condé Nast Publications, Inc.; 145: Copyright © 1946 (renewed 1974) by The Condé Nast Publications, Inc.; 146 above: All World Photos, Westport, Conn.; 150, 151: photograph by Ted Croner; 162: Copyright © 1948 (renewed 1976) by The Condé Nast Publications, Inc.; 163 left: Photograph by David C. Laughon; right: Copyright © 1948 (renewed 1976) by The Condé Nast Publications, Inc.; 166: Courtesy Eleanor Lambert; 167 left: Copyright © 1943 (renewed 1971) by The Condé Nast Publications, Inc.; 168: Copyright © 1946 (renewed 1974) by The Condé Nast Publications, Inc.; 173 above: Copyright © 1951 (renewed 1979) by The Condé Nast Publications, Inc.; below: All World Photos, Westport, Conn.; 174 above: The Bettmann Archive; below: Copyright © 1954 (renewed 1982) by The Condé Nast Publications, Inc.; 176: Copyright © 1951 (renewed 1979) by The Condé Nast Publications, Inc.; 178 left: Courtesy Eleanor Lambert; right: Copyright © 1951 (renewed 1979) by The Condé Nast Publications, Inc.; 181: Courtesy Eleanor Lambert; 182: Copyright © 1950 (renewed 1978) by The Condé Nast Publications, Inc.; 183, 184 left: Courtesy Eleanor Lambert; 185, 186: photograph by Ted Croner; 187: Courtesy Suzanne and Lilly Daché; 190 left: Courtesy Betty Furness; right: Copyright © 1957 (renewed 1985) by The Condé Nast Publications, Inc.; 192: Copyright © 1950 (renewed 1978) by The Condé Nast Publications, Inc.; 193 above left: Courtesy Betty Furness; center, right: Courtesy Eleanor Lambert; 194 left: Courtesy Janet Leigh Figg; right: The Bettmann Archive; 195: Copyright © 1953 (renewed 1981) by The Condé Nast Publications, Inc.; 196: Courtesy Scaasi; 197 left and right: The Bettmann Archive; center: Courtesy Eleanor Lambert; 203: Courtesy Betsy Pickering Kaiser; 204: photograph by Ted Croner; 205: Courtesy Betsy Pickering Kaiser, Copyright © 1960 (renewed 1988) by The Condé Nast Publications, Inc.; 208–9: Copyright © 1966 by The Condé Nast Publications, Inc.; 210: photograph by Howell Conant, *Life* Magazine © 1967 Time Inc.; 211–17, 221–30: Courtesy Eleanor Lambert; 232: Courtesy Scaasi; 234, 237 center, 244 above: Courtesy Eleanor Lambert; 239: Courtesy Francesco Scavullo, New York Studio; 244 below: photograph by Ted Croner; 245 above: Courtesy Bill Blass; below: Courtesy Eleanor Lambert; 246: Courtesy Janet King McClelland; 250: Courtesy Eleanor Lambert; 252: Courtesy Francesco Scavullo, New York Studio; 253 above: Courtesy Janet King McClelland; 253 below: Courtesy Perry Ellis; 254: photograph by Ted Croner; 255 left: photograph by Pierre Scherman, Courtesy Eleanor Lambert; right: Courtesy Charles Kleibacker; 256 left: Courtesy Janet King McClelland; 256 right: Courtesy Eleanor Lambert; 258 left: Courtesy Eleanor Lambert; right: Courtesy Mary McFadden; 266: Photograph by Phillip Smith; 267: Courtesy Janet King McClelland; 268: Courtesy Ralph Lauren; 269: Courtesy Perry Ellis; 270–71: Copyright © 1985 by The Condé Nast Publications, Inc.; 272 left: Courtesy Victor Costa; right: Courtesy Cathy Hardwick; 273: Courtesy Robert Lee Morris, Artwear; 274: Courtesy Carolyne Roehm; 276: Courtesy Sheila Metzner; 277: Courtesy Scaasi; 278: Courtesy Donna Karan, New York; 280 above: Courtesy Adolfo; center: photograph by Lois Greenfield, Courtesy Adri; below: Courtesy John Anthony; 281: Courtesy Bill Blass; 282: Courtesy Perry Ellis; 283: Courtesy Fabrice; 284 above: Courtesy Cathy Hardwick; below: Courtesy Carolina Herrera; 286: Courtesy Calvin Klein; 287: Courtesy Ralph Lauren; 288: Courtesy Isaac Mizrahi, photograph by Ted Croner; 289: photograph by Ted Croner; 290: Courtesy Giorgio di Sant' Angelo; 291: Courtesy Adele Simpson; 292: Courtesy Stephen Sprouse; 293: Courtesy Koos van den Akker; 294–95: Courtesy Adrienne Vittadini; 303: Courtesy Mish Jewelry; endpapers: Copyright © 1985 by The Condé Nast Publications, Inc.; back cover: Copyright © 1943 (renewed 1971) by The Condé Nast Publications, Inc.

Endpapers: Calvin Klein paired a full silk skirt with an off-the-shoulder T-shirt for this evening ensemble of 1985. Photograph: Sheila Metzner. Courtesy *Vogue*

Page 2, above: The bustle-backed street and visiting costumes published by Butterick as pattern designs in 1875 were set against the background of Central Park. Museum of the City of New York

Page 2, below: These glittery brocade theater suits by (left to right) Nelly De Grab, Customcraft, and Junior Sophisticates were photographed by Gordon Parks in front of the Helen Hayes Theatre on Broadway in 1958. Courtesy *Life* Magazine

Pages 4–5: Skating in Central Park in the 1890s called for gigot-sleeved coats and street-length skirts. The Leonard Hassin Bogart Collection, Museum of the City of New York

Page 6: This 1962 Burke-Amey day dress appears with the Seagram Building on Park Avenue in the background. Hat by Lilly Daché. Photograph: Horst. Courtesy *Vogue*

ACKNOWLEDGMENTS

All of the following people were helpful in putting this book together, and it has been their enthusiasm for the project that has meant the most to me and for which I am the most grateful. For reading the manuscript thanks to: Anne Schirrmeister and Seymour Rennolds. For their knowledge and their generosity in sharing it: JoAnne Olian, Phyllis Magidson, Dorothy Hanenberg, Sandy Schreier, Eleanor Lambert, and Betsy Kaiser. For talking to me about their work: John Anthony, Harvey Berin, Tom Brigance, Donald Brooks, Victor Costa, Lilly Daché, Mr. John, Charles Kleibacker, John Moore, Mildred Orrick, Eva Rosencrans, Gloria Sachs, Giorgio di Sant' Angelo, Scaasi, Carolyn Schnurer, Stavropoulos, Pauline Trigère, Koos van den Akker, and Gustave Tassell. For help with illustrations: Betsy Kaiser, Eleanor Lambert, Horst P. Horst, Richard J. Tardiff, Richard Ely, Suzanne Daché, Marjorie Miller, Deirdre Lawrence, Jean Druesedow, Bob Kaufmann, Phyllis Magidson, Diana Edkins, Tom Fallon, Thom van Aken, Judith Straeton, Fred Tarabas, Irving Solero, Betty Furness, and Miles Barth. For copy photography: Ted Croner. For research and office assistance: Carol Chow, Jan Reeder, Alex Bowe, Caitlin, and Jennifer Kaiser. Many thanks also to my editor, Lory Frankel, and to Ray Hooper for his design of the book. To my agent, Miriam Young, to my sister, Margaret Blythe Rennolds, for constant assistance and guidance, and, finally, to my husband.

Golden metal bow necklace designed in 1988 by Mish Jewelry